JACK OF ALL TRADES

An Alaskan Word Wrangler's Collection
of Poetry and Prose for Regular Folks

By Sydney Huffnagle

*To Derek & Jocelyn
from your Poor old
Homer-Sapiens Buddies*

DeVon Dee & Sydney A. Huffnagle

PO Box 221974 Anchorage, Alaska 99522-1974
books@publicationconsultants.com—www.publicationconsultants.com

ISBN 978-1-59433-156-5
Library of Congress Catalog Card Number: 2010937303

Copyright 2010 Sydney Huffnagle
—First Edition—

All rights reserved, including the right of
reproduction in any form, or by any mechanical
or electronic means including photocopying or
recording, or by any information storage or
retrieval system, in whole or in part in any
form, and in any case not without the
written permission of the author and publisher.

Manufactured in the United States of America.

Dedicated to my wife
Devon

Devon and Sydney's 50th wedding anniversary,
April 11, 1996

Contents

Dedication 5

Prologue 15

Chickens Didn't Eat Pot Pie Way Back Then 17

My Father's Willow Chair 20

Let It Be 22

You Can Always Tell A Dyed In The Bull Politician But You're Just Wasting Your Breath 'Til He Closes His Mouth 24

Virtual Reality 28

A Letter To Mama 32

A House By The Side Of The Road 35

Pride 42

Aw Gee Dad, Do I Haf'ta? 43

Above All Else 49

Court Of Last Resort 50

Do You Ever Wonder Why 53

A Special Breed 54

Here's Lookin' atcha, Jack 58

Little Things 62

Jist A Dang Ol' Funeral 66

Best Way I Know T'find Out How A'man Thinks Is T'walk A'mile 'Er Two In 'Is Tracks 68

On Whom The Bell Tolled 88

Th' Rites'a Passage 90

Dear Ol' Deer Huntin' Camp 92

Showdown At The Rio Grande Western-Southern Depot 94

A Heavy Load 103

Stealin' Out Th' Door 104

Old Ed Was A Hard Man To Put Down 105

Call Girls, What Would We'a Done Without 'Em? 111

Mists Of Memory 115

Into The Valley 116

Harvest What You Will 118

Make Room For Me, Columbus! 119

Things A Man Can't Seem To Forget 125

Ol' Man Hockley 127

Agnostic Agony 133

Tricky Business 134

24 Carat Memories 140

It's No Sin T'Grin, Y'Know..141

Tommy, The Thirty And One Cat 142

I Believe 146

Holy Shit, Amigo! 148

Th' Walleyed Mule 158

A Gathering Of Yule Logs 166

My Love.. 173

To My Love 175

A Tribute To Doris 176

Bosom Buddies 177

My Christmas Prayer... 194

Oh The Pain Of It All 195

Yet Another Butch And Me Escapade 196

Buckerooooooooo Butch.. 206

Flying Free My Love... 210

The Highway...211

It's Your Bet.. 212

Writing Machine 213

'Tis Nought But Fate 214

A Poem To Roast Your Toes On	215
Tom	216
Ode To My Poor Wife	217
It May'a Been Fate, But 'Tain't Fair	218
A Thirsty Business	220
Smoke Signals	223
A Call In The Night	230
Ain't Life Somethin'?	231
Miz Martin, Our Southern Belle	232
To My Pen	237
An Odious Ode That's Truly Owed An' Long Overdue	238
One Cold Sonovagun	240
With Visions Of Grandeur or Sugar Plums, anyhow	250
Hey Doc, What's Up	252
Make Use Of All That You Possess	261
Stealin' Out Th' Door	262
Cabin Fever	263
Jist Minin' My Ghosts	269
Ron's Green Monster	274
Rustic Refuge	279
Things That Go Bump In The Night	281

Singin' a Scrofulous Song 291

An Ear For Music 293

Am I Too Profound? 298

Bottoms Up, My Friend 300

Who Gives A Stinkin' Damn? 302

Loon's Legacy 303

Just In Case Someone Wants To Know 310

It Sure Ain't Th' Paint 311

Rat Reagan's Ace In The Hole 312

Straight Out Of The Blue 321

Silent Soliloquy 323

Cat-Scanning The Neighborhood 324

Thanks A Lot, Doc 326

A Wee Bit' a Doggerel 328

Bits Of Fluff And Stuff 329

Two For The Price Of One 330

Same Song, Second Verse (At Least) 332

Dadblame Birds 335

That's Th' Way Th' Ball Bounces 337

Proceed With Caution, My Love 338

Take Jessica Please 340

Around And Around She Goes	342
Hardrock Hill	344
Go Ahead Sucker, Jist Make My Day	346
Here's T'fanny	349
Afognak Sojourn	351
There'sa Hare In My Stew, Dang It!	366
In Search Of Glory	368
A Stammerin' Man	373
With Eyes That Shine	376
Riding The Red-Eye Special	378
Ain't That Jist Ducky	382
Ballad Of Mean Mouth Mack	388
If You Knew Su Like I Knew Su	392
Th' Ol' Tin Bucket	395
Just Another Day In Paradise	396
The Ballad Of Big Bold Benny	398
Love's Not Really Blind You Know	404
Alaskan Storms	409
Clairvoyance, Or Dementia	410
Moonhead	412
Cloudy Weather	417

T'ol' Moonhead's Darlin 419

Potted Potential.. 422

Ol' Gert's Night To Howl... 424

Now I Lay Me Down To Sleep 427

Shady Deals From Out Of The Past 433

Three Cheers For Candy.. 436

Epilogue For A Collection Of Stories And Poems......... 440

Prologue

In so far as my wife, DeVon D. Huffnagle, passed away on May 16th, 2009, after spending the last 15 years of her life as a victim of Progressive Supra-Nuclear Palsy, otherwise known as PSP, it's my intention to donate fifty percent of the proceeds derived from the sale of this book to the CUREPSP Foundation, whose address is –CurePSP Executive Plaza III 11350 McCormick Road, Ste. 906 Hunt Valley, MD 21031 For simply because she spent at least the last three and a half years of her life confined to a wheel-chair, totally unable to either stand or walk without support from myself or someone else, as far as our family is concerned, PSP is absolutely the nastiest form of Parkinsonism in existence today. Because even though she got a certain amount of benefit from the medicine called "Sinemet", it was confined solely to what's known as the "Restless Leg Syndrome", which results from the patient's inability to use their legs.

But neither it nor most of the so-called "Agonist medications" that have thus far been developed had any effect at all on her sense of balance, or her ability to speak clearly enough to allow others to understand what she said without a great deal of difficulty. And for the final 6 or 8 months of her life, she was unable to read anything except the captions in the newspaper articles she'd formerly derived so much pleasure from. For even though I'd begun reading as much of the paper to her as my other duties allowed, it was an extremely poor substitute.

During this same period of time she'd been having so much difficulty in swallowing her food and drink without choking, she began using a suction-pump to get rid of food particles and excess saliva in the rear of her mouth, then when that no longer took care of the problem, our doctors advised us that she needed a feeding-tube installed just below her chest-diaphragm, which I'm firmly convinced was what caused her to give up. For the past four years or so she'd been unable to move her eyes voluntarily, so our Eye-specialist installed a frosted lens for her left eye, since her vision in it wasn't as good as it was in her right eye, which relieved the effects of her astigmatism.

But even though we'd been installing saline-drops in both her eyes ever since she'd been diagnosed as having PSP, during the last four months of her life, her saliva glands and those in her nostrils began working overtime. For just because the doctor that installed her feeding tube told us she could still eat whatever she wanted by mouth whenever she felt like it, if you've never had the opportunity to sit at the table with someone you love with all your heart, and watched the mucous streaming down into their food without their realizing it, you just don't know what heartbreak is all about.

Unless, that is, you too have just returned home from having your second shoulder-replacement surgery the night before your loved one dies, and are in so much pain that you've just told the woman you'd been married to for slightly over sixty-three years, that you think she'll rest better if you sleep in the adjoining bedroom, barely three feet through the wall from where her pillow is. Particularly since all she needs to do is press the inter-com button located no more than a foot from her hand, or call the girl whose bed is no more than three feet away from hers.

And you've then had that same girl pound on your door to let you know your wife is cold and doesn't seem to be breathing, and you've then spent somewhere between fifteen and thirty minutes giving your wife "mouth to mouth" while the girl calls 911 and asks the operator to send help as soon as possible, you can't possibly know what real heartbreak is all about.

Which is the main reason I'm also donating at least five percent of the proceeds from the sale of this book and however many others God gives me the time to write, to "Hospice of Homer" P.O. Box 4174 Homer AK 99603.

But if you know of anyone who has this hideous disease, won't you please make at least a small donation to the CUREPSP Foundation if you can afford to? I'm all too well aware that there are many worthwhile charities in need of help though, so I really hope you don't have too much trouble mucking your way through my goofy southwestern Colorado vernacular. Unless, that is, you speak the same dialect of Prawper Bawstonian jibberty-jabber lingo my poetry Perfessor did, all those many long years ago.

Chickens Didn't Eat Pot Pie Way Back Then

As difficult as it may be to believe, for those of you who've reached maturity since jet-propelled aircraft first made it possible for man to go skipping hither and yon at the drop of his gilt-edged plastic passport to practically everywhere, the world was so large back when I was a runny-nosed kid that even traveling to the next town was worthy of mention in the local newspapers. And anyone who was either foolhardy or brave enough to undertake a trip all the way from my little hometown to Denver was a leadpipe cinch for frontpage coverage both going and coming.

Because if you had the kind of money that would allow you to make that six-hundred and some mile round trip more than once in the same year, you sure as the devil were a whole heck of a lot better off than most of your neighbors. But if you didn't own your own business, or at least have a wealthy relative who did, there was a better than average chance that our county sheriff would be finding some kind of an excuse to pay your neighbors a visit fairly soon, just to ask whether they'd noticed anything peculiar going on around your place lately.

Why with gasoline selling for somewhere close to twenty cents a gallon, about the only man I ever saw who dumped a whole ten-gallon glass cylinder's worth into his car at one time, was George Perkins, the guy who owned the garage where that antiquated old pump stood at attention. Practically everyone else made ol' George quit pumping just as soon as the gas got up to the five gallon mark, which was the halfway point on the cylinder.

You see, back in those days gasoline was pumped up into the cylinder by hand, then gravity took care of getting it into your car's tank. This was because folks considered gasoline to be such a dangerous commodity that they just weren't even about to take a chance on an electric spark frying either themselves or their jitney, at least before they'd had a chance to go wherever it was they had it in mind to go. And believe you me, none of the folks who lived in our neck of the woods would even think of letting George pull the trigger on the hose until after all the air-bubbles had made it to the top of the glass, just so they could be absolutely, positively sure that they were going to be getting their money's worth of go-juice. Thrift wasn't just a once-in-awhile thing in those days, you understand, it was what made the difference in having to eat gravy all by itself, or in having something to put it on.

Why I can flat-out guarantee that about the only folks living in our little town who didn't raise a garden, were the ones who'd moved away, or already been hauled off to the cemetery. There weren't many who didn't have a little flock of chickens in the backyard either, or at least a couple of rabbit hutches. And up until I was about ten years old, there were at least half a dozen families who kept a milk-cow or a few goats out behind their house. There were also a pretty fair number of horses kept in the numerous barns and sheds, since there were still enough diehards around town who stubbornly refused to acknowledge that anything that didn't run on steam or oats could possibly be a dependable form of transportation.

And if you think folks didn't get hot under the collar when someone got careless with a cigarette butt and set the town-dump on fire, it's high-time you learned a thing or two about what life was like back then. Why I can even remember seeing our local banker prowling around up there from time to time. Because there was just no way of knowing when some poor fool might have gotten so fed up with hefting junk-buckets around in his storage shed, that he'd finally carted everything up to the dump but the fool shed. But you really had to be quick on the draw, just to get up there before everyone else could make off with the best bucketloads. As well as just about anything else that folks with an inventive nature might be able to find a use for.

So that's why I decided to call this hodge-podge of essays and verse what I did. Because no matter when or where any of us are born, most of us wind up resembling nothing more, nor less, than a beat-up old pot that's been filled to the brim with all the bits and pieces of blood, bone, sweat, and tears of the folks we've rubbed shoulders with along the way.

And way back in one of the more remote sections of my memory, there still sits a picture of a blue-enameled old pot, in which its owner stored most of the leftovers from his table. There's also a pretty fair possibility that the vessel may actually have been what was known in those days as a chamber-pot or slop-jar. For even though I know for a fact that it possessed a lid, I'm no longer completely sure whether it had a tightly rolled flange at the top, the way bail-handled kettles all did, or whether this particular one had the wide, inward-sloping flange that was found only on chamber-pots. Regardless of that though, this versatile vessel very often contained as much as a week's accumulation of the odds and ends of food that were still too good to throw out to the hogs or chickens. But once its owner grew weary of lugging it back and forth between the kitchen and his spring-house, since there was never enough room for it in his icebox, he just added some biscuit dough to its contents and called the resultant concoction pot-pie.

I think, that more than any other one characteristic which went into the making up of my being, it was this habit of hanging on to what they had until they'd exhausted virtually every possible use for it, that I inherited from the folks in my hometown. None of them fit the category you could call stingy or tight-fisted, for I doubt that there was a single one who wouldn't give you the shirt off his back if he liked you, and felt that you really needed it. It was just that by living through the so-called Great Depression, and all the other calamities that Life had seen fit to pile on their shoulders, they'd become about as self-sufficient a group of people as you could find.

There will always be events in our lives that leave a great deal to be desired, and I'm reasonably sure that most of us have wasted far too much time just feeling sorry for ourselves. This much I've learned though, there's almost always someone around who's got it one hell of a lot rougher than we ourselves do.

But out of all the things that might have happened otherwise in my own lifetime, I can't help wishing that I still had the opportunity to tell the people this book is about just how much I loved and respected them. A few of the names contained herein have been changed, solely to protect any descendants these particular individuals may have from the possibility of embarrassment. And since it has evolved almost entirely from my memory of the events depicted, there is more than a remote chance someone may remember things differently than I've told them.

I'm also fairly sure that a few of you will find places where the language and so-called humor are a little too down to earth for your tastes. But just as one can't expect a cook to come up with an authentic pot of gumbo or Texas-style chili without using the proper spices, you have to realize that a writer must use the same words and dialect his characters did, otherwise there's just no way he can honestly portray them. So grab a spoon an' dig in before it winds up gittin' too moldy.

My Father's Willow Chair

On a certain summer's evening, back around nineteen hundred and thirty-nine or so, there came a knock upon our front door.

And my father, a look of weary annoyance upon his face, pushed back his plate and rose slowly to his feet.

For, as both mother and father to my younger brother and me, he'd been up since dawn and was rightfully tired.

Yet he smiled upon reaching the door, I swear that he did, for I could sense it in his voice.

"Yes, my friend", he asked of the ragged hobo who was standing there, "what can I do for you?"

And the hobo, in a tone sounding ever so mean and surly, replied "Fer ten dollars cash, ya kin buy this here chair."

Now my father, who toiled at least two days for a similar amount, knew we had no need for yet another chair, for times were hard.

So he said "I can see that it's well made, my Friend, I'm sure you'll sell it before very long, somewhere on down the street."

The hobo's voice rose to a hoarse shout now, "On down th' street y'say? Th' Bloody Hell I can, I've already tried, man!"

"It's took me a solid week y'know, down in th' jungle b'low th' tracks an' watertank, t'fashion this."

"An' now I've lugged it from one end'a this lousy town t' th' other, just t'eat th' same ol' slop at ever' door."

"What's a guy like me s'posed t'do, I ask ya, beg like all th' other bums? Th' stinkin' Hell I will, I work fer what I get."

"So unless ya've supped t'night, as I have, on Ma Futility's stingy tit, how's about just givin' me five fer th' chair?"

But when he stalked off down the street some ten minutes later, two well-wrinkled portraits of Abraham Lincoln were snug in his pocket, and a bag of Dad's groceries was under his arm.

And for twenty-eight long years after that, the willow chair sat, in all its rustic glory, right there on Dad's front porch.

T'was an ever-present reminder to every vagrant who followed, that the man residing within our house had a kind heart.

And I, at least, was beginning to learn that even though they too can rest as uncomfortably at times as that willow chair, a person's dignity and pride in his work are two of the things he can least afford to lose.

Let It Be

Have I come this way before?
Has there ever in some far distant time,
Been the chance that my eyes have seen,
These wondrous sights? If not, then why do I feel
I sometimes know what lies in store?
Could there just possibly be, some reason sublime,
For mortal man to be reborn, and clean?
Please don't say there's not, just let it be real,
So that loves I've known, I'll know once more,
With friends to walk, and hills to climb,
Midst trees and flowers, on slopes of green,
Where sun and rain, and shadows steal,
Oh let me believe, I've been here before,
And just possibly will, at least once more.

GROVER C. HUFFNAGLE
& JOSIE COOPER
@ RIDGEWAY; CO. IN 1942

You Can Always Tell A Dyed In The Bull Politician But You're Just Wasting Your Breath 'Til He Closes His Mouth

A short time after deciding to run for the office of Town Treasurer, due to a substantial number of his little community's voters being scattered some distance out in the hills, Dad had rented a saddle-horse from the Ridgway Livery Stable and ridden clear out to the upper end of what was known as Beaver Creek valley. And since he'd discovered during the preceding weeks, while thumping his own tom-tom, that many of the country people seemed to take offense whenever he balked at sharing their midday hospitality with them, he'd begun timing his trusty steed's progress so that he could arrive at one of their homes as close to lunchtime as possible. Or at least just close enough to it so that he didn't appear to be looking for a handout, which was no doubt what everyone expected to be the case anyhow. But back in those days, thrift came a lot closer to being an admirable asset than it is today, as far as most politicians go, anyhow.

So after telling this Henry Cuddigan character why he was out and about, and letting him know that his vote would be appreciated, Dad chalked up another "Well, I dunno whether I'm gonna be goin' t'town that day er not, but I guess if I do, I might jist as well vote fer you as anybody else."

While Dad stood there trying to come up with some way to continue the conversation without making it too obvious that what he would like every bit as much as one more vote, would be an invitation to come inside for lunch, Henry beat him to the punch by saying "But so long as yer here, ya might jist as well c'mon in an' chew some vittles while yer chewin' th' fat! I was jist gittin' ready t'eat some stew an' biscuits, an' they're already warmed up, so it won't be no bother."

So while Dad was looking around for a place to put his horse, the old man said "But I'm jist about outta oats, so yer nag's gonna hafta be satisfied with some'a th' grass under that tree out there acrost th' road. Ya kin use that halter by th' gate t'tie `im out, if ya wanta."

And by the time Dad had gotten that done and had entered the small two-room log cabin, his host had already set another tin plate and cup on the table, along with a knife and fork. Feeling the necessity to compliment his host on his culinary abilities, as Dad sat down at the small rough-board table he said "I can't remember ever seeing fluffier-looking biscuits Henry, what's your secret?"

The old man beamed at this of course, saying "Ain't no secret to it, I jist gotta be sure I don't git carried away with m'fork when I'm stirrin' `em up, an' wind up overloadin' `em with flour.", referring to what was the more or less standard practice among work-conscious male cooks in those days, to save dirtying a bowl by mixing the dough right in the sack.

One of the highly prized pictures, albeit only the mental one that comes floating out of my memory at times, is of a certain high-heeled cowboy cook by the name of Harvey. And when I squint my eyes just right, I can still see my six-year old form hovering there beside him, in the soft, kerosene-glow of the lamps at hunting-camp. And if I hold my breath just long enough, I can also hear him saying "Y'see, Buzz, y'gotta make sort of a bowl right here in th' flour, then ya put in `bout this much bakin' powder, an' this much salt, an' ya pour in `bout this much milk. Then ya jist stir it around `til it's thick a'nuff t'flop out on th' cuttin'-board. There now, wasn't that easy?", and as a general rule, I still have a tendency to brush away the coating of flour his callused fingers always left on my nose, as he gave it his usual friendly pinch.

But whenever I start thinking of Harvey, I invariably arrive at the time when he finally became so disillusioned with his world that he decided to take his own life, and when I then have to blink back the tears this produces, the picture fades away into the dust of all those long-ago years.

Before I get too carried away, though, while Dad was sitting there at Henry's table he became aware of the tabby-cat that kept sidling up against his left leg and purring. Obviously the mother of a recent litter of kittens, she kept alternating between Dad's leg and his host's, until he finally said "She's sure a friendly cat, Henry, is it alright if I give her a little bite of biscuit?"

Henry snorted and replied "If ya do, she'll be up on yer lap b'fore ya know what's what." Then he reached down and shoved her toward the doorway of what was obviously his bedroom, saying "Go on now Missus, leave `im be. Ya need t'look after them brats'a yer's anyhow. Now scoot!"

Turning back to Dad, who'd just helped himself to another biscuit, which was somewhere around the fourth or fifth one he'd taken since sitting down, Henry said "I bin meanin' t'tell ya, ya might find one of `er hairs in them biscuits now an' then, th' damn little snip. While I was out doin' chores a'few days ago, she d'cided my flour-sack there on that box under th' window, was 'bout as good'a place t'birth 'er kittens as any. S'when I come back inside, she had their butts all dusted up real good. A'course I hustled 'er right on inta th' bedroom there, t'th' nest I'd already made up fer 'er, then I throwed out at least'a gallon'a flour. But there's still'a chance I might'a missed'a hair er two, I guess."

Dad had a little difficulty cleaning up his plate after that, but since the new mama had disappeared by this time, he saw very little alternative. Unless he wanted to risk offending his host, that is. By swallowing each bite at least twice, though, he eventually got the deed done. Then he lied through his teeth by saying "It's been a real pleasure, Henry, but I really need to get started back down the road, unless I can give you a hand with."

Being a polite sort of host, Henry just said "ya don't need t'worry 'bout th' dishes, I allus let Missus lick 'em off b'fore I wash 'em anyhow, an' she's busy feedin' 'er tribe right now. Go on an' take off."

Which was precisely what Dad said he did, like a Fourth of July rocket. He only made it around the first bend in the road though, before his stomach caught up with him. But as he always said, each time he related the story, "At least the trees kept Henry from seeing me vomiting everything he'd fed me. I sure didn't have much of an appetite for biscuits for a long time after that either. But I learned a really valuable lesson that day, believe you me!"

And whenever some member of his audience would ask "And what was that, Grover?" he'd laugh and say "Politics is so often such a disagreeable business to get involved in, I knew I just didn't have the stomach for it."

MARY GENEVIEVE HUFFNAGLE
GROVER F HUFFNAGLE SYDNEY A. HUFFNAGLE
(KAYO)   DOG-LADDY   (BUZZY)
PICTURE TAKEN APPROX. 1932

Virtual Reality

By the time I'd reached the ripe old age of four and a half, I'd grown accustomed to the idea that Mom and Dad could probably protect me from virtually anything that might happen, simply because they'd done a pretty good job of it thus far. So when Mom loaded Kayo and me into the back seat of our six year old Chrysler just a few days before Thanksgiving in 1932, after telling me we were going out to Venus and Scotty Rose's to pick up the turkey Venus had just called and said they had ready for us, I was about as ill-prepared for what was right on the verge of taking place as I could possibly have been.

So when I asked "Can Laddy come too, Mama? There's plenty'a room back here with us." she just said "No, honey, he can't. He'll just end up starting a fight with Scotty's dog, or barking his head off every time Buck comes close, so he's just going to have to stay home! We won't be gone all that long anyhow."

"Then how come yer not tyin' him to the big tree? Ya know he's jist gonna follow us!"

Wagging her head from side to side as she slid into the driver's seat, she responded with a highly impatient "Just because I'm pretty sure he'll turn around and come back before we start up the hill, that's why! Now please quit arguing and try to keep Kayo from falling off the seat and getting dirty before we even get out of the driveway!"

She sounded just cranky enough to make me think I'd probably said enough already, so once we'd started down the street toward the church, I devoted my attention almost entirely to Laddy, who was now trotting along about fifty feet behind us. Whispering somewhat conspiratorially to my little brother, who was just barely tall enough to see out the rear window, when I told him that I was "purty sure Laddy ain't gonna turn around.", Mom heard me and snapped "Then if you'll just sit back down where he can't see you, maybe he will!"

Consequently, since there wasn't much doubt as to my having strained her patience almost to the breaking point, I did as directed. At least for as long as it took her to drive halfway up Ridgway Hill. But then, when her attention seemed to be equally divided between shifting gears and dodging as many chuckholes as possible, I twisted around just far enough to see that even though Laddy was still coming, he was almost a full block behind, which was when I turned to see Mom grinning at me in the rearview mirror.

So when I now informed her "He's still comin', Mama." she winked and said "That's just because he's every bit as stubborn as you are, Sweetheart! But once we get to the top of the hill, where it's not so rough, I'm pretty sure he'll give up and go home. Anyhow, since I'm well aware of much you love that goofy old dog of yours, I'm sorry I was so cranky."

After telling her "That's okay Mama, I know you do too.", I was fairly sure it would be alright to get back on my knees and look out the rear window again. But despite her having gained at least another hundred yards on Laddy by the time we reached the top of the hill, when Kayo began mimicking my soft entreaties by yelling "Wun fassa Waddy, wun fassa!", she announced "Alright you guys, if he's still coming when we get to Sherbino Lane, I'll stop and let him in, even if he is going to get mud all over everything!"

We'd made it around the long curve to the first swale when I once again caught sight of Laddy, loping along in the ground-consuming gait that collies usually fall into once they've made up their mind it's the only way they're going to catch up with the object of their affection. Which in this case, just happened to be me.

He was still a good hundred yards from the swale when I saw a black Model-A pickup come over the top of the hill, roughly two hundred yards behind him. Concerned that Laddy might not hear it coming, I yelled "Mama, a truck jist came over the top'a the hill, we better stop an' let Laddy in before it ketches up with `im!"

Glancing quickly into the mirror, she said "I see the pickup, but where'soh, there he is, just coming out of the swale. Don't worry Honey, he must've already heard the truck, see how he's moving clear down off the shoulder into the grass. I can't stop here anyhow, the road's too narrow for the pickup to get past. We'll just go on up to the lane and wait for him there."

Reasonably sure Laddy was probably going to be alright, I felt the Chrysler leaning gently to my right as Mom turned off at Sherbino Lane. Then, all of a sudden, the black pickup swerved sharply to its left and headed straight toward Laddy, who by now was at least six or eight feet beyond the shoulder of the road.

Convinced that the little truck's driver must intend to run over my dog, I screamed "MAMA, THAT TRUCK'S GONNA HIT LADDY, YA GOTTA DO SOMETHIN' RIGHT NOW!"

I was vaguely aware of her saying "Oh my God!", just as the pickup's left front wheel struck Laddy. And by the time the little vehicle had bounced back up onto the gravel once more, Mom had jammed the Chrysler's gears into reverse and backed out into the middle of the road. Slamming on the brakes as she threw the door open, she yelled "You boys stay where you are, the rotten bastard's going to have to run over me before he gets past!"

Then, as the first tears began coursing down my cheeks, she raced around to the other side of the car and started waving her arms and jumping up and down, almost as though she was trying to fly. Which even if it did nothing else, must have made it pretty apparent to the man driving the pickup that she'd either seen what he'd done, or had gone completely off her rocker.

As unlikely as it may sound, there are times even now, over seventy-five years later, when all I have to do to bring the whole scene back into focus, is just to close my eyes. Perhaps that's only because as soon as he saw that he had no choice but to stop, the pickup's driver adopted such a look of feigned innocence, it was impossible to forget.

As soon as he rolled down his window, though, and said "Hi, Gene, what's got ya so stirred up?", Mom screamed "You know damned good and well what's got me stirred up, Ray, you rotten sonovabitch!"

Drawing her hand back then, she slapped him as hard as she could, demanding "What in God's name made you run that dog down the way you did?"

Looking almost as though he intended to deny that he had, he grabbed her hand just as she was drawing it back to slap him again. While struggling to jerk her hand loose, she yelled "Don't you dare try to lie your way out of this, gawddam you, I saw it with my own eyes. And what's even worse, my two little boys saw it too!"

Glancing momentarily toward where I had by now managed to roll down the window of our car, and was yelling "Hit 'im again, Mama, hit 'im again!", when he saw Kayo's and my tear-streaked faces, he must have decided to try and reason his way out of it, saying "Aw fer Christ's sake, Gene, it was only'a lousy dog! An' besides, ya didn't have any bizness lettin' 'im run loose, the way he was doin'."

This last barb apparently struck an exposed nerve in Mom, because she just stood there looking straight at him for several seconds, then her shoulders sagged as she burst out crying.

Wasting no time in taking advantage of his new situation, Ray growled "If yer through makin' a damn fool of yerself, I got bizness t'take care of on down the road."

When he let go of her hand to roll up his window, Mom just stood there staring at him for several more seconds, wagging her head as though she simply couldn't believe anyone could act the way he had. Then, as he began easing his still idling pickup around the front of our car, she walked over to stand close to Kayo and me.

Ducking her head through the open window, she whispered "I'm sorry boys, so sorry! If I'd just taken the time to tie Laddy up, or had stopped sooner, none of this would ever have happened."

Finally, after looking at me as though she was wondering how long it would be before I too would begin blaming her for Laddy's death, she said "But since I didn't, I guess I'll just have to live with it!"

Withdrawing her head then, she walked around the car and climbed in behind the steering-wheel once more. Starting the engine, she pulled far enough forward to allow room for turning toward town, then she drove slowly back to where Laddy's body was lying. After getting out to make sure he was indeed dead, she got back in and drove the rest of the way home, where she called Dad on the telephone and told him what had happened.

Consequently, when he hurried straight home from his office and took the car to go get Laddy, approximately one and a half hours later he came back and told us he'd buried our faithful friend beneath a large cedar tree on a little knoll across the road, a couple of hundred yards back toward town. The very next time we went out to Venus and Scotty's, though, I insisted on his stopping to show me where it was.

So even though he brought a new collie puppy home one night, barely a month after Laddy's death, I was never able to forget our first one. And by the time both Champ and I were big enough to be allowed to go pretty much wherever our legs would take us, Mom too had died.

But simply because her grave was nearly a mile and a half further down the road, up until another low-life bastard saw fit to run over Champ too, it was fairly common for the two of us to hike on over to Laddy's tree whenever we went up to the dump to look for pop bottles to turn in at Duckett's store, or to sail lard-bucket lids as high as they'd go, or just about anything that kids and their dogs used to do. And every so often, by the time we'd leave, there'd be a small bouquet of bluebells and tiny white daisies in the little mustard jar I'd brought over from the dump the first time we'd stopped to spend a little time with Laddy.

A Letter To Mama

Dear Mama,

I'm tryin' t'be good, but I bin cryin' quite'a lot
Well maybe not right at first, like I prob'ly should'a
But I did after I climbed inta bed an' Daddy turned out th' light
'Cause when ya didn't come kiss me er say "Sweet dreams lil' man"
I knew ya really must be dead, th' way Daddy said ya was
An' Mama, since I knew ya jist had to be up there in Heaven
After I fell asleep I dreamed I found th' stairs that go up there
An' even tho I knew that I sometimes fergit t'say my prayers
Th' way ya said God always likes fer us kids t'do
I started climbin' up t'see if maybe th' reason He was s'mad
Was 'cause He thought I really was bad most'a th' time
But when I got up t'th' top, some guy with long white hair
Was standin' there in front of'a great big gate
An' he said "Go 'way lil' boy, ya can't come thru 'til ya die
S'even tho I told 'im I jist wanted t'talk t'God fer'a minute
He said I couldn't, but then, when I started t'cry s'more

He said "I prob'ly shouldn't do it, but if ya promise t'be quiet

Ya can go knock on God's back door jist this once"

An' ya know what Mama, when Missus
God seen me standin' there

She smiled ever s'nice, an' asked if I'd like t'come inside

Jist fer'a minute,

So I said "Yes Mam" th' way ya always told me t'do

An' right there in her kitchen was this great big stove

That looked jist like ours, s'when she went t'tell God I'd come

T'ask if you was alright, I sat down b'hind it, 'cause I was cold

But ya don't need t'worry none Mama, er scold me neither

'Cause I didn't slide on down underneath of it

Th' way I usta do, when you was here at home

But since I fell asleep anyhow, I didn't git to talk t'God

Er ask 'im if it'll be alright t'come back agin after I'm seven.

Oh yeah Mama, if Laddie's up there with ya, please give 'im a hug

An' pat 'is head ever now an' then, 'cause he always liked that

A House By The Side Of The Road

Resembling a seed that's taken root simply because an errant breeze chose to deposit it in a specific time and locality, my earliest recollection of the old two-story white house was planted firmly in place one sunny Sunday, during what was more than likely my fourth summer. Sitting just a short distance north of the dam that has so recently turned the Uncompahgre River into one of Western Colorado's more popular playgrounds, the house looked a great deal smaller the last time I passed by it, than it did that long ago day when Dad parked our 1926 Chrysler beside the gate leading to Frank and Mamie Hafley's front door. By then of course, our old gas-wagon had been stirring up Ouray County's dust a full two years longer than I had.

And as I went charging toward the porch, Frank stepped out onto it, bellowing "Gitcher gun quick, Mamie, the dad-blamed renegade jist got here!"

Then, after several minutes of serious rough-housing, he led me inside and pointed toward a brightly-wrapped box resting on one of the plates ringing the perimeter of the large table in the center of the kitchen. And he told me "If ya don't clean that box off'a yer plate before Mother Leisey's chicken gits done fryin', yer jist gonna be outta luck, Kiddo!"

So by the time the last shred of paper had fluttered to the floor, I'd jerked the lid from the box and discovered the pair of cowboy boots it contained. A fraction the size of those on Frank's feet, they were identical in every other respect, making it quite obvious that they'd been produced as a result of his orders to his personal boot-maker. And if I wasted more than a second or so in jamming my feet inside them, it was only because my shoes wouldn't come off until he'd extracted my fumbling fingers from their tangled laces.

So after we spent the next few minutes seeing if they'd go as fast as his, and as loud, it was only by dint of Dad's threat to remove them by force, that I finally agreed to belly-up to the table when Mother Leisey announced that her chicken was ready to eat. But a few minutes later, when Frank saw fit to inquire as to whether I'd perfected my whistling yet, and I'd managed to blow chicken-crumbs all over the tablecloth in a not too successful attempt to prove that I had indeed, Dad informed me that whistling at the table was a sure-fire way of bringing on a spell of bad luck. Since I was already wise to the way he could twist any proverb's tail into doing what he wanted it to, I didn't have too much trouble in figuring out he was once again threatening to take my new boots away from me.

During the course of the next few years though, we made the trip down to Frank and Mamie's house a great many times. So many in fact, it's nothing short of miraculous that the Chrysler survived as long as it did, considering the roughness of the road and the number of times it had to negotiate all the Rio Grande Western railroad-crossings there were in those days. And during these visits I learned that the Hafleys had once been part of Buffalo Bill's Wild West Show. Then they'd started one of their own, naming it California Frank's Wild West Show, no doubt because such shows were then in vogue.

But by the time it was eventually disbanded, it had played not only in New York City's Madison Square Gardens, it had also appeared in England and numerous cities in Europe, just to show all the kings and queens who lived in that part of the world what a grand and glorious place the American West truly was. So if you think I wasn't impressed with the stories I heard in that old white house, it's been entirely too long since you were a kid.

In her heyday Mamie had been billed as the World's Champion Trick Shot, and their daughter Rene supposedly held the title of World Champion Trick Rider. At least that's what I was told, as well as what was printed on some of the old posters hanging on the walls of their living room. Pretty heady stuff for a kid to digest, wouldn't you agree?

So just how, you might well ask, did a runny-nosed twerp like me happen to get so lucky as to be hobnobbing with such important folks. Well sir, it was simply because Dad owned the one-man real estate agency that arranged for them to buy their little ranch. And during the time it had taken to find property that suited them, Dad took them down to look at Charley Marlow's place. And just in case you weren't already aware of it, Charley himself would one day be portrayed by none other than Dean Martin, in that rootin' tootin' Hollywood epic, *The Sons of Katie Elder*.

Of course it was John Wayne who got to play Charley's older brother, Frank. For some reason or other though, the movie's director didn't include what had happened to Charley the day Dad brought the Hafleys down to look at his ranch, even though Dean would probably have gotten a real charge out of it.

Because after they'd spent the whole morning walking all over his fields and pastures, Dad said that Charley insisted they have lunch with him. Naturally enough, once she got inside the house and saw some of the rifles Charley had in his gun cabinet, Mamie just had to comment on them. And since this gave her host the opportunity to elaborate at great length all through lunch, as to his prowess with the various weapons, the hour passed all too quickly. So due to the fact that Charley was busy doing most of the talking, Frank didn't have the least bit of trouble in finding plenty to eat.

Well before he'd gotten his fill, though, he'd also found the means for setting up one more performance of his beloved *Wild West Show*. So he wasted no time in suggesting "Maybe Mister Marlow will let you borrow one of his rifles for a few minutes when we finish eating, Mamie, and you can show him you know a little about guns yourself."

Since he was totally unaware of his guests' background, Charley swallowed Frank's bait without even batting an eye, by responding "Sure thing Miz Mamie, jist take yer pick'a anything in the cab'net, they all shoot straight." Then he continued regaling them with stories about all the various deer, bear, and other animals he'd taken with the rifles, right up until Frank finally got through with his fork.

Once Mamie had chosen a little pump-action 22 caliber rifle from the cabinet, and they'd filed out the door to the backyard, Frank picked a rusty condensed-milk can out of the trash-box, saying "Now when I toss this in the air, Mamie, I'd like to see you put a hole in it."

Of course this caused Charley to protest "That's askin' an awful lot of 'er ain't it? 'Specially since she ain't even had a chance t'try it out yet! Fact'a the matter is, I ain't too sure I could do it myself!"

Dad said Frank just grinned and replied "I've never believed in making things easy for folks, even when they happen to be women, Charley, and most especially when the woman is my wife.", then he tossed the can up and Mamie took a shot at it.

After Frank had picked the can up and inspected it, he said "Ya musta got lucky, Kiddo.", before tossing it over for Charley to look at.

According to Dad, Charley responded with something like "Well I'll be damned!", but that was all he could manage before Frank got another can from the box and said "Alright Missy, let's see you hit this one twice."

And sure enough, when Frank tossed the can to them after Mamie shot two more times, once just before the can reached the top of its arc, and once more as it started down, there were two sets of holes in it.

But this time, even though Charley couldn't seem to come up with an appropriate comment, Dad said he stared at Frank as if he was finally beginning to realize he'd jumped square in the middle of a rigged game.

Apparently Frank didn't believe in making things easy for men either, because after selecting another milk-can, he said "I think maybe you've got their attention now, Missy, how about adding a little bonus this time."

Dad swore that Mamie's three shots were so close together he could hardly distinguish between them. And after Charley had seen the result, he walked over to where Mamie stood grinning at them, almost as though she'd just grabbed the biggest slice of pie, and he said "I sure would appreciate it Miz Hafley, if ya'd jist try an' fergit ever'thing I told ya about my shootin' awhile ago. But if it ain't askin' too awful much, would ya mind tellin' me how in jumpin' blue blazes ya learned t'aim that fast?"

Once she'd explained that there's never enough time to actually aim with that kind of shooting, a person just has to point and pull, she went on to explain how she'd fired as many as five hundred practice rounds a day while they were touring with their show, just to keep her skill honed to perfection. Then she apologized for allowing her husband to do what he had, shaking her finger at Frank as she admonished "You really should be ashamed of yourself, you know. Especially after making such a hog of yourself at lunch!"

But since the primary intent when I started shooting off my mouth at the start of this, was to pay homage to one of the sweetest ladies I was ever fortunate enough to know, it's about time to let you hear some more about Mother Leisey.

According to the small stone at the head of her grave, she'd been christened Fannie C. at birth, but shortly after she'd been hired by Frank and Mamie to provide the nursing necessary for keeping the performers of their show in shape, everyone had begun calling her Mother. And by the time the show eventually closed, since she'd already spent so much of her life ministering to the needs of the Hafleys, it's my understanding that they offered to provide her a place in their home for as long as she needed it, in return for her help in looking after their interests.

But if there was ever a lady more deserving of the image the title "Mother" evokes for most of us, I've no idea who it could possibly be. For the only fault I ever discovered in her character, if it could actually be called that, was that she was positively the most unimaginative fibber I'd ever encountered. Otherwise she surely would have been able to come up with a more plausible sounding explanation as to what had brought about the sudden demise of Billy the Kid, the pet goat I'd very reluctantly allowed Dad to leave with her a few weeks earlier. Presumably, so she could teach him some manners in return for his help in keeping the weeds out of her front yard.

Honestly now, have you ever encountered a single five-year old boy who'd even come close to swallowing a cockamamie yarn about how the goat that had butted his rump until he could hardly stand to sit down, had actually broken his fool neck by trying to knock a dumb old hitching-post out of the ground? But I'll readily admit that my tears had more than likely caught her with her guard down, since she'd undoubtedly been expecting Dad to explain to me that when a headstrong boy-goat isn't needed for the perpetuation of the species, the only prudent thing to do is to turn him into goat-chops.

Although it took me awhile to accept the fact that she wasn't quite as perfect as I'd thought she was, I eventually forgave her for not letting me know what was brewing, in time so that Billy and I could run away and join a circus, just in case we couldn't locate another show like Frank's.

For when he and Mamie had discovered that the sedentary life of a farmer lacked virtually all the excitement they'd enjoyed while touring the world at the helm of the covered wagon bearing the banners of "California Frank's Wild West Show", every few months they'd find some reason to go gallivanting off into the sunset, leaving Mother Leisey to keep the home fires burning until they returned.

And due to the fact that their little farm was somewhere around eight dusty miles from her nearest source of supplies, Mother Leisey soon had ample reason to take to the road on her own. Her travelling was done via Shank's Mare though, since there'd been no need to keep a team of horses around after Frank leased most of his land to one of his neighbors. For even if he'd provided her with an automobile, it's not too likely that she'd have agreed to try and learn how to drive it. So the only other option she had, was to do without until she could find time to start hoofing it up the road to Ridgway.

Because even though most of the little ranch's land was being farmed by the man leasing it, a fairly good-sized pasture for Frank's saddle horse, as well as a large garden-plot, was apparently Mother Leisey's responsibility. At least virtually every time I can remember going down there during the summer, she was either out hoeing the garden, or tromping around the pasture in her black rubber irrigating boots, with a shovel in her hand. Of course the garden and front yard were also irrigated in the same manner. You see, the world of mechanization hadn't yet progressed much beyond automobiles and trains in our neck of the woods. So it would still be several years before the term "running-water" meant anything other than running to the pump or spring-house with a bucket, for most of Ouray County's farmers.

And as a general rule, at least after Mom died, once Mother Leisey had gotten what she needed from the store, she'd swing on up the street to our house, just to make sure we were getting along alright. Then, after satisfying herself that we were doing as well as could be expected, she'd pick up her shopping bag and head for the door. And unless Dad could come up with an acceptable reason to check out a prospective real estate listing somewhere in the vicinity of where she was going, that would be the last we'd see of her until the next time she needed something from the store.

But whenever she got the idea he was doing it solely to save her from making the long walk, she'd jerk her shoulders as straight as they'd go, poke her knobby-knuckled finger about an inch from his nose, and say "Grover, you know good and well the only reason I came by was to see how you and the boys were getting along. These old feet of mine have have walked across an awful lot of the ground this world is made of, and they've still got a good many miles left in them. So don't you dare rob me of my pride, by trying to invent some fool excuse for taking me home!"

From time to time, though, providing he couldn't sell her his first bill of goods, she'd consent to wait long enough for him to call a few neighbors who might be getting ready to drive at least part of the distance. But if he wasn't able to find anyone, out the door she'd march, her old navy-blue straw hat perched squarely on top of her white head, its silken flowers bobbing in time to each and every resolute step. And as the years crept slowly by, she was eventually forced to rely upon a willow walking-staff. Then, after the passage of a few more years, the staff was replaced with a store-bought cane.

So even though I truly hate to admit it, I can't remember just when it was that I last saw her clipping off the miles on that long road home. Because by then I'd progressed all the way through the age of Ovaltine, to that of gasoline, and I was no longer as thoughtful of her needs as I should have been. And by the time I'd finally learned that love freely given can only be repaid by regular doses of love returned, it was too late to tell her how much she'd added to my life, simply because she cared enough to come by and ask "How're you fellas gettin' along?"

But Mother, I really did love you!

Mother Leisey.

Pride

It's a priceless thing you know, the honest kind at least
For without it, man would be no better than the mindless beast
But one of the most truly amazing things about it, or so I think
Is that just when it seems to have been pushed on over the brink
By all the many political clowns who seem to endlessly scheme
And rob you of it, you'll note, for the price of your vote
It can never be killed, at least not in its entirety
So long as one man, or woman, is willing to be an anomaly
And stand out in the crowd, by yelling long and loud
"Keep yer handouts sucker, I still got my pride!

Aw Gee Dad, Do I Haf'ta?

The number of times that the above question is asked by small boys may not actually equal the number of stars in the sky, fish in the ocean, or leaves in a forest, but there's a pretty fair chance that most fathers might be inclined to argue the point every now and again. I know mine quite easily could have. Because despite Mom's assurance that I'd eventually get to where it would no longer be necessary, he seemed to feel it was up to him to see to it that I brushed my teeth every morning and night, washed my hands before each meal, then ate the spinach that he loved and I hated. All of this just so I'd be healthy and look as much like a gentleman as possible, when I finally reached that elusive goal.

But whenever he handed me a dime as he was heading out the door to go to work, I knew my hair had finally gotten long enough so that I could head down to Mister Charlie Chapell's Barbershop again, at least just as soon as Mom said the hands on our clock were close enough to nine so that I could be sure of covering the three block distance in time to be the first in line. Now even though the top of Charlie's head fell at least an inch short of reaching up to the point where most men's tonsils begin, you've no doubt already reached the conclusion that I considered him something of a tonsorial artiste, if not actually a bona fide virtuoso.

So since he and his family lived in a little apartment at the rear of his shop, the first thing he'd see when he'd raise the blind on his door that morning would be my back, draped in the blue suspenders of my bib-overalls. That is unless I'd heard the floorboards squeak under his feet, or had felt them vibrate slightly beneath my rump, and had corkscrewed erect without falling down. Then, of course, he'd get a glimpse of what Dad had seen some two hours earlier, when he'd not only checked to see if my face was clean enough to go through our daily oatmeal and toast ritual, but whether there were also enough teeth left in the gap to get everything herded in the direction of the gulley leading to the bottomless pit.

As a general rule, once he'd gotten the door unlocked, Charlie would barely have time to get his freshly shined shoes out of the way before I'd have it pushed all the way open and would be yelling "Hi Mister Charlie, is this'a two-fer-one day?"

So he'd walk over to his big Burgher Brothers Barber Supplies calendar and run his finger back and forth and up and down for a few seconds, then he'd grin and say "By golly, it sure 'nough is! Guess this's yer lucky day agin. S'jist climb up on th' board an' git comf'table, while I git this here ol' straight-edge sharp a'nuff t'slice off that beard, b'fore yer hair gits plumb down t'yer chin an' I can't see what I'm doin'."

Feeling like I must have been born under just about the luckiest star in the whole world, at least as far always landing on one of Charlie's two-fer-one days went, I'd jump up onto that brightly chromed scroll-work reminder of why Burgher Brothers always sent him a new calendar every year. Then I'd grab hold of one of the genuine marble armrests with both of my hands and haul myself on up to the white-enameled board that was now waiting for me. So once the stropping had been completed, and he'd held the razor up so that I could look for any nicks in the blade, without being able to reach it and ending up with some nicks in my finger instead, Charlie would lay it on the counter and take the cape from its hook.

And if it was the one with candy-cane stripes, instead of the sissy-looking one with the little blue pansies all over it, you'd be safe in betting that I was feeling especially lucky by the time it had been tucked tightly around my neck, "Jist so none'a them sharp ol' whiskers a'yers wind up down inside yer B-V-D's."

After he'd put a little warm water in his soap-mug and whipped the brush round and round, until the mug was so full of foam that he'd say "Lordy, I bet there's a'nuff suds in there t'shave a'full growed grizzly bear! Ya think maybe that'll be a'nuff?", the real show was just about ready to begin.

At least it was, once I'd gotten to say "It might be Mister Charlie, if ya don't git any on my nose agin."

So then he'd waltz around the chair like it was an artist's easel, dabbing soap on my chin and cheeks until they just wouldn't support another drop. And right at the very last second, he'd go "Ah-ah-ah-ah-ahhhhh-choooooo", and almost as if by magic, I'd wind up with a dollop of soap on my nose that looked as big as a basketball. At least to my crossed eyes, it did. But even though I hated to get more than a trace of soap on my face at home, Charlie could have iced me up like a birthday cake and I'd be loving every speck of it.

Then he'd say "Land sakes, I must'a breathed in'a feather er somethin', it sure did tickle.", and he'd pick up the razor. But despite how many times he'd already performed this same virtually identical ritual, I'd always draw back away from that wicked-looking razor until my head was pressed against the chair-back and would go no further. Then he'd lay one hand on top of my head and say "Okay, close yer eyes tight now, so we don't git any soap in 'em. An' set real still, I sure would hate t'slice that nose a'yers off."

But once I'd feel him shave the soap off my nose, and would reopen my eyes, he'd say "That come off s'slick it might be best if ya shut 'em agin, an' jist let me tell ya when it's okay t'open 'em. What'a ya think?", so of course I'd do as he said.

I eventually learned that once my eyes were squinted as tightly together as I could get them, he'd swap the razor for one of the combs in the pocket of his smock, or use the back of the razor itself. But it was so much fun playing the game his way that I never let him know I'd peeked through my eyelashes just that one time. So after he'd wiped my face with a damp cloth, he'd point toward several bottles sitting beneath the big mirror and ask "Okay, which one's it gonna be t'day, th yella one, th' green one, er th' red one?"

And when I'd invariably pick the red one, he'd pick up the yellow one. So just as soon as I'd yell "Mister Charlie, ya got th' wrong one agin." he'd say "I don't know why I even bother t'ask ya what one ya want, since ya must be color blind, er somethin'."

Then he'd shake a drop or two into his hand from that yellow bottle and say "Okay, hang on tight, this is purty powerful stuff an' it might burn a'little.", then he'd rub my cheeks so fast they'd turn pink and my teeth would rattle. So he'd say "See, didn't I tell ya it was powerful?"

And once I'd gotten my eyes refocused again and had said "Boy, ya sure was right Mister Charlie.", we'd each have a good laugh.

So by the time he finally got around to cutting my hair, he'd already have devoted at least fifteen or twenty minutes on me. And in those days, unless a person was as bald as a billiard ball, he could bank on spending at least thirty minutes in the chair, while his hair was being cut. But even though I can't say for certain that Charlie didn't charge the men fifteen cents for cutting theirs, I know for an absolute fact that he collected only a dime from kids like me. They just don't seem to make that kind of bargain nowadays, you know.

There was another reason I thought Charlie was pretty special though, three of them actually. For out behind his little apartment he had a kennel that contained three very large and, so we kids were firmly convinced, extremely dangerous bloodhounds. And since most of the time they'd lay there in the straw and dust of the kennel floor, with their eyes seemingly closed, most of us were certain that they must be every bit as cunning as they were dangerous.

Consequently, since Charlie was brave enough not only to enter the kennel with their feed and water, but also to attach leashes to their nail-studded collars and then take them out for a run, in my eyes at least, he ranked as an equal to old Bring-em-back-alive, Frank Buck. But I don't suppose there's much chance that most of you latter-day squirts have ever heard of him, either.

Located as that little kennel was, on the side of a dilapidated old assortment of boards and battens that looked just like most of the other storage sheds around Ridgway, it pretty much sat right in the center of us kids' universe. For diagonally across the insection of the alleys, in the southwest quarter of the block was our Community Church, where most of us attended Sunday School. In my case, most frequently under duress. North of the church and just west of the kennel was Perkins' Garage, the sole supplier of vehicles for our annual Tire Racing Derby.

Which, just incidentally, could occur on each and every day of each and every summer, at least as long as we could find enough tires in George's garbage pile to hold one. And if you think those old tires of his weren't the next thing to greased lightning, it's just because you never had to dig one out from under all those supposedly empty oil cans.

Anyhow, before I get sideswiped by an altogether different train of thought, the quarter block east of the church and south of the kennel contained the Oddfellows Hall. And whether you care to believe it or not, there probably wasn't an odder bunch of fellows in the whole country, than what collected there every time they had their weekly get-together. Why if us kids had ever even come close to making as much racket as what came blasting out through the walls of that old building, when they got all wound up inside, we wouldn't have been able to sit down for a month.

Hanging on the north wall of the hall though, more or less like the tailend of an afterthought, was the local creamery. But whether it was just because it didn't smell so hot or not, most of us kids didn't waste much time hanging around there. Seventy-five feet or so back up the street though, on the southeast corner of the block, was one of the little rusty-red, corrugated metal sheds that housed one of the hosecarts our volunteer firemen used in those days. So when we didn't have anything more exciting to do, two of us would latch onto the hand-shafts, which were designed so that a single fireman could pull the cart to a fire without too much effort. Then we'd snort and nicker our way to several highly imaginary blazing infernos during the course of the next fifteen minutes or so. Unless something more promising showed up in the meantime, that is.

But the quarter-block that Charlie's shop and kennels were in, also contained Wade Carmichael's Grocery, where a friendly inquiry of "Hi Mister Wade, how ya doin' t'day?" almost always produced three or four saltines from the large wooden barrel at the end of his cash register counter. And if we held our mouths just right, and there weren't more than two or three of us, we could usually count on ol' Wade for a generous dollop of peanut-butter, to go along with the crackers.

But whenever the contents of that big, wide-mouthed jar of his had been ladled out too many times without adequately remixing the oil that had separated, the two or three inches of goo it contained looked as though it might have come from the same barrel as the gear-grease at Perkins' Garage. Then the dollop became a wallop and we really had to hustle to get back outside before we dripped peanut-soup all over Wade's floor.

Down on the other side of Charlie's shop was the Sherbino Theater, where Dad ran the projector part of the time. Most of the movies that I recall seeing at this little theater were the silent variety, or at least they were supposed to be. But when Jack Holt or Tom Mix were starring in one of them, they were anything but silent. And this was only partly because the piano player played faster and faster, as the action got hotter and hotter. Why about the only reason that Tom or Jack didn't get elected president in 1932 and 1936, instead of Franklin Delano Roosevelt, was just because us kids weren't allowed to vote.

And right smack between the theater and the northeast corner of the block, our town's founding fathers had left just enough room for Sam Boucher's Drugstore and Soda Fountain. But since us kids didn't need a whole lot of artificial stimulation to get all hopped up over life in those days, we just called it Sam's Soda Fountain. Why if any of us had ever gone in there and said "Gimme'a hit'a Castoria, Mister Sam, an`a coupl'a jolts'a calcidine.", he'd have swallowed his wad of tobacco right then and there. But that should give you some idea of how much we knew about the really high-powered drugs he sold.

And now that you've found out why my little world revolved around Charlie Chapell's Barbershop, we might just as well go all the way to the dogs, together. In order to do that, though, you're going to have to make believe it's six o'clock in the morning and we're lying side by side in bed. You're probably already half asleep anyhow, so you shouldn't have to strain too hard to get in the proper mood.

"But wait a minute, that sounds jist like Mister Charlie's mean ol' bloodhounds right now. I'll bet he's let `em outta th' pen agin! Golly, but I hope he don't let go'a their leashes, er trip an' git drug t'death, er somethin'. They're gittin' closer, too, s'he must be comin' straight up th' alley from his place this mornin'. Oh criminy, would ya jist listen at `em howl? They must be right down at th' end'a th' street now, by Gramma Cohen's house. I sure hope she don't open `er door er nothin', b'fore they git past. Er I'll hafta find someone else t'witch off th' next wart I git."

"Whew, sounds like it's ooh oh, they must'a jumped Miz Stevens'es big tomcat agin. C'mon Mister Charlie, hang on tight. Hey, hold on doggone it, if I'd known ya was gonna hog th' pillow, I wouldn'ta let ya git in here with me. Oh well, here then, take th' darn thing, I'll plug up my ears with my fingers."

"Guess Brutus must'a got away from `em okay agin, er they'd be makin' lots more noises b'sides them plain ol' "awoooo awoooo, awoooo's", I bet. Boy! I don't know what they latched onto one mornin' last week, `less maybe it was'a skunk er somethin', but they sure did make'a racket. Well, sounds like they made it clear `round t'th' schoolhouse, s'I guess we can git back t'what we was fixin' t'do b'fore they started all that yowlin'."

"Last one t'th' outhouse is a'sissy!"

"Wow! Yer a'lot faster'n ya looked. But ya jist better not go dribblin' on th' seat, `cause Dad likes t'set an' look at th' catalogue awhile, `specially since he knows it's last years an' he don't haf'ta worry `bout sendin' off fer none'a th' stuff. Man-oh-man, would ya jist lookit them nifty boots, with th' pocket-knife holder? Wouldn't they look neat with'a pair'a them tight-legged britches there? One'a these times I'm gonna ask Dad."

Above All Else

If I've learned a solitary thing, while
traveling Life's often lonely road

It's just that it doesn't really matter worth a Tinker's diddly damn

How well I'm dressed when at last I
stumble over that old finish line

Or whether my speech is sometimes
sprinkled with too salty a curse

No, what matters the very most I think, is
whether I've carried my end of the load

And have taken the time to lend some poor
devil a helping hand, when he's in a bind

For if there's anything that could possibly be
worse, than just winding up all alone

T'would only be in knowing I'd left not
a single soul back there behind,

Just to whisper "I'll miss you, My Friend!"

Court Of Last Resort

Although there's a very remote possibility of my being mistaken, I'm fairly sure the little pushy-pully doohickey that was at least partly responsible for that somewhat ominous sounding title at the top of this page was located on the dashboard rather than the shift-lever. For just because yours truly was the 9-year old knothead that pulled the goofy knob out in the first place, as well as the 73 year-old windbag that was originally responsible for writing this thing for the sake of posteriority somewhere in the neighborhood of 9 years ago. All of which ought to make it fairly apparent as to how far some of us are willing to go for the sake of as much notoriety as we're able to achieve by working our fingers to the bone on a dang fool keyboard, not to mention a severely chafed hemorrhoid that's been caused by sitting on our rump 8 to 10 hours a day. Anyhow, it pretty much looks like you're stuck with knob staying on the dashboard for the duration of this thing. Unless, of course, you're willing to take a chance on my old buddy, Judge Jelsma's coming back from the grave long enough to fine you for Contempt of Court!

But since none of this would even have happened if Dad had just taken my little brother and me fishing that morning, instead of forcing us to wait until after he'd had a chance to con our new County Judge and his wife into buying the piece of property he'd recently received the right to sell. So it was just as much his fault as mine that the pushy-pully doohicky got pulled. Because when you come right down the nitty-gritty of the whole fiasco, if he hadn't went and traded our perfectly good 1926 Chrysler in for a dang old 1935 secondhand Chevy that had a whole gob'a stuff on it that neither one of us knew a dang thing about, it sure as the devil seems like he really should'a knew better.

Anyway, since the knob had "Free-wheeling' wrote right in plain sight on it, it just seemed like it should be pulled all the way out, instead'a shoved all the way in, since it was really difficult way back then to get practically anything for free. For just on account'a the way that dang George Perkins was chargin' at least 15 cents a gallon for gasoline at that time, ya really had to watch 'im close to make sure he let all the air-bubbles get to the top'a the globe before he pulled the trigger on the hose. An' that's for double-dang sure! But just because Dad an' the Judge hadn't much more than took off through the toolies before Missus Jelsma told Kayo an' me she was just gonna hike on over to a little grove of Quakies to see if there was any Indian paintbrush or columbines growin' among 'em. So I told Kayo that all she was prob'ly tryin' to find was someplace to take a leak without comin' right out an' sayin' so.

She hadn't gotten much more than fifty feet from the car though, before we'd crawled up into the front seat, where I promptly slid under the steering-wheel and began doing my darnedest to beat Barney Oldfield to the finish-line, zooming and vahrooming all over the countryside without even raising a speck of dust. But after my motor started misfiring and threatened to just cut out altogether, I told the twerp that as long as he promised not to tell Dad how fast I'd been going and wouldn't honk the horn or mess with any of the knobs and shifters, he could drive awhile. Otherwise I was flat-out gonna knock his dang block off!

Consequently, due to his actually keeping his big mouth shut for once, by the time we finally got started back down the road toward town, the Judge had already asked his wife what she thought about the property. So when she said she thought that as long as he thought it was alright to go ahead and buy it, it was okay with her. So I pretty much decided that everything was prob-ably gonna work out alright. Which, even if it proves absolutely nothing else, just goes to show how dad-blamed easy it is for a kid to get in trouble when his Dad's dumb enough to go ahead and buy a dang ol' car he don't know nothin' about.

Because when we got to where the road started down off the top of a dinky little hill that wasn't even close to bein' anywhere near as steep as the one after that turned out to be, an' Dad had to stomp on the brake 6 or 8 times to slow us down enough to finally git stopped, he shook his head from side to side and said "I don't know what in the world's gotten into this thing today, but first thing Monday morning I'm taking it down to Perkin's Garage to get the brakes fixed.

Judging from the way the Judge kept glancing over his shoulder at me though, just like he figured I could prob'ly shed some light on the case if I was so inclined, it was beginning to look like I was either gonna have to come right out an' admit I had a pretty good idea as to what might be responsible for our current state of affairs, or take a chance on his being a lot more lenient than he looked.

Anyway, by the time I finally decided the latter of the two options had a lot more going for it, we'd already passed the point of no return an' seemed to be headed for "HOLY COW, Dad, if ya don't watch out, we're gonna run right smack into that big ol' pine tree an'MAN OH MAN but that was closeOh oh, here comes another one, over on the other siJimminy Chris'mas, I bet we didn't miss than one more'n a inch erJudas Jumpin' up Priest, Kayo, ain't Dad jist about the very best driver ya ever seen", which was as far as I got before Dad bellowed "Buzz, will you just shut up and sit back down where you belong, before you get us all killed! It's hard enough to keep my mind on what I'm doing without having you screaming in my ear like that!"

So in spite of the fact that the Judge didn't come right out and say anything, when he turned sideways just far enough to barely wink at me, I was pretty sure he must have decided I'd already learned my lesson, or had most assuredly suffered enough for one day. In any event, due to our having reached the bottom of the hill by this point in time, he waited until Dad had pulled over to the side of the road and stopped, before saying "That was as fine a job of driving as I've ever seen, Grover. For a little while there I wasn't at all sure you'd be able to pull it off. But even though it's plain to see that you really know what you're doing, while I was watching you twist that wheel every which way, I couldn't help noticing that the Free-Wheeling knob seems to have worked its way out, more than likely from the vibration of bouncing around on these rough old roads all the time. So even though I've never owned a car that was equipped with one, I cant help wondering if that might not have been what the problem was all along. And since the quickest way of finding that out is just to go ahead and shove the fool thing in, it seems to me that it might be worth a try"

Needless to say, two of the most important lessons I learned that day were that it's hardly ever too good an idea an idea to mess around with stuff you know nothing about, and just because Justice, such as it is, almost always prevails, there really isn't any point in tossing in the towel until such time as you flat-out have to!

Do You Ever Wonder Why

So much of mankind finds less to favor in the bellow of the impotent ox, than in the throaty roar of the caged and castrated lion?

And why does the laboring beast's awkward stance seem to signify he is incapable of experiencing pain, and also joy, to the same degree as the graceful gazelle?

Or why the dull wetness of the oxen eye seems to mean its host can neither recognize the beauty of a misty morn, nor find his peace within the velvet folds of night?

I do.

But then I too have raised my hoarse voice, seemingly in vain, stumbled wearily while longing only to dance. All so I might eventually discover that until such time as a man has slaked his thirst on the bitter water flowing from the fountain of futility, he can never hope to gain the peace he seeks!

A Special Breed

Our little town lost several men during the fighting of World War II, but there's one in particular who comes to mind every so often. For despite the fact that each of them gave everything they had to give, it's always seemed to me that Jack dug just a little deeper than any of us had a right to expect of him. But America seemed to be a different place back then, even though it probably really wasn't, since a person's age has always had such a lot to do with the way he looks at things.

And being slightly less than fourteen years old when Japan bombed Pearl Harbor that Sunday in December of 1941, my tender age undoubtedly had a lot to do with my spending the first three years of the war hoping it wouldn't end until I'd gotten old enough to help pay the Japanese back for what they'd done. So with all the foolish bravado of youth, I went down to Hockley's General Store on December eighth, after school let out, and spent my entire nest-egg on as much 22 caliber ammunition as it would buy, also purchasing several five cent tubes of bee-bees for my air-rifle, just to sharpen up my marksmanship with.

The nest-egg itself came from peddling the excess eggs that were produced by my father's flock of laying hens, which just incidentally would probably have layed a lot more eggs if my brother and I had taken the kind of care of them that Dad wanted us to.

Anyhow, patriotism being such an easy thing for young shoulders to adapt to, during the next year or so one of my schoolmates and I spent most of our free daylight hours roaming the hills around town, pretending that the numerous fat prairie dogs were either the Japanese, Italian, or German generals whose demise would bring about a near miraculous end to hostilities when we eventually got to the front lines. But even though killing prairie dogs was deemed necessary back then, in order to prevent beef animals and horses from breaking a leg in their burrows, I couldn't help feeling we weren't really doing everything we should, since the only person I knew of that ate the little rodents was a Navajo Indian who worked for one of the local ranchers. The Indian's name was Grover, the same as my father's.

The rancher's name was Forrest Binder, but we all just called him Frosty. Ranching wasn't really Frosty's field of expertise, even though it was in one of his fields that Butch Nickleby and I spent so much of our time, either plunking prairie dogs with our little rifles, or diverting enough irrigation water into their burrows to force them to the surface. Because then, if we were quick enough, we could either club them with a stick, or grab them with our bare hands, the way Grover got most of the ones he ate.

Brutal as it may sound to those of you whose animal indoctrination came about from watching or reading Walt Disney cartoons and assorted other fairy tales, I tended to lean more toward the Teddy Roosevelt method, by trying to walk softly, while carrying a big stick. At least after my sole attempt at emulating 'Bring 'em back alive, Frank Buck' had ended up with my having to choke one of the little varmints into submission, just so I could extract his chisel-like front teeth from my extremely bloody finger.

And even though I take very little satisfaction in it at this point in time, being able to drop a robin back then, with one well-placed beebee, usually meant that our parents would be able to harvest enough strawberries so that they wouldn't have to buy something else from the grocery store. Even if we did have to eat them with a little honey instead of sugar, which of course was rationed, the same as all the meat and many of the other things we had to buy.

But as the months wore on, and the Gold Stars began going up beside the names emblazoned on the side of Frosty's Hardware Store, down on mainstreet, the fact that some of our boys were dying far from home had a decidedly sobering effect on all of us. It's a whole different ballgame, you know, looking at a name you've been familiar with all your life, and realizing that the person it belonged to will never again yell "Hi guys, how ya doin'?, or stop to tell you about the big trout he caught a day or so earlier, out on Cow Creek, or maybe up in Gore Slough.

I suppose this must have been what caused Jack to do what he did. For even though we'd all grown accustomed to the fact that his extremely poor eyesight would undoubtedly keep him out of the armed forces, he had an ace up his sleeve. And he eventually played it for everything it was worth.

A relatively quiet boy, whose family always seemed to be just barely getting by, he'd gotten a job on Frosty's little ranch. And unless I'm mistaken the time would probably have been during the Spring of 1943. Frosty was buying ponys from the Navajos then, down on the reservation, trucking them over to his ranch, where Grover and Jack would break them to the saddle. And if I remember correctly, he then sold them for anywhere from twenty-five to forty dollars apiece, at least doubling his original cash outlay.

Jack apparently had taken a liking to a little pinto mare, which he told us Frosty had let him have at cost. And at times I can still bring back his unlikely image, at least late at night when sleep eludes me, with his long legs dangling well below the pinto's belly, and his old slouch hat cocked rakishly above his thick, wire-rimmed spectacles.

Butch and I hadn't seen Jack for a couple of weeks or so, when this one particular morning, while we were out hunting up more prairie dogs, he came riding toward us on his pinto. He didn't have a saddle of his own, simply securing a blanket to the mare's back with a rope-cinch, Indian fashion, the way Grover had apparently taught him to do. And after stopping beside us, he said "Hi guys, Frosty's really tickled with th' way yer wipin' out s'many prairie dogs, even though Grover claims he's havin' one heckova time findin' a'nuff t'eat anymore."

We had a good laugh over that, of course. Then Butch asked "Where ya bin hidin' out th' last ten days er so? Frosty send ya down t'th' reservation fer another load'a ponies, er somethin?"

Jack's grin looked almost like it stood a good chance of lopping off the upper two-thirds of his face, and he said "Naw, I bin kinda busy, but I also went off t'Denver an' took my physical."

And after allowing that to sink in for several seconds, he threw his shoulders back and practically yelled "An' I passed th' sucker too, s'what'a ya think'a that?"

Unable to believe this, I said "Aw baloney, Jack, you can't see th' end'a yer own nose without them specks, an' I know good an' well they wouldn't let ya use 'em t'read th' eye-chart with. Ever'body knows by now that ya got t'be able t'read at least part'a th' thing without glasses. Unless they changed th' rules, er somethin'?"

He laughed then and said "Naw, they ain't changed th' rules yet. But I managed t'get hold'a one'a th' charts ahead'a time, an' I had th' dang thing memorized backwards, forward, an' sideways. s'what'a ya say t'that? I'll haf'ta buy my own specks, er at least th' first pair, but after I bin in fer'a few months I'm purty sure I can prob'ly get th' army t'do it. We'll just haf t'wait an' see, I guess."

And after we'd talked awhile longer, he said "Well guys, I'll try t'send ya a postcard from Africa er someplace, if I can find one that's wrote so's ya can read it. But keep on pottin' th' prairie dogs, will ya? Frosty's gonna keep little Sweetheart here until I git back, an' I sure would hate it if she broke'a leg b'fore then. Be seein' ya!"

Watching him ride off then, I couldn't shake off the feeling that something bad was going to happen to him. But I was mostly just envious that he was going to get to do what I could only dream of doing, so I yelled "Hey Jack, yer taken a big bag'a garlic along with ya, ain'cha?"

Realizing that I was referring primarily to his habit of eating raw garlic, in order to avoid catching a cold, he broke out laughing, stopping the mare long enough to answer "Naw, I don't think that'd be too smart. 'Cause even if it did keep me from gittin' sick, it'd just make it easier fer th' Germans t'home in on me. But I'd prob'ly be in'a whole lot more danger from th' guys on our side, don'cha think?"

And he gigged the mare's flanks just as I answered "Yeah, ya prob'ly sure as th' devil would be."

As the pinto crossed a shallow gully, a large flock of red-winged blackbirds left the willows lining its bottom, loudly protesting the intrusion. Watching them circle high overhead for a moment, Jack raised his arm and waved a final time at us, then he and the little mare disappeared behind a low rise.

I was very much aware for the rest of that day that we could quite easily have talked to Jack for the last time, but the way things turned out, we got a chance to see him for a few minutes when he came home on leave a couple of months later, just before being sent overseas. The army had managed to put a little meat on his bony frame and he really looked sharp in his uniform, even with those thick glasses of his.

Every so often after he shipped out, his younger sister, Bernice, would let us know that they'd gotten another letter from him, and that he was getting along alright. So whether I ever knew or not, I no longer remember if he made it to Africa, since neither Butch nor I received the postcard from him. I have to assume that he didn't, though, since I'm fairly certain the fighting in Tunisia was over well before he could have been sent there. And to the best of my recollection, it was on the beaches of Anzio, Italy, where he was killed.

By then, I understand that he'd received his Corporal's stripes, and when the death of each of his superiors left him in charge of his unit, it was reported by those few men who survived, that he'd led them forward right up until he was no longer able to crawl. And they said he'd had to crawl, since his bullet-riddled legs would no longer support him. A final bullet eventually put an end to his struggles, shattering one of the thick lenses in those homely wire-rimmed specks. But homely as they may have been, they were what had made it possible for him to see just far enough, and long enough, to keep his appointment with Destiny.

So rest in peace, Jack, you haven't been forgotten.

Here's Lookin' atcha, Jack

The last time I saw 'im was right close to sixty years ago

Naw, that ain't quite right, it was the next to the last time

I'm talkin' about, that I really remember the best

Because even tho' they'd sent 'im home on furlough before they shipped 'im overseas, I'll never ferget how proud he looked, settin' with that blanket-clad pinto clamped between 'is knees

Just grinnin' for all he was worth, about how he'd pulled the wool over th' U.S. Army's eyes. Because since he'd been cheated at birth, he'd figured it'd be just as fair for 'im to memorize

The chart he'd talked as fast as he could, to convince some buck-hungry buck-private out of. So even tho' he almost got tripped-up, by trippin' over 'is own feet at that ol' induction-center

He wound up passin' all their tests with flyin' colors! All in spite of the fact he was dang near blind as a bat without the specks he'd hid in 'is pocket at the start of the line!

But that was Jack for ya, always findin' a way to even the score.

And even tho' he was singin' when he rode away that day, I couldn't help wonderin' if he'd ever be ridin' back our way.

He didn't either, but just because of what he did awhile after that, quite a few Nazis didn't make it home neither. So altho' I never knew the full particulars about that particular fight

What I heard made me feel Ol' Jack'd really done alright, just crawlin' forward on `is gut when `is legs got shot so fulla holes he couldn't stand on `is own two feet.

So in spite of where his bones are still layin', in that far-away foreign land, I can't help feelin' we should all be prayin' that our country never runs short of near-sighted boys like Jack!

Jack Brummitt.

Jack Brummitt.

Little Things

After spending a good deal of the past forty-eight years having to listen to my little woman rant and rave about how most normal adults are able to discard the odds and ends cluttering up the inside of their heads by the time they reach maturity, I've finally come to the conclusion that normal must be just one more category I can forget about qualifying for. Especially since none of the restaurants she insists on dragging me to will hardly ever let me get away with ordering the "Children's Special", even after I've gone to all the trouble of making it plain that I feel the prices they're asking for their regular fare are positively exorbitant. But since the waitresses at each of these little establishments all seem to share Mama's opinion that anyone with a headful of gray hair is just about as mature as he's ever going to get, it's still a pretty bitter pill to have to swallow, don't you know?

But even though I've almost gotten to the point where I wish I could just pull a chain or press a lever, and flush the sucker down the tube, some goofy memory is constantly crawling out of the muck between my ears. And after it's managed to poke its nose into whatever I happen to be involved in at the moment, it seems like I always wind up wondering what might have happened if I'd just done this, or that, instead of what I really did, way back when I should have been planning what I actually wanted to do with my life. And then, of course, Mama almost always ends up yelling at me, just because I never seem to find time to finish what I've already gotten started.

That's what happened just the other day, you see, right after I'd promised her I was going to straighten up the mess in our garage. I'd gone down there with every intention of following through on my promise too, then while I was trying to remember where I'd left my shovel and wheelbarrow, out pops another one of those stupid memories. So while I wind up wondering what my life might have been like if I'd just been born left handed instead of right handed, the rest of the afternoon pretty much slipped out of focus. And since I've always had a hard time focusing on more than one thing at a time, you'd just better believe that the little woman's jaws got a real workout when she came down to call me for supper, fully expecting that I'd have made at least a little progress on my cleaning project.

So even though I did my best to explain what had happened, while I was wading through my second helping of her Meatball Stew, she just flat-out refused to believe that there was a good possibility my frustrations might come from a whole lifetime of doing everything with the wrong hand. Man-oh-man, but women sure can be unreasonable at times!

But before I completely forget what I was going to tell you about, I suppose I'd better go ahead and get it over with. You see, it involves the very first rock that I can really remember throwing. And since I was probably somewhere between three and four years old at the time, that would mean that it just about had to have happened either in 1931 or 1932. Anyhow, I was trying to make the rock skip down the sidewalk in front of George and Esther Milly's house. So if I'd only been born lefthanded instead of. Oh well, it doesn't make too much difference I guess, since I wasn't.

But considering my tender age and all, I already had pretty darn good range and velocity, even though my aim was sorely in need of extra work. I hadn't learned to tell time yet, you see, so even if the dinged-up old Ingersoll pocket watch I'd found in a neighbor's garbage barrel a few days earlier had been full of ticks instead of rattles, I couldn't have known I'd picked the worst possible time to practice on improving my aim.

Old George was home from his run on the railroad and had conked out on the couch under the big double windows in their living room. I guess I must have been using my Dizzy Dean windup, since I apparently got a little too wound up by the time I let loose of the rock. At least I wound up landing on my rump on the sidewalk, while the stupid rock wound up flying straight away from it. It really wasn't a very big one either, but the hole it made in ol' George's window was such a whopper that I could hardly believe my own eyes. But when he poked his head and shoulders right out through the hole and started yelling, my ears convinced me it was either time to do some fast thinking, or get my feet in gear. And since I've always had sort of a hard time thinking in anything but low gear, the next few minutes went more or less as follows;

"Did you throw that rock, Buzzy?"

"I guess so, Mr.Milly."

"Do ya know what I did t'th' last little boy that threw a rock through my window?"

"I don't think so, Mr. Milly."

"Ya see this here pocketknife, don'cha?"

"I sure do Mr. Milly, an' it really looks like'a dandy."

"Well I cut off 'is reason fer standin' up in th' outhouse, an' jist as soon as I ketch ya, that's exac'ly what I'm gonna do t'you."

So that's when I jammed my feet in gear, but since my aim hadn't improved all that much while I'd been standing there on George's grill, I started running directly away from home. By the time I got to Jay and Mamie Phillips' yard though, I realized my mistake, since I wasn't entirely stupid. But George was closing the gap with every jump, and still howling like a wild Apache. So even though I was pretty sure I was a goner anyhow, when I got to the end of the Phillips's fence, I zigged into a hard right turn.

George had a fairly big belly that just sort of bounced up and down whenever he tried to hurry, you see, so that must have been what caused him to skid a little on the zig. And by the time he got back on my trail again, I'd circled around Granma Cohen's big box elder tree and was now headed back down the street toward home. By that time though, George's wife, Esther, was out on the sidewalk, jumping up and down with her mouth wide open and just waving her arms for all she was worth. So I almost threw in the towel right then and there, since I was concentrating mostly on running instead of listening.

But when I finally realized it was George she was yelling at, instead of me, I heard her say "George you fat old fool, you leave that boy alone before you have a stroke or something. Now I mean it, George! Do you hear me?", so I knew I still had a chance to go on living a relatively normal life. At least out in the outhouse.

And by the time he wheezed out "Yes Esther, I hear ya.", I'd already made it around her and was headed for our front door.

I sort of think that might have ended things too, if only I hadn't gone and stuck my tongue out at him just before I ducked through the door. From that day on though, at least up until they finally moved away, practically every time he'd see me, that pocket knife would fly into his hand almost like magic, and here he'd come, yelling at the top of his lungs; "I'm gonna getcha this time, I'm gonna getcha now fer sure." Then he'd cut loose with that crazy high pitched cackle of his, and the hair on the back of my neck would stand straight up.

In all honesty though, I have to admit that I was fairly sure he wouldn't really use his knife on me, since he never had its blade open, and he was always dropping by our house to leave a little bag of licorice jellybeans for Mom to give me. But there's some things that a fella just can't afford to gamble on, don't you know?

But since this all took place back before Dad bought our big secondhand cast-iron bathtub, with the legs that held it just high enough off the floor so that if you weren't really careful with the soap, it would wind up ricochetting off the wall and then go sliding just far enough underneath so that you had to get out of the tub and lay down on the cold linoleum to retrieve it. And one day while Mom was giving me a bath in our kitchen sink, since that so was much easier than dragging out one of our galvanized laundry tubs, old George came barging through the front door without bothering to knock, or even yell, until he was already inside the livingroom. And as soon as he saw me sitting there on the drainboard in all my raw majesty, he jerked out that knife and started yelling that he was really going to fix me this time.

Mom only had a bar of soap in one hand, and the wet washrag in the other one, but she managed to keep him away from me with just the two of them. Because every time he'd try to duck around her, she'd swat his face with that wet, soapy rag and konk him over the head with the bar of soap. And after a few noisy lunges, during which time he began looking like he had rabies or maybe even something serious, she finally got so tickled at him that he forgot all about me and started in laughing too. But since I still had soapsuds all over me, and they were really starting to itch, I sure couldn't see much of anything particularly funny about the situation.

I have to admit though, that life seemed awfully dull around our neighborhood for a long time after the Millys finally moved away. But I've always had a pretty special affinity for nuts and licorice jellybeans, you see, and if he was anything at all, Ol' George was a really first rate nut!

Jist A Dang Ol' Funeral

Huh? Oh, hi kid. Yeah I guess it'll be alright, but fer cryin' out loud hurry up an' climb down off th' top'a that fence b'fore them folks over there see ya. No need t'upset 'em anymore'n they already are ya know, t'wouldn't be right.

Yeah, it's jist another dang funeral. Sure seems like we been havin' a bunch of 'em lately, don't it? C'mon now, plop down here on this little headstone b'side me. Then that big 'un over there should keep us outta sight.

Aw Lordy, will ya jist lookit that poor fella? Naw not that'un, th' big'un there, hangin' on t'that skinny little gal's arm. Now wouldn'cha think she'd a'been th' first t'cave in? But I tell ya boy, size don't have nothin' a'tall t'do with bein' strong.

What's that y'say? Holy cow kid, ya don't hafta yell. I ain't plumb deaf ya know. Naw that long black car don't b'long t'no rich man. It b'longs t'that gawky lookin' drink-a-water there, th' one wearin' that snappy red bow tie.

His name's Dooley y'see, an' he's th' undertaker. Naw I don't know whether th' reason they call 'im that is b'cause he puts folks down under th' ground. Kind'a makes sense though, don't it? But it's 'bout th' only sense these shindigs has goin' fer 'em.

Folks sure seem t'think we gotta have 'em though, no matter how much hurt they cause. Guess that's why ol' Dooley d'veloped what he calls his funeral philosophy. Says it's all that keeps 'im goin' at times, exposed like he is, t'sharin' other folk's pain.

Huh? Naw I don't own this place. Leastwise no more'n what it'll take t'lay th' ol' lady an' me out in, when our time comes. This here rock garden b'longs t'all of us boy, an' even them as don't have a dime t'their name still gits planted here when they die.

Ah Judas Priest! Will ya jist look at that sky? Sure as shootin' it's fixin' t'rain. Man! If that won't be some kind'a mess. Oh oh, th' preacher must'a seen it too, b'cause he's already windin' 'er up. Now that's what I call a real down t'earth kind'a guy.

But soon's th' mourners all git gone kid, I'm gonna haf'ta give Dooley a hand with 'is gear, not that I mind. B'cause he sure is one swell ol' boy, an' if anythin' ever goes wrong with one'a these shows, I can flat-out guarantee it won't be his fault.

Why ya know what he done a couple weeks ago? We'd jist finished sealin' up'a vault when he walks over to th' big ol' pile'a flowers, an' b'fore I know'd what he was doin', he'd picked one here, an' a'nother'n there, then he ups an' hands 'em to me.

Well sir, I says "Dooley, jist what in Hades am I s'posed t'do with these? 'Tain't right t' take flowers from dead folks ya know!" Then he looked me right square in th' eye, an' I swear, both'a his was plumb tin-tub full'a tears.

An' he said "What ain't right, Charley, is when jist a'little bit a'beauty can't come from somethin' as hurtful an' ugly as'a dang ol' grave. Why flowers is fer th' livin', man, 'stead'a th' dead. Even though they're the ones as usually gits most of 'em."

"Now you knew poor Bill down there ever' bit as good as me, but if you can make me b'lieve he wouldn't jist flat-out hop up an' down fer joy, over knowin' that'a few a'his flowers was gonna grow'a smile on Annie's face t'night, then I'll put 'em back."

Annie's my ol' woman ya know. Has been fer over forty years too. So since I knew Dooley knew she prob'ly hadn't got many flowers give to 'er in all that time, I went ahead an' took 'em on home. After I'd shoveled ol' Bill's grave full, that is.

An' at first, when I told 'er where they'd come from, I thought sure she was gonna throw 'em out th' door, me right along with 'em. But then I says "Jist set down a minute, ol' woman, so's I can tell ya how come I brought 'em on home to ya."

An' ya know boy, by the time I finished tellin' 'er what all that dang Dooley'd said, she was bawlin' jist like a baby. After she'd made'a reg'lar mess outta my bandana though, she says "Charley, that's jist about th' nicest thing I ever heard tell of."

Ah wouldn't ya know it, there he goes, doin' it all over agin. Homely bird ain't he, with that big ol' Adam's apple pokin' out 'most as far as 'is chin? Jist goes t'show ya boy, real beauty sure winds up in some funny lookin' buckets at times.

Best Way I Know T'find Out How A'man Thinks Is T'walk A'mile `Er Two In `Is Tracks

It may indeed be the best way, but it sure isn't always the quickest one, because even though I walked a lot of miles in my father's tracks when I was a boy, it wasn't until long after I'd reached maturity that I really got to know him. And it wasn't until well after he died that I truly came to appreciate what I knew about him. That's the way the buck jumps at times, though.

I was just young enough when Mom passed away, so that all I really thought about was how it affected me. Which was natural enough, I guess, but it sure didn't come close to making it right. Because my little brother and I always seemed to be first and foremost in Dad's thoughts, in most everything he did. Although I'm fairly certain my brother wasn't too sure that was the case, the morning we took him and Mrs. DeVore down to the depot in October of 1935.

She'd been keeping house for us ever since Aunt Margaret went back to her home in Texas shortly after Mom's funeral. And since she had a sister living in the adjoining town, taking my four year old brother with her not only made it possible for her to stay on Dad's payroll, it also allowed Dad to take me to deer hunting camp with him. So you can just bet that I'd been giving Kayo a real pep talk on how much fun he'd have riding on the train, all decked out in his twin six-shooters and cowboy hat. And he hardly ever went anywhere without taking his double-barreled cork-gun along for backup.

For several days prior to when we were scheduled to go our separate ways, the poor kid had been wavering halfway between "Aw gee Dad, I'll be quiet if ya'll jis' take me with ya.", and full-blown rebellion. So Dad sweetened the pot by first adding a movie at the Fox Theater, which was soon followed by the promise of a root-beer float afterwards. Then while Kayo and I were waiting for sleep to come on the night before D-Day, I delivered the coup de grace by saying "If ya'll jist quit bein' s'stubborn, ya kin have my cowboy boots t'wear on th' train."

So when he asked "Ya mean fer keeps?", I sort of skipped right on across the fact that my feet had outgrown them at least a year earlier, and I said "Yeah, fer keeps, but ya know how much I've always liked 'em. So ya gotta promise that yer gonna git on that train t'morra an' not start blubberin' all over th' place, th' way ya bin doin' lately, understand?"

By then I was feeling kind of guilty about tricking him, so I said "Ya kin borrow my good neckerchief too, as long as ya promise not t'lose it. An' ya want'a be sure an' take yer lariat along, jist in case ya gotta help th' conductor hogtie some robbers er somethin'."

So as you can see, the poor little dude was just about as railroaded as it was possible to get, before actually getting on the train. And the last thing he asked before he drifted off into dreamland was "D'ya think it'd be alright if I wear my sheriff's badge too?", to which I replied "A'course it'll be alright, ya little nut, how else're th' robbers gonna know they better not mess with ya?"

The following morning though, if the conductor hadn't seen how close the poor kid was to caving in, and asked him to help collect the other passengers' tickets, Dad's and my hunting trip would have been washed out with tears before it even got started. And even then, if the engineer hadn't gotten the train rolling when he did, Kayo would more than likely have jumped ship in another minute or so.

It didn't take Dad and me more than thirty minutes to get home and load our things into the back of our old Chrysler, which was piled so full, that all the way up the hill out of town, I kept asking "Is she gonna make it, Dad, er d'ya need fer me t'git out an' push?" But that was one thing about our old car, no matter how loud it moaned and groaned, it always seemed to get the job done.

When we got about halfway up Dallas Divide though, it was making so much noise I really had to yell to make Dad hear me. And by the time he finally pulled off to the side of the road, it was all I could do to keep from wetting my pants before I could get my door open. It's awfully difficult to apply much force when you're concentrating as hard as you can on clamping your knees tight enough together so that you can hold back the tide and still push.

After seeing how the Chrysler gushed all over itself while we were parked there, I didn't feel quite as bad about splattering my shoes a little. It might have been a different story I guess, if my radiator had just been as big as the Chrysler's. Dad soon got both of us recharged from the canvas water-bag that was slung from the Chrysler's right-hand headlight.

But when we finally got over the top of the Divide it didn't take us very long to get to the old railroad station where we left the graveled highway behind and started up a narrow dirt lane. There were white-faced Hereford cows

Me with a four point buck.

grazing behind the barbed-wire fences on each side of the lane, and every few minutes I'd ask "Are those some of Roy Case's yet, Dad?", and as soon as he'd reply "No, not yet.", I'd hit him with "How much further is it t'Roy's, Dad, are we gonna git there b'fore dark?"

By then the road-dust was swirling in through the window I'd rolled down so I could look for brands on the cattle, and it was so thick I'd nearly knocked Dad's hat off once or twice in my efforts to fan it back out the window. So when I began coughing too, Dad said "If you'll just roll the window up, Big Partner, I'll stop at the next wide spot and see if I can find our cider jug in one of those boxes in the back seat. I'm getting pretty thirsty, myself."

I always liked for him to call me that, but this time it made me remember how I'd tricked Kayo, or Little Partner, into thinking I'd given him my boots out of the goodness of my heart. So after Dad stopped the car I told him what I'd done. He looked at me for several seconds, until I was beginning to think he must be mad, then he placed his arm around my shoulders and said "There are some things that just don't seem fair in life, but you and I both know Kayo was just too little to come with us this year. It would have been a different story if your Mother", and when his eyes filled with tears at this point, he seemed to lose the ability to say anymore.

Then he blinked hard a time or two and said "But that's the way things happen at times, and there's nothing we can do about it. So we'll just keep this between you and me, what'a ya say t'that, Big Partner?"

I couldn't say anything, because the lump in my throat was so big that I knew I'd start bawling if I even tried. So I just nodded my head. If you'd been watching a few minutes later though, you'd have had a hard time believing so much cider could find its way around even a little lump.

It must have been at least twenty minutes later when Dad pointed to a fork in the road and said "Up there's where we turn into Roy's place, it isn't much further to camp now. I don't think he'll be back from town yet, so there'll probably just be Joe and Marion and Harvey for you to pester. Do you think you can handle that?"

My grin was all the answer he needed, since he already knew how much I liked Joe, one of Roy's older boys. And even though Marion and Harvey were much quieter and less rowdy than their employer and his sons, the last time we'd shared their camp with them they'd soon made me feel like I belonged there. And a kid just can't ask for a better deal than that.

Unless maybe it includes being turned upside down and tickled until he's so out of breath that all he can do is wheeze "Aw c'mon Joe, cut it out! Er when I git as big as you, yer gonna be sorry. 'Cause I'll…."

But I never did learn enough to let well enough alone, because when Joe finally released me this time, I tried to stomp on his foot and wound up with both of his pinning mine to the porch floor. Then he grabbed me by the ear and led me on into the cabin, where he said "Harvey, dump th' water-bucket inta th' kettle an' throw some wood in th' stove, 'cause if he don't work some'a his ornery off b'fore supper, I'm gonna need plenty'a hot water t'scrub it off after we eat!"

And just like that, I was back in the swing of things. For keeping the wood-box and water-bucket filled were chores I was expected to do. Because in a working cow-camp, if you didn't carry your end of the load right from the start, you didn't get invited back for another try at it. Another of my tasks was making the bunks, or at least the bottom ones, since I was too short to reach the top ones. The only sweeping they'd let me do was out on the porch, where the resultant dust-cloud wouldn't make any difference.

In addition to doing most of the cooking, since no one else could make biscuits that compared to his, Harvey worked a full day outside, just like everyone else. So he'd always let me do things like scrubbing potatoes and setting the table, and once he showed me how it had to be done, I also got to put the biscuits into the pans as he'd cut them out. And every evening there were at least two large pans that had to be made. Store-bought bread just wasn't a viable option in those days, you see, so it took a lot of biscuits to feed a crew of hungry cowboys and deer-hunters.

It was in that same ramshackle little cabin that I first learned to like oatmeal, since I was just as prone to turning up my nose at it as most kids are today. But when I'd made an issue of it a year or so earlier, Joe had said "Hey little Buzzard, that stuff might look like oatmeal an' raisins to ya, but what it really is is bear-sign. So whacha hafta do is dump in'a couple spoons's brown-sugar an' mix it all up. An' by golly, if ya don't like it then, it's plain t'see ya jist ain't never gonna be'a cowboy."

Anyhow, the following morning Dad and I headed out into the woods just as it was getting light enough to see where we were going, without making an undue amount of noise by stepping on every dry twig we came to. Which is more than likely what Dad thought I was doing, even after it got completely light. Because every time we'd stop to rest that day, he'd whisper advice like "A good hunter learns to walk without looking right at the ground all the time, since he needs to use his eyes to watch for game. But you'll eventually learn to feel where you're going with your feet, most of the time at least."

And I did too, although it wasn't that day, or even that year. Rather than biding my time quietly and following Dad's example of talking in a whisper, whenever I thought of something to ask him about, I'd hurry to catch up with him and then blurt out whatever it was that I wanted to know. Consequently, for most of that first day all of the deer within a country mile of us probably thought we were the advance team for Barnum and Bailey's Circus. Because the only thing we saw that even looked as though it might be attached to a deer, was a small patch of white that disappeared almost as soon as we noticed it.

We hunted to the south of camp the whole day, working our way along the edge of a relatively open draw that got progressively deeper and wider the further we went. So it wasn't until mid-morning that we reached the point where the draw had almost become a canyon, and that was when I caught the reflection of a small pool of water down in the very bottom. It would probably be more correct to call it a puddle I suppose, but at least it served to remind me that I was getting thirsty, since I hadn't had anything to drink from the time we left camp. As far as that goes though, Dad hadn't either. Which just goes to show you what an overly leaky radiator will do to a guy.

But rather than hike down to see if it was fit to drink, Dad pointed to where half a dozen cows were lying in the shade, about seventy-five feet up the draw from the puddle, "You see those cows lying there don't you? Well if you'll look real close, you should be able to see how dirty the lower part of their legs look, and that makes me think it's probably because they've been wading around through that water you're looking at. What do you think?"

Since he put it that way, I said the only thing a normal seven year old could say, "Yeah Dad, but I'm still thirsty."

To which he replied "So now you're learning that hunting isn't always as much fun as you thought it was, aren't you? And what's the reason you got to come hunting with me, and your brother didn't?"

While struggling to come up with an answer that would still allow me some latitude for checking out the puddle, I thought I detected a grin lurking just behind the semi-serious look in his eyes, so I did a quick about-face and said "B'cause I'm old a'nuff not t'make'a fuss ever' time I don't git my way, right?"

His grin at that moment almost made me forget about how thirsty I was, and when he said "Right, Big Partner, why don't we go sit down in the shade under that pine over there, where we can watch the draw while we eat a couple of the apples I stuck in our knapsack this morning?", I decided I really wasn't as thirsty as I'd thought I was. But that yellow-transparent sure went down easy a few minutes later, especially when I found out there were still several more in the sack for later in the day.

Dad pulled another surprise out about twenty minutes later, when he stood up and said "Okay, now it's time to learn something else. And while we're at it, maybe we'll learn whether I knew what I was talking about a few minutes ago."

Seeing the look of confusion in my eyes, he said "C'mon, let's go down and check that water-puddle out, now that you know there's more than one way to satisfy your thirst. Then we'll climb up to the other side of the draw, where the sun'll soon be behind us. That way we won't have to look into it, and any deer that we jump will."

After discovering that my water-puddle was barely an inch deep and so muddy on the bottom that even if it hadn't been swarming with thousands of

Me with my brother Kayo.

the tiny, wriggling larval forms of some insect, there was just no way that my thirst had yet reached the point where I could have considered drinking from it. So I had to admit there were lots of things I could learn from Dad. But all I said was "Wow, Dad, I don't see how them cows can even stand t'drink it!"

By late afternoon my feet were really dragging and Dad kept stopping every few minutes to let me catch up, although he made it look as though he was just watching for a buck to show itself. But when I heard the faint sound of bawling cattle and cowboy's voices, I perked up in a hurry, asking "Gee, Dad d'ya think one'a th' guys'll let me ride `is horse fer'a little bit when we git t'camp?"

Chuckling softly, he said "Not if we don't hurry, they won't. It'll be dark soon, and I'm betting we still have at least half a mile to go, judging from the sound of things."

But even though it was nearly dusk when we came out into the cabin clearing, when I went charging through the screen door to see whether Joe was inside yet, Harvey said "He's still out at th' barn, brushin' down th' horses. If ya hurry though, maybe he'll let ya help. But don't take too long, I'm `bout outta water an' wood. An' if Marion don't git t'crackin' with them spuds, yer gonna haf t'give `im a hand with `em, er figger on eatin' em half ra"

By then though, I was on my way to the barn, yelling "I'm comin' Joe, I'm comin'! Boy, wait'll ya hear how far me an' Dad walked t'day, I bet it was at least twenty miles."

Joe's response to that was "Then I reckon yer jist too wore out t'let ol' Buck here show ya he ain't fergot what a good job ya do at brushin' out `is mane. Why th' goofy sucker won't hardly even let me touch it, now that he knows yer here. So what'a ya think?"

What I thought was "It's gonna be too dark t'even think about askin' fer'a ride, when I git done.", but what I said was "I think yer still as full'a hot air as ya always was, `cause all Buck thinks I'm good fer is sugar-lumps, an' I fergot t'git one from Harvey."

He laughed and said "Well jist as soon as ya git done brushin', ya kin give `im this'n.", as he pulled one out of his shirt pocket.

So a few minutes later, after Buck's sugar-loving lips had exhausted all hope of finding any more in my small hands, Joe had hoisted me onto the buckskin gelding's back and was leading us through the first of several circuits around the pole corral. A great many times, in the years since that night, I've wished it was possible to go back and actually do it just once more. Mostly, just so I could say "Thanks, Joe.", since I'd forgotten to say it that night.

By the time I'd carried the wood and water into the cabin, and eaten a large enameled plateful of Harvey's biscuits and chipped-beef gravy, I fell asleep before I'd managed to drink half the hot-toddy Dad had set before me. For even though he didn't put as much whiskey in mine as he did in those of the other guys, he always tried to make sure I was included in everything that went on. But when he carried me in and helped me into my bunk awhile later, I roused just enough to say "G'night Dad, I sure had a swell time t'day!" His "Me too, Big Partner.", would be pretty nice to hear once more, too!

The next morning as I was hurrying back from the outhouse, a loud "Who-wh-wh-whoooo" coming from one of the tall pines out by the barn, sent me charging back inside the cabin so fast that Marion grinned and said "I wish somebody'd shoot that goofy sucker. He 'bout made me pee all over myself th' other mornin' when he cut loose jist as I was tryin' to. Man-oh-man, my hackles stood up s'dang fast they almost knocked my dang fool hat off."

Then he winked at me and patted the bench beside him, saying "C'mon Buzz, sit here b'tween me an' Joe. Maybe then he'll mind 'is manners an' not hog all th' dang biscuits. I swear, he must'a ate four th' other mornin' b'fore I even got one."

So my day was off and running in more ways than one, without my having to feel embarrassed over letting one of the resident owls scare me half out of my wits. And when everyone laughed at my response of "He jist better not try it t'day, er we'll throw 'im in th' water-trough, hunh Marion?", I felt at least ten feet tall, and more than ready to wade into the biggest and meanest looking bowl of bear-sign Harvey ever dished out.

That day Dad and I hunted even further down the canyon than we had the preceding day, in hopes that we might find a buck holed up under the massive ledges of sandstone lining both sides of it. But even though we did see two different does go racing for cover across the canyon from us, they were the only deer we saw. And by the end of the day, most of the soreness in my leg muscles was beginning to dissipate.

The following morning we headed away from camp in a more or less northerly direction, hunting through one grove of white-barked quaking aspen after another. Consequently, when we began finding a number of trees with initials and dates scarring their trunks, as though at one time someone had nothing better to do than to daub them up with a blackened paintbrush, I was soon applying as many of the initials to my school chums as they'd fit. But since most of the dates accompanying the initials ranged from 1905 to 1928, the year I was born, it was quite apparent that none of the carvings could be attributed to my somewhat narrow range of acquaintances.

When I began asking Dad who he thought might have been responsible for them, I soon found that he knew a lot more about the local history than I'd given him credit for. After all, here we were, right out in the middle of thousands and thousands of square acres of wilderness, at least forty or fifty miles from home, and more often than not he seemed to have a good idea as to who had done the carving. The one that I got the biggest charge out of though, was the one that read "Hugo V. Sept. 15, 1919".

And that was because Dad told me how he and three of his hunting buddies had stopped at this Hugo's place one fall during the early 1920s, to purchase a gallon jug of moonshine from him. He said that several days latter, after shooting three nice bucks, they'd each returned to camp early in the afternoon. So after passing the jug around a time or two, until some of the resultant stories were beginning to sound a little far-fetched even to them, they'd gone outside to let this Ray character show them just how expert he was with his lariat.

After boosting him into his saddle two or three times and having him slide straight off the other side, they soon decided to hitch up their spring wagon and let him throw his loop from it. Since it was a lot easier to let him throw it at the large hitching post in the clearing at the front of the cabin, rather than at one of the bleary-eyed cows out in the pasture, my future Uncle Jimmy soon convinced everyone else that "Since it was my idea t'use th' wagon in th' first place, it's only fair I should drive th' sucker."

So when the wagon was eventually hooked up, delayed somewhat by the necessity to check on whether the aforementioned jug's contents had begun to evaporate, simply because someone had left the cork out, the circus was finally ready to take to the road. Stationed as the wagon was, some fifty yards from the post, Ray lost several valuable seconds by losing his balance when Jimmy jump-started the horse with an overly enthusiastic "Whaaapppp" of the lines on the poor animal's rump. But he soon showed he had the makings of a champion in his blood, as well as several ounces of distilled spirits. Because just as they were racing past the post, his loop flew straight and true, dead-center around the crafty critter.

Even though Ray immediately applied his brakes by bracing his rump firmly against the seat-back and planting both boots on the wagon floor, he was soon flying through the air at just over the speed of sound. Or at least Dad said he must have reached that speed, since his "Whooooaaaa" sounded as though it was trailing his trajectory by several yards. It was soon drowned out though, by an extremely emphatic sounding "Kerwhooomp", when he fell from orbit in a nearly perfect one-point landing. As it turned out though, when the others reached where he lay and pried his hat off, the peeled spot on his bald-head was a good five degrees out of perfect alignment.

Dad said it really didn't make much difference, since his eyeballs had seemingly gone clear off the screen. But at least he was still breathing when they laid him out on his bunk a short time later. Dad also claimed that, except for the peeled spot on his head, Ray's headache didn't seem to be a bit worse than anyone else's the next morning. Which jist goes t'show ya, what tankin' up on too much high-octane moonbeams'll do fer ya!

Anyhow, when he'd finally finished the end of his story, I popped loose with my old familiar standby of "Boy, I sure am thirsty, Dad, ain't you?"

Chuckling, he said "Yes, I am, and there's a good, clean spring about three-quarters of a mile north of here. But if we hike on over to it at this time of day, we're very apt to spook any deer that are headed that way too. And we'll also have an additional mile and a half to back-track. So what'a ya say, will an apple do for now?"

Not especially anxious to put in any additional mileage, I grinned at him and said "I guess so, Dad. An' anyhow, we can always check it out t'morra, right?"

His "Right, Big Partner." was then followed by thirty minutes or so of additional information about the lay of the land around the spring. But when he told how two different trails came together just a short distance down a shallow draw from it, I said "It sure sounds like a good place t'ketch a buck, Dad. Maybe we ought'a try an' git to it t'night, we could always build a fire an' camp there if we had to, as long as there's water t'drink."

Laughing again, he said "But since Joe and the others will be expecting us in camp, that will mean they'll be worrying when we don't show up. You don't want that to happen, do you?"

Once I'd said I hadn't even thought about that, we soon headed back the way we'd come, detouring to the south after awhile so that we could intersect the road from town and have easier walking. Then just before reaching it, I heard what sounded like a pickup in the distance. At least I hoped that's what it would prove to be, since Dad had said there was a good chance that Roy would be coming in before dark, if he hadn't already arrived.

So when I began walking faster in an effort to reach the road before whoever it was had passed, Dad said "Sometimes it would be pretty easy to get the idea that you think as much of Roy as you do of me, the way you're always so anxious to see him, you know.", but when he saw the instant look of guilt this produced, he hurriedly added "But I know that's not the case, even if it is him this time. Go on now, hurry up and catch him before he gets by! I could stand a ride myself."

As soon as the burly driver behind the windshield of the old green pickup saw me running toward him, he slammed the brakes on so hard that all I could hear was the loud squealing they made. Then almost before the wheels stopped turning, the door flew open and Roy hit the ground running, his "Hi roughneck, how ya doin', did ya gitcher buck yet?" so loud that the guys in camp should have been able to hear it with no problem.

And by the time Dad reached where the two of us were tussling, both of us were so out of breath it was all Roy could do to gasp out "Don't know why ya don't try t'teach this kid some manners, Grover, he's' a real mess, ya know. Acts like some dang half-wild Injun all th' time. Looks like one too, with his hair all fuzzed up like it is.", he grabbed my head in both his huge hands then and dry-scrubbed it until my ears were ringing.

Dad just laughed and said "Don't know what get's into him Roy, unless maybe he's picked up a case of the Crazy Cases somewhere along the line."

Roy Case.

Roy snorted and asked "Ya want some'a th' same as he's gittin', er'a ride in my damn chariot? Thought ya was smarter'n t'go insultin' me b'fore we even shook hands.", he let go of my head and grabbed Dad's hand in his, pumping it as though he was trying to get water from a dry well.

After making sure everything was well with our family, or what was left of the one he was familiar with, he said "That big box'a steaks in th' back th' truck's gonna spoil if we don't shake a stick an' git t'camp b'fore Harvey starts fixin' somethin' else. An' I really bin countin' on one of 'em fer supper, how 'bout you, Roughneck? That sound okay?"

When I responded with "Jist as long as it ain't mostly fat!", he asked "If ya don't like fat, then how come yer s'damn fat yerself?", and the wrestling match began all over again, until we were both so covered with red dust that we could easily have passed for Indians.

It eventually ended though, when Roy wheezed "Okay ya little varmint, a'nuff's a'nuff. We're both gonna be lucky if that pertic'lar damn Harvey don't make us take'a bath in th horse-trough b'fore he even lets us in th' cabin. C'mon, git in th' truck, b'fore I drive off'n leave ya.", and he limped around to his side as though he was barely able to navigate.

As we negotiated the half mile or so of road that remained, he asked whether we'd seen any bucks. So when Dad told him we hadn't, Roy said "Hell Grover, I seen a damn nice four-point jist b'fore I headed down t'th' ranch th' other day. He was jist fatter'n hell, too, th' way 'is hide wrinkled up when he run down th' draw from th' spring you guys was comin' from awhile ago."

Before he could say any more, I burst in with "See Dad, didn't I say we should'a gone all th' way? We prob'ly would'a seen 'im if we had. Now somebody else'll prob'ly git 'im b'fore we do."

Roy came to Dad's defense before I could say anything more, saying "Whoa Tiger, there ain't nobody else huntin' on this place but th' two of ya, leastwise they'll be awful damn sorry if I ketch 'em. S'jist quit layin' inta yer ol' dad that way, he's prob'ly jist bin lettin' ya learn yer way around b'fore he takes ya up t'th' spring. Ain't that right, Grover?"

To which Dad replied "Not really, Roy, but thanks anyhow. It was mainly just because the last time I was over there was when Gene"

Seeing the hurting look on Dad's face, Roy suddenly shoved his elbow into my ribs so hard it nearly knocked the breath out of me, then he yelled "Christamighty, we jist made it in time, Roughneck! Here comes Harvey an' th' others right now. In a'nother five minutes he'd'a had 'is head set on fixin' fried mush er somethin' jist as awful."

So by the time Roy informed Harvey that he'd "damn well better figger on T-bones fer supper, er find somebody else t'gum down them damn doughgods yer allus pullin' out'a th' oven.", Dad had ample time to regain control of his emotions. And before very long at all, Harvey had another big batch of his 'dough-gods' in the oven, and two huge skillets of steak sizzling away on top of the stove. And when Roy asked whether we were having potatoes to go with them, Harvey grinned and said "Not unless ya want'a git off a yer lazy butt an' fix `em, we ain't."

Then he winked at me and added "An' th' only way I'll sit still fer that, is if ya d'cide t'scrub that scaly old hide'a yers in th' trough out at th' barn first."

Which caused such an outburst of laughter, that all Roy could do was sit there shaking his head. When it died down enough so that he could be heard though, he said "Gawddam cooks er all th' same, don't make no diff'ernce whether they're wearin' skirts er chaps, they all `spect ya t' kiss their butts like they was Gawd's gift t'mankind, er somethin'.", then he glared at Harvey and yelled "But by gawd, ya better not ruin them steaks, I worked my ass off a`cuttin' `em!"

Profanity was as much a part of Roy as his bellowing voice was, but everyone who knew him, also knew that both were nothing but a smoke-screen to hide a heart that was as big as a feather-tick, and twice as soft. And if he'd ever stopped his cursing, or teasing those around him, they'd undoubtedly have rushed him straight to the hospital, just to ask the doctor if he was dead. So when he went stomping out of the cabin as soon as supper was on the table, climbed into his truck and started it up, we all knew he was up to something. But when he started the engine and took off in a cloud of dust, I'm pretty sure most of us were wondering if he really was mad this time.

About three seconds later, though, the screeching of brakes made it plain that he was just up to his regular routine, and when the truck came backing into view once more, it had our full attention. And when Roy jumped out onto the ground, there was a big grin on his face, as well as a quart of whiskey in one hand. Tromping back into the cabin, he shook the bottle at Harvey and yelled "An' by gawd ya better not'a burned th' toddy water, neither, `cause as soon as supper's over, we're gonna have some real doozies!"

Winking at me, he said "You too, Roughneck, yer prob'ly gonna need it, jist t'melt th' lard off a yer teeth. Gawd, would ya jist look at that pile'a meat, don't hardly look like he even got it warm, does it?"

But even though there's been an awful lot of beef that's slid down my chute since that night, none of it has ever left a warmer feeling that what that steak did. The toddies weren't bad, either. And when I finally gave up and crawled into my bunk, the sweet sound of the laughter coming from around that long table in the other room was the last thing I heard.

There was frost on the ground when I ran to the outhouse the next morning, and even though the owls were having a real gab-fest, it sounded kind of nice. So did the lowing of the daily increasing number of cattle out in the pasture behind the barn. For while Dad and I had been hunting for deer, Joe and the others had been rounding up Roy's cows and calves and bringing them into the fenced pasture in preparation for their return drive down to the home ranch.

Up until the sun softened it, the frost made for noisy walking that morning, as well as slow progress. So we didn't get to where Dad and I had turned back the previous day until mid-morning. And in addition to being thirsty, I was also becoming convinced that we'd lost our only chance for a buck, by not going on to the spring when I wanted to. But even though I made sure Dad knew how I felt, he insisted on stopping every little bit to watch the various clearings we came to before proceeding across them. When my complaining about how thirsty I was finally induced him to spend nearly twenty minutes at one of these stops, he made it fairly evident that he was losing patience with me. I didn't especially care right then, though, since mine was getting pretty thin too.

As so often happens when a person is busy making an ass of himself, Fate decided to intervene. For we hadn't much more than just barely started across this last clearing, when we heard the sharp crack of a dead limb as a large buck went racing across the far end of the clearing. But just as Dad's 30-30 got to his shoulder, the buck reached a little island of oak-brush, halfway across the clearing. After standing there for what seemed like an eternity to me, Dad's arms finally got so heavy that he had to lower them.

That was all it took to put the buck in motion again, but before he'd covered half the remaining distance to safety, Dad's 30-30 slug caught him in mid-stride and down he went. And up I went, over and over, mouth wide open and screaming "Ya got `im Dad, ya got `im, ya got `im. Boy-oh-boy, he's really'a beauty, c'mon, let's go see how many points...Oh criminy, Dad, he's tryin' t'git back up. C'mon, I'll hold `is horns so ya kin shoot"

Dad's "Buzz, stay out of the way!" was so urgent that I came back to earth in a hurry, remaining there until another sharp report from the little carbine put an end to the deer's struggles. And when we got to where he lay, close examination revealed that Dad's first shot had broken the buck's back, just behind the chest cavity. But at least the pain caused by it had ended within only a few seconds, since the next shot broke the deer's neck, immediately in back of the ears. And by the time we saw there were four tines on each side of the antlers, not counting the inch-long brow-points, the buck's eyes had already glazed over.

The death of such a magnificent animal had a somewhat sobering effect on me, but since death had always walked hand in hand with the food that graced our table, it was of very short duration. And within the matter of only a few moments, I was fully involved in helping Dad dress the buck out, my mouth once more going a mile a minute; "Gosh, he's a beauty Dad. Is he th' biggest one ya ever got? Boy-oh-boy, I can hardly wait t'git back t'camp an' tell th' guys what'a good shot ya are! I bet even

Roy can't shoot any better'n that. I bin meanin' t'ask ya, Dad, will ya git me'a beebee-gun one'a these days, s'maybe I can kin git t'be a good shot someday too?"

The only time the words ceased during the next hour or so was when we finally made it on up to the spring and I bellied down on the ground to suck up some of the coldest, and sweetest tasting water I'd ever had. But since it was no longer necessary to be quiet to avoid spooking any deer, even Dad quit whispering and did a substantial amount of gum-bumping too.

We made it back to the cabin just as Joe was coming out the door with one of Harvey's cold biscuits in his hand. He said he'd just brought several head of cows into the pasture and had decided to grab a quick bite before going out to look for more. But when he saw some of the blood I'd failed to wash off at the spring, he grinned and said "Okay Lil' Buzzard, tell me all about what's gotcha so excited, b'fore ya up an' bust'a gusset. It's plain t'see ya must'a found yer Dad a buck.", then he stood there while I gave him a lengthy and very graphic recounting of my morning.

When I finally stopped for breath, he looked up toward where the sun was already about halfway between noon and the rusty-red barn roof and said "Well one thing's fer sure, if we don't git that sucker packed in b'fore dark, there ain't nobody gonna git any sleep around here t'night."

Looking at Dad then, he said "If ya think ya kin manage t'git by, ridin' back out on a packsaddle, I'll throw one on Harvey's big gray mare while yer gittin' somethin' t'fill this kid's mouth with, b'fore he runs plumb out'a gas. Harvey won't care, 'cause he knows ol' Buck here jist don't hold with luggin' raw meat on 'is back. But we're gonna hafta git a move on, er it'll be dark b'fore we much more'n git there."

When he pulled me up behind him on Buck's back a few minutes later, and we headed away from the cabin in a different direction than the one I was familiar with, I began jerking on his arm and yelling "Yer goin' th' wrong way, Joe, our buck must be at'a diff'ernt spring than th' one yer headin' for. We gotta go that way.", and I pointed off at right angles to the way we were headed.

Chuckling good-naturedly, he said "Simmer down, Tiger, there's more'n one way t'skin a cat ya know, jist like there's more'n one way t'th spring. An' mine's lots shorter'n yers, which is gonna make a big diff'ernce on how sore yer Dad's rump is when we git there. That wadded up sweater'a his ain't doin'a whole lot'a good ya know, with no stirrups t'put 'is feet in."

Dropping his voice to a whisper then, he said "Which is th main reason I ain't tried real hard t'git Buck used to a packsaddle. My b'hind jist don't fit them them suckers worth a dang."

Although I couldn't help feeling guilty over my disloyalty, for much of the thirty-five minutes it took us to reach the spring, I kept twisting around to see how Dad was faring, then I'd snicker and whisper "Boy, Joe, he sure is bouncin' all over th' place. If he had on a pointy hat, like that clown at th' rodeo did last month, I bet he could git `is job."

Every time it became necessary to find a new location for my own rump though, I'd have adequate occasion to regret my lack of compassion. But there have always been things that strike a kid as being funny, even when they're really not.

When we finally reached the spring though, and I saw that it was indeed the correct one, I whispered "Maybe we ought'a git off an' walk th' rest'a th' way, Joe. It's only a little ways from here, an' Dad looks like he could use a rest. B'sides I could stand another drink'a water, it sure tastes good."

Once we'd all recharged our radiators and Dad had gotten some of the kinks and dents worked out of his rumble-seat, we headed on down the draw toward where we'd earlier covered the buck with an assortment of branches from a nearby clump of oak-brush. And just before we reached the little clearing where we'd left the buck, a virtual cacophony of sound erupted from directly ahead of us, causing both horses to snort and pull back on their reins. Then at least fifteen or twenty magpies took to the air at once and began flying in circles, plainly disturbed by something we hadn't yet seen.

Joe turned toward Dad and said "Christamighty, Grover, d'ya think maybe a bear", and just at that moment there was a loud screech as a large and extremely agitated hawk came rocketing into the air with what looked like a fifteen inch length of deer-intestine dangling from his talons. Dodging and twisting from side to side, he led nearly half of his black and white tormentors off toward the south, flying just above the tops of the clumps of oak-brush. Watching until the feathered entourage disappeared behind several tall pines, Joe said "Sucker sounded real pissed-off, didn't he. Sure hope him an' them dang racket-wranglers didn't make a mess'a yer meat."

But when we reached the teepee of brush we'd erected around the buck, we discovered that the birds had apparently devoted most of their efforts toward the pile of entrails, which we'd dragged several yards away from the buck. And when Joe got a look at what had gotten me so wound up earlier, he gave a loud whistle and said "Holy cow, Buzzard, no wonder ya got s'blowed up this mornin', he's gotta be th' biggest four-point I ever seen. An' I know fer'a fact that I never seen a purtier rack!"

All of which couldn't have been said any more eloquently, at least as far as I was concerned. Dad didn't look as though he was inclined to find fault with it, either. Because if his grin had gotten any bigger it would more than likely have lopped off the top of his head.

Before our little Mutual Admiration Group could reap the full benefit of our labors, there was a considerable amount of work to be done. So as soon as Joe had tied Buck back out of the way, I spent the next several minutes trying

Joe Case.

to keep my body out of the way of the gray mares much larger one. Because with both Joe and Dad trying to hoist the heavy deer over her back, I was the most logical choice for a hitching-post. But every time they'd manage to get the deer almost ready to slide over the packsaddle, the mare would execute a fancy, four-footed foxtrot and I'd either wind up dangling from her bridle like a poor unfortunate dwarf struggling to salvage his virginity from the overly-amorous advances of some sex-crazed Amazon, or she'd jump backwards, as though she was trying to protect hers from me. And for several minutes it was anybody's guess as to who was going to have their way with who.

When Joe finally took his sweat-soaked shirt off and tied it over the mare's head, just like privacy was what she'd been wanting all along, the goofy four-legged ostrich decided to behave herself. And within just a few minutes, Joe had the buck lashed to the saddle with the still attached head tied back over the top of everything else, so that the antlers couldn't gouge the mare's flanks. But it was equally as much just to keep them from hanging up in the brush and getting broken, for Dad had already made it very plain that they had an appointment to keep with a taxidermist.

For the first mile or so Joe walked along with Dad, both of them leading a horse. But after commenting several times that "these dang boots sure ain't made fer walkin'", he got back into his saddle, moving me behind it once more. Still sweating from the ordeal of loading the deer, Dad had earlier given me his wool sweater to hang onto and I now wedged it between my legs and the cantle of the saddle so that I could wrap my arms around Joe's waist. It had been a long day and as the sun dropped below the horizon, my eyes also began to droop. And the last thing I was aware of was Joe's arms clamping tighter on mine.

When I eventually roused, it was completely dark and we were just coming into the clearing by the barn. Before Joe had much more than lowered me to the ground though, I was wide awake and headed for the cabin, yelling at the top of my lungs "Hey you guys, come see what me an' Dad got t'day!"

They'd already heard us ride in though, and were coming out the door with a lantern when I reached them. So after grabbing Roy's hand in an effort to hurry him along, I launched a non-stop verbal barrage of what they were in store for; "Man-oh-man, you guys ain't never seen'a deer like me an' Dad got t'day! I bet he weighs five hunderd pounds, Roy, an' jist his horns alone must weigh'a hunderd, er at least fifty. Boy-oh-boy, are they ever big...C'mon, hurry up, will ya. Joe an' Dad could use some help ya know."

So it wasn't until after they'd all had a chance to inspect our trophy and agree with my assessment of it, that the buck was hoisted up and tied off to a rafter in the granary room of the barn. Just so, as Roy put it, "Th' damn packrats don't all git in cahoots with each other, an' bust'a gut tryin' t'lug that ol' boy off somewheres b'fore mornin'."

So it was as we were heading back to the cabin that Dad remembered his sweater and asked me what I'd done with it. But even though I dropped down out of the clouds in a hurry, all I could come up with was "Ah golly Dad, it must'a slipped out from b'tween me an' Joe on th' ride back. But it couldn'ta bin 'til after I fell asleep, honest. Soon as ever'body gits t'th' cabin, I'll take th' lantern an' see if I can find it."

Luckily for me though, my altogether spur of the moment offer was firmly rejected when he said "No you won't, I couldn't even find my own way back over the trail we came in on, with just a lantern. It'll still be there in the morning and it won't take me long to find it then. So don't worry about it."

I did though, at least until I fell asleep with my head on the table, while still trying to down my first helping of Harvey's beef stew. When I woke up in my bunk the next morning, wondering how come I still had my coveralls on, the very next thing I thought of was Dad's sweater. So I was halfway to the outhouse before I realized that I'd just seen the sweater hanging from its usual nail as I'd rushed past where the other guys were sitting around the table. At least it looked just like Dad's sweater. But right then I had far more urgent business to attend to.

And sure enough, once I got back inside I saw that it really was the missing sweater. And after I'd taken my place on the bench between Marion and Joe, Marion whispered "Ya looked s'upset about it last night, that me an' Joe was all saddled up at daylight. But we didn't hafta go more'n a quarter mile t'find it. S'that ought'a make yer bear-sign taste'a little better, hunh?"

Grinning up at him, then at Joe, I said "It sure will! Thanks'a lot guys, yer jist about th' best friends a kid could ask for."

Joe's "Yer not s'bad neither, Lil' Buzzard!" slid down even easier than Harvey's bear-sign did, too.

But after the buck had been retrieved from the granary, and draped over the right-front fender of the Chrysler, where everyone we'd meet on our trip back to town would be sure to see it, what the guys all made very plain as we were getting ready to leave, was even sweeter to my ears. For one at a time, they each shook my hand. Then each of them pretty much echoed Joe's words of "S'long Lil' Buzzard, try an' talk yer Dad in'ta stayin'a little longer next year!"

After hanging in Dad's living-room for the next thirty-five years, that beautiful deer head has now graced a wall in my own home for the past thirty-seven. It's beginning to look a little shop-worn now, but I am too, and there's just no way I could stand to part with it. Dad's hunting license is still stapled to the back of the base, offering proof that for one dollar and fifty cents, in 1935 it was possible to buy a memory that would last a lifetime. Maybe even longer.

On Whom The Bell Tolled

Although the poor lady was only doing what she was hired to do, when Gertrude Milly rang her little bell to let my second-grade classmates and me know that recess was almost over, that April afternoon in 1936, she unwittingly set off a chain-reaction that proved to be only slightly less catastrophic than the birth of the atom bomb would eventually be, at least for me.

Because for the first and only time in my life, I'd managed to send a kite streaking toward the ionosphere, or at least as close to it as the two large balls of string I'd purchased down at Wade Carmichael's Grocery Store would allow. The string had cost me a whole nickel, but the kite itself had been free, since before it became only a black speck in the cosmos, it was wearing the reddish-brown coat of arms of the Lipton Tea Co. upon its glossy-green surface. And any kid who'd gotten up early enough the previous Saturday to get down to Wade's before they were all gone had received one just for going in and saying "Hi Mister Wade, how ya doin' t'day?"

Anyhow when Miss Milly rang that fool bell of hers, it caused such a rapid exodus among my once admiring audience, that even Bobby Nicholson deserted me. And without his support, when my eyes and arms eventually got completely dizzy from trying to wind up all that expensive string, there was no one left to spell me off. Consequently, I was already sweating up a regular downpour when Miss Milly saw fit to come out the door of the schoolhouse and call "Sydney, you'll have to come inside now, recess has ended.

That was the straw that rally opened the floodgates, you see, for by the time I decided that I had no alternative but to jettison my kite, unless I wanted to be sent to the principal's office for disobeying a direct command from my teacher, both legs of my corduroy pants were even wetter than the armpits of my shirt. And even though I tried to catch up with Miss Milly before she got to our room, so that she could see why I needed to be excused for the balance of the afternoon, I was fighting a losing battle.

And little dunce that I was, I'd peeked through the doorway and seen that everyone's attention was focused on the blackboard, where Miss Milly was even then writing down our reading assignment for the afternoon, I still decided I had a fifty-fifty chance of making it to my desk without being seen.

But of course I was no more than halfway through the door be when the first "Tee-hee began, and before my corduroys were able to utter "snick-snick, snick-snick" the third time, my world of make believe had come tumbling down around my crimson ears. So when Miss Milly turned around an saw what everyone was laughing about, she came to my rescue by telling one of the girls to begin reading the first paragraph of the assignment, then she took me out into the hallway and told me I could go home and change clothes, and she'd expect me back in class the following morning.

But after the passage of nearly seventy-five years has eased the pain of that fateful day, I still find it difficult to believe that I could have been lucky enough to have been born in Ridgway, where this fantastic lady spent so many years of her life. Because you see, after Mom had died the previous year, this Guardian Angel of Ridgway's League of Wayfaring Waifs always seemed to realize that whenever I was reluctant to head for home, it was usually because we were in between housekeepers and there would be no one there to look after me. This tine, though, I was able to tell her "Yeah, Miss Milly. ol' Missus Gage'll be there." So she knew that my reluctance was probably due to nothing more serious than an acute case of embarrassment.

Th' Rites'a Passage

Ones th' greatest mysteries a'life, at least
fer this ol' grey-bearded goat,

Is jist how far a'knuckleheaded kid can see
`is way clear t'tote `is fishin' pole

On'a sunny summer's day, when there jist ain't
no way a'dang hoe handle'll fit in `is fist.

An' when ya git right down t'th' brass tacks a'things,
if there's one solitary thing that's any slower

A'runnin', than'a kid-powered lawnmower, I sure ain't
got even'a ghost of'a notion as t'what it might be.

Most `specially when that same goofy kid's mind
is jist settin' on sunnin' `is bare buns b'hind

Up th' river an' around th' bend a'piece, where fer some
unknown reason, except t'him an' `is chums a'course,

A'well-knotted chunk'a rope dangles from th' tangled limbs
a'th' gnarled ol' cottonwood that's leanin' right out over

What flat-out has t'be, th' very best swimmin' hole a'guy could
ever hope t'see, leastwise if `is eyes're in tune with June

Er fer that matter, `most any month'll do, jist as long
as it falls pretty much of anywhere, in b'tween

"Oh golly Freddy, I jist hope we both live long
a'nuff fer summer t'git here, don'chu?"

An' "Aw Holy Cow, Dad, are ya absa'lutely, pos'a'tively
certain school starts next week? AWREADY?"

Dear Ol' Deer Huntin' Camp

There was a place we used t'go, dear ol' Dad an' me
That seemed near'bout as close t'Heaven as a place could be
Fer even tho' t'was jist a rag-tag two-room shack
With a single-hole chick-sales a'settin' out back
That little cabin would git so flat-out rife with life
Whenever our pal Short decided t'bring Marge, 'is goofy wife
Why it's barely short of a miracle the walls didn't fall down
When that runty little female nut'd start in clownin' around
Because even tho' t'was plain t'see that Short was 'er only guy
T'was dreamin'a ways t'devil poor Harvey that gleamed in 'er eye
An' despite it's bein' more'n sixty years ago, I can see 'em yet
Her a'hootin' at Harvey's scootin', his face red as it could get
Round an' round that rough ol' table they'd go
With Marge yellin' as loud as she could
"Aw c'mon Harvey, WHOA!"

But even tho' Harvey was a cowboy an' knowed what she meant

T'was only faster an' faster them bowlegs a'his went

But after awhile his buddy Joe'd poke out `is toe

An' down that six foot four bag'a bashful bones'd go

So he'd no sooner come crashin' t'the deck

When Marge'd be on top of `im, both
arms wrapped around `is neck

Jist nuzzlin' `is crimson muzzle with `er puckered-up lips

Rasslin' `round `til it'sa wonder she didn't bust both `is hips

But that's the way the race ended `most ever' night

That crazy woman jist howlin' with all `er might

"Aw c'mon Harvey, kiss me, please"

"Cuz ya sure do turn me on, Sweetie Pie

With them cute bow-legged knobbledy-knees!"

Showdown At The Rio Grande Western-Southern Depot

Due to my being unable to convince my father that his stories about the various events that occurred in Ouray County after his arrival in 1908 really should be written down while he was still able to do so, all I have left to rely on is my memory of the incidents he said he took part in. So just because one of them involved both Charlie Marlow and his older brother, George, who have already been mentioned in the story about Mother Leisy and the Hafleys, I've decided to include it in this collection. I readily admit that my version may not be quite as factual as Dad's would have been, but there's adequate reason to believe that most of it took place as follows:

After Dad and his first wife returned to their jumping-off spot once again, when he rented a small office adjacent to the local barbershop and went into business for himself, it looked as if they just might be on their way up the ladder at last. Not very high perhaps, but at least far enough to allow him to begin placing ads in the Real Estate listings of both The Denver Post and Pueblo Chieftain, two of the state's most influential and prominent newspapers at the time.

Its difficult to say what impact this might have had on the welfare of the little town, but when a certain United States Marshal purchased the current issue of the Denver Post from a news-stand a few doors down the street from his office in the "Mile-High City", and noticed Dad's listing of a ranch for sale over in Ouray County, stating "If property is not found as herein represented, I will refund your railroad fare. G.C. Huffnagle, Ridgway, Colorado.", the lawman soon decided there was a good chance this realtor might either be acquainted with the two Marlow brothers he needed to talk to, or should at least know where they could be found.

Since he'd long ago learned that the quickest way of getting things done the way you wanted them, was to do them yourself, he was soon headed down the street to the telegraph office. For despite knowing that he might have been able to reach this Huffnagle fellow by telephone, he couldn't help feeling that by the time he'd yelled himself hoarse, then strained to decipher what the man said, it was much simpler to do it in the same manner he always had. That way at least, there'd be documented evidence that he'd done what he could to give the marshal down in Texas a hand.

Therefore, since even telegrams sometimes took several hours to reach their destination, the marshal (who shall hereafter be known by the purely fictitious handle of Jack Holt) returned to his office to write a letter to the marshal in Texas (who for the purposes of this narrative shall be given the alias of none other than Tom Mix, due to his being another of the author's idols at the time he first heard this particular story), informing him of what had thus far been done regarding his earlier request for information about the Marlow brothers.

The man who'd replaced Grover as Ridgway's jack-of-all-trades station agent and telegrapher was too busy sorting the freight that had arrived on the Western's morning train, and was doing his best to accommodate the various farmers and ranchers who kept coming in to ask if the articles they'd been expecting for several weeks had finally gotten in, so it was nearly four o'clock before he realized he still hadn't let Grover know he'd received a telegram. And since the "Bang-bang-bang, you're dead!" erupting from the mouth of the kid that kept jumping out from behind the new manure-spreader that had been sitting on the loading-dock for the past few days was wearing pretty thin by this point, he yelled "Hey Buster, if ya think ya can hustle up to Grover Huffnickle's real estate office without gittin' lost, an' tell `im he's got a telegram down here, I'll give ya a nickel when ya come back!"

Although he was somewhat out of breath by the time he brought his stick-horse to a stop in front of the screen-door leading into Grover's little office, Buster was nevertheless able to fulfill his end of the bargain by panting "Mister Huff-Huff-Huff-a-nickle, the guy down at the depot said he'd give me a nickel if I'd tell ya he's got a telegram fer ya. But since my horse's really outta breath from runnin' all the way up here, d'ya think ya could maybe gimme the money yerself, an' jist sorta tell `im it's okay t'pay ya back, since I done what I was s'posed to?"

Chuckling as he got up from his desk and walked over to open the screen-door, Grover said "I'll tell you what, son, since I don't usually keep that much cash on hand, would it be alright if I write you a check instead? I know that'll probably mean running down to the bank and cashing it, at least if you intend to spend it today, but unless you think that poor old horse of yours can make it all the way back to the depot, I just don't know what else to suggest."

Not at all sure Mr. Huffnagle wasn't just teasing him, when Buster turned to stare back down the nearly three block distance to the depot, almost as though he was wondering why dealing with grownups always had to be so darn complicated, Grover quickly pulled the proper coin from his pocket. Then he bent down and pretended to pick it up from just behind the heel of the boy's shoe, exclaiming "Well, would you just look at what you almost stepped on, this sure enough must be our lucky day!"

After an instantaneous inspection of the step and sidewalk failed to detect any additional coins, Buster squinted up at Grover and said "I should'a knew better than t'fall fer that goofy trick, since the guy down at the hardware store's always doin' the same thing. But one'a these days when I git as big as you guys, I'm gonna think'a some way t'git even, you jist wait an' see if I don't!"

Dropping the coin into the boy's outstretched hand, Grover replied "I don't doubt it for a minute, son, but since you and your horse both look pretty thirsty, it might be a good idea to lead him on down to Boucher's before Sam runs out of soda-water or decides to lock up early, which is what I'm going to have to do in order to go see who in the world could have sent me the telegram that started all this foolishness."

By the time Grover removed his sleeve-protectors and put on the suit jacket he'd draped over a chair-back upon returning from lunch some three and a half hours earlier, then locked the door of his office and walked down to where he could see Buster perched on one of the stools visible through the window of Boucher and Sons Drugstore, the boy had already consumed three-fourths of the drink his hard-earned wages had purchased. Grover was several feet past the door before memories of his own somewhat austere childhood caused him to turn around and enter the building.

Extracting another nickel from his pocket as he walked over to where the boy sat eyeing him in the large mirror behind the fountain, he said "Son, if I'm ever lucky enough to have a boy of my own, I sure hope he turns out to be as honest and hard-working as you seem to be. So stick this in your pocket and save it until you get thirsty again."

As he walked on down the street a few minutes later, passing the building that would eventually house not only his real estate and insurance business, but would also be the spot where he would spend nearly thirteen years serving as the little community's postmaster, it's extremely doubtful that he had anything on his mind other than wondering whether one of the ads he'd placed in the Denver Post a few days earlier had actually borne fruit. If he'd had the slightest idea that the fruit would be coming by way of the United States Marshal's office, there's an excellent chance he'd have walked across to one of the saloons on the north side of the street before continuing on to the depot.

Just because he didn't, he was about as unprepared as he could possibly be for his friend Bob's wide-eyed inquiry of "What in gawd's name was ya involved in before ya showed up in Ridgway, Grover? Did ya rob a fool bank or shoot somebody, or somethin', to give the U. S. Marshal the idea ya might'a been doin' stuff ya shouldn'ta been?"

Completely taken aback by the question, as well as by the incredulous tone of the other man's voice, Grover failed to detect the twinkle in Bob's eyes, and he stammered "I-I-I-uh, I don't know what the devil you're talking about Bob! The boy just said you had a telegram for me, he didn't say one word about what was in it!"

Unable to contain himself any longer, Bob burst out laughing, then said "Man-oh-man, Grover, if ya just could'a seen the look on yer face when ya thought the law might be after ya, I swear, ya'da swore off doin' anything that wasn't strictly on the up an' up fer the rest'a yer life!"

Reaching into the basket beside the telegraph-key, he continued "Before ya up an' bust a gusset, though, all this guy want's to know is if ya can give `im a hand in settin' up a meeting fer him an' another marshal from off down in Texas, with George an' Charlie Marlow. I don't really know a hellova lot about it, but I seem to remember somebody's tellin' me how some Texas Ranger come up here after `em quite awhile back, an' before all the dust'd settled, a bunch'a George an' Charlie's neighbors got their heads together an' wound up tellin' that ranger he dang well better bring some help with `im the next time he come back. But since it's pretty plain that this ain't got a dang thing to do with anything you might'a done, how come yer still lookin' so pale?"

Not quite ready to let his friend off the hook yet, Bob waited until Grover had studied the telegram for several seconds before saying "Fer somebody that's always goin' on about honesty bein' the best policy, ya sure as the devil look awful guilty about somethin' right now! Are ya absolutely positive there ain't at least a couple clinkers layin' in yer tracks back down the line a ways?"

Realizing Bob would more than likely keep right on needling him if he didn't put an end to it in some manner, Grover finally said "When you sent that boy up to tell me there was a telegram down here for me, he said you've been forcing him to run errands all over town for quite awhile now. So I told him that if that really is what's been going on, I'd send a letter to the company headquarters and let them decide what to do about it, which was when he said he'd go on home and see if he could remember how many times it's happened. So all I can say is HOW DOES IT FEEL TO GET A DOSE OF YOUR OWN MEDICINE FOR A CHANGE?"

Grinning as he stood there wagging his head from side to side, Bob's response of "Yer a hellova lousy liar, Grover, I know dang good an' well that kid never said anything of the kind, it's wrote all over yer face!"

Jack of All Trades by Sydney A. Huffnagle

When Bob then asked "Well, what're ya figgerin' on doin' about what this Marshal Holt's askin' of ya? Since I'm almost positive neither one of the Marlows has a phone, an' I'm fairly sure you ain't broke down an' bought an automobile yet, it looks like about all that's left is rentin' one'a the nags from the guy up at the livery, or lettin' me sell ya a ticket on tomorrow's train to Montrose, which jist might mean spendin' the night camped beside the tracks an' catchin' the train back the next morning.", Grover exploded "Then it pretty much looks like I'm stuck with renting a horse, doesn't it, my fine-feathered friend?"

Due to an all but total lack of familiarity with Ouray County's four-legged means of transportation, by the time Grover finally reached the little farm he would one day be partly responsible for Frank and Mamie Hafley's buying, his mood was a lot closer to sour than sunny when he at last saw one of the brothers who'd been responsible (albeit unknowingly) for his thoroughly uncomfortable journey.

Charlie's "Howdy friend!", as he straightened up from his irrigating chores and splashed his way over to the fence paralleling the road, sounded a whole lot more friendly than otherwise, Grover groaned "Mister Marlow, I sure hope you don't end up thinking I'm some kind of troublemaking busybody, but simply because the United States Marshal over in Denver must have seen one of my real estate ads and decided towell, anyhow, hehehe wants me to ask if you and your brother will be willing to come up to Ridgway and talk to him and another marshal from Texas in the next week or so!"

Realizing the other man almost had to be the owner of the real estate agency that had first opened its doors in Ridgway a year or two earlier, Charlie laughed and said "Will ya jist relax Mister Huffnagle? George an' me's already told our side of the story these guy's are gonna be askin' about, more than enough times t'know they're prob'ly jist gonna keep right on askin' an' askin' 'til they fin'ly git it through their thick heads that we've been tellin' the truth all along. There ain't a dang thing you or anybody else can do about it, so jist simmer down an' climb offa that nag long enough t'give yer rump a rest! From the way yer squirmin' around, it almost looks like the fool saddle must be hot."

Grimacing as he attempted to extract his right foot from the stirrup, Grover said "I'm not at all sure I'll be able to get back on once I get off, Mister Marlow, but right at this moment walking all the way back to town seems to have a lot more going for it than riding. I can tell you this much, though, if I'd had to ride a horse all the way out here from Ohio, I never would have lived through it!"

Chuckling as he stuck out his hand, Charlie said "Part a'yer problem is them short stirrup-strapsuh, Grover, ain't it? So if ya'll jist drop the Mister Marlow stuff an' call me Charlie instead, I'll be more than glad t'let the fool things out fer ya. That way the trip back t'town's gonna seem a whole lot shorter'n the one ya jist made. When ya do git back, though, tell that livery guy I said he oughta knock off at least half 'a what he's chargin' fer this hunk'a buzzard bait, jist because he was too dang lazy t'let 'em out hisself."

Watching the ease with which the other man lowered the left stirrup approximately three inches, Grover said "If you'll let me do the other one uh— Charlie, maybe I'll still remember how the next time it becomes necessary. If that ever happens, anyhow!"

After visiting for nearly twenty minutes, during which it was decided that ten days ought to allow the lawmen adequate time to get to Ridgway, Grover remounted his horse and said "Even though this saddle fits a whole lot better than it did a while ago, if that marshal in Denver isn't able to convince the other one that he's got to be here when we say he does, they can just find someone else to run their errands from now on, because I'm not even about to ride all the way down here again!"

By the time he'd returned to Ridgway and sent a wire off to the Denver marshal, then waited until late the following afternoon to find that the terms were acceptable, he'd once more begun worrying about his role in the forthcoming meeting. Which, naturally enough, his friend Bob had promptly begun referring to as "The big showdown at the Rio Grande Western-Southern Depot!"

So as the days dragged slowly by, Grover's earlier bravado was replaced with some truly serious doubts as to whether he ought to send another telegram off to Denver, with word that he had to go back to Ohio for some family emergency, or maybe out to California, or just about anywhere else, the day of reckoning finally arrived. But after listening to the "tick-tock, tick-tock, tick-tock" of his office clock, he slammed his ledger-book shut and stood up so abruptly that his chair fell over, crashing to the floor just loudly enough to make him wonder if it was remotely possible to hear a pistol-shot before its bullet would already have started him on the way to his grave.

As he undoubtedly should have expected, he'd barely entered the depot before Bob noticed his more or less haggard appearance and said "Yer lookin' pretty green around the gills this mornin' Grover, what'd ya do, soak up a little too much liquid courage before ya went t'bed last night?"

Glancing at the big clock hanging above the door leading out onto the loading dock, he then added "The train was a good fifteen minutes late gittin' outta Montrose, so it ain't too likely that it'll have made it as far as the bridge by Charlie's place yet. So even if him an' George didn't take it inta their heads t'dynamite the sucker", by this point the object of his baiting was already heading through the door toward the north end of the dock, where he was relatively certain he'd be able to spend his final moments in peace. Unless, that is, Bob decided to tag along.

Just to avoid as much likelihood of that as he could, when Grover reached the far end of the freight-room, he stepped around the corner out of sight.

But simply because he was much too tense to stand still for more than a few minutes, he soon began pacing back and forth across the end of the dock. Fairly certain it was totally ridiculous to think there was any chance at all the Marlows would be so concerned about meeting the marshals, they'd actually consider blowing up one of the railroad's bridges, he still couldn't help feeling it might indeed be possible.

But since that would amount to virtually the same thing as admitting they were guilty of whatever it was that had ultimately resulted in the marshal's decision to involve Grover in something he had absolutely nothing to do with, it was hard telling what might happen when the train finally arrived. Why even if it didn't actually turn into another fracas like the one down in Tombstone, Arizona thirty or forty years earlier, once the word got out that he'd been involved with two men that a United States Marshall was willing to come all the way from Texas to talk to, well, it really was hard to tell how much longer he'd be able to stay in business!

About that time, though, just as a faint whistle indicated the train was approaching what almost had to be the Old Dallas crossing, he saw two riders coming toward him from the direction of the stockyards, roughly a quarter of a mile north of where he stood. Not having expected the Marlows to be coming from quite that direction, another minute passed before he finally realized they must have forded the Uncompahgre River just above the railroad bridge approximately three-quarters of a mile north of the depot and one and a half miles south of where the first puffs of smoke were now becoming visible above the thick stand of cottonwoods lining both sides of the river.

When the rider in front raised his hand in acknowledgment just as his horse broke into a trot, Grover knew it was already too late to slip out of sight, so he waved back. But due to the fact that both of the brothers were wearing hip-length jackets, it wasn't until they'd halted their mounts a few feet from the edge of the platform that he was able to see the barrels of their large caliber revolvers protruding several inches beyond the bottom of their coattails. As if that wasn't bad enough, each of the men had apparently felt it advisable to carry a Winchester carbine in the scarred leather scabbards secured to the right-hand skirt of their saddles.

Upon seeing the stunned look this observation had produced on Grover's face, Charlie grinned and said "George an' me learned a long time ago that it ain't too smart t'give the other side the idea they're holdin' the best hand, so even though the hardware's mainly fer show, we figgered we prob'ly better bring it along. There shouldn't be any trouble though, unless the marshals start it. An' since that ain't too likely t'happen, ya might as well try wipin' that sick look off yer face while we're tyin' our horses t'the rail out front."

Not the least bit happy about the way things seemed to be turning out, as Grover stood there watching the puffs of smoke drawing closer and closer, the front of the locomotive suddenly emerged from the trees and the puffs quickly turned into a long black plume, more than somewhat reminiscent of the widow's weeds his fashion-conscious wife might soon be wearing.

Realizing he'd never as yet spoken to the older of the two brothers, he started toward the far side of the depot just as they came back around the corner. Extending his hand as George came toward him, he said "I hope your brother told you how I managed to get involved in this, Mister Marlow, because I sure as the devil don't want you or anyone else to think I'm here because I want to be, becausewell, just because I really don't!"

Chuckling as he shook Grover's hand, George said "That's pretty easy to see, Mister Huffnagle. But since there's nothing to be gained by letting the marshals know how nervous you are about this, why don't you take Charlie's advice and try to relax a little before they get here. And while you're at it, it'll sound a whole lot friendlier if you use our first names when you introduce us. Alright?"

Winking at Grover at this point, Charlie quipped "That's alright fer `im t'do with you an' me, George, since we ain't used t'havin' folks treat us like we're any better than anybody else. But since you know as well as I do that most sheriffs an' marshals pretty much like t'think they sit jist a little higher in the saddle than reg'lar folks, don't ya think he better call them Marshal Mix an' Marshall Holt instead? As long as he can do it without gittin' the Holt an' Mix part all mixed up, anyway!"

As he stood there eyeing Charlie and wagging his head from side to side, George finally said "As you'll probably find out once you've known him a little longer, Grover, my brother has always seemed to think he's a comedian. And even though some of the things he says and does really are funny, there have been a good many times when both of us would have been a lot better off if he'd just tried to be serious for a change."

"Well if that's the way ya feel about it" Charlie now snorted, "maybe I better jist go grab my Winchester before the train gits here! That way the marshals're bound t'know I'm jist as serious about this deal as it's possible t'git!"

Reasonably sure Charlie must be joking, just as Grover was opening his mouth to say that's what he truly hoped he was doing, the train's locomotive drew abreast of the platform, accompanied by more than sufficient "Chuff-chuff-chuffing" and "Clang-clang-clanging" to drown out everything but the short, shrill toot-toot-tooting of it's whistle, which very nearly succeeded in causing Ridgway's only licensed real estate broker to run right over the top of the men he was facing.

Despite his eventually calming down enough to introduce George and Charlie to the marshals with only a marginal amount of stammering and stuttering, during which all four of the men got so amused at his discomfiture they could barely maintain their composure, when Marshal Holt finally thanked him for his help and said he was free to go, he wasted very little time in so doing. So little in fact, that he would ever after proclaim he made it all the way to the corner of Field's Brother's Hardware without turning to look back even once, despite his fully expecting to have lead zinging past his ears at any moment.

He was so out of breath by the time he got to the doorway of his favorite saloon, though, that he took a quick peek back toward the depot, where Charlie seemed to be pointing and waving his trigger-finger directly in the Texas marshal's face, almost as if he might actually be scolding the poor man for causing so much trouble for everyone else. More than somewhat inclined to feel that the marshal probably had it coming, he nevertheless felt he too had something coming, which was when he shoved the door open and said "I'd like a shot of the usual, Pete—uh no, on second thought, why don't you make it a double instead?"

A Heavy Load

The man was old and stooped, his thinning crown all silver gray, Just shining like a halo, in the brittle light of the damp and cheerless day.

And as he stood alone, his deep voice choked "Tisn't right LORD, an ugly black hole in this damned frozen clay. YOU know I hate its sight.

An' even though it's not really for me t'say, what's fair or foul Or might'a been th' better way, I only know that one so young, so sweet an' small,

With her gentle smile an' teasing eyes so clear an' shiny bright, She deserved better by far, LORD, than what she got!

For now she'll never know another sun-warmed morning in early Spring, or watch th' waxing moon waltz with th' clouds on a starry night.

Nor will she hear th' piercing cry of th' Black-crested Jay As he heralds yet again th' return'a day.

Now she'll never smell that rose I placed in her hand, an' they'll both just wither here, in this all forsaken pile'a clay.

AW NO, LORD, damn it all t'hell, it's just not right!"

Stealin' Out Th' Door

What's the matter Honey, why are you getting up?
Can't sleep Babe, so I might jist as well.
What time is it? It's still awfully dark.
4:30, but don't you fret none, I think I'll drink me a cup,
n' jist set fer'a spell. There must'a bin'a moose messin'
around out in th' yard, leastwise somethin' made ol' Pard
growl. You go on back t'sleep now, n' I'll be all right,
cause it's really kind'a nice, jist loafin' in th' easy chair listnin'
T' my Willy tapes, n' watchin th' Anchorage light,
a'glistnin off th' Inlet ice. Th' shadow shapes a'th' trees
up on Skyline Ridge are purty too, n' oh yeah, I meant t'ask
you, are those purple grapes still in th' fridge?

Old Ed Was A Hard Man To Put Down

Although I'm not sure just when my first face to face encounter with old Ed Fisher actually took place, it almost had to have occurred during one of my initial prospecting trips prior to 1935. I probably was making more than my normal amount of racket that day, since I was using my favorite hammer to crack rocks open, just to see if there was any gold inside. The main problem with having a favorite hammer in the first place, you know, is the necessity of having a really good back-up plan for fixing the fool thing whenever the head flies off. Because I know for a bonafide fact that just slipping the pieces back together and pounding on the end of the handle with a rock hardly ever gets you more than three or four licks before you've got to do it all over again.

But when you're bound and determined to find out how much paydirt's lying around, you've just got to keep whacking away with what you have. And what I had, at least after ol' Ed showed up, was a pretty darn nosy audience. So even though I'm no longer absolutely certain about everything that was said during the ensuing few minutes, it probably went pretty much as follows:

"Hey Boy, how come yer makin' so dang much racket?"

"I'm jist lookin' fer gold Mister Fisher, do ya know if these're the right kinda rocks to find it in, er not?"

"What I know, Boy, is that if ya keep bangin' away on them things long enough, yer prob'ly gonna wind up with a blind eye, same as this one'a mine!"

This said, he bent over and pointed a stubby finger at one of his eyes, just which one I no longer recall. To the best of my recollection though, the iris had a fairly large area of white at one side, and the pupil was a cloudy-gray color. But there's a good chance this memory may have been acquired in the years that followed. Whatever the case, though, Ed Fisher was the first person I remember as being blind in one eye.

If I had to hazard a guess as to his height, it would be somewhere close to 5 feet eight or nine inches, possibly a little less. He was fairly stocky, and at least in all the mental images I've been able to conjure up, his cheeks and chin were always covered with a short, heavy stubble of gray whiskers. Relatively gruff sounding, he was the type of man most kids have a hard time being at ease with. At least that's how he usually affected me.

His son Bryan was one of the biggest teases I ever knew, so he was a lot easier to get along with, as far as I was concerned anyhow. One of the first memories I have of Bryan occurred one afternoon when my dog, Laddie, and I were just minding our own business out in the street beside his house. Unless, that is, you call trying to learn to pop the little circus whip your Mom bought you just a couple of days earlier, not minding your own business. Bryan had just come home from his ranch over across the Uncompahgre River, so when he suddenly grabbed my whip and started acting like he was going to use it on me, neither one of us had any idea as to what was about to happen.

They'd been living there long enough by then so I knew he was only teasing, but Laddy was an entirely different matter. And before the whip was drawn back for a second swing at my rump, there was a full-grown collie hanging from Bryan's wrist. Once he dropped the whip, though, Laddy let go of his wrist right away. It was just barely bleeding, and since his wife, Jean, was a registered nurse, at least he didn't have to pay for the little bandage she put on it. But you can bet your bottom dollar he paid close attention to where Laddy was, whenever he started teasing me after that.

One of my favorite memories of Jean involved something that happened every summer, when the hogback we called Ridgway Hill was positively bristling with the creamy-white blossoms of the yucca plant. But since the area's first white settlers had used the blossoms for making soap, most of us called it Soapweed. Jean was the only person I knew who still made her own laundry soap, and all I have to do is close my eyes to once again bring her sun-bonneted image into focus, hiking along that dusty, hot old hillside for the sole purpose of harvesting just one of the ingredients in another year's supply of⎯yeah, that's all it really amounted to I guess, just so many soapsuds.

And even though I haven't the slightest idea as to what all was involved with converting those flowers into soap, I know it was a darned good thing there weren't any EPA nuts running around loose when she had her mind set on rendering out the suet she needed for her recipe. Because one morning back around 1937 or so, upon seeing a plume of thick, black smoke suddenly erupt from her back yard, I went racing over to see what was going on.

About halfway between the backdoor of her house and the rear of their garage, which sat out beside the alley, hung one of the biggest and blackest cast-iron stew-pots I've ever seen, bar none. Jean had discarded her bonnet prior to my arrival, for it was lying on the ground some distance away. And the only thing that could possibly have made her look more like a witch, would have been if she'd had on one of those wide-brimmed, pointy hats they always seem to be wearing, at least in the funny-papers. Her hair had come unpinned and it was so frazzled you'd have sworn she'd never combed it in her life. Beads of perspiration were glistening all over her face and neck when I skidded to a stop a few feet away, blurting "Holy Cow, Miz Fisher, what's goin' on? When I seen all that black smoke shootin' up, I was scared yer house must be on fire, or somethin'!"

Wagging her head as she grinned at me, she swiped at her face with the back side of one arm before saying "Buzzy, I've been trying to get this fool fire to burn the way it needs to for the past hour. So when it just wouldn't do it, and I couldn't find anymore coal-oil out in the garage, I just decided to use a few chunks of this suet instead."

Chuckling wryly at my second "Holy Cow!", she said "I guess that means you think I could probably have gotten by without quite as much, hunh?"

Since I didn't want her thinking I really was thinking what she thought I was thinking, I decided to play it safe by just saying "But it sure is burnin' good now, ain't it?"

Then, after a couple of somewhat uneasy moments of silence, I added "Well, now that I know ever'thing's okay, I better git on back home. Dad said if I git enough weeds chopped this mornin', I can prob'ly go fishin' up at the slough with some'a the guys after lunch. Be seein' ya!"

Consequently, since that's the extent of my knowledge about Jean's soap recipe, I'd probably better just go ahead and tell you what happened when old Ed eventually died. Because that really is what I've been trying to get around to ever since I started wagging this little tale.

I'm fairly sure it was during the early summer of 1942, when I was fourteen. Dad was one of three members on the board of the Dallas Park Cemetery Association, and the previous year he'd persuaded the other two guys into giving me and my cousin, Wayne Grooms a shot at the sexton's job. Wayne's mother had been Dad's sister, so when Wayne's father died three or four years after she did, Dad brought Wayne out from Ohio to live with us. But just because he was approximately nine months older than I was, the fur had begun flying almost as soon as he showed up. And even though we'd managed to make it through the first summer at the cemetery without killing one another, when Wayne found a job with a rancher out in Pleasant Valley the following summer, I finally convinced Dad there was no reason I couldn't handle the sexton's job all by myself. Needless to say, the fact that I would no longer have to share the $35.00 per month salary with anyone else had a lot to do with my being so persuasive. And since I'd also be receiving the entire $10.00 that was then the going rate for digging a grave, you'd just better believe I was convinced that I'd be the richest kid in town by the time school started again. At least if enough people cooperated, by dying when they were supposed to.

Consequently, when Ed eventually got around to giving up the ghost, Bryan offered to send his hired man, Kent Dickson, out to help dig the grave. Free of charge, no less. So it's little short of a miracle that the handle of my shovel was long enough to reach the ground when Kent showed up. And just because he was pretty darn handy with his too, by somewhere around 11:30 that morning we were down about four and a half feet. Which was when water began oozing up from the bottom of the grave. Dad showed up a few minutes later, just to see how we were getting along, so he told us to go ahead and eat our lunches while he high-tailed it back into town to get Bryan.

We'd just barely finished eating our sandwiches when they pulled through the cemetery gate, trailing more than enough dust to bury Ed in, at least if all of it had settled right there on the Fisher family's lot. So after acknowledging that even though most of the folks in the area already knew a good seventy-five percent of the cemetery had always been plagued with the seepwater that began percolating in from the surrounding hayfields as soon as the irrigating season began in the Spring, Bryan said he still didn't think it would look right to drop his dad's earthly remains into a foot or two of water, right smack in front of everybody. But since there was just no way to delay the funeral until Fall, when the irrigating would end for another year, he finally decided the only feasible thing to do was to install Ed temporarily on one of the vacant plots at the upper end of the cemetery, where we could be fairly sure we wouldn't encounter any water. Then when it was safe to do so, we'd just have to dig him up and move him back to where he was supposed to be.

But since we didn't dare leave the hole we'd just dug open for the next three months, Kent and I wound up getting stuck with filling it in, while all Dad and Bryan had to do was find a suitable location for disposing of our by now mutual problem. So it was somewhere in the neighborhood of 1:30 P.M. when we began digging Ed's home away from home. Of course, as soon as I'd seen the spot Bryan and Dad picked out, I told Kent "I sure hope yer as good with a pick as ya are with a shovel, because we're gonna need it before we git more'n a foot deep! Right over there where that little metal marker is, is where Wayne an' me spent dang near four whole days diggin' our very first grave, jist last summer. Of course it was fer a vault, an' we wasn't too swift with our shovels an' picks yet, but this ground up here is H-A-R-D, hard, an' that's fer dang sure!"

It was somewhere around 5:30 that evening when Dad drove back out to get us, carrying three well chilled bottles of his do-it-yourself rootbeer, so you'd just better believe that Kent and I were thirsty as heck by then. Because by taking turns at swinging that miserable pick for the past four hours, one of us had usually managed to recover enough breath to start shoveling just as soon as another two or three inches was pried loose. And by the time Dad appeared on the scene, we'd made it down to the four and a half foot depth again, or three-fourths of the way to the finish-line.

But after practically chug-a-lugging the contents of his bottle, Kent said "Boy howdy, that tasted so darn good I'm gonna see if I can finish pickin' this next layer loose all by myself!"

So after jumping down into the hole and raising the pick clean up over his back, he brought it crashing down with all his might. And since Dad and I were still sitting on the mound of dirt that had already risen from the grave, so to speak, we had pretty much of a ringside seat to the action. But even so, it happened so fast it really didn't register until several seconds after Kent's yelp of "**OH MY GOD!**" was followed by his flat-footed exodus up to the far side of the hole.

Unsure of whether I was actually **seeing** what I thought I was, I hopped down into the grave to make certain. And sure enough, almost smack-dab in the upper half of the twelve inch opening that had nearly succeeded in swallowing Kent's pick-head, lay a head that had originally belonged to another human being. And even though the neck bones were covered by the dirt that had fallen in, I was able to make out a few ribs just below where the shoulders would have been. But when a small cloud of what appeared to be some kind of gnat began spiralling round and round the skull down in the hole, I vacated the premises almost as quickly as Kent had. So it wasn't until after we'd begun refilling what was to become only the second of the three graves I was personally involved in digging for Ed Fisher, that I became more or less convinced I'd also seen what appeared to be a patch of long, rusty-red hair still attached to the top of the skull.

And whether you choose to believe it or not, after pouring over the Dallas Park Cemetery's so-called record-book to help find another likely spot to put Ed in lay-away in, and get him out of our hair for a little while, the spot where Kent and I spent the following day sweating up a regular storm, came within a subterranean gnat's eyelash of producing exactly the same result its predecessor had. But after Dad once again high-tailed it into town to get Bryan to come take a gander at the exterior and extremely decayed end of yet another ancient rough-box, which had shown up at the very edge of this hole, it was unanimously decided that the best thing to do was just to mix up a bucket of mud and plaster it over the board.

So when Ed's exhumation took place later that Fall, in order to lay him to rest for the rest of eternity, at least hopefully, you'd just better believe it didn't hurt my feelings one iota when Bryan decided it wouldn't be right to ask Dad if I could skip school long enough to give them a hand.

It ought to make it somewhat easier to understand how all this could have occurred, though, when I explain that due to the fact it had taken several years for the area's first white settlers to get their little cemetery association organized, quite a few folks wound up getting planted before a really serious attempt was made at jotting down just where those first graves were located. This was supposedly just because it had become necessary to threaten to lynch the bull-headed sucker that claimed the graves were on his homestead, if he didn't agree to relinquish his claim to that portion of it. So when you stop to consider that the surviving members of the families involved had often loaded their wagons and moved even further west by then, as well as the fact that the life of a simple wooden cross is relatively short, it's fairly easy to see how something like this could happen.

I'll tell you this much though, if I live to be a hundred and ninety-nine and two thirds, I will never forget how much trouble we went to, just getting that dang ol' Ed Fisher to stay put!

Call Girls, What Would We'a Done Without `Em?

Despite its small size, my little hometown of Ridgway undoubtedly had just as many call girls as most of its sister communities, and believe me, we kept them busy right around the clock. The madam of the whole shebang was a big ol' gal by the name of Rita, but we all just called her Reet. Called her a lot too, not that our appetites was all that much greater for her line'a expertise, than those of our more sophisticated cousins in the bigger towns. And life sure wouldn't a'been much more than just barely bearable without th' service those gals gave us, either.

And when I shut my eyes, I can still see each and every one of them sitting there beside their open window, at least during the summers of my youth, waving at all of us down below and just yelling "Hi" like they really meant it. Their place of business was located on the second floor of what was called "The Bank Building", directly above Mac's Drugstore, and to get to it you had to climb up a long and unbelievably creaky flight of stairs. And even though the large red-brick structure still had "The Bank Building" inscribed across its somewhat ornate facade, the bank itself had gone broke during the so-called "Great Depression", not that any of the adults I knew thought it had been so dang great.

About the only business us kids had up where the girls worked though, since we seldom had more than a couple of pennies in our pockets, was just to go up and watch them do their tricks. But as long as we were quiet when we got up there, and hadn't tried to come up the stairs with our roller skates on, it was perfectly alright with them for us to watch them perform.

There was never more than one girl on duty at a time, since our switchboard was so small, but it was still kind of fun watching them sit there with their headphone clamped on top of their hair-do, just waiting for someone to ring in. And after they'd say "Hi Bert" or "'Lo Mamie" or some such thing, they always seemed to know just which gizmo to plug the plug into.

But what was really exciting, and also the biggest reason most of us kids went up there in the first place, was when whoever happened to be on the other end of the gizmo was yelling "Fire" loud enough so that we could hear it too. Because just as soon as Reet, or Riva, or Ila, or Joanne, or Beverly, or Gloria, or whoever was on duty, had found out what was on fire, and where, they'd jump up and run over to turn the siren on, all but scalping themselves whenever they forgot to take their headset off first.

Riva was just as teeny as Reet was big, you see, but she could yell every bit as loud, and I never could figure out why either one of them even bothered to turn the fool siren on. Especially since neither could afford to lose anymore hair than what they already had. But that part about hair reminds me of the day Mable Craig rang in to let them know she had a fire at her place, so I suppose I'd better go ahead tell you about it.

Just to help you get a little better idea of the way ol' Mable was put together though, since the video button on this chapter blew a fuse a long time ago, and I haven't been able to come up with a replacement, even though she wasn't all that hard to look at, she sure hadn't been shorted the least bit when **heavy** and **volume** were being passed out. So on the day of her fire she didn't have the least bit of trouble in making Reet understand what her problem was, even if she did still fall a little shy of capturing Reet's title for **heavy**.

Anyhow, when that siren went off up there on the roof of the Bank Building, within three shakes of a snake's tail ol' Reet was poppin' plugs on that switchboard jist fit t'kill, as all th' volunteer firemen rang-in t'find out where th' fire was, along with th' usual assortment'a busy-bodies that soon got their ears blistered fer tyin' up th' lines again. An' you just should'a seen those big ol' arms'a hers fannin' air. You'll also have to make a few allowances for me, since that fool siren always did tend to get me pretty wound up.

But after I got knocked flat on my duff at the foot of the stairs, just because the Chief of the volunteers hadn't been able to get through on the phone, and had reached those big old double swinging doors a split second before I did, it was pretty plain to see that I wasn't the only one in our town that got turned on by that dang thing.

So by the time I got my roller skates clamped back on, the street down below Reet's window looked just like a pee-ants nest on the Fourth of July, right after a 4-Star Salute had gone off on top of it. Folks were yelling up at her, and she was yelling back down at them, and coupled with the noise of that god-awful siren, it's a flat-out wonder anyone made it to Mable's in time to help put out her fire.

Her husband, Ralph, wasn't going to be any help in that respect either, since he was out on his regular job with the railroad. But the way things turned out, it was just as well, because it not only gave Mable a few days of grace, just to get herself cleaned up, it also meant one less grownup for me and the other kids to have to stay out of the way of. But anyhow, by the time the firemen and the rest of us got up to her place, ol' Mable was squirting her garden hose at two holes in the roof over her kitchen, and the fire seemed to be already out.

But so was the left hand half of the new permanent she'd gotten just a day or so earlier, over at Edna's Beauty Shoppe. Boy-howdy, was she ever something to look at. I meant Mable, not Edna. Smelled even worse too. Kind'a like a fire in a feather-tick factory probably would, if you know what I mean.

She had soot all over her face, apron, cotton stockings, and hands, but that was only a fraction of what was plastered all over the inside of the house. Which ol' Ralph had just incidentally finished re-painting the last time he was in town. So in spite of the way she was always messing up us kid's tire-races an' stuff, jist because she thought we were making too much noise, I couldn't help feeling kind of sorry for her, at least after I found out what had caused all the commotion.

But I might jist as well let Mable tell you about it herself, since she knows better than anyone else jist what happened, Lord rest `er poor departed soul. She always did do a pretty good job of talking long-distance though, whether her nose was shoved right up tight t'yours, or not. But there sure ain't no disrespect intended Mable, so jist go ahead an' let `er fly.

"Still a smart-mouthed little whippersnapper, ain't ya, Buzzy Huffanickle? Never could understand why yer dad didn't swab it out with'a little Fels Naptha now an' then. But I guess he done `bout as good a job as he knew how, at teachin' ya some manners, poor ignernt man.

Why I use'ta see `im out there in `is garden early ever' mornin', jist choppin' weeds er waterin', an' I knew dang good an' well you two little whelps was prob'ly jist layin' in bed an' waitin' fer `im t'come inside an' fix yer breakfast fer ya. An' then when he'd leave fer work, after linin' ya out with an hour er two's worth'a chores, why it wouldn't be no time a'tall b'fore ya'd be scootin' past my place, headin' fer some kind'a devilment. But that's kids fer ya, I guess.

As far as that goes though, it's most men fer ya too, allus a'wantin' more'n they got a right t'expect. Why, even with Honey Boy sellin' fer only a dime a'loaf down at Wade's Market, that dang Ralph allus expected me t'bake `im homemade bread. Claimed there wasn't a'nuff flour in th' store bought kind so's it would stick to `is ribs. An' that's jist ex'ac'ly what caused my dang-blasted fire, ya know.

'Cause by th' time I'd got a'nuff dough mashed out th' second time, fer six more loaves, th' dang fool oven had cooled down.

An' since Ralph never would set still fer my usin' much coal in th' summer time, there wasn't a'nuff coals left in th' firebox t'set off th' kindlin'. So I had t'pull th' spud off th' coal-oil can an' give 'er a couple'a squirts, don't ya see?

Then th' boys went t'scrappin' out in th' front yard an' I had t'go yell at 'em, so I jist barely made it back t'check th' stove in time t'almost git myself killed. It sounded sort'a like th' fool thing had a case'a th' hiccups, don't ya know? So I'd jist grabbed hold'a th' lifter, when there was'a big ka-boom that sent them dang stove-lids flyin' all over th' place. It was two a'them ya know, that knocked th' holes in th' roof. An' ya can jist talk 'bout fire 'til yer black in th' face, boy, ya ain't never seen fire like what I had squirtin' at my ceilin'.

But I knew I'd better crank Reet up b'fore I did anything else, so I did. An' ya know, by th' time I done that, th' fire comin' outta th' stove had jist about up an' left. I was scared though, that it might'a left by way'a th' attic, so that's why I was outside shootin' water on th' roof when all of ya showed up.

But boy howdy, if ya think that dang Ralph didn't make a fuss when he got home a couple days later, ya sure got a'nother think comin'. An' th' biggest part of it was all b'cause I'd let that stupid fire burn off half my new six dollar permanent, if ya can b'lieve that. Wasn't near as concerned 'bout 'is new paint job, er fer that matter, th' rest'a me. Dang-blast men all t'smithereens, anyhow, they just don't seem t'preciate all th' trouble us women go through, lookin' out after 'em!"

And now that ol' Mable's more or less had her say, I'd like to point out that it's not just the men who tend to take things for granted, in this race with the clock that all of us seem to be involved in. Because I still remember how enthusiastically our whole town looked forward to being able to dial whatever number we wanted, without having to bother with cranking up whoever was on duty, and then waiting for them to do their thing.

But it was a lot more reassuring, I can guarantee you, back when I could give the crank a couple of turns and ask "Would you plug me in to 17-J, Reet? I need to ask Dad how long it's gonna be b'fore he's comin' on home."

And after she'd rung the number a couple of times without any response, she'd usually say "Just a minute, Buzz, let me look across the street to see if his light's still on."

And a second or so later, I'd either hear her scream "Hey Grover, Buzz want's t'know how soon yer gonna be home.", if Dad just happened to be locking the door at that moment. Or she'd come back on the line with "Th' lights're already out over there, Buzz, so he must be on 'is way. But gimme a call in a few minutes if he don't make it, an' I'll ring th' store er th' garage fer ya, just t'see if maybe he's stopped off there."

We sure do pay an awful price for progress at times, it seems to me.

Mists Of Memory

Standing this morning in the stillness of my home,
I watched out the window as the shapes of the surrounding trees
Seemed to come and go,
Moving, yet standing still as the faint
Sound of the gentle rain that fell, likewise
Faded and then returned as the mists swirled
All round-about.
Standing there, alone and still, yet not alone
But moved by the
Precious mists
Of Memory.

Into The Valley

In silence they slowly descend,

Welcomed neither by beast, nor friend,
Cold and starkly, thru Popple they march,
Behind, unseen are the slopes covered with larch,
Ignored, unheralded, even by the raven,
The hounds of their pack, seemingly craven.
A kestrel too, soars down and away,
From a mate that sits, while he searches for prey,
The signboard of the Inn hangs awry,
While beneath, a small child begins to cry,
And the washer women go about their weekly toil,
As one scrubs on the board, removing the soil,

Does the trio dread their reception?
Is this why their heads hang in dejection?
Knowing that most of the many can hardly share,
In their one, single, flea-bitten hare,
Will their neighbor's back-bending load of fuel,
Once more warm only a pot of thin barley gruel?
Or have the fishermen met with success,
Have the two village-ponds yielded up with a mess,
Of carp, that bony but succulent fish,
Will there be a piece for each and every dish?
Oh! What will they find, what will they learn,
When the wandering three,
The Hunters return?

Harvest What You Will

When a garden of cheer is freely hoed,
Why then is anger so commonly sowed?
When frowns make such a burdensome load,
Why aren't smiles sown by the road?
Where fields of hate are tiresomely mowed,
Chariots of Love could so easily be towed.

Make Room For Me, Columbus!

I wasn't much more than knee-high to a bowlegged hornytoad when Fate granted me my first audience with Isabella. And due to the timidity of my tender years, far too much time would elapse before I'd actually come to understand how unique this lady truly was. But since I've always had a tendency to be a trifle slow around the ladies, particularly those with enough gumption to look a guy square in the eye as though they're just daring him to hand 'em a little sass, that's the way it goes.

Always one to say precisely what she thought, the only time I ever knew Izzie to beat around the bush about anything at all, was when she was rooting out some varmint that was pestering her chickens or other livestock. On those occasions she almost always had a big club in her hand and an ornery look in her eye, and I was too chicken-hearted to ask if she needed any help. But far and away the biggest deterrant to an earlier development of our friendship was her boy Freddie's description of what she was probably going to do when she found out I was the one who'd ruined his shirt. I'm getting a little ahead of my story though, so let's back up a few days to the first really vivid scene in my rusty little bucket of Izzmobilia.

I'm fairly sure I was eight years old at the time, so this would have made it sometime during the summer of 1936. And if memory serves me correctly, I was hot on the trail of the biggest grasshopper I'd ever seen, down in the vacant lot on the west side of our Community Church. During the summer this was a real good place to catch bumblebees with a fruit-jar, or chase butterflies as they flitted around among the purple blossoms of the wild onions that always seemed to thrive there. Since there was also an abundance of tiny white daisies and the scarlet variety of Indian Paintbrush at this particular location, it was frequently necessary to share the spot with two or three of the neighborhood's more obnoxious residents, ever so frequently referred to as 'girls'.

Since none had as yet made an appearance on this particular morning, I'd become so engrossed with keeping my eyes on the spot where the grasshopper had landed, I hadn't even heard Izzie's buckboard rattling down the alley at the rear of the church, much less seen it. Then all of a sudden, just as I was almost ready to pounce on the long-legged varmint, it sounded like a darn wooly-booger had blown his nose right smack in my left ear. And just because something like that is pretty hard to ignore, when a no-nonsense voice bellowed "Fer cryin' out loud, kid, are ya tryin' to git yerself killed?", I came real close to stripping a few of my gears.

It may have been because of my proximity to the church, but for some reason it took several seconds for me to realize the voice wasn't coming directly from God, so I just plain froze in my tracks while that rustic little chariot was forced to detour around me. None of my Sunday School teachers had ever said one word about God or any of His angels riding around in a buckboard, let alone wearing anything other than long white nightgowns, so I finally decided the noisy lady and the kid on the seat probably hadn't driven straight down from Heaven to get me. Which was when I finally backed a couple of steps out of the way. Still slightly awed by the authority of her voice, I now proceeded to follow the rig to the hitchrail at the back of Wade Carmichael's grocery store.

After helping his mom carry all their butter and eggs through Wade's back door, the boy came back out and said "Hi! My name's Freddie and I'm thirteen, how old're you?."

So even though I kind of hated to admit it, simply because I still wasn't entirely convinced he might not have some invisible connection to God, I wound up admitting I was only eight. Despite the fact that it was plain to see his opinion of my relative importance was somewhat diminished by this revelation, he nevertheless asked if I'd like to ride back out to his place and spend the rest of the day playing. Once his mom got through swapping her home-grown stuff for some of Wade's canned goods, that is.

A few minutes later Wade and the lady came back out the door, each carrying a big box of groceries, both of which were promptly stowed behind the seat of the buckboard. So I guess the main reason Freddie eventually got as big as he did, was just because his mom kept his mouth crammed full of food, more than likely just to give her ears a rest. After listening to Wade and her visit for several minutes, during which she seemed to laugh at least as much she talked, I decided it was probably safe to accept Freddie's offer. So by the time time Wade yelled "See ya next week, Izzie.", then disappeared inside the store, I'd been dragged up over the tailgate by my potential playmate.

Even though she now had a name, I was only slightly less intimidated by Freddie's mom, so I decided it would probably work out better if I just let him do all the talking. Which resulted in his saying "This is Buzz Huffnagle, Mom, he wants t'know if it's okay t'come out t'our place an' play this afternoon. I think he's kinda lonesome er somethin', poor kid. I know I was s'posed t'hoe the garden when we git back, but would it be alright t'wait an' do it tomorrow, jist this once?"

Izzie stared at me for several seconds, almost as if she might be wondering if I was bright enough to say anything on my own, or whether Freddie was just using me in order to avoid using their hoe that afternoon. Wagging her head at last, she said "I guess it'll be alright, but I've got too damn much work t'take time t'haul him back inta town, so he'd better understand right from the start that he's gonna be hoofin' it."

Looking at me like he thought a little help was probably in order, when I nodded my head somewhat doubtfully, he finally said "He knows it, Mom." Then he whispered "I'll show ya a shortcut, so jist don't worry about it!"

The two and a half mile ride out to their house seemed to take considerably longer than the time we actually spent playing after we got there. And other than for sliding off a haystack in back of their little barn several times, chasing some geese until they got cranky enough to start chasing us, I no longer recall doing anything that was particularly exciting. Then Izzie hollered "It's four-thirty, an' if that goofy kid wants t'make it home in time fer `is supper, he better git started."

Since Freddie's shortcut turned out to be the tracks of the Rio Grande Southern Railroad, and I turned out to be the only traffic on them that afternoon, it must have been somewhere close to six o'clock when I finally left them behind and began limping down what was then called `Stringtown' road, with a good long three-quarters of a mile yet to go. I don't have the slightest idea how many times I'd already stopped to dump the cinders out of my low-cuts and pull the cheat-grass stickers and hoarhound burrs out of my socks, but it was a whole bunch and that's for double-darn sure.

By the time I finally staggered through our back door just a few minutes after seven, the only thing that kept me from getting a licking was the speed with which I mobilized my mouth. And even if Izzie had been there at the moment, it's not too likely that she'd have believed I was the same tongue-tied little dummy who'd just wasted the last half of Freddie's day.

Despite everything I'd been through, though, I apparently hadn't acquired any additional smarts, because the blisters on my heels hadn't much more than gone flat when Freddie rode back into town on their old gray mare a few days later. And before I'd even had a chance to figure out what was going on, his darn motormouth had talked me into coming back out to his place for another fun-an'-games afternoon. Since he already had a gunnysack full of groceries tied to his saddlehorn, he hauled me up behind the cantle and away we went.

We were barely halfway to the top of the first hogback when my rump began feeling like my B-V-D's had either shrunk, or I'd picked up a hitchhiking cockle-burr enroute. Consequently, the second really stupid thing I did, unless you count getting out of bed that morning, was to talk him into stopping for a few minutes.

Approximately fifty feet straight up the hillside, you see, a large pinon tree was shedding just enough shade to make me think it would be a lot cooler up there than it was down on the road. So just because I was dumb enough to bring this to Freddie's attention, by the time that fool horse had hopped across the bar-ditch and then started leap-frogging up the bank toward the tree, I'd begun losing several inches of rump with every jump, figuratively speaking, anyhow. So just as mine parted company with the mare's, I latched on to something that felt fairly secure.

At least it did for the first couple of seconds, then a long drawn out rippp-ppppppppping sound sent me rolling head over heels back down into the ditch. Once all the dust had settled, and I'd spit most of the dirt out of my mouth, my eyeballs had pretty much begun to refocus. Or at least enough so that I was able to make out the big wad of blue chambray rags in my right fist.

For some reason, though, more than likely because my brains were still slightly scrambled, I couldn't seem to comprehend how I'd wound up with the dang things. About that time the mare either farted or snorted, so when I looked up and saw her perched on a little knob halfway between me and that lousy pinon tree, there sat Freddie, looking just as cool as a slightly anemic cucumber.

As you may already have begun to suspect, other than for the collar, yoke, and sleeves, about all that was left of his shirt were the two strips containing the buttons and buttonholes. And even though there were quite a few stray strings dangling from each of these, it's rather doubtful that even a highly skilled weaver could have found much use for them.

For what was quite possibly the only time in his life, it took another thirty seconds or so for Freddie to get his mouth fired up. And by the time he'd launched a whole raft of the horrible things I could expect to happen when his Mom found out it was me that had made such a mess of his shirt, I was already a hundred yards down the road, leaving at least four feet of gravel between each puff of dust.

Consequently, for the next twenty-odd years, although some turned out quite a bit odder than others, I tried to avoid stirring up too much dust in Izzie's presence. So it was a long time before I worked up enough courage to say much more than "Hi", and I never did get brave enough to ask if she'd believed Freddie's story about the shirt.

Time rolled by, though, the way it always seems to, and I eventually moved my family to Alaska. Then a few years later Freddie called to let me know he'd moved North also, and was living in Eagle River, roughly twenty miles from my trailerhouse in Anchorage. Even though we seldom bumped into one another during the next few years, since we both subscribed to our hometown paper, we more or less kept track of each other in that manner. From time to time I'd read where he'd been back to visit Izzie, and whenever I'd go home to see my folks, I'd usually swing by her place just to say "Hi" again.

Dad passed away in 1968, then just a couple of years later we received word that my stepmother, Doris, had too. My wife and I caught the first available plane, of course, and soon found ourselves in the empty old house where I'd grown up. After a relatively sleepless and tearful night of it, a loud hammering on the back door succeeded in prying me out of bed. My watch was doing its best to convince me it was eight in the morning, but since it was still 6:00 A.M. back in Anchorage, it took me a minute or two to figure out where I was, and why. I managed to get my pants pointed toward the noise in a few seconds, though, and by the time I'd stumbled out to the back door, both them and my shirt were buttoned up enough to pass for decent.

There on the other side of the glass stood Izzie, her arms overflowing with pots and pans. Grinning apologetically as I pulled the door open, she wasted no time in transferring the entire load to my arms, but just flat-out refused to come inside, saying "I'm real sorry to wake ya up this way Buzz, but when I seen the lights was on up here last night, I figgered ya must be down from Alaska. And since I knew that more than likely there wouldn't be too many groceries in the house, since Doris'd just got back from California when the stroke hit 'er, I roasted up a chicken and all the fixin's. There's an angelfood in that cake-caddy too, so once yer done with the pans an' stuff, ya can either drop 'em off at my place or let me know, an' I'll come git 'em."

When I insisted that she come on in and at least wait for the coffee to perk, she just said "I'd really like to, but I caught a damn flu-bug the other day an' I don't wanta take a chance on givin' it t'you kids."

Yet that remarkable lady had risen at daylight, killed and dressed a chicken, cooked it and the fixings, and also baked one of her famous angelfoods. Then she'd lugged the whole works for nearly three blocks and still felt the need to apologize for waking us. Consequently, my lifelong image of a tough as rawhide, hard-as-nails and hell-bent-for-leather old sister was washed straight down the drain in the next few seconds, by the tears I couldn't hold back. By the time my voice found a way around the big lump in my throat, though, and my vision had cleared a little, Izzie was already "hoofin' it" back down the sidewalk.

After spending the next few years wondering why it seemed to be the folks that had the least, who'd often contributed the most to my life, I finally decided it was high time I tried to let some of them know how I felt. So even though it took quite a bit longer than I'd had any idea it would, I was eventually able to pay my respects to a very special friend. For when the original version of the preceeding story appeared in the February 23rd, 1989 issue of The Ridgway Sun, another good friend wrote to tell me Izzie had asked one of her neighbors to pick up ten additional copies for her, just so she'd be able to send them to friends and relatives who didn't subscribe to the paper. Since I was fairly sure that must mean she liked what I'd written, I wound up feeling pretty dang good about it too.

She hoofed it on over the top of her last hill only a few years later, so just to phrase it in the manner a lot of us used back in the days when it wasn't supposed to be macho for a guy to get overly mushy, "Izzie, ya ornery ol' batt, ya might be gone, but ya sure as the devil ain't fergot!"

Things A Man Can't Seem To Forget

His mama's voice, saying "Go back to sleep
Little Man, it was only a bad dream."

The pungent smell of his daddy's sweat, as he was
carried across a favorite fishing stream.

The harsh sound the tire-chains made on a neighbor's
black Model-A, the day his mama died.

And how truly devastated he felt as his daddy knelt to tell him,
and he thus learned that even grownup men sometimes cried.

Or how quickly recess ended the April afternoon
he at long last got his first kite to fly.

As well as how long a piece of string can seem when it's tied
to that heretofore impossible dream up there in the sky.

Or the look of surprise in his Sweetheart's eyes, the
night he asked her "Honey, will you marry me?"

And how positively incredible it felt, to have the clerk at their
little honeymoon hideaway, hand him their room key.

Or how susceptible he would be, to feelings of
jealousy, after the birth of his first child.

But altho' t'was only a natural reaction to the loss sustained
by gaining an heir, at times it could drive him half wild.

For of all the many things a man will ever
know in his life, both good and bad,

Few have the power to make him madder, sadder, or
gladder than those connected to that oh so innocent
sounding little word we know simply as "Dad."

Isabelle "Izzie" McDonald.

Ol' Man Hockley

Despite how much he may have been revered by his children and grandchildren, all that old F. B. Hockley had to do was poke his fringe-topped head out the door of his little general store, and my bib-overalled companions and I would be off and running. And by the time he'd yelled "Git outta here ya little varmints, go bother somebody else fer a change.", we'd be fifty yards down the street, our holey-toed sneakers scattering gravel with every jump.

Unless of course, we were wearing our roller skates that day. In which case, since tennis-shoes weren't much better than bare feet for clamping skates to, there was better than a fifty-fifty chance that at least half of us would be doing a hippity-hop-duck-waddle down the sidewalk, with our dangling skates adding a few more pockmarks to the surface of the cement, as well as even more scrapes and scabs to our shins and ankles.

Prior to achieving the ripe old age of eight or nine, none of us actually knew whether the old man was really as ornery as he sounded, but just because he looked ornery and talked ornery, it didn't seem like a good idea to take too many chances with a two out of three batting average. By the time we'd graduated to the fourth grade though, most of us had learned we could safely enter his store as long as we had a penny or two to spend.

Once we'd ventured so far as to actually close that creaky old door behind us, of course, we'd make a beeline straight to the candy cabinet and give the glass a couple of healthy raps with the edge of our penny, just so there'd be no doubt about our actually having money to burn. And providing that our tapping was discreet enough so he didn't immediately jump up from his chair, yelling "Take it easy on that glass, ya damn little egghead, a'fore ya crack it!", the old man would then amble on over to stand behind the case while we decided just which kind of candy we were going to dicker for.

At times, though, if we'd ventured into that dark and dusty little emporium without benefit of moral support from at least one of our peers, and seemed to be in a complete agony of indecision as to whether we wanted to sacrifice our solitary coin for the wintergreen, cinnamon, or maple flavored candy, he'd rasp loose whatever was hung up in his throat and croak "Fer cryin' out loud, ya little dodo, I ain't gonna wait here all day. But if ya'll promise t'come back the next time ya got an extry penny t'spare, I guess maybe ya kin have two fer the price'a one t'day. But jist don't figger on its bein' a reg'lar thing, or go blabbin' t'all yer snot-nose buddies about it!"

Naturally, we'd immediately respond with "Gee Whiz, Mister Hockley, that's awful nice of ya! An' I promise, jist as soon as I find a Coke er Nehi bottle t'turn in over at Duckett's grocery store, I'll come pay ya back."

Since most of us weren't necessarily shiftless or overly dishonest, once we were safely back out on the sidewalk we'd more than likely spend the next hour or so searching through the weeds bordering whichever street or alley we figured might produce one or two of those lucrative but highly elusive pop bottles. But if an unusually large grasshopper happened to go racketing off to safety, or an overly warty toad picked that particular moment to hop into view, our promise and debt was swiftly forgotten. At least until we crawled into bed that night, at which time it was fairly common for most of us to review the day's events and start planning the ones for the morrow.

But in the event that the night's encounter with Morpheus hadn't erased all memory of Mister Hockley's generosity the previous day, and I didn't dally in our outhouse long enough to miss it, the sight of his tall figure returning to his little store was generally sufficient to send me up to the town dump right after breakfast, just to resume my search for bottles. Perched as it was, on the side of a hog-back hill that was itself comprised of the refuse of some prehistoric ocean, the hillside surrounding the dump was one my favorite places to spend time. Which, as you no doubt realize, was about all I had to spend.

For up there, despite its somewhat distinctive aroma, my companions and I could almost always find a wealth of lard-bucket lids to send sailing toward the sun, just to see if they'd come close enough to scorch the paint on their upper side, or render the rancid lard loose from the one beneath. But even though none of them ever attained sufficient altitude for that, they almost invariably caused the resident crows and magpies to loft themselves into the air from the scattered pinon pines growing there, squawking loudly enough to satisfy our all but insatiable need to be noticed.

Once our arms grew weary from launching those homely predecessors of the flying saucers a fairly hefty number of our generation would one day profess to encounter, and we'd given up on finding a treasure-trove of bottles that could be converted into candy-cash, there was the hill itself to explore. For the shale beneath the dusty gray soil was soft enough so all that was needed to pry loose an abundance of fossilized clamshells and once lacy fern fronds was one of the numerous pieces of scrap-iron to be found in the dump, or one of the sun-hardened limbs from the pinon and post-cedar trees.

And even though the fossils invariably crumbled within a few hours of being exposed to the light and air of our alien world, it didn't matter to us in the slightest. For with the entire bulk of that primitive graveyard towering several hundred feet above even the tallest of our homes, there just didn't seem to be any way possible that we could ever run short of fossils to dig.

There was also a good chance of finding what we'd been told were petrified shark teeth, whether they actually were or not. Most of them were bluish-white in color, extremely hard, and they were also nearly identical in appearance to the nipples commonly found on the underside of every pig I've since had occasion to scald and scrape. Consequently, Mister Hockley's grandson, Don, who was approximately four years older than me, and who also seemed to consider himself far above any of the rest of us as far as intelligence was concerned, told us they'd come from the mouths of the extremely dangerous and bloodthirsty Pig-tit Shark.

One hot afternoon in the summer of 1938, after several hours of crawling around on the hillside, dodging the clumps of prickly pear cactus and yucca that also thrived there, I'd gone racing home to show two of the teeth to my new stepmother. Because after the death of my natural mother some three years earlier, it really didn't take an awful lot to send me homeward that summer, just to make sure my new mom was still there. So after I'd dumped my assortment of broken bits and pieces of arrowheads and pottery out onto the kitchen counter, which she made all the desired comments about, I'd brought forth the teeth while attempting to say "An' jist look at these two pig-tit shark's teeth!"

Quite possibly because she'd had a very proper upbringing and had also been a schoolteacher, but <u>most</u> definitely because my tongue had gotten tangled up in my own teeth, what had slipped out of my mouth brought a totally incredulous look to her pretty face. It also brought a relatively incredulous "WHAT DID YOU SAY THEY ARE?"

By then of course, I realized I'd actually said "pig-shit tark's teeth", and face flaming, I quickly corrected my mistake. Upon seeing how mortified I was, she burst out laughing and wrapped both of her extraordinarily freckled arms around my neck. Taking great pains to correctly enunciate each of the troublesome syllables, she said "Honey, I don't know just what they really are, but I can assure you they certainly are not **pig-tit shark teeth**."

Even though both of us spent most of that evening giggling every time we looked at one another, causing Dad and my little brother to look as if they thought we'd taken leave of our senses, I vowed never again to believe anything Mister Hockley's know-it-all grandson had to say.

I don't know just when the old fellow had first arrived in Ridgway, but it was undoubtedly not too long after the town itself came into existence, in 1890. He'd apparently acquired almost two hundred acres of grazing land by filing for it under the Homestead Act. Located approximately five miles from town, the land lay at the upper end of what eventually came to be known as Happy Hollow, a winding and relatively steep little canyon containing a tiny, spring-fed stream of crystal-clear water.

All during the period of years when my peers and I were keeping a critical eye on the doings of the town's adult population, it was common knowledge that the old gentleman made at least one pilgrimage a week up the Hollow's dirt road to his homestead. And since we were seldom out of our beds early enough to observe his upward passage, all I have to do is close my eyes to bring his homeward-bound image once more into focus.

Because of his generally stern demeanor though, unless we'd blundered blindly around one of the countless bends in the road and had nearly been run over by him, we'd usually be hunkered down in a patch of chokecherry bushes or scrub-oak, just far enough off the road to allow us to feel invisible. This was always highly preferable to visible, of course, since invincibility was a commodity his sharp tongue stripped from us as easily as one shucks an ear of corn or a cottontail rabbit. He was fairly tall, as I've already mentioned, but as is so often the case with those of above average height, over the years he'd developed a very noticeable list.

And since patience was an attitude he seemed to have missed out on entirely, that list was always aimed straight ahead. So unless the road was muddy and slick as spit, as it frequently was, he'd be clipping off nearly four feet with every step, leaning a good ten degrees into a nonexistent headwind. I'd not be afraid to bet, either, that those steps came every bit as regularly as the ticks spilling from the shiny, old watch he carried in the little pocket directly beneath his right hand suspender buttons.

No matter how softly we whispered, down under those leafy green branches, he frequently seemed to sense our presence. And on two separate occasions that I was involved in, the old rascal came to an abrupt halt directly adjacent to where we were hiding. Then, with all the aplomb you might expect from someone standing in the sanctity of his own outhouse, he turned toward us and very deliberately began unbuttoning the fly of his pants.

From the safety of my present vantage point at least, I feel certain the likelihood of his actually urinating into the bushes we cowered under was virtually nonexistent. But back then it was a whole different ballgame, and long before he'd had a chance to complete the unveiling, we'd have erupted into the road, yelling "Hi Mister Hockley, we was jist playin' Indian. See ya' later!", as we hightailed it somewhere else just as fast as our visibly, but not actually dampened dignities would allow.

Of course, since our line of retreat was invariably in the opposite direction of where he was headed, this gave the old man a chance to yell "You egghead-ed little snots better stay offa my prop'ity, because if I find where ya bin messin' around my cabin, or mashin' down the bobwire fence, yer liable t'wind up spendin' the next couple days jist tryin' t'pull my boot outta yer butt!"

That accomplished, I rather imagine he made the remainder of his journey while chuckling over how effectively he'd flushed us from our lair.

Although I didn't reach maturity in time to form more than a very reserved relationship with the old man, the story my father told me numerous times will stay with me as long as I live. For whether there was anything he needed or not, Dad made fairly regular visits to the little store, just to chew the fat awhile. And on this one particular day, Mister Hockley had gotten quite involved in giving Dad his views on life in general. Which, as you'll no doubt agree, is just about as broad a subject as any you're likely to find.

He said "Grover, I'll be the first to admit there's lot'sa folks smarter'n me, but ya know, I've allus figgered that so long as a feller treats folks honest, like he wants t'be treated hisself, it don't matter a whole helluva lot how smart he is. I know there's plenty'a people around here as thinks I'm jist a cranky ol' bastard, an' I `spose I really am. But by golly there ain't a dang soul in this whole valley that can honestly say I've ever cheated `em outta one red cent, an' that's the flat-out gospel truth!"

After Dad had admitted this was undoubtedly so, the old man continued, "An' that's what burns me up with so many'a these dang high-minded preach-ers. They're allus poundin' their fist on some pulpit or other, yellin' about how we're all faced with Hell's fire an' damnation if we don't do what they tell us is right. Why Judas priest, Grover, you know as well as I do that most folks ain't nowhere near as bad as them loud-mouth fools'd have us believe we are."

Dad said that by now Mister Hockley was so worked up he was actually pacing up and down one of the store's narrow aisles, pounding his fist on the counters in exactly the same manner he'd just criticized the preachers for doing. Upon seeing Dad's struggle to maintain a straight face, though, he came to an abrupt halt, grinning sheepishly as he said "Hellova one t'talk, ain't I?"

"No foolin' though, Grover, I honestly believe that we need mosta these dang preachers about as much as we need another hole in our heads. Because it seems t'me they jist stir up ever' bit as much trouble as they cure. So that's why I've worked out what I call the Hockley recipe fer jist gittin' by."

Once again noting Dad's struggle to keep from grinning, he said "Now jist hold on a minute, dang it. An' while yer at it, stick out both'a yer hands. Rightside up, the way they're allus doin', jist like they're waitin' fer somebody else t'fill `em fulla money."

Extending his hands, palms up, Dad did as he'd been told.

"Okay now," the old man said, "jist figger that fat sucker on the left rep'asents one'a these dang soul-savers I'm talkin' about. Way off down there at the other end'a the line is another fat S.O.B. that ya kin call the devil, er most any other kinda stink-stirrin' hell-raiser ya want. An' stuck right smack-dab in the middle'a them two troublemakers is eight more fingers, rep'asentin' us ordinary folks. So with eight outta ten of us jist tryin' t'live an' let live, I figger ya can't hardly ask fer much better'n that."

Then he chuckled and said "But maybe we oughta ask Santy Claus, er God, er whoever the hell's pullin' the strings on this show, t'kinda go easy on them two fat guys. Whatta ya think? That's fair, ain't it?"

So right or wrong, fair or foul, that's the way I'll always remember ol' man Hockley. And even though he was close to ninety-five when he finally died, I've never yet talked to anyone that said he'd ever cheated them "outta one red cent."

Agnostic Agony

Unless you too have known the bone-chilling fear that comes from sliding quietly and alone, beneath the chrome-clad skirt of a crackling wood-stove, and have then cowered there, numb with the knowledge that your dead mother's ghost was now alert and had once more crept from the crypt-like and dusty closet near the bed where every night the blankets soaked-up your cries, tears, and sweat, as you lay agonizing over what had brought it all about.

And while your very Ears still throbbed with the sound of your Aunt's words that fateful day when you struggled and thrashed in her well-meaning arms, as she held you over that perfumed, yet oh so hideously foul-smelling casket to "Just kiss your mama Honey, this one last time."

And unless you also have arrived at the age of ten and felt the almost unbelievable joy of Spring, simply because you have just succumbed to the charms found within the arms of your new Mother, and have then had Death's serpent-like tongue flick coyly from its foul lair beneath Autumn's discarded leaves and the first snows of winter, thus devouring her also. And unless you too have stood center-stage in that pure-white blanket, to curse, dare, and plead with a supposedly kind and benevolent SAVIOUR to "Oh please, just get out of my life and leave me alone.", then you will no doubt find it difficult to understand the almost overwhelming sense of loneliness an ageing agnostic so often feels, as he contemplates the day when he may once again stand forsaken, this time for all eternity.

Tricky Business

One of the main drawbacks that I can see to getting old, is that by the time most of us finally manage to scrape up enough cash to convince ourselves we can afford to do a few of the things we've always wanted to do, we've either forgotten what the heck we were actually going to do, we've become afraid of getting sued if we're caught, or we're just plain too dang tired to take a chance on finding out whether we can still cut the mustard. And, of course, by this stage of the game it's almost always a good idea to check our calendar before we try to do anything at all, just to see if we've got time to get it done before our next doctor appointment.

For like it or not, most of us over the hill duffers eventually get to the point where if we even so much as sneeze, we grab the phone and make an appointment, just to see if we can find out why, thus wasting a big chunk of the cash we worked our butts off to accumulate. Because as a general rule, once we've searched through the yellow-pages long enough to find a doctor that isn't some kind of exotic specialist, who'll undoubtedly charge far more than we can see our way clear to part with, and have actually made an appointment to go see him, well before that date ever arrives we'll no doubt have recovered from whatever it was that caused us to sneeze in the first place.

Believe me, life was a heckova lot simpler back when I was a kid! For even though it was sometimes necessary to entrust my personal posterior to our little town's only prod, prick, and pry practitioner, I almost always knew just where to find him. Since if he wasn't in the little cabin where he ate, slept, and took care of whatever business came his way, he was practically guaranteed to either be coming from, going to, or already at the only other place he seemed to spend much time.

This ol' coot was a bona fide character you see, although the local Ladies Aid Society more than likely felt that character was his biggest failing. And even though he had a regular name, just like everyone else, nearly all of us just called him "Doc."

His office was a ramshackle little log cabin, like I said, with his living quarters attached to it in various locations, more or less like warts on a toad. To the best of my recollection though, the waiting room, examining room, and operating room were one and the same. But since the single, bare bulb dangling from the low ceiling didn't offer too much in the way of illumination, that's probably why the doors at each end of the main cabin were left open, just to let in a little light. The biggest trouble with that though, since all of our streets were gravel in those days, was that it let in a lot more dust than light.

So it's entirely possible that the dust was what caused Doc to drink a little more than he really should have at times. Be that as it may, it wasn't too good an idea to get in his way whenever he was headed for that other place I mentioned a moment ago. This beeline flight usually occurred about the middle of the morning, more than likely immediately after a close inspection of the assorted glass containers in the cabin had convinced him there probably wouldn't be any medical emergencies that were a bit more pressing than the one he was now faced with.

So as soon as the screen door banged shut behind him, he was off and running. And if my friend Freddie and I hadn't been delayed by some errand of lesser importance, we were almost always in a position to observe this exodus and thus predict the time of the return flight with enough precision to allow us to be at our post when it began.

For by the time Doc had soaked up enough fluid to alleviate his parched condition, he'd invariably fly straight out of the hanger and into difficulty, which would thus necessitate a certain amount of staggering around, just to get his bearings. That was when we'd move in and begin flying escort, just far enough to either side so as to be safe from his wildly flapping wings. And since there were almost always a few touch-downs that made it necessary for us to clear the field of all the pink elephants and alligators, as well as the equally invisible snakes, as a general rule the noise emanating from our laboring engines was usually sufficient to keep the balance of the town's inhabitants free from harm.

As you've probably already surmised, the initial leg of Doc's flight was much more direct, involving a total distance of approximately two blocks. But with all the sorties to either side, as well as the sudden loop-de-loops and corkscrew turns, just to make sure our back-trail was clear, the return leg covered considerably more distance. But whenever we managed to bring him in for a safe landing at his home base, he was almost always good for a nickel, maybe even two. Being but eight or nine years of age at the time, Freddie and

I hadn't yet learned the value of thrift. So within barely more than a minute or so after collecting our wages, we'd be bellied up to the bar at old Sam Boucher's soda fountain, planning our strategy for the balance of the day.

One activity that filled a good percentage of our time in those days was the racing organization all us kids belonged to, although if you'd ever watched one of our races, you probably would've noticed a good deal more disorganization than anything else. Freddy and his family lived with his maternal grandmother, so most of our activities were centered near her well-seasoned, old two-story house. The street it was on had a slight down-grade to it, beginning about fifty feet to the south, right in front of Billy Sower's little yellow house. From there it went down past Granny's to Edna's Beauty Shoppe, which sat at the corner of the block. Edna's place was two-stories high also, and every bit as old as Granny's, but its coat of white paint always made it look practically brand new.

Our high-speed races generally ended at Edna's corner, but the endurance races made a hard right turn at that location, and depending on the endurance of the participants involved, as well as Bobby Craig's mother, went on past the alley to yet another down-grade. Mabel was just plump enough so we didn't have too much problem outrunning everything but her yells of "Quit makin' so gawddam much racket, you dang-blasted kids!", but naturally enough, Bobby always dropped out as soon as she started yelling. And since he was a couple of years younger than all the other drivers, and hadn't yet developed as much skill behind the wheel, this meant that the rest of us really had to pour on the coal in order to keep from being the last one to cross the finish line.

I doubt that it's ever been mentioned anywhere in the Guinness Book of Records, but we kids then owned just about the fastest tires on the western-slope, one per racer, of course. Most of the smaller kids had sleek little sport models, while the larger, and ever so frequently dumber, ones drove the big powerhouses that really tested your skill, as well as your endurance. Me and my racer were in this latter category you see. And not just because I was all that much larger, either.

On one particular day that sticks in my mind, we were all revving our motors up on the starting line, and even Granny's endurance seemed to be approaching the breaking point. So as soon as the flag dropped, away we went. I managed to get clear of the slower machines within the first fifty feet or so, and just as I was pulling into the number two position, I romped down on the throttle with everything I had, just to see if I could overhaul the kid who was number one.

I must have given it just a little too much gas, because before I could do anything about it, that big ol' rig of mine started fish-tailing all over the place. And by the time I finally figured out what was going on, it was too darn late to do any good, since that good for nothing outfit had already taken off through the toolies all by itself, immediately after ejecting me head-first into the wooden culvert that ran under the sidewalk beside Craig's house.

Once all the dust had settled, and I'd finally managed to extract my head from the culvert, it didn't take hardly any time at all to figure out why all the lubricating fluid was leaking out the end of my left ring-retainer. For just because a one inch piece of the broken beer bottle I'd rammed it into was still stuck in the lacerated meat beneath the nail, if you think my motor didn't jump straight out of idle into wide open when I saw that, you don't know beans about us red-blooded tire-racers.

And even though helicopters hadn't even been invented yet, if I could just have gotten my right arm synchronized with my left one, I know good and well I'd have gotten a whole lot further off the ground than just three feet. But as it was, I was still lifting off and coming back down in the same spot when Granny zeroed in on me. And as quick as she got a good look at my damaged digit, she started towing me straight down to Doc's. My motor was misfiring all the way down the street, due to a fairly severe case of vapor-lock, but it was only a few minutes before she had me parked on his examining table, with most of the other contenders wedged into the doorway behind us.

So once he'd spent a couple of minutes wrestling with me, as well as however much medical propriety he still adhered to, Doc muttered something about needing Dad's approval for any repairs involving needlework. But after observing my thoroughly agitated response to his mentioning the possibility that he might actually be thinking about poking a dadblamed needle into my finger, he finally said "As worked up as the as the little fart is right now, Alta, he's gonna start pukin' all over the place as quick as he git's the first whiff'a ether. So I think we'd prob'ly better jist settle fer tapin' it up the best we can, an' call it good."

But since Granny was still huffing and puffing like a runaway locomotive when he eventually got through with me, he walked over and tilted her head up with his knobby-knuckled, nicotine-stained forefinger and asked "Are ya gonna be alright ol' woman?"

After she'd responded with "A'course I'm alright, ya crazy ol' quack, why wouldn't I be?", he snorted and came right back with "Jist because yer gittin' too damn old t'be runnin' footraces all over town, ya silly ol' witch! One'a these days yer gonna pull a stupid stunt like the one ya jist done, an' that wore out ol' ticker'a yers is jist plain gonna stop tickin'. What in hell ever gave ya the idea it's up t'you t'play nursemaid t'all these little snots anyhow? Freddie's the only one'a this pack that's any kin'a yers, an' fer all the damn good he is, ya might jist as well stick `im in a gunnysack an' drop `im in the river!"

Turning slightly, to wink at Freddie then, he continued with "Even if he does manage t'claw `is way outta the fool sack, at least the next time him an' this Huffanickle brat decide I need `em t' escort me home, his face ought'a be a whole lot cleaner than it usually is!"

Wagging his head at this point, as though he knew he was just wasting his breath, Doc looked down at me and said "Okay ya little fart, ya've wasted enough'a my time already, but if ya think ya can make it outside an' up into my ol' hoopy, there's prob'ly enough gas left in the tank t'haul all of ya back up t'Alta's place."

Pausing just long enough to heave a thoroughly exaggerated sigh of resignation, he took Granny by the arm, before adding "Ya know somethin', ya sag-titted ol' rip, one'a these days you an' me are both gonna wind up bitin' the dust, an' I'd almost be willin' t'bet there won't even be one'a these little snots that'll remember half'a what we done fer `em. What'a ya think?"

Within the passage of only a few more minutes, though, we'd all piled into that high-wheeled, canvas-curtained old car of his and gone putt-putting up the street to Granny's house. I suppose there's a pretty fair chance my memories of the incidents involving these two people have somehow become adorned with a few extra frills during all the years since those long-gone days, but this much I know for an absolute certainty, I will never, ever, forget either one of them.

I've no recollection whatsoever of Doc with anything other than a field of quarter-inch stubble on his face, and whether it was his beard or his razor that suffered from suspended animation, I really can't say. But whenever one of us kids sucked into a still struggling bee in our almost daily dollop of free honeycomb down at Cecil Stowell's bee-house, we'd invariably head straight for Doc's. And sometimes when I close my eyes just tight enough, I can still see that grizzled old gray head, peering down at me as he says "O.K. ya dumb little fart, quitcher gawdamn blubberin an' poke out yer tongue." Then he'd dab some tincture of cloves on it and send us packing.

One evening I began whining about a toothache, the way most kids have a tendency to do. And just because I hadn't eaten much in the way of supper, Dad figured I must have a relatively valid complaint. But since the only available dentist was ten miles away, and he'd long since closed his office for the day, I was soon sitting in the dust of Doc's examining table.

Naturally enough, when I saw him uncork the familiar clove bottle, I opened my mouth and dropped my guard all at the same time. Consequently, the sneaky old devil slipped his pliers in right behind the cloves, and all of a sudden it felt like he was bent on snapping my neck. He just might've succeeded too, if the pliers hadn't slipped off when they did.

I lit on the floor in high gear, of course, but Dad made a lucky grab and soon had me plopped right back in the dust. I must have inherited a substantial share of my dumb from him, I guess, because when he relaxed his hold just enough so I was able to slide right back down to the floor before he could stop me, within less time than it takes to tell I was out the door and around the corner of the cabin, where I slid down under a big lilac bush. It was just dark enough by this time so they might not have found me if I'd been smart enough to shut my mouth and stop yowling.

But since I didn't, they did. And this time I wound up spread-eagled in the dust, with Dad laying across my chest and one of Doc's arms threatening to smash the bridge of my nose. If I'd possessed any smarts at all, of course, I'd have started sucking in enough air to get by on, through the cracks between my teeth. But since I didn't, when the pliers clamped on this time, they didn't slip off. And by the time that darn tooth finally let go of my jaw, it felt like there was a good chance my big toes were right on the verge of turning inside out.

My jaw stopped hurting almost immediately, but since it felt like there was enough blood coming out of it to paint at least one side of a large barn, I finally closed my mouth. Then, after waiting long enough for it to get fully loaded, I puckered up and let `er fly, all over Doc's ratty old linoleum.

For the next few seconds he just stood there with his lower jaw hanging almost all the way down to his adam's apple, looking like he could hardly believe all that slop had come from one half-pint kid. Before he had a chance to think of some way to get even, though, Dad noticed I was already working on another load, and he jammed his handkerchief in my mouth just in time to prevent a repeat performance.

Needless to say, while he was towing me back up the street to our house a few minutes later, he said that even though I probably thought I was justified in doing what I had, he truly hoped I'd eventually come to realize what an asset Doc had always been to our little town.

So for whatever it's worth, now that it's too late to do any good, I sure hope Doc and Granny realized how much it really meant, just knowing I could almost always count on their being there whenever things got a little too rough for me to handle by myself.

24 Carat Memories

Back in the days when I was brash and bold,
I spent a lot of time just mining for gold
And the other equally glamorous metals lying
Buried in those ever so dark and dank old holes,
Where we crawled around far under the ground
Like ridiculous two-legged gophers and moles
Searching for the wealth that so often is found
In places of such danger, I didn't know much
And cared even less, that I'd never get rich
Scratching away as I did at another man's itch,
Slowly spending my youth, as well as my health.
But now that time has passed, and I'm out at last
And I've finally begun to perceive something much
Stranger than fiction, for the truth of the matter is
Now that it's over and done, I'm beginning to believe
I was much happier back then, just being so young.

It's No Sin T'Grin, Y'Know

In spite'a th' fact that it's s'easy t'fall out'a
bed an' get up with a frown,

Ya really ought'a be aware that life's seldom
s'serious that ya ever need t'be down.

At least fer any longer'n it takes t'pry yer chin open with'a grin.

An' jist simply b'cause they're always s'downright contagious,
Hardly anyone'll ever be umbrageous, er feel yer not bein'
courageous, er are bein' outrageous, when one'a yer shoes
is green, an' th' other'n's brown, so long as ya'll jist tell folks
yer main claim t'renown lies in th' fact that ya was doin'a
hoedown in uptown Motown when that downtown Edsel Ford
clown got `is comedown an' nearly had'a nervous breakdown
b'cause of'a lowdown slowdown in th' countdown'a th' initial
shakedown rundown over in ol' Chinatown! S'untangle
yer fool tongue an' cut loose with'a big ol' grin, dang it,
b'cause they're always jist s'doggone good fer what ails ya!

Tommy, The Thirty And One Cat

If Tommy ever entertained any thoughts about the unjustness of his lowly station in life, he kept them well hidden from my young family and I. He'd come by Hardrock Hill one afternoon, the name I'd given the small, rock and thistle infested farm we were living on at the time. I'd figured he was just looking for a night's lodging and a bite to eat, and would no doubt be gone by morning. But even though his coat was a little threadbare, his pride was intact and he soon made it plain that he was willing to work for whatever we were willing, or able to give him.

All my three little girls had to offer him in the way of compensation was an abundance of love, and the chance to share in their daily activities. He found that as acceptable as the milk that Dee had given him and he was soon taking all their ministrations in stride. And as a general rule he seldom circled around our rickety old house more than two or three times before he was once again ready to submit to getting all gussied up in a doll's dress and sunbonnet. If he experienced the slightest shame over having to spend such a substantial part of his day thus attired, this gray-striped tiger kept that hidden also. The fact of the matter is, I really think he enjoyed it, for he'd lie there in their coaster wagon purring, or napping whenever that was possible.

His workday began when theirs ended, you see. For that was when all the mice, which far outnumbered anything else we raised, came out to play. And since there weren't a great number of cash outlets for our rocks, thistles, and mice, I spent a good deal of my own time working in one of our local mines. This not only allowed us to buy grain to supplement the chicken's diet, it also made it possible for us to buy a few groceries for ourselves. And since the grain we thus bought was also what kept the mice fat and happy, I have to admit that my efforts were more or less counter-productive, even way back then. But I was young and also reasonably happy, so I didn't worry about it all that much.

There were but two shifts at the mine, day-shift and night-shift, so every week I was either going to bed just before the mice got up, or I was just getting up when they were going to bed. So as you can see, it was up to Tommy to take care of them for me. His work was somewhat easier when I was on nightshift though, for when I'd get home at 4:00 A.M., before I could go to bed it was necessary to milk the cows, do the irrigating in the summer, or feed our flock of sheep in the winter. I also had to dump several gallons of that expensive grain in the chicken feeders 365 days a year.

But it was the filling of those chicken feeders that soon became the highlight of Tommy's day, and mine too really. He was always waiting on the porch for me to drive up, you see, and I soon found myself reversing my schedule and filling the feeders before doing anything else. For just as soon as my lunch-bucket hit the porch floor, Tommy would race toward his, stopping first at the grain-room so that I could get the buckets of grain. And although this little scene from out of the past may very well make me seem even more odd to you, it usually sonded something like this;

"Holy cow, Tommy gimme'a chance t'git th' bucket filled, will ya?"

"Rowrrr." This favorite phrase of his was deemed suitable for any and all occasions, but the intensity with which it was uttered was usually sufficient to let me know whatever he wanted me to know.

So by the time my buckets were ready, Tommy would literally be dancing in circles and looking for all the world like a cat on a hot-tin roof, if you'll allow me at least this one moth-eaten old cliche. And as soon as I was able to get the door to the scratch-pen open, he'd make a bee-line for the feeders, generally stopping several feet short and waiting for the fun to commence, his tail lashing from side to side like the pendulum of a metronome. And even though there was no tick-tock-tick-tock to break the early morning stillness, I knew for a fact that the last few seconds of time were running out for at least one unlucky freeloader.

"Okay Tommy, I'm gonna turn `em loose, are ya ready?"

"Rrrohrrrr!"

As a rule, just as soon as I lifted the feeder-lid, one or more mice would erupt from the tray at the bottom like rats fleeing a sinking ship. (Some of us just plain think in cliche-time you know.) And before the first one out had gone more than two skips and a jump, Tommy would have it in his mouth and would be galloping after the second one, at least if there was a second one. Ordinarily this one would be held in place with his paws, while he administered the coup de grace to the one in his mouth.

But on two separate occasions, when the second mouse chose to run up the sloping sides of the feeder and then leap for his freedom, much like some of the rockets that later began blasting away from Cape Carnival on a fairly regular basis, I saw this feline space-walker shoot aloft in hot pursuit, nailing the mouse in mid-air with claw-clad paws that were as deadly as any laser-beam our scientists will ever come up with. He was some kinda' cat, Ol' Tommy was.

One beautiful spring morning I was sitting out on the front steps, enjoying a day off from the mine, as well as the warm sunshine, when I heard one of the most heartfelt "Rrrowrr's" you can imagine. Then I saw Tommy hobbling up through the cow-lot toward me, so I ran down to see what his problem was. The whole side of his head and one leg was jam-packed with wicked-looking porcupine quills, and he was in so much pain that he was trembling all over. But even if we could have spared the money for gasoline, so I could drive him the twenty-five miles to our nearest veterinary, we damn well didn't have enough to cover the bill this would generate.

So I got my pliers and sat back down on the step with Tommy on my lap. During the next fifteen minutes or so, he lay there and let me yank thirty of those filthy, miserable things out of his body. And for the whole time, the only sound or struggle he made was when I'd touch that thirty-first quill. It had been driven completely through the center of the large pad on his right front foot, you see, and it was poking out the top as well as the bottom. Every time I'd touch it, he'd snarl. But finally, it was the only one left and he seemed to realize that the show had to go on.

So as I sat there talking to him, I was squeezing his leg between my fingers, just trying to slow the circulation enough to make it grow numb. And when he at last allowed me to clamp the pliers onto the quill, it only took a fraction of a second to pull it out. Tommy had been a little quicker though, and the blood was already oozing from my left forefinger as I lay the pliers down on the step beside me. But there was just no way I could hold a few drops of my blood against someone who'd just gone through what Tommy had, so I sat there and continued to hold him. And after a little while, a rather ragged sounding purr began rumbling deep inside his chest. Although my vision got a little misty then, nobody but Tommy was around to notice.

For a day or so he limped around the farmyard, avoiding the girls as well as his other soulmate, Queenie. He'd wasted no time that first day he came to the house, you see, letting this bob-tailed shepherd mongrel know that as long she quit yapping at him, he'd allow her to continue sleeping under the front porch and eating from her dented-up old enamel washbasin, just as long as she was willing to share them with him. Their cease-fire had been pretty shaky for the first week or so, but by the end of the second one we'd grown accustomed to seeing them curled up side by side, or eating from the pan simultaneously.

But other than for those few days of limping off in search of seclusion, Tommy was soon back to being his congenial self. The weeks continued rolling by, until several years had eventually passed and our oldest girl had been enrolled in school. When the mouse population had finally gotten to the point where we hardly ever discovered one in the chicken-feeders anymore, my good buddy was gradually forced to roam farther and farther afield. For even though we always made sure there was plenty for him and Queenie in the food pan, he still seemed to feel that he had a job to do. But you needn't get the idea that he'd become such a workaholic that he didn't make time for a little romance every now and then.

And at these times he'd be gone for several days or even a week, then one morning we'd find him once more sunning himself on the porch. His ears and face would be covered with scratches, and once he even had a nasty looking cut under his ribs. But that too healed up and we grew accustomed to his comings and goings. Then he finally disappeared for over a month and I'd about decided that he'd either been killed by a bobcat, or had been run over by a car.

But one afternoon while my two youngest girls were taking their nap, I once more heard a long, moaning "Rrrrowwwrr" coming from the direction of the cow-lot. In a few minutes I saw Tommy staggering toward me, barely able to walk, so I ran down and picked him up. This time though, I was even more sickened by what I saw than I'd been the other time. Fully two-thirds of his body was covered with weeping scabs, and the blood and puss were literally dripping from every one of them. Looking back from this present point in time, I suppose there may have been a chance that a veterinarian might have been able to do something for him, but at that moment all I could think of was ending his agony as quickly as possible.

So after making sure the little girls were still napping, I slipped quietly outside again, with my revolver stuffed inside my shirt. Then I picked Tommy up and carried him some distance up the little canyon behind the house. When I lay him down in the shade of a clump of oak-brush and felt him trembling, I was so sure that he knew what I was going to do I could hardly stand looking into his eyes. But all I could hope for was that he'd understand that I loved him and would forgive me. After I'd jerked the trigger and felt, rather than heard the blast of sound, I was tempted to hurl the gun a far as I could. But I realized that wouldn't change anything, so I just sat down beside his pathetic little body and bawled.

After awhile I got to my feet and headed back down to the house for my shovel. I lied to the girls that night and told them I'd found Tommy already dead and had buried him. They naturally wanted to know where, so the next morning I showed them the little mound, and every so often after that they'd carry a few flowers up to lay on it. In time, several of their dolls were buried there beside him.

Although that was well over thirty years ago, to this day I seldom see a cat but what my old friend comes stalking back into my thoughts.

I Believe

Back in the days when I was a wee small child
An' a trav'ling show would come t'our little town
Mom an' Dad an' my baby brother an' me was sure t'be
Just settin' right there, on our hard ol' foldin' seat
An' up until th' curt'n went up, us kids'd sound half wild
We sure got quiet tho', when th' lights started t'dim down
An' by th' time th' first act was thru', I'd be in ecstacy
Waitin' for th' pretty lady t'begin sellin' Kisses So Sweet
While th' man on th' stage called out "An' I repeat, my friends
You'll find a prize in ev'ry box, or th' next one's free!

Well I've grown older now, an' quieter too, I fear
So what little wisdom I've gained, has come at th' cost
Of the youth I've left behind, but one thing I've learned
While listening to those now muted voices from out of my past
Is that when you cease to believe, you loose something so dear
That despite all you've attained, your soul is surely lost
So it gives me great pleasure to think that I've earned
Th' right to proclaim loudly to one an' all, at last
Yes! Oh yes my friends, there truly is a prize in ev'ry box!
But you will have to stretch for it, so be sure you always
Wear a spiffy new pair a'those nifty universal socks!

Holy Shit, Amigo!

Although the names of the mine and individuals involved in the following story have been altered to prevent the possibility of embarrassment to the families and friends of the men herein portrayed, due to the author's being the man who has long been known as "Buzz" to both his family and friends, the reader can rest assured that I had first-hand knowledge of everything that happened that day. But since you also need to be aware that even though I've deleted the biggest share of the hard-core obscenities that have long been part and parcel of miners and most blue-collar workers down to earth speech characteristics, there is still more then enough profanity contained in the story so that most of you probably won't want your younger children exposed to it. So now that you've been made aware of it, you're now on your own.

Based entirely upon that somewhat tenuous bit of evidence, almost anyone would have considerable difficulty in concluding that the dark complexioned young man who'd just uttered those words was particularly profound. But positioned, as I was, directly across from where he sat, looking for all the world as though he was completely satisfied he'd said it as well as it could be said, I wasn't too inclined to argue the point.

Simply because "HOLY SHIT, AMIGO!" pretty much exemplified my own feelings regarding what had prompted his outburst. Returning his toothy grin with one far less dramatic in appearance, since my sun-starved complexion was almost totally devoid of the warm, brown tones creating such a vivid contrast between the color of his face and that of his teeth, I'd responded "You ain't just kiddin', Pard! Today's inch and a half is gonna make our next paychecks look ever' damn bit as good asaswell pretty close, at least, to what ol' Sophia's knockers would, if I had one of 'em plugged into my ear, an' was jist layin' there whisperin' sweet nothin's into th' other one."

Just as the sound of laughter erupted from his throat, though, the abrupt lurch of the steel-mesh-wrapped rail-car was immediately followed by the clickity-clack vibration of the eight flanged wheels positioned only inches below our neoprene-encased rumps. Inhaling deeply as we entered the gloom of the snow-shed, which extended approximately one hundred feet along the steep mountainside from where the rails exited the main portal of the Mountain Maid, I'd watched Ramon follow my lead. For even though the air within the mine would become considerably warmer the further we progressed, it just never seemed to smell as sweet, as that which had been touched by the late-winter sun. Which only moments before had climbed from behind the lofty spires of San Juan Peak and its closest neighbors.

Within a few seconds the dusky interior of the shed was exchanged for the all-encompassing blackness of the tunnel itself. But in those same scant seconds, virtually every man on the two long, open-topped man-cars had switched on the lamp that was clamped at the front of his muck-encrusted hardhat. Which was perched on top of his oh so vulnerable hairy head.

As the electric-locomotive at the forward end of our rusty metal snake began picking up speed, the clickity-clack, clickity-clack, clickity-clack of the wheels, as they rolled over the jointed rails, began sounding almost as if some strategically placed machine-gun bunker was firing a constant volley of armor-piercing shells, in its attempt to prevent us from penetrating deeper into its alien domain.

For as the low-slung locomotive's trolley-wheel bounded and bounced along the bare-copper cable, suspended barely two feet above the motorman's domed hat, the wildly arcing sparks it produced gave the appearance of being nothing more, nor less, than white-hot tracer-rounds, ricocheting off the rough-hewn surface of the tunnel's walls and ceiling. Or as most of my compadres and I would have said, the ribs and back of the drift.

Yet for all the seeming mayhem taking place, there was hardly a man among us who wasn't positively relishing the thought of what the ensuing eight hour's worth of overtime pay was going to do to the amount of his next paycheck, most particularly my Chicano partner and myself. Back in those days, though, few if any of us were aware of what the term Chicano stood for. And as a general rule, depending upon the closeness of our relationship, we Gringos almost always referred to our Mexican counterparts as Greasers, or Wetbacks. But on the rare occasion when we were really pissed-off with them, we usually resorted to something such as "Aw fer shit-sakes, ever' damn one'a you lousy Mexicans ought'a be run right off the mountain, since all yer good for is sittin' on yer asses, yabberty-jabberin' away in that chicken-chatter lingo. While us white men do all the really hard work!"

We seldom had to wait longer than a second or so, of course, for them to respond in kind. But despite the connotations an ordinary member of society could most certainly be expected to attach to such degrading language, most of us would have crawled all the way to hell and back for those recipients of our verbal abuse. Not always cheerfully perhaps, but we sure wouldn't have waited around for an engraved invitation.

Be that as it may, since that's the way it was, the only bone that was stuck in my craw right at that moment, was in not knowing how much trouble Ramon and I were going to have in accomplishing the task lying ahead of us. To be as precise as possible, though, since we'd only travelled about a hundred and fifty yards by then, the task was still lying some two and one half miles ahead of our mechanical beast's probing penis of light.

For that's what it resembled, more than anything else, as it thrust tirelessly forward, as though lusting for contact with the Maid's hymenal membrane, whose bursting would at last release the sweet, golden nectar that had been dammed since the beginning of time, deep within the protective folds of her sacrosanct and cavernous womb. And by the time we reached the first fold, 11,000 feet from the portal, virtually every man on the train, with the possible exception of the one at the helm of the locomotive, swiveled his head astern, just to catch that faint and ever so tiny gleam of sunlight. Because there wasn't a man among us who wasn't fully aware that this one brief glimpse might very well be his final one.

There were a number of folds after that first one, or bends if you will. And as our cumbersome beast traversed every last one of them, its wheels shrieked in protest, each in its turn, as the guiding flanges grated and ground their way around the slender parallel ribbons of steel, whose wooden cross-ties were so deeply embedded in the drift's muddy floor. The train moved considerably slower now, needless to say, for it always thoroughly irked Joe, our motorman, whenever one of the sets of wheels would ride up and off its rails, to go thumping and bumping along until one or more of our number would bellow "Aw shut th' sonovabitch down, Joe, we're off the lousy track again!"

This didn't happen very often, of course. But whenever it did, we'd all climb down from our rusty little chariots and try to find enough room between the sides of the errant car and the rough, rock ribs on either side of it, just to bend our backs and strain in unison until the car was once more back where it belonged. And once we'd reached our destination, you could bet your pair of knee-high rubber hard-toes that the track-gang would be getting an ass-chewing within a matter of moments, via the shift-boss's telephone.

Unless of course, they were already en route, in which case the chewing would be delayed until their arrival. Which may or may not precede that of the first ore-train.

It didn't really make much difference, though, because until that first train of the day had been loaded and was once again sent on its way outside, there wasn't going to be a hell of a lot done to those troublesome rails. Simply because ore was ever and always the order of the day, and that ravenous reduction-mill rumbling away beneath its huge ore-bins just had to be satiated before any serious repairs would be undertaken by the Maid's underground gandy dancers.

Which was the only reason Ramon and I could see, that had made it possible for us to work on this particular Saturday. Because due to the fact that the mill had been shut down the previous evening so that some long overdue repairs might take place, there would be no ore-trains moving back and forth beneath the ancient and long unused chute we were scheduled to install a sheet-steel liner in.

Lester Carl, or Letch as we all called him, was the Maid's superintendent in those days. And since Ramon and I had been hounding him to hell and back, to give us first crack at driving the scram-drift beneath a recently discovered block of ore that was located several hundred feet above the main drift, he'd finally agreed to let us have it. But just from knowing the big bastard as well as we did, we were pretty sure there'd be some strings attached. Don't go jumping to conclusions too soon, though, because even before this particular deal, Letch rated an A-Okay as far as we were concerned. In spite of his longtime reputation as being a two-fisted, kick-`em-in-th'-nuts-if-ya-have-to brawler for most of his life. Or maybe it was just because of it, how the hell would I know?

Anyhow, it had turned out that those damn strings were tied tighter'n a virgin's twat to this lousy ore chute, which he figured was the best way to dispose of the rock we'd be blasting out of the scram. Because it didn't make a stinking bit of difference, you see, whether that rock turned out to be waste or millable-ore, every last ounce of it would have to be hauled straight outside. And as far as Letch could see, that meant Ramon and I were going to have to install steel plates on the bottom and sides of the chute, just in case the planking was too rotten to stand the pounding it would be getting.

This isn't intended to be anything but a shortcut to what you're going to have to know, in order to see what we were up against. So I wouldn't recommend your rushing up to some mine right away, to try and rustle a job. But whenever possible, most mines utilize gravity for getting their rock from point A to Point B, just because that's the cheapest and fastest route. So a series of ore-passes is the usual method of getting this rock down from the upper levels, to where a gated chute then allows it to be loaded into tram-cars. The chute is almost always constructed of heavy planking, which is supported by a framework of much heavier round timbers, or posts and stulls.

Since the tremendous weight of the rock mass in the ore-pass above the chute mandates that some form of restriction be applied where they join, a bulkhead of logs is constructed to divert the ore (or waste), so that it must flow horizontally for a few feet before entering the throat of the chute itself. Most of the older chutes terminated in a stepped series of three or four gate-boards, which allowed the trammers a reasonable amount of control over how fast the material then dropped into the car that was positioned beneath it, as well as how much. Whenever there was a significant amount of water involved, though, as ever so frequently occurred, and the muck itself was made up mostly of small particles (or fines), a certain amount of spillage was common. And since this had to be cleaned up with a muck-stick (shovel), making sure the cars were full enough to satisfy management was always an extremely dicey deal.

Approximately one hundred feet before reaching the chute that morning, the train stopped to let us off, since most everyone but Ramon and me needed to climb aboard the man-skip that would then take them up to whatever level they were to work on. But since we had to wait ten minutes or so for the train to pull on down out of our way, we followed Pat Franklin through the short, narrow passage connecting the main drift with the spur-drift, where his hoist-room was located.

Several years earlier, upon realizing that Pat's age was making it more and more difficult for him to keep up with the younger miners, Letch asked him if he'd fill in for the current hoist-man, who was supposedly going on vacation. The man had actually quit, but by letting Pat think it was only a temporary situation, Letch not only gained enough time to satisfy himself that Pat was probably the most qualified man for the job, Pat had actually begun dreading his return to the far more strenuous activities he'd earlier been engaged in.

For even though his new position paid less, once he'd hoisted the various crews to wherever they worked, he was then free to sit there and dream up the poetry that now seemed to hold priority over the higher wages he might earn while driving a drift, raise, or stope. But as he told us that morning while he was hoisting the first six-man load, "Why Hell's bells boys, I've already put more'n a'nuff time in, hangin' onta th' shitty end'a ever' damn machine Ingersoll an' Gardner-Denver's ever dreamed up! S'when I can sit in here where it's nice an' warm an' quiet, why should I bust my ass anymore, an' take'a chance on gittin' it smashed flatter'n one'a yesterday's cold ol' pancakes? No siree, I don't miss that part one little bit!"

Grinning at him just as the signal lamp and buzzer announced that the men who'd been on the skip had all gotten off, Ramon waited until Pat had released the brake and the cage was on its way back down, to comment "I can't say as I blame ya on that score, Pat, because if there was any damn way I could buy a'nuff pinto beans and spuds t'feed my ol' lady an' kids, on what this job pays, I jist might be inclined t'wrestle ya for it. But with mama poppin' new editions out of `er chute as reg'lar as she's been doin', there jist ain't no way in hell I'm gonna be buckin' fer yer job. Fer th' next twenty years er so, anyhow."

Watching the hoist's cable-drum closely, for the mark that would let him know the cage was almost down, Pat began applying ever increasing pressure to the long brake-handle, so that by the time the mark at last appeared, the drum was just barely turning.

And as the cage eased to a halt, directly in front of the group of men who were waiting, one of them shouted "Pat, ya damn ol' fart, why'n hell don'cha drive th' bastard like that all th' time? I swear t'Christ, ever' damn time I'm on th' sucker, ya always seem t'bang it down s'hard it feels like yer jist tryin' t'see how high we're gonna bounce, or somethin'!"

Winking at Ramon and me, the old man yelled "Charlie if ya ever get smart a'nuff t'let someone else yank that damn bell-cord, ya might find out what a really smooth landin' feels like. But ever' time ya start jerkin' on it, I flat-out know who it is, an' that more'n likely ya'll be bitchin' when ya get here, so that's why I make sure ya touch down a little extry hard!"

At that moment, though, the motorman stuck his head through the door to let us know he was getting ready to move his train out of our way, so Ramon and I headed down the short spur-drift that provided the Maid's supply-trains with access to the raise. And as soon as the man-train had rolled well beyond the wye, we threw the switch that allowed us to push a string of five tram-cars out onto the mainline, using the small locomotive that had been left for us by the night crew.

Within the next two or three minutes, we'd pulled the cars down to where our chute was located, parking the car nearest to the locomotive directly beneath the chute, which was almost exactly halfway between the wye and the short pedestrian-way serving the hoisting area. So if you can visualize a letter Y, whose two arms are fairly elongated and running parallel to one another, when you add that little connecting link at the upper end of the arms, you've produced a reasonable facsimile of the Maid's mainline layout.

The last time any muck had been pulled out of the chute, had probably been at least thirty or forty years earlier, according to what Letch told us. So it must have taken a good forty-five minutes to pick, pry, and cuss enough material loose to fill the first car. By the time Ramon climbed down to pull the second car into place, both of us had long-since removed our shirts and neoprene jackets. And our tee-shirts looked for all the world as though they'd just spent the entire forty-five minutes in the drum of a mechanized cement mixer. Even though they were actually hanging on the outside of two flesh and blood varieties.

The air temperature was somewhere close to fifty-five degrees, but you wouldn't have had the slightest problem convincing Ramon and me that it was a hundred and fifty-five. The sweat was leaking out from under his hard-hat in such quantities that his face now resembled what I'd always imagined the stern-end of a zebra must look like. Except for the fact that the brush above his chute was considerably shorter. Needless to say, it was his intake chute, rather than the one at the lower end of the line.

Once we had the next car in place, we decided a short stint on the feed-bag was in order, so we both wolfed down a sandwich. But in barely more than five minutes time we were both toiling and cursing away again. And by the time that car was half full, we'd begun thumping our heavy, six-foot pry-bars against the underside of the bulkhead timbers in a somewhat futile attempt to dislodge enough muck from the topside, just to finish filling the car.

Letch had told us he didn't think the ore-pass had much muck in it, and since almost every time our bars would slam against the bulkhead, a little water would come spilling down on us from between the timbers, we felt he was probably right. But a miner just doesn't dare take a chance on probably. Not if he wants to live long enough to get one more peek at the sunshine at the end of the tunnel.

Which was what prompted me to growl "I sure as hell wish there was a damn air-valve close enough so's we could use a blowpipe, Pard! Why I'll bet we'd have this mess cleaned up in plenty'a time t'spend an hour er two, jist swappin' lies with Pat."

The words were barely out of my mouth, though, when a sufficient amount of muck came cascading down from above the bulkhead, to fill the car. By this time, the only gate-board still in place was the one at the very bottom of the chute. Because in order to prod and poke our bars at the area just below the edge of the bulkhead, it had been necessary to remove the two upper boards.

Consequently, when a ten or fifteen-gallon quantity of slop came spilling down while we were in the process of rolling the third car of our string into position, as soon as we'd climbed up into it, I said "Amigo, it jist might be a real good idea t'put at least one'a them damn boards back where it belongs. It's hard tellin' jist how much shit's still up there, but if it's even a car and a half, I ain't in any mood right now t'hafta muck it up!"

Which was why that top board was partially blocking our view approximately thirty seconds later, when a wall of muck suddenly came WHOOSHing down over the top of it. It happened so quickly that all either one of us could do was just stand there, watching it come. But I can close my eyes even now, almost fifty-five years later, and still see it. My whole life didn't flash before my eyes, the way some folks say has happened to them. But I was sure as hell thinking "This is as far as she goes, Sucker, it's th' end'a th' stinkin' line fer both of us!"

After I was hammered flat against the bottom of the car, I remember wondering why it was still possible to move my arms, for I was certain I was being buried alive. I couldn't see anything, of course, so I stretched my right arm as far as it would go, and felt what I was sure must be the end of the car. Pushing against the opposite end with both legs, which for some unknown reason still worked, I finally managed to grab hold of the upper edge of the car with my right hand. My whole body felt as though it was being pummeled with an endless flow of coarse gravel, yet even though I was conscious of the force with which some of the rocks thudded against me, I don't have any recollection of feeling any particular amount of pain.

But since I didn't seem to be able to breathe, I knew I was a goner if I didn't get some air as soon as possible. So somehow or other, I forced my left hand up until it too had hold of the car rim. And a second later, I was draped over the drawbar at the bottom of the cars.

I still couldn't see a damn thing, of course, so I started crawling down the drift, running my left hand along the side of the tram-cars until I eventually reached the far end of the locomotive. Grabbing what my fumbling fingers told me was probably the throttle lever, I followed it to where it seemed to be fastened in place, then pulled myself erect. I'd been reluctant to take a chance on moving the lever, you see, because of the possibility of setting the train in motion. I needn't have worried, though, for by this time the Maid was every bit as powerless and in the dark as I was.

I'd been aware of something rattling along the drift beside me, all the time I'd been crawling. And since an occasional tug at my waist had given me ample reason to think it was caused by my lamp, I now ran my left hand up along the case of the battery that powered it. Reaching the cord, I traced it for its full thirty inch length until I discovered that the protective lens and bulb were both smashed. But since the shell was still clamped to my hardhat, I knew the hat must have come off my head when I'd fallen down between the cars. Yet all I'd been aware of was the need to put as much distance as I could between myself and that damnable metal coffin, as soon as I could.

But it still wasn't until after I'd put my hat back on, and determined that the goop covering my eyes and cheeks was probably mud, rather than blood, that I realized Ramon was very likely still in the car. It seemed almost as though everything from that point on jumped right straight out of the fat and into the fire. Because without being able to see, I didn't have the slightest idea how I was going to find him in time, even if he wasn't already dead. I just plain went into orbit then, screaming his name over and over, and over again.

I was facing in the direction of where the last of the chute's contents were still splashing and rattling down in the darkness, when I heard someone behind me yell "Oh Jesus, Buzz, is that really you? I was scared shitless ya jist had t'be dead.", it was only a matter of milliseconds before we were in one another's arms.

By the time all the back-slapping and breathless yabberty-jabbering ended, I'd learned that the deluge had washed Ramon right out over the other end of the car. So once he'd scrambled to his feet, he'd had a ringside seat to most of what followed. Even though with all the water, rocks, and mud flying through the air, he'd missed seeing me crawl out the far end of the car.

For as he said "There was just s'damn much shit flyin' all over th' place, there wasn't no way in hell I could get t'where I figgered ya had t'be. But when I seen th' way th' whole side'a that damn car was red-hot, on account've its slammin' inta th' main power cable hangin' there on that side'a th' drift, I flat-out knew ya must already be fried! So I run up t'th' wye, then down th' spur t'th' hoist room. Because I knew Pat wouldn't hardly dare leave it, in spite'a th' power bein' off by then. Judas Priest but it seemed like it took a long time fer them damn outside fuses to blow, after th' car shorted out th' line that way."

Stopping to catch his breath finally, he blurted "Holy Shit, Amigo, I sure am glad ya ain't really fried!"

After telling him I was pretty happy about it myself, we headed down toward the little passageway leading to Pat's hoist-room. Because by that time my teeth were chattering like a set of castanets and my legs were beginning to feel like they wouldn't hold me up much longer.

Since the only source of light in the entire mine at the moment was what came from the tiny lamps on the other miner's heads, as they reached the hoist-room one by one after their long climb down the ladders of the raise, Ramon and I had ample time to bask in the spotlight before Letch too showed up. He was huffing and puffing as though he'd just run a footrace, after finally running into something his fists couldn't put down.

Once Pat filled him in on what had happened, though, he waltzed over to where Ramon and me were huddled side by side, rammed his thumbs between his belly and belt, then asked "Can either one'a you sorry bastard's give me one good reason why I shouldn't run yer asses clean off'a this lousy mountain?"

Ramon tilted his head back until the beam of his light was centered on the other man's chin, and replied "Th' best one I can think of, Boss, is jist because if ya do, yer prob'ly gonna wind up gittin' th' shit knocked plumb out'a ya, when our ol' ladies hear about it."

So after waiting at least thirty seconds for the resulting uproar to settle down, he added "Oh yeah, since yer th' sucker that started this round'a question an' answer bullshit, can **you** give **me** one good reason why ya didn't bother tellin' us that Swede Nelson and 'is partner finally broke through into that ol' winze last night, way up above where Buzz an' me's gonna be drivin' yer crummy scram-drift. Because since all them jillions'a gallons'a water that come out've it, is what damn near washed us t'kingdom come, ya jist better believe we're more'n a'little pissed off right now ourselves!"

Which, as it was fully intended to do, created so much laughter that even Letch had tears running down his cheeks when he finally came up for air. But since he just couldn't seem to resist Ramon's challenge, he slowly swung the beam of his light across every face in the hoist-room, before loudly proclaiming "Well if that ain't par fer th' damn course, I'll kiss yer ass! Th' only time in his life that this lousy Wetback's ever had fer turnin' hisself into a white man, an' not only was he too lazy t'scrub hard enough t'get th' job done, he winds up blamin' me fer it! Boy oh boy, some days it jist plain don't pay t'get out'a bed!"

Since one of the first men who'd climbed down the raise had immediately begun hot-footing it down the drift toward the portal, just in case the people outside put two and two together and came up with five, or maybe even seven, and still couldn't figure out what had blown the fuses, we were fairly sure there'd be someone coming to get us before too much longer.

While we were waiting for them to show up, though, Letch came over to me and asked

"How come yer damn bottom lip's s'swole up, ya sorry sack'a shit? Did ya fin'ly swaller a'nuff'a that nasty snoose-juice t'poison yerself, er what?"

Coming right back at him with "How in th' Hell d'ya s'pect me t'know ya' goofy Bastard, I ain't got eyes in my lousy chin!"

Bending closer now and running his right forefinger gently across my lower lip, he burst out "Judas Jumpin' up Priest ya simple clown, that ain't snoose, it's blood! It looks jist like ya must'a bit all the way through th' damn thing!"

Running the tip of my tongue gingerly along the inner surface of my lip now, I said "Yeah, I guess that's what I done alright, but I'll tell ya fer definite an' damn sure, as rough as them lousy teeth are right behind it, it almost had t'be one'a them lousy rocks that was hittin' me in th' face that done it. But jist on account'a how sore my damn lip is, if ya got an extry ten bucks in that suitcase ya pack around in yer hip pocket, I got half'a can'a snoose left that I'll let ya have. Jist as long as ya don't screw around too long, anyway."

Wagging his head as though he thought I was completely hopeless, he took everyone but Pat, Ramon, and me up to the chute, where they cleaned up just enough of the mess to allow them to roll the cars out of the way. Just so the Maid's electricians wouldn't have to wait to waste time repairing the broken cable, once they arrived on the scene. But when that battery-powered locomotive at last came rattling up the drift toward us, pushing two more man-cars ahead of it, you'd just better believe that every one of was standing right on top of ready.

But if you don't at least have an inkling of what that Wetback partner of mine had to say, when we rolled around the bend at the 11,000 foot mark and caught sight of that tiny little beacon at the end of the tunnel, as far as I'm concerned there isn't a hell of a lot of hope for you!

This time, though, he even added a bonus to the tail-end of it, which was "Now ain't that jist really somethin'?"

And it just really was, too!

Th' Walleyed Mule

He was called Smokey, y'see, among a number'a other things
altho' some'a them wasn't eg'zackly too awful po'lite
at least if there happened t'be much mixed comp'ny about

But since there was almost never any'a that up there at th' mine
where that contrary, long-eared, moon-eyed critter worked
he flat got accustomed t'hearin'a whole lot'a swearin'

Not that any of it ever done all that much good, I hafta agree
b'cause ever' time he'd come clippity-cloppin' out'a th' portal
I swear, ya could'a swore he already had th' idea fixed

Square b'tween them flippity-floppin' ears, t'put th' mortal fear
in th' heart'a th' poor stupid suckers that was waitin' fer 'im
an' since that jist happened t'be me, an'a kid called Floyd

There wasn't no earthly way we could even hope t'avoid
what prac'tickly always was plumb bound t'occur,

No sir there sure a'nuff wasn't, not by
any stretch'a yer `magination

B'cause even without too much illumination, other'n fer th' lamp
attached t'th' headhand on ol' Smokey's
halter, which jist incidentally,

is purty much of'a speech anomaly

Simply b'cause that simple-minded fool mule's built-in halter
never seemed t'work, at least in time so's
we could unhook `is traces,

from th' train'a ore-cars strung out b'hind `is rump

But quick as he'd slam on `is brakes, even tho' t'wouldn't be
in time t'do th' good it should, ya'd hear'em go bumpity, bump
right smack as they smacked that goofy jackass in th'uhh

Tail-end. That is if it's alright with you, Mam, t'call it that?
but anyhow, once that dang dunce'd caused that t'happen, t'was
us as had t'near bust'a gut, gittin' them cars clear of `is butt.

An' even without rear-view mirrors b'side `is ears, Ol' Smokey
always got'a charge out'a watchin' that, b'lieve you me.
Fer he'd stand there a'makin' funny noises
way down inside `is rotten hide

Jist fannin' `is swatter from side t`side
like he was th' king a'th' Pride.

That was th' name'a th' mine, ya know.
Er t'be more purely precise,

t'was ac'shally called Th' Pride'a Th' West!

Which as far as me'n ol Floyd was concerned, at best,

Ol' Smokey sure as heck wasn't. But anyhow,
after we'd bawled' `im out real

proper, we gener'ly had t'stay purty clear of `is train-stoppers.

Jist t'keep `im from plantin' `em thumpity-
thump-thump on one er

th' other of our own rumps, y'see. B'cause wowie, did that sucker

ever pack'a wallop with them steel-toed shoes he wore!

Why jist thinkin' about it fair brings tears t'my eyes.

But since ya might have sort of'a hard time
jist tryin' t'realize what it felt like,

I prob'ly best jist git on with th' rest'a m'story.

Even tho' from here on in, it comes purty close t'gittin' gory.

it don't quite make it tho', so you nervous lookin' dames can

jist quit fidgittin' that way. At least if that's yer problem?

But solely in th' interest'a brevity, since I ain't a'tall sure

how much levity yer equipped t'handle,
lets jist shoot on by th' less

pertinent details an' git t'th' nitty-gritty heart'a th' matter.

Since that's purty much what matters. I
sure hope none'a ya wind up

fallin' in th' dang grizzly thoughNow hold
on jist'a dang minute Mam!

Didn't I jist warn ya stuff might be gittin' rough?

But if I was you, I'd watch how hard I plopped
back down in that there chair,

th' way ya jist done. My doctor told me jist'a while back,

it's stuff like that as'll git yer piles all puffed up.

Which r'minds me'a th' time I chunked'a hunk'a ore right square

in Ol' Smokey's back door. Why considerin'
th' way `is swatter swung shut,

it'sa miracle he didn't wind up gittin'a pilectomy.

Er whatever it is ya call them things. All I know, though,

is it'sa purty fancy dang name t'jist hang onta somethin'

that ain't really nothin' more'na plain ol' pain in th'uhh

Anyhow, I guess most'a ya prob'ly know what I mean,

so we better git back t'ol' Smokey, b'fore
he makes anymore of'a mess.

But since them cars was rollin' right along
when we got `im unhooked

It didn't have no effect a'tall when he set `is
brakes, so he winds up that swatter'a his

an' jist flat hops, square over th grizzlyDammit
Mam, I sure wish ya wouldn't squeal like that,

It flat makes my `lectric ears feel plumb awful.
Fer cryin' out loud, what I'm talkin' about

ain't got hair, er claws neither, it's jist' th' chute-
hole me'n Floyd dumps th' ore in.

Or? Or what, Lady?Oh! Well, let's jist say
ore's th' stuff th' cars're full of,

an' let it go at that. This ain't s'posed t'be no crash
course in plain ol' common sense, ya know!

Judas jumpin' up Priest, where in heck was
I, anyhow? Oh yeah, I r'member

so there that clown stood, jist grinnin' like
he was plumb proud'a outfoxin'

that ol' train. Stupid fool as he was

But when it jist kept on rammin' `is rump,
`til `is breast was pressed tight

Against what amounted to'a two by eight
bandeau, fastened at th' end'a th' tipple

aww, Holy Hannah, Lady!

Awright awready! Let's jist call it'a skinny shed with stilts on,

er we're both gonna be here all night. So
about th' time Smokey's brassiere

pops loose at each end, he starts goin' EEEEEEEEEYONK

But by th' time th' yonk part was out of
`is mouth, he was clean out in

outer space, jist makin' like Ol' Peguh
Pigasses, er whatever that horse

was named. You know, th' one with wings?

An' if you think that sucker's feet wasn't
churnin'An' ya jist should'a seen

`is ears! They must'a bin doin'a good ninty
miles`a minute! Why if he jist could'a

throwed `em in reverse, he might'a

But since he couldn't, he wound up doin'a
nose-dive right smack down

on top'a th' ore-chute, which lucky fer
him had'a lid that let `im skid

fer'a good forty feet, b'fore he went off th' edge.

Ol' Floyd'n me couldn't see no way he
could avoid bustin' `is fool neck,

y'see, but when he cut loose with that next big ol' blast'a

EEEEEEEEEEEEEEEEYONKKKKKKKKKIN',
t'was plain t'see he hadn't.

An' whether ya want'a b'lieve it er not, even
tho' he'd flat-out flattened `is headlamp,

he must'a seen jist a'nuff light out there
in outer space, t`convince `im

he dang well ought'a change `is ways.

B'cause once he'd recoopilated'a week er so in th' mule-shed,

that egg-headed sucker turned inta th' best doggone mule

ya could ever hope t'see.

But b'fore ya go Mam, I feel like you'n me ought'a cut'a deal

Cuz there's this guy right down th' street a'ways, as has been

copyin' my stuff of late, so if I slip ya five fer th' gate

Would ya mind too awful much, jist catchin' his show next time,

instead'a mine? Why I could prob'ly even
cough up'a extry dime er two,

fer th' popcorn, so what'a ya say?

Hunh? Aw awright Lady, ya ain't playin' fair,
but if ya'll promise t'call us square,

I'll even see that ya git'a refund fer t'night.
BUT PLEASE, AW PURTY PLEASE,

JIST DON'T COME BACK!

Dee and me on our wedding day.

A Gathering Of Yule Logs

As Buzz stepped out onto the floor of the narrow, open porch, the rough boards groaned and creaked under his feet while several shards of thin ice erupted into the air from their surface. Descending the steps to the driveway, he hurried across it toward where a thermometer was attached to a twenty foot pole with a yard-light at its top. Upon entering the circle of light radiating outward from the pole, his head was cocked to one side as he strained to hear whether the wind was still howling up on the rim of the mesa, roughly three-quarters of a mile to the north. Reaching the pole, he began scraping the glittering frost particles from the slender glass tube of the thermometer with a fingernail, stopping when he found the point where the short thread of red color ended.

It had been two degrees above zero shortly after sunset. Now, slightly more than an hour later, it was fifteen below and there was every indication it was going to get even colder. Tommy, the gray, tiger-striped tomcat that had stopped by for a handout one sunny day the previous summer, and had then decided to hang around, kept lifting one foot after another off the frozen ground as he rubbed against Buzz's leg. Saying "Whats'a matter Tommy, you tuned in to a mouse out in the chicken coop?", the young man stooped down and patted the animal's head.

As he'd begun doing shortly after he'd arrived, when the cat now heard the word "mouse", he immediately ran to the screened in scratch-pen and peered in at the hopper of chicken feed. Laughing softly, Buzz followed and opened the door for him. And as soon as the long spring that held it closed gave off its metallic 'sproinnng', a fat, brown and white field mouse darted from the feeder toward some hidden exit. Before it had covered more than a few feet, though, Tommy had it firmly in his jaws, its tail whipping violently about his nose. Asking "Got room fer another one in there, Little Buddy?" Buzz lifted the lid of the feeder and a second mouse ran up the sloping side of the hopper and launched itself into the air.

Like some major league ballplayer, Tommy caught it neatly between his two front paws while it was still airborne. A soft crunch put a stop to the threshing of the first tail, then the second mouse was swiftly dispatched in the same manner. "Okay Hotshot, I got work t'do, so let's go.", and Buzz held the door while his accomplice deposited one hot lunch in the snow, then dashed back for the second one. Saying "Enjoy yer feast ol' Buddy.", as though he felt the cat understood every word, Buzz headed over to the dented-up log-truck parked in the driveway.

It had been standing idle for over three weeks, while the county road crews had cleared the road to the mesa day after day, only to have the wind drift it full again within an hour of their passage. So Buzz had serious doubts as to whether the battered old truck would even start when he turned the key. The starter whined like a banshee for several seconds, until its own heat finally softened the caked grease on the Bendix spring, allowing the small ring of steel teeth at the end of the shaft to begin its uneven, David versus Goliath battle. Protesting loudly, those eight descendants of Henry Ford's ridiculous dream began sucking gasoline vapors as though they didn't care whether they were toxic or not. But each successive draft seemed to call for another, then another, and another. Finally, with a loud hiccup, the frigid assembly of nuts, bolts, and odd-sized chunks of metal belched its way into life, and Buzz whispered "Atta girl, Lizzie, yer fin'ly gonna earn yer keep tonight."

When he was sure the engine would continue running, he slid off the seat and headed back into the house, making a curving detour to see if the temperature was still dropping. In slightly less than fifteen minutes, the thread had grown shorter by almost two degrees. Stomping his feet as he re-crossed the porch, he entered the warmth of the kitchen, wrapped in a swirling cloud of fog. His wife, Dee, looked toward him from the sink, where she was rinsing the last of the supper dishes in the final quart of water remaining in the large teakettle she held. "I was just about ready to call out the Search and Rescue bunch, then I caught a glimpse of you and Tommy coming out of the chicken-house. You guys ought to be ashamed of yourselves, you know, ganging up on those poor little mice all the time. I suppose you're gonna tell me our favorite cat's still in contention for the Fielder of the Year Award. How many did he pick off this time?", then she laughed before Buzz could answer, and asked "Is that the truck I hear running?"

"Yeah Babe, it's the truck. The bottom seems to be droppin' plumb outta the thermometer, so the stinkin' wind has finally stopped, at least fer a little while. Since I saw the County crew come down the hill jist before quittin' time, I know the road'll be open to the gate into the woods. So I'm gonna git at least one load out before Christmas, er bust. The girls're gonna have a present or two to open if I have to chase my butt around the clock fer the next three days, and that's a promise."

Looking at him like she knew it was useless to try talking him out of it, Dee walked over to the phone hanging beside the door, cranked the handle twice, then gave the operator the number of their nearest neighbor. A few seconds later she said "Hi June, would it be alright if Susan came up and spent the night with our three girls? Their dad's finally gone clear off his rocker and is heading up to the woods in a few minutes, to see if he can get some logs out before the wind starts raising Cain again. I may not be able to keep him from breaking his fool neck, but I intend to be there if it happens." Getting an affirmative answer, she said "Thanks Hon, I'll be watching for her." then she hung up.

Roughly fifteen minutes later, two heavily bundled figures climbed into the now warm cab of the truck, the smaller of them carrying an unlighted Coleman lantern. Silhouetted in one window of the ramshackle old farmhouse, three small shadows and a larger one stood waving their arms. Looking over at his companion, Buzz shook his head and said "Ya dumb Broad, yer twice as crazy as me, ya know.", then he put the truck into gear and they began rolling down the driveway.

When they eventually got to the gate where he had to leave the plowed road, Buzz left the truck idling, with its park lights on. Then he told Dee "That ol' tractor'll start jist as long as I can turn the fool crank, but it's a good long quarter-mile away and from the looks'a those drifts out there, it's gonna take me awhile to plow one pass back to the truck. So whatever ya do, don't let the engine die. An' be sure t'leave the park lights on, so I can see where ya are."

Then he lit the Coleman, opened the barbed-wire gate and started off across the drifted snow. For most of the way the surface had been packed hard enough by the wind so that he only broke through into the soft powder beneath occasionally.

For the next hour and twenty minutes Dee was able to follow his progress with the aid of the lantern. It hadn't taken him much over fifteen minutes to get to the old crawler tractor, and when Buzz set the Coleman on a nearby stump she'd watched his huge, shadowy outline move to the front of the tractor. He'd turned the crank over a couple of times, walked around to adjust the hand-choke again, and had then returned to the crank. Another turn or two had sent a large cloud of exhaust shooting into the glittering, frost-filled air. And during the next hour she'd been able to see where he was whenever the tractor passed between where she waited and the lantern.

Back at the gate finally, Buzz turned the tractor around and waved his arm for Dee to follow him with the truck, as he began widening his somewhat erratic trail through the drifts. Dee had unconsciously flipped the headlights on when she got behind the wheel, and he soon stopped the tractor and walked back to open the truck door. Saying "This second-class help ya git these days don't seem t'know what end's up.", he shoved the light switch back to the park position. Then his mitten-clad hand slid across Dee's knee as he asked "Couldn't interest ya in'a little starlight stroll, could I Lady?"

Laughing, she said "I'll stroll you, Romeo, but it won't be tonight, so get that cold hand off my leg. It's almost ten o'clock you know, and if you're at all interested in getting home before daylight, you'd better crawl back on that tractor."

Buzz grinned at her and growled "You darn floozies're all alike ya know, always flauntin' yer wiles at a guy, then when ya git `im turned on ya go an' say somethin' dumb like `Git yer cold hand off my leg'. I'll be danged if I know why we put up with it."

Then he walked back and climbed onto the tractor seat. With the glare of the headlights now gone, the dim radiance of the stars on the snow allowed him to see well enough to do what he had to.

But even with the blade on the front of the tractor angled slightly away from the already cleared trail, an especially hard-packed section of snow would slue the machine violently in the opposite direction every few feet. Buzz would have to back up then and slam into the edge of the drift until it broke off and rolled up onto the undisturbed snow at the side. The high-pitched squeal the tracks and blade created was in direct contrast to the throaty roar of the engine, and every so often it seemed to Buzz that the engine noise faded away altogether. Finally, he reached the edge of the pine growth and the depth of the snow diminished to little more than a foot, which was only slightly crusted.

Lying scattered about among the smaller trees were several logs, most of them sixteen to twenty feet in length and two to three feet in diameter. Obviously no big-time operator, Buzz ordinarily cut a load of logs in the morning, then loaded and hauled them the thirty-five miles to the sawmill. Some days he was able to get back to the woods in time to cut a second load and haul it off the mesa to his house. Then, after gulping down his supper, he'd get back in the truck and make the remaining sixty mile round trip to the mill and back.

And even though many of his days added up to eighteen hours or more, he and Dee had been unable to accumulate any savings. It seemed like every month a new tire had to be purchased, or something broke and needed welding, and the gasoline bill almost always exceeded whatever was left over. Yet he enjoyed working in the woods more than anything else he'd been involved in during the ten years he and Dee had been married.

By the time she parked the truck in a small clearing near the logs, and Buzz had propped the loading-poles against the log-bunks, it was nearly midnight.

And although he had no way of knowing just how cold it actually was, he felt sure it had to be at least twenty-five degrees below zero. Now that the wind had stopped, the frost was building up rapidly on the needles of the trees, and the small universe surrounding the hissing lantern glittered and flashed as though it had been drenched with diamond dust. And as the young couple stopped to gaze upward for a few seconds, Dee remarked "In spite of the cold, you couldn't ask for anything more beautiful, Honey. It looks almost like the sky's completely filled with diamonds, rubies and emeralds that are floating down to Earth from the stars."

After Buzz skidded the first three logs to the truck and had rolled them up the poles with the tractor blade, it was necessary to use a pair of cables and cross-haul the balance of the logs into place. This would have been a fairly simple process with a team of horses, even in the darkness, but with the tractor it was anything but simple. For with the engine noise drowning out Dee's shouts to turn this way or that, the logs had a tendency to begin rolling crosswise and then one end would come crashing back to the ground. Buzz would have to unhook the cables then, re-hook the skid chain to the log and drag it back into place at the lower end of the poles. Then the seemingly endless battle began again.

Although Dee could walk over to the lantern from time to time and absorb a little of its warmth, or climb into the cab of the idling truck for a few minutes while Buzz was dragging a log out of the woods, it was easier for him to step up onto the hood of the tractor and hold his numbed hands close to the glowing exhaust stack. In this way he was also able to draw a little heat through the soles of his boots and warm his feet a little . But by shortly after three o'clock, when the last log was finally rolled into place, both he and Dee were so thoroughly chilled that their teeth were chattering.

As soon as they'd gotten the chains tightened securely around the mound of logs, Dee picked up the Coleman and turned the valve to the off position, then they both climbed into the truck. As he sat there relishing the warmth on his face, his still mittened hands gripping the steering wheel, Buzz looked over at his wife's huddled figure. Seeing the still warm lantern clamped securely between her legs, he snorted "I never thought I'd wind up playin' second-fiddle to a smelly damn lantern Babe, but I want ya to know it sure would'a been Hell up here without yer help tonight."

His voice was so choked with emotion and nearly total exhaustion, that it had broken at the last. And when he leaned over to kiss her, the wetness of his cheek made it apparent just how much her coming with him had meant. As he turned back to put the truck into gear, she said "I love you too, you big galoot."After wiping her eyes, she sniffed audibly and said "See what ya do t'me, when ya go gettin' all sedimental like that?", obviously mimicking the speech mannerisms that came so naturally to him.

And as the truck bounced slowly back toward the County road, Buzz couldn't remember ever being more exhausted, but the warmth of Dee's hand as it caressed his right knee was very pleasant, nevertheless. So was the knowledge that now their three little girls would each be unwrapping a doll on Christmas morning. There would undoubtedly be enough money for some stocking stuffers as well and just maybe, there'd even be enough for a bag of sweet potatoes and a can or two of cranberries to go along with their home-grown chicken and canned garden vegetables.

Tilting his head back slightly, his rasping voice filled the truck-cab. "Oh if it's chicken on Sunday, an' even Christmas too, ever'things gonna be alright Momma, ever'things gonna be okey-dokey Babe."

Then Dee's voice joined in with his "Eeeyahoo!" just as they rolled out onto the County road once more and he opened the door to go close the gate. An' even though well over fifty years've passed since that long-ago night, the goofy ol' Broad's still hangin' onto my hand an' helpin' me over whatever rough spots we manage to run into. But I didn't marry `er jist because I thought she was smart, in spite'a what she likes to think. Man-oh-man, but that ol' him an' her chemistry stuff sure is one fantastic commodity!

Dee and me on our 50th anniversary.

My Love

By DeVon D. Huffnagle

I've often thought I'd like to write
A poem, my love, to give you an insight
You are dear as can be
And the reason I'm happy you married me.

One of the things I admire most about you
Is your integrity to see a dream through.
You sometimes cannot come up with the means
To accomplish immediately one of your dreams
But little by little, things start to take hold
And another of your dreams begins to unfold.
I think of your dream and your wish to come north
Your setting of posts, stringing of wire and so forth.
It seemed there were lots of obstacles to me
But you made it happen with your integrity.

Another dream that you shared with me
Was a cabin on a lake where there would be
Room enough to go and things to do
And lots of privacy for just us two.
I remember our delight when the shore was deep

The late boat ride before we went to sleep.
Then came the plans and lumber cost
The loading of the raft and the night we got lost.
Hut it was fun and now our cabin stands
My love had accomplished another of his plans.

Another of your ways that is dear to me
Is your innermost basic honesty.
When you tell me something I know that it's true
If you say I love you, yes I know you do.
With other people your feelings don't unfold
But I could tell them I know you're pure gold.
At this you'd scoff and tell me I'm blind
But listen, my love, it's true and I find
A person that questions himself as you do
Will only make commitments that he'll see through.

I am beginning to understand your way of life
And I find that to my delight as your wife
I like the fishing and camping we do
Of course the camper helps there a bit too.
But what I am finding in this sort of life
Is that it's so nice to get away from the strife.

Your sense of humor is dear you see
Although some of the jokes embarrass me.
But I like the banter that we share
It tells me just how much that you care.
So go ahead laugh, kid and have fun
I'd miss it a lot if it wasn't done.

And now my love, my poem is ended
I hope you know the wish I intended
On our 24th Anniversary I wanted you to know
I love you very dearly and I wrote this to tell you so.

Your wife

To My Love

By DeVon D. Huffnagle

Another few years have passed, my love
Since last I took my pen in hand.
To share with you my deepest thought
And dream our dream of what life's brought.

I just wanted to let you know, sweetheart
How much you've given to me.
The happiness I feel while sharing your life
The contentment that comes from being your wife.

The smile that we share with no words spoken
And even the teasing I often endure.
The thought that you are always there
Lets my heart know that you still care.

And now another dream is done
A home you've built for us.
With lots of work and stubborn pride
And a proud, happy woman at your side.

I cherish the times we've had together
Twenty-eight years have passed by so fast.
Our days have been full, our dreams only begun
Many more will happen before our setting sun.

With love,
Your Babe.

A Tribute To Doris

By DeVon D. Huffnagle

We called her Doris because you see
Anyone can a mother be.
In our lives she was always there
Some one to turn to, someone to care.
We didn't have to ask for her hand
It was always there, she would understand.

One could knock at her door and be sure and find
A special greeting, the warm and friendly kind.
And then a cup of coffee or a spot of tea
It was there for you, it was there for me.
An attentive ear you would always get
Young or old, someone she had just met,
She was your age and so much fun
A lovely visit and lively visit was sure to come.

Our road of life she helped to pave
She had so much to give and gladly she gave.
We know she is still there just around the bend.
Much more than a mother she was our friend.

Bosom Buddies

As the two boys waded barefoot through the shallow water along the banks of the little municipal reservoir, the distant chattering of magpies caught their attention and they grinned knowingly at one another. Buzz removed the mud-splattered wire-rimmed glasses from his nose, and after pulling a red bandana from the right rear pocket of his bib-overalls, he began cleaning the twin ovals of glass. Saying "Sounds like yer Uncle Art's about ready t'put a kink in our frog-huntin' again Butch.", he squinted near-sightedly toward the ongoing eruption of flailing wings, several hundred yards down the hillside from where they stood.

Then, just as a tiny cloud of blue smoke began rising from the willow-thicket the birds were circling above, the sound of violent coughing reached the boy's ears and Butch burst out laughing, before saying. "Wouldn't ya think that if th' goofy clown really wanted t'catch us, he'd leave his dumb Camels in his pocket until he got th' job done? An' if he had any smarts at all, he'd throw th' fool things in th' brush, circle around th' pressure-box an' come straight on up here."

Buzz laughed softly, saying "That's fer sure, them magpies know good an' well they can count on `im fer a water-dog feed ever' time he hikes up th' hill though, that's why there's always s'many of `em waitin' fer `im in that clump'a willows."

Butch and his divorced foster-mother, Bonnie Nickleby, were at that time sharing a house with her two unmarried brothers, Art and Dutch Rohmelle. Dutch had undoubtedly been given a more conventional name at the time of his birth, but that had been just long enough ago that even if there was still anyone around who knew what it was, nobody used it to address him.

At some time in his youth he'd suffered a fairly severe blow to the top of his head, which had necessitated the installation of a silver plate. And from that day on Art had made no secret of the fact that, as far as he personally was concerned, at least half of Dutch's intelligence must have leaked out the hole in his skull before the doctors got it plugged. But even if he was a little slow on the uptake most of the time, out of the three adults in Butch's household, Dutch was the one for whom he felt the greatest affinity.

Coming as he had from an orphanage, and then having his adoptive parents reach a parting of the ways a short time later, Butch's inner shell seemed to have a hole or two in it also. And given the additional fact that his mop of whitish-blond hair generally resembled an explosion in a straw-factory, while his quite prominent ears more or less looked as though they'd been pasted to his head as an afterthought, he'd somehow become convinced that his appearance was the primary reason his natural mother had abandoned him, and was also at least partly responsible for the separation of his foster parents.

And since his own mother had died just shortly before he was seven years old, Buzz could readily understand the sense of loss Butch felt. For even though his father did his best to find housekeepers to help look after him and his younger brother, Kayo, there had been numerous periods during the past six years when the three of them had been forced to shift for themselves until another housekeeper could be found.

And in order just to avoid the possibility of the gossip a small town is so often prone to, it was almost mandatory for Buzz's father to find a woman whose advanced age had a tendency to discourage most, if not all, talk of romance. Unfortunately though, the abundance of gray hair on these women's heads often caused them to become weary of dealing with the pranks of two young boys in relatively short order. So even if they didn't decide within the first few weeks to try to find employment elsewhere, their dispositions often turned so sour that the boys usually preferred to spend most of their time outside the house. And since Kayo was nearly three full years younger than Buzz, both of them had totally different circles of friends.

So as the frog-hunting duo stood on the hillside watching, the distant birds began diving toward the ground, and within the matter of only a few seconds, Art's agitated yells reached their ears. "Awright ya damn pinto vultures, at least gimme time t'git `em shook outta th' screen, fer cryin' out loud."

Then, after a few second's of silence, they heard him scream "Dammit all t'hell, now see whatcha made me do? That big bastard's headed down th' pipe fer sure. My phone's gonna be jumpin' right off th' stupid wall fer th' next two days, ever' time some old biddy finds a hunk of `im in `er damn drinkin' water. Aw shit, I might jist as well a'stayed in bed t'day!"

The two boys got so amused at Art's tirade, that by the time another cloud of cigarette smoke began drifting up out of the willows, they were both practically gasping for breath. But when Buzz finally caught his, he said "That oughta give us jist enough time t'work th' big clump'a cattails down at th' other end'a th' reservoir, Butch. 'Cause by th' time ol' Art finishes that weed, an' hikes up t'th' big rock under th' red-cedar tree fer 'is next one, we should have plenty'a frogs fer a real mess'a legs. Then maybe we can get th' redwings t'make jist a'nuff racket so's we can squeeze'a little more fun out'a yer fav'rite uncle."

So as they stepped from the ankle-deep water to the grassy shoreline, a fat frog arced into the air, hitting the water with a loud 'ker-plop'. And since Butch was closest to it, he eased several feet down the bank, to the point where two eyes and the tip of green snout were now floating in the center of an ever widening series of rings. Slowly raising the willow-club he carried in his right hand, he brought it crashing down at the same instant the frog dove toward the grassy bottom. And during the few seconds it took the resultant geyser to rain back down around it, the greenish-white underbelly of the frog rose slowly to the surface. Grasping the four-inch rear legs firmly between his thumb and first two fingers, Butch rapped the frog's head sharply against the club he'd now switched to his left hand. Then he dropped the still quivering form into the burlap bag that was slung about his neck on a length of cord.

Winking at Buzz, he stepped back out of the water once more, directly onto a patch of dry soil where he felt sure the wet outlines of both his feet should still be visible when Art eventually arrived. Then he said "I git blamed fer messin' around up here all th' time anyhow, so I might jist as well give 'im somethin' that'll make 'is blood perk a little faster."

So after the boys retrieved their shoes and socks from where they'd left them awhile earlier, they made their way along the top of the earthen dam to the north end of the reservoir, where the large clump of cattails grew. And as they walked, they both made a concentrated effort to leave as much evidence of their passage as possible, even going so far as to stop several times and re-wet their feet, just so their tracks would be that much more visible. The light breeze flowing up the shallow ravine below the dam was filled with the scent of chokecherry blossoms, and Buzz said "Smells like there's gonna be a'big bunch a'berries this fall, Butch. An' if there's anything that tastes better on hotcakes than chokecherry syrup, I sure don't know what it could be. Th' jelly's one'a Dad's fav'rites, too, but most'a th' goofy housekeepers we get don't seem t'be able t'figger out how many crabapples they need t'mix in with it, t'make it thicken up, so we almost always wind up with plenty'a syrup."

Upon reaching the cattails, both boys continued on down the bank to the point where a small ditch emptied into the reservoir. The ditch itself originated roughly a mile further on around the hillside, where it drew water from a small stream that was known locally as East Beaver Creek. And due to the fact that the stream flowed for some distance along the Happy Hollow road, where most anybody who came by could see at least a dozen cows wading around in it on any given day, Ridgway's town councilmen had decided several years earlier that it might be best to heed the State Health Department's advice and add some chlorine to the water in the reservoir.

Orlie Imes had been Constable at the time, and as such, his primary duties involved keeping the town's sidewalks free of snow in the winter, and water running from the faucets all year long, preferably minus as much evidence of cow-manure and waterdog remnants as humanly possible. But since there was almost never more than enough money in the little town's coffers to do anything but pay Orlie's wages, the contraption that had been devised for injecting the chlorine, through the combined efforts of Orlie, the councilmen, and the Mayor, was somewhat primitive to say the least. Consequently, by the time Art Rohmelle replaced Orlie, the amount of poisonous chemicals dripping into the town's potable-water supply was in direct proportion to the number of complaints received on any given day.

Because if most of the telephone calls indicated there was too much chlorine, Art just shut the dripper-valve off and left it that way until he'd heard from an appropriate number of his waterdog and cow-manure sentinels. And the number of turns he then gave the valve was pretty much dictated by how abusive the calls had been.

So since the boys could hardly be accused of being stupid, they'd soon learned that if they washed the mud from their feet several yards up the ditch, well above the chlorine gadget, they weren't quite as apt to be accused of fooling around in the reservoir. Once they decided they had nothing better to do than go on home, that is. So after depositing their footgear beside the ditch's safe zone, they hurried back to the reservoir and once again waded out into the water. Butch began working his way through the cattails to the south of their point of entry, while Buzz headed through those to the north.

So for the next fifteen minutes the silence was broken only by the periodic smacks of their willow-clubs striking the water. Then a much louder spasm of coughing convinced the boys that Art must already have left the shade under the red-cedar tree, and be headed up the last hundred yards of trail to the reservoir. But since the steepness of this section of trail never failed to keep him coughing all the way to the top, they knew he'd have to stop for breath several times before reaching the crest of the dam.

And as they hurried back to where they'd left their shoes, Butch whispered "I got eight more saddles in my sack Buzz, an' a couple of `em are real doozies. How'd you do?"

Buzz grinned and whispered back "I beatcha this time Ol' Buddy. I got an even dozen, an' Ol' Croaker's one of `em. Th' big sucker almost made it under that log'a his again, but this time I was jist too darn fast fer `im. Man-oh-man but he's a real monster. We're prob'ly gonna hafta put him in th' skillet all by hisself."

Never having seen a true bullfrog, since the extent of his worldly wanderings had so far been pretty much limited to an occasional trip either to Grand Junction or Durango, both of which were less than a hundred miles from where he'd been born, Buzz was nevertheless prone to some enthusiastic bragging about the size of his `monster'. And even though Butch had been brought to the area from Denver, his response to a statement about froglegs the size of chicken drumsticks would more than likely have been "Yeah, and yer fanny's suckin' air too, wiseguy!"

But by the time they'd washed most of the mud off their feet and had begun wiping the balance off with their socks, Butch caught sight of Art just breasting the hill at the other end of the reservoir, and he whispered. "Holy-cow, there he is already. Don't stand up er he'll see us fer sure. It bugs `im a whole lot more when he can't really be sure who's made th' tracks an' riled up th' water, 'cause then all he can do's wonder if it's us er not. Hurry up'n git yer shoes on, so's we can git down over th' edge'a th' bank where th' brush'll hide us. We don't dare start shootin' donies at th' redwings until we do!"

So as soon as they'd gotten safely behind a large clump of buckbrush, and had each collected an assortment of marble-sized rocks, both boys pulled slingshots from their hip-pockets and began pelting the fifteen foot high growth of haw-brush at the far end of the cattails. And within a matter of seconds the air was filled with dozens of shrieking birds, which immediately succeeded in getting Art's attention.

So as Ridgway's current Guardian of Law and Order now began trotting along the crest of the dam, his eyes riveted on the swirling birds, some sixth sense must have alerted him to the fact that there were fresh footprints preceding his own. Either that, or the rush of smoke-free air had allowed his peripheral vision to begin functioning again. To the watching boys though, it looked almost as if the poor man had stepped on the strings of both his shoes at the same moment. And when he thrust his arms out to either side and began rotating them counter-clockwise, in an effort to regain his balance, they both snorted with glee.

"Watch this.", Butch whispered. And after taking careful aim with his slingshot, he launched a rock toward Art, whose attention now appeared to be devoted entirely to the wet footprints.

But when the projectile hit the water a good ten feet behind him, and he whirled around to see what had made the splash, Buzz pulled the heavy strips of innertube on his slingshot back as far as they'd go, then released them. His rock hit the water a full hundred feet further down the shoreline, and as Art looked toward it, Butch's second shot smacked into the chokecherry bushes just below the dam. Immediately whirling around to see who, or what was skulking in the brush, the poor man had taken several steps in their direction by the time Buzz's second shot splashed down in the water, this time no more than five feet behind him.

Finally realizing what was going on, Art made three complete revolutions with his right hand shading his eyes, then he yelled "Gawddam you Butch, I know yer out there somewhere. If I ketch up with ya, I'm gonna peel th' hide right off'n that smart ass'a yer's. An' if that four-eyed damn Huffanickle kid's with ya, he's gonna git a dose'a th' same thing."

A violent fit of coughing brought an abrupt end to his verbal barrage then, so the boys grabbed their frog-sacks and began crawling as fast as they could toward a large clump of brush that would keep them hidden. Once behind it though, they stood up and began trotting along the ditchbank toward the Happy Hollow road. But as soon as he was sure they were safely out of ear-shot, Buzz stopped and turned toward his companion in crime, saying "Ya know Butch, when he starts coughin' like that, it kinda scares me. I sure would feel awful guilty if we was th' cause'a him chokin' t'death sometime. Wouldn't you?"

"What's gonna cause 'im t'choke, is them dumb Camels in 'is pocket! An' if he's too dang stupid t'know it, then it's jist his tough luck. But yeah, I guess I'd feel bad if he up an' croaked while we was messin' with 'im." Butch replied.

The sudden chattering of a chipmunk above his head caused the boy to raise his gaze toward the branches of the pinon tree they were standing under, and he fell silent.

A moment later though, he said "But I'd think a whole lot more of 'im, ya know, if he jist wasn't s'dang ornery to Dutch all th' time. I know Dutch's drinkin' bugs heck outta Art an' Bonnie, but I bet they'd drink too if they had headaches almost all th' time, th' way Dutch does."

Stopping for a breath of air, he then added "I'll tell ya this much, though, Dutch's th' only one that ever slips me a nickle fer a candy-bar, an' he almost never gits mad, er yells at me th' way they do. So if he ever d'cides t'move out, I swear, I'm gonna be movin' right along with 'im."

Then he resumed walking again, saying "But c'mon, ya never know when that sneaky Art's liable t'decide t'go home this way, jist t'see if he kin fin'ly ketch us."

But upon reaching the Happy Hollow road some ten minutes later, without seeing or hearing any evidence that they were being followed, the boys felt sure Butch's uncle had gone the other way. Walking down the road until they reached the point where a small ditch passed beneath it, they stopped to see if they might find yet another frog to add to their supply. The wooden culvert under the road had gotten so choked with mud and debris though, that at least half the water had begun flowing over the lower ditch-bank, and was now running down the arroyo paralleling the north side of the road.

And just as they dipped their frog-sacks in the deeper water at the upper end of the culvert, a two foot long watersnake glided out of the lush grass on the near bank and began swimming rapidly upstream. Dropping his sack on the ground, Butch hopped into the knee-deep water and soon had the violently writhing reptile in one hand.

And as he splashed back to where Buzz stood, he said "Lookit `im, ain't he a beaut? I gotta good notion t'take `im on down t'th' house an' turn `im loose in th' pantry. Bonnie's been howlin' up a reg'lar storm 'bout all th' mice in there, an' I kin always say I done it t'help git rid of `em. Can't ya jist hear th' noise she'll make when she sees `im flickin' that red tongue out at `er?"

Buzz laughed and said "What I'll prob'ly be hearin', ol' buddy, is how yer gonna sound with yer right ear danglin' by jist'a bloody thread. She's gonna be ticked-off a'nough when she see's yer wet shoes anyhow, have ya stopped t'think about that? I thought we was all set t'go up t'th' Devil's Dinin'room an' cook these legs. S'jist how d'ya figger on convincin' her t'give ya th' okay fer that, if she's sore because'a that snake?"

Glancing down at his oozing footwear, Butch said "That's what makes me s'much smarter'n you, ya know. While yer busy stewin' 'bout th' little stuff, ol' Butch's makin' sure he don't git boxed inta no corners. Th' main reason I jimmied th' catch on my bedroom window, ya know, was jist so's I kin git in an' out without anybody knowin' 'bout it, whenever I need to."

Stooping down to retrieve his frog-sack then, he continued "Jist b`cause it's upstairs don't mean nothin' neither, at least when yer smart a`nough t'keep'a shinny-pole around fer emergencies. Why by th' time you hotfoot it down to yer house after a couple of roastin' spuds an' some bacon, I'll already have my ol' shoes on an' be headed back up here with th' bread an' skillet an' other stuff. So's ya better not go takin' all afternoon jist b`cause ya know I'm gonna be busy cleanin' our frogs."

Then, wanting to make sure Buzz didn't in some way trip him up, he added "As far as Bonnie's concerned though, she's gonna think we're fryin' some trout we caught down at th' slough. That way ol' Art'll jist about hafta think it was someone else zingin' rocks at `im awhile ago."

So after the snake had been released, and they'd hidden their frog-sacks in the fork of a fairly large cottonwood sapling, the boys parted. Making sure he wouldn't derail Butch's plans by letting Bonny see him, Buzz slipped past Butch's house by detouring clear around the far side of the old McClellan farm-lot. But then he was forced to go nearly a half-mile further out of his way, in order to avoid getting his own shoes soaked in the irrigation water running down across the field. Consequently, he was so out of breath by the time he got home that he had to repeat the number of his father's office phone three times, before the operator was able to understand him.

And when his father answered, rather than tell an outright lie, Buzz asked "Would it be alright if me an' Butch had a cook-out up on th' hogback t'night, Dad? We jist want'a roast some spuds an' maybe fry'a little bit'a bacon. Butch is gonna bring th' bread an' some other stuff."

So when his father asked if he'd spent any time hoeing the weeds in the garden, or done his evening chores yet, Buzz said "I promise I'll chop weeds in th' mornin' Dad, but I'll git th' eggs an' fill up th' woodbox before I go. Huh? No, I ain't seen Kayo all day. But he was headed fer Bobby Craig's when he left th' house this mornin'. Please say I can go Dad, because ya know he always shows up in time fer supper anyhow."

After several more minutes of lecturing his older son about how vital it was for a person to keep his word and not just fritter his days away, doing nothing, Buzz's father said he could go. Just as long as he was home by dark.

Which quite naturally elicited an immediate protest of "Aw Dad, can't I stay at least `til 9:30 er so? We like t'sit around an' tell ghost stories fer'a little while after it gits dark. An' it's always lots'a fun watchin' th' bats an' moths swoopin' down around th' fire. Anyhow, ya'll be able t'look out th' backdoor an' see right where we are, since we're jist gonna be up at th' Devil's Dinin'room."

But when this brought a chuckle of amusement over the wire, then his father's consent, Buzz couldn't help feeling somewhat guilty over not being completely truthful. Now the preparation of the evening meal would be left entirely up to his father, since Kayo's field of expertise didn't allow him to do anything beyond setting the table, whenever he made it home in time, that is. But after Buzz had raced out to the chicken-coop to gather the eggs, and discovered that he was also going to have to pack a bucket of drinking water for the flock, his feeling of guilt began evaporating quite rapidly.

And by the time he'd carried two arm-loads of wood into the house, without completely filling the box, he debated for several seconds over whether to get a third load. But then he decided it wouldn't be right not to, so once that was done, his conscience was entirely unburdened.

And when Kayo came through the back-gate with Bobby Craig, just as Buzz emerged from the cellar with four potatoes and a good-sized chunk of bacon in his hands, the older boy answered his brother's query of "Is that what we're havin' fer supper agin t'night?" with an extremely impertinent "No it ain't what yer havin' fer supper, this's fer Butch an' me. But if ya don't git th' chip-bucket filled b'fore Dad gits home, ya probably won't be havin' any supper. Butch an' me're gonna be up at th' Devil's Dinin'room eatin' frogI mean trout."

The younger boy looked puzzled for only a second, then he grinned impishly and said "I'm gonna tell Dad you guys've bin up at th' reservoir agin, then we'll see who ketches heck. Ya know he told ya not t'fool around up there, jist because grownups don't like fer kids t'wade around in their drinkin' water."

To which Buzz replied "An' how would ya like it, runt, if Dad was t'hear `bout what you guys was doin' with Margie an' Barb'ra out in th' barn th' other day? Both'a ya were s'dang busy tryin' t'talk `em inta lettin' ya look in their bloomers, that ya didn't even know Skinny an' me was out in th' alley, watchin' th' whole show through'a couple'a knotholes."

Pausing to let this bombshell soak in, he then added "An' Skinny said he's gonna tell their Mom th' very next time Barb'ra d'cides t'git smart with `im, too. S'jist go on an' tell Dad on me, an' see what happens. Because I kin flat-out guarantee that ya won't be settin' down fer'a whole month, wiseguy!"

Buzz went into the house to get one of their spare sets of salt and pepper shakers then, and when he came back out the door several minutes later, with all his plunder in a brown-paper bag, the two younger boys were still standing where he'd left them. And both of them were looking as though there was a chance they might consider running away from home, at least if they could just figure out which way to run. Grinning maliciously at them, he said "Be seein' ya, twerps.", then he ran up the driveway and out the back gate.

So by the time he eventually made it to the ditch where Butch was waiting, he was again panting heavily. This time he'd detoured to the north of the other boy's house, in order to keep Bonny or Art from seeing him. And this meant that he'd had to climb halfway up to the Devil's Diningroom, before dropping down the backside of the steep slope. Butch had half a dozen freshly peeled frog-saddles lying in the bottom of a clean lard bucket, but with well over four times that many still to go, it was quite apparent he'd mostly just been killing time until the other boy got there to help him.

So when Buzz caught his breath and then asked "Okay, how many arrowheads did ya find?", Butch grinned and said "Jist a couple'a chips, but they're both big a'nough t'see what they was. I'll show `em to you after we get th' rest'a th' frogs cleaned."

Prior to the time the first white settlers had swarmed into this part of Colorado, probably during the late 1870's, the Ute Indians apparently had a small encampment at the lower end of Happy Hollow. And sitting as it did, in a protected cove at the base of what would one day come to be known as Miller Mesa, it would have been difficult to find a prettier spot in which to camp. For approximately ten miles to the east, Courthouse Mountain and Chimney Rock Peak have been standing guard for countless centuries, daily awaiting the moment when the rising sun exits its nest among the ragged spires of the Sawtooth Range, only a short distance further east.

But long before the Utes found the little valley, and quite likely before even the mountains themselves came into being, the mists rising from the tidewaters of an ancient ocean had no doubt been turned pink by the early-morning sunlight. For the low hill bordering the old campsite on the north is comprised almost entirely of the soft-shale sediment that had accumulated at the bottom of that ocean. And inter-mixed throughout these deposits are the remains of the countless shellfish and lush plant-life that thrived there.

Though it too has now eroded away into the mists of memory, back in the late 1930's and early `40's, what the little town's younger generation knew as the Devil's Diningroom was nothing more than a ledge of that same shale. Mostly rectangular in shape, its dimensions were somewhere close to fifteen by twenty feet. So although the crest of the hill itself gained roughly another hundred feet in elevation, from the Devil's Diningroom it was possible to see just about forever, or at least that was the way it seemed to its young habituates.

And on any given evening, whenever enough growing bodies had been willing to carry firewood up from the cedars and pinons down below, Ridgway's adult population was almost invariably treated to the sight of the leaping and cavorting silhouettes of their offspring. For from where they danced around the flames, the shadows the children cast were long indeed.

But by the time the boys finished cleaning their frogs and started up the hillside away from the ditch, Buzz remembered that he hadn't even thought to bring along any drinking water, so he asked Butch if he had.

The other boy replied "Yeah, I got a`nuff fer both of us. That is if ya don't git too piggy. I always keep one er two'a Dutch's empty wine bottles stashed away, jist t'carry water in. But it sure didn't take me very long t'find out I might as well use th' Tokay bottles fer target practice. Boy-howdy, I don't know how he can stand t'drink that stuff. I kind'a like th' taste'a th' Mogen David though, an' th' Virginia Dare ain't too bad neither."

Grinning at Buzz, he now added "That's what we're havin' t'night with our froglegs, ya know. I don't hardly ever bother washin' th' bottles out, at least as long as I know they was Dutch's."

Seeing his companion's expression change slightly, he immediately said "Aw don't go gittin' all huffy on me, Huffy, I washed th' outside off good after I took it outta th' garbage barrel, so ya shouldn't be suckin' in any fly crap!"

The sudden snapping of a twig above their heads caused both boys to look upward then, just as a large hawk soared away from the limb it had been perched on. The lower branches of the tree, a Juniper, or red-cedar as it was locally called, were completely covered with pea-sized, silver-blue berries. Which prompted Buzz to say "Dad told me an old bootlegger he usta know used them berries t'make gin. He said it was purty good stuff t'drink a little bit of, `specially if ya had a backache. But he said th' main trouble with it was in knowin' a'nuff t'stop before ya wound up gittin'a headache too."

Grinning at the humor of what he'd just said, he added "An' he said that back b'fore him an' Mom got married, he usta git quite'a few headaches. So I guess he must'a done his share'a drinkin' too, same as Dutch. All I ever see `im drink anymore though, is jist'a Hot Toddy, an' that's mostly jist when it's real cold outside. He always fixes Kayo an' me one too, but he don't put as much whiskey in ours."

Butch gazed at him for several seconds without comment, then said "Yer purty dang lucky ya know, havin' yer real dad. All I got is Bonny an' 'er brothers. An' even if Dutch does treat me okay, about all that dang Art ever does is yell at me."

He started chuckling then and said "Man-oh-man I thought he was gonna bust'a gusset th' time I got 'is ol' blunderbuss out, but I guess I already told ya 'bout that, didn't I?"

Buzz grinned and said "Yeah, but it's okay t'tell me agin, I allus gotta kick out of it th' other times."

Butch snorted and said "Ya jist think ya gotta kick out of it, that sawed-off little sucker sent me rollin' fer a good twenty feet. An' then, when my eyeballs quit spinnin' around an' th' dust'd settled, all I seen was Art runnin' right smack through th' screendoor. Bonny must'a hooked it t'keep th' bees out er somethin', I guess, 'cause by th' time Art figgered out it was hooked, he was already clean through it."

Chuckling delightedly at the thought of this, he continued "An' Gawd but was he ever mad. Why as quick as he seen me settin' there in th' dirt with that ol' antique'a his, his mouth popped wide open 'bout four times b'fore he could start cussin'. I hadn't never even heard some a' th' things he said that time, b'lieve me."

By now Butch was fully engrossed in his story and both boys had come to a complete halt on the hillside.

"It was right down there, between th' outhouse an' that big ol' fencepost." he said, pointing his finger toward where a well-weathered outhouse sat, its rusty-red, corrugated roof barely visible through the branches of a large pinon tree. "I'd set one'a Dutch's empty wine-jugs on th' post, then I opened up that ol' sheephorn flask an' dumped in 'bout as much powder as I seen Art do one Fourth'a July. I guess maybe I must'a put'a little more in than he did though, 'cause it sure made one awful racket when I pulled th' trigger. Not right away though, b'cause right after that ol' gooseneck hammer hit th' flint, it seemed like it went 'ffsssssstttt' fer at least five minutes, an' I was startin' t'wonder if th' powder was any good. Then all of'a sudden it jist went KAAABLUUUUEEE!"

At this point Butch pursed his mouth and expelled a blast of air, to emphasize his story, spraying Buzz with several droplets of saliva in the process. And when Buzz immediately jumped back a foot or so, then began wiping exageratedly at his face and shirtfront, Butch said "Aw ya don't haf t'git s'dang carried away, ya know good'n well I didn't mean t'do that. Anyhow, judgin' from th' way that sucker kicked my shoulder, I think I must'a dumped in way too many ball-bearin's too. Even though none of 'em wound up hittin' th' dumb wine jug. An' I was usin' that goofy tripod thing it's got too. Sure beats me how them ol' Pilgrims ever killed anythin' but theirselves with them cannons. But one a' these days I'm gonna git th' sucker out agin. At least if I can find where Art hides th' key to th' trunk he keeps it in."

He fell silent then, and after several seconds of watching the bemused expression on his face, Buzz said "C'mon Miles Standish, let's git on up th' hill b'fore someone beats us t'th' Dinin'room. If ya think ya can carry this bag'a mine th' rest'a th' way, I'll round up a'nuff limbs t'cook supper with."

And by the time the two reached the bare ridge comprising the final fifty yards of the trail to their destination, Buzz's arms were filled with an assortment of pinon and cedar limbs. And clutched in his right hand were several long strands of white-cedar bark. From where they climbed, the boys were now visible to anyone who happened to be looking up from down below. So even though they were both breathing heavily by now, the instinctive pride of their youth made it all but mandatory for them to complete the final push without stopping to rest.

Consequently, by the time they finally reached the ledge, both boys were so winded, and their legs were trembling so violently, that it was all they could do to remain erect. But judging from the grins on their faces, at least once their wide-open mouths returned to normal, you'd have thought they'd attained the golden arches of Valhalla. Then they both dropped their loads to the ground, tipped their heads as far back as possible, and yelled in unison, "EEEEEYAHOOOOO."

So providing that none of the folks down below had suddenly gone completely deaf, they'd know that Ol' Satan was entertaining guests for supper.

And once they'd rearranged the fire-blackened ring of stones in the center of the ledge to their satisfaction, Buzz ripped the cedar bark into shreds, twisting the strands into a large, loose ball while Butch broke several of the smaller limbs into short pieces. Placing the bark precisely in the center of the circle of stones, they then piled the sticks around it to form a miniature teepee.

Extracting a kitchen-match from his shirt pocket, Butch made several unsuccessful attempts to light it with his thumbnail, finally giving up and striking it on one of the stones. And almost as soon as the match touched it, the ball of bark began shooting off sparks, much the same way a Fourth of July sparkler does. So as the first wisps of smoke began spiraling upward around them, both boys inhaled deeply. For despite its sharply biting aroma, burning cedar bark is far from unpleasant to a person's nostrils, at least in moderate amounts.

And by the time the little teepee had collapsed into a pile of glowing embers, and more limbs had been added to the fire, Buzz had taken the potatoes from his sack and placed them in the small space left between the fire and the stones. Then, while Butch arranged three more stones within the outer ring, this time in the shape of a triangle, Buzz cut the bacon into cubes with his pocketknife and put them into the long-handled skillet, finally setting the soot-blackened utensil on the triangle.

Then, while the bacon was beginning to float in its own juices, Butch dumped the frog-saddles into a paper bag that contained roughly two cups of flour, which he'd filched after getting Bonny's permission to take four slices of bread from the half-loaf that was left in the pantry. He then shook the bag so vigorously that the saddles not only wound up being well-coated, they came very close to being ejected through the rapidly growing assortment of holes in the walls of the bag.

Saying "Get ready t'catch `em so's they don't jump outta th' pan.", he began dropping them one by one into the now bubbling grease.

The instant the saddles hit the liquid, both legs shot out to the side almost as though they were still alive, often sending one of the adjoining morsels flying against the side of the skillet. And by the time the bag was empty, the pan was so full that Butch had to exercise considerable care to avoid knocking any of it's contents into the flames. So while he slowly stirred them round and round with the blade of his pocketknife, both he and Buzz kept bending forward to savor the smell of the steam rising from the pan, licking their lips and closing their eyes in ecstasy each time they did so.

Finally Buzz could stand it no longer and he said "If you don't pull that dang skillet off a th' fire right this minute Ol' Buddy, I'm gonna do it fer ya. I'm s'hungry I almost bit a hunk outta yer ear th' last time ya sniffed th' pan. Let's eat `em b'fore they dry plumb up, fer cryin' out loud!"

So after retrieving the potatoes, which turned out to be only slightly more than half cooked, the boys moved out to the brink of the ledge, where they could better observe the coming and going of their distant neighbors while they ate. And from time to time, as the first lights of evening began winking on, they were able to catch the somewhat muted sounds of life down below. Most of the voices were too faint for them to actually hear what was being said, but when Bobby Craig's mother stepped out onto her porch to call him and his little brother, Billie, home for the night, Butch and Buzz were able to hear almost every syllable.

There was just no denying Mable's volume, you see. But in spite of this, during the next ten minutes it was necessary for her to call her boys two more times. Then, when one of Granny Hotchkiss's roosters decided to add his voice to Mabel's, and several dogs also began barking, Butch tilted his head back and cut loose with his coyote yodel. And before the last throbbing note had faded away, nearly every dog in town was howling. So Buzz joined in with his version of Johnny Weismuellar's "Tarzan of the Apes" yell.

Consequently, for the next several minutes it sounded almost as though the whole town had gone completely mad. Then Mable put an end to it by screaming "If you dang-blasted little smart-alecks don't shut yer mouths right this instant, I'm gonna hike up there an' give ya somethin' t'think about b'sides makin such'a dadblame nuisance'a yerselves."

She sounded just angry enough to carry out her threat too, so even though the two boys were relatively sure she had no idea who they actually were, they decided to let tranquility try to find its way back into the cluster of lights below. But thanks to the diehard attitude of various members of the canine population, it was several more minutes before that happened.

Both boys had been plucking the sweet-meated saddles from the skillet one-by-one, until finally only the largest of the lot was left. And since it undoubtedly had belonged to Buzz's "Old Croaker", he now took his pocket-knife and severed the pelvic bone so that both halves were as nearly equal as he could make them, then he took one and shoved the pan toward Butch.

So as they sat there watching the last hint of rose-colored light disappear from the tops of Courthouse Mountain and Chimneyrock, Buzz made several false starts, before finally asking "Butch, if I tell ya somethin' I never told anyone b'fore, will ya promise not t'make a 'big deal out of it, er go blabbin' it all over town?"

Sensing that his friend was really bothered by something, Butch simply said "Scout's honor.", then he waited quietly for Buzz to continue.

"Are ya ever afraid I mean, does it ever bother ya t'be all alone when it gits dark?"

Feeling somewhat uncomfortable because of the nature of the question, Butch made an attempt to add some humor, by saying "Only if I happen t'think th' first thing I'm gonna see when th' light comes on is Art's ugly face."

"Aw c'mon Butch, be serious fer once. What I mean is, does it bother ya t'be th' only one in yer house when it gits dark, er d'ya ever jist hang around outside so's ya won't have t'go in `til someone else is there?"

"Well, I don't really like goin' inside when I know Bonnie an' th' others ain't home, but once I git t'my room an' shut th' door, it's okay. Why'd ya ask?"

"Because even though I know good an' well there ain't s'posed t'be any such thing as ghosts, ever since Aunt Margaret made me kiss my Mom at 'er funeral, an' I made such'a big fuss about it, I bin havin' dreams about 'er ghost hidin' in my clothes closet. I know it sounds kind'a crazy, but even in th' daytime I'm almost scared t'open th' door t'git out a shirt."

"Well why don't ya jist leave th' dumb thing open all th' time, then?", Butch asked.

"Because that makes it even worse Butch. Then it feels like she's watchin' ever'thing I do, an' even though I know she loved me before she went an' died, I can't help feelin' like she's mad because I bawled when I had t'kiss 'er, right there in front'a ever'one in th' whole dang church. Have ya ever smelled someone who's dead, though? It's really awful!"

The anguish Buzz was feeling caused his voice to take on a huskiness that made Butch feel uncomfortable, and his answer of "No, I don't guess I have." was just barely audible.

"Well it's got t'be th' worst thing I ever smelled, that's fer sure. An' that was th' main reason I made such'a fuss, er at least I think it was. I couldn't even breathe until Aunt Margaret finally put me back down on th' floor. But now, ever' time I have one'a th' dreams, I can smell 'er agin. An' then I wake up bawlin' like a dang little snot-nose. Not very loud I guess, since Dad never seems t'hear me."

"Well why don't ya jist up an' tell 'im about th' dreams then?", Butch now asked.

"Could you do that Butch? Really? Jist up an' tell someone that, even though yer thirteen whole years old, yer scared'a yer own mom's ghost?"

"Well yer tellin' me ain't ya?"

"Yeah, but that's differ'nt, yer th' same age as me an' it's easier t'talk t'you. I keep thinkin' each dream's gonna be th' last one, an' then it won't make no diff'ernce anymore. But then after'a couple days er so, I wind up havin' another'n. I didn't have a single dream th' summer Dad an' Effie got married, then she had t'go an' die too, an' they started right in agin."

Buzz turned then to look directly at Butch, and there was defiance in his voice when he said "Well go on an' say it, why don'cha? Say I'm jist'a crazy dang bawl-baby, er somethin'."

"Hey, this is yer ol' buddy Butch. I already know ya ain't no cry-baby."

Getting to his feet then, Butch walked back to toss a few more limbs onto the dying coals. And with Buzz still watching him, he got down on his knees and blew on the embers until the wood began putting off a few hesitant flickers, plus an abundance of smoke. Satisfied at last that it was going to burn, he came back to sit down with his feet once more dangling over the edge of the bank.

Then, after squirming around to relocate some of the pebbles beneath his rump, he said "Now I'm gonna tell ya 'bout'a dream I have ever' so often. But if ya ever breathe'a word of it t'anyone at all, I'll tell 'em yer jist'a lousy liar."

So once Buzz too had uttered the sacred 'Scout's honor', the other boy continued, "I don't r'member ever seein' what my real mom's face looked like, y'know, since I was jist'a baby when she d'cided she didn't want'a keep me. But I've sure seen what 'er back looks like a'lot'a times since then, at least in these crummy dreams. I'm allus settin' there on th' sidewalk with nothin' on but'a dirty diaper, jist bawlin' up a reg'lar storm while she goes marchin' down th' street away from me. An' there's allus'a whole bunch'a other people standin' there an' laughin' 'bout how funny I look, too, with my ears stickin' out an' my hair standin' straight up."

Grinning then, he shook his head as though he found a certain humor in the image his words were painting. "But I guess I'd laugh too, if I seen hair an' ears like mine on'a little tiny ol' baby."

A second or so later, though, he slapped his leg for emphasis and said "No by dammit, I wouldn't neither! I'd pick th' poor little bastard up an' chase `is mom `til she couldn't run no farther."

Looking straight into Buzz's eyes then, he said "That's what I prob'ly really am, ya know, jist'a dang bastard. Art called me that once, so I got out that big ol' dictionary at school an' looked until I found it. It's s'posed t'mean yer folks wasn't married, so ya don't never know who yer dad really was. I guess that makes me kind of'a double bastard though, since I don't even know who my mom was."

Butch's short chuckle had a bitter ring to it that Buzz had never heard before, but he knew he'd never forget the harsh sound of it. And he had to blink his eyes several times just to keep the tears from rolling. So when he felt he could once more trust his voice, he just said "Thanks fer tellin' me Butch, an' ya don't haf'ta worry none, I won't go blabbin' it t'nobody."

And in the weeks and months to follow, whenever Buzz's dreams made further sleep an impossibility, he'd lie there in bed, wondering if perhaps Butch too was awake. For simply by sharing their two separate, but nevertheless very similar secrets, they'd succeeded in forging a bond that would bind them together through the balance of their adolescence. And just the fact that they had the other one to draw courage from was often enough to cause them to venture out on trails that approached, but never quite reached, disaster. But at least there was always someone to share the blame, as well as the glory, whenever they got caught.

And over in far off Europe, a man by the name of Adolph Hitler had also been seeing just how far his imagination and ambition would take him. And although they'd known it was only a matter of time before the United States would finally be forced to jump into the fighting, a great many of her citizens still harbored enough of a grudge against their British cousins so that they'd been content to sit on the sidelines for however long it took England to ask for assistance. Indeed, much of the sentiment could well have been summed up us "Let the snooty bastards get down on their knees and beg for our help if they really want it, maybe they'll appreciate it enough to thank us for it this time!"

But on Sunday, the 7th day of December 1941, the Japanese bombed Pearl Harbor and brought an end to the waiting game. Buzz and the other members of his family were sitting in the Fox Theater in Montrose when the screen suddenly went black, and before the afternoon audience had much more than begun hooting, the lights were turned on and the theater manager walked on-stage. And in a voice that was positively trembling with emotion, he solemnly announced had taken place only a few hours earlier.

Consequently, since I was the "Buzz" involved in the preceding pages, and would be having my fourteenth birthday in slightly more than two months time, for much of the ride back to Ridgway that evening I was involved in trying to remember just how much money had been in the old Band-Aid box hidden beneath the clean underwear in my chest of drawers the last time I'd counted it. Acquired through the sale of the excess eggs from Dad's flock of hens, I'd long been in the habit of squirreling my half of the egg-money away, rather than blowing it on candy to share with my buddies, the way my little brother almost always did with his.

So although none of us had any idea at that moment as to just how long the war would last, or whether the Japanese forces might actually invade the American mainland before they were stopped, I fully intended to spend every cent I'd been saving, just to buy as much ammunition for my 22-rifle as I could. And anything that was left over would be used to purchase bee-bees for my air-rifle, since daily practice with that would allow me to keep my aim as sharp as possible. For right then, with every fiber of my oh so naive being, I began hating a race of people I'd never yet so much as lain eyes on, but had high hopes of doing so as soon as possible, preferably through the sights of a rifle.

The truly sad part though, at least for me, is that despite the way America's bloody fighting with Japan eventually ended, on August 15th, 1945, a full six months before I would become old enough to enlist without my father's consent, I'm fairly sure it will be an extremely cold day in Hell before that anger ever completely leaves me.

My Christmas Prayer

FATHER

Knowing that this day we are truly blessed,

This humble prayer is to THEE addressed,

So hear it, and grant it, if THOU will LORD,

When we turn away, lead us instead, toward,

Help us to bend, rather than break,

Teach us to give, rather than take,

Help us to be wise, rather than witty,

Fill us with compassion, rather than pity,

Give us strength, rather than power,

We ask not for beauty, but help us to flower,

And when `tis THY will, to show us our place,

Grant us the ability, to accept it with grace,

Amen.

Oh The Pain Of It All

Oh dear Mother in Heaven, how dids't thou fail but see
When first my tiny body was placed within thy loving arms
The dull gleam of lunacy within my blue and newborn eyes?
And how oh Mother mine, could'st thou help but perceive
That lying buried deep within my childish charms
Was a spark that would'st ever flare, yet seldom achieve
The peace and harmony dredged forth with ecstatic cries
Just from knowing I'd finally created a bit of simple
Poetry.

Yet Another Butch And Me Escapade

I always prowled around the countryside with my friend Butch Nickelby whenever I could. And even though the ammunition cost a good deal more, we seldom lost a chance during duck season to go hunting for them with our twelve-gauge shotguns whenever we could. And at least we were able to compensate for the higher cost by shooting most of our ducks when they were swimming in a group on the water, thus making it possible to bag two or three with a single shell.

Some of you diehard sportsmen will no doubt have a tendency to turn up your noses at such a thing, but economy had every bit as much to do with the way Butch and I hunted as sport ever did. Probably a great deal more, since I seem to recall that Mister Hockley charged us right close to three dollars a box for twenty-five twelve-gauge shells. So when you compare that to one cent apiece for twenty-two caliber shells, you should be better able to appreciate our position.

And this one particular afternoon, after we'd hiked a mile or so up the Uncompahgre River, Butch's position came awfully close to being downright hazardous. For while sneaking along the riverbank, just a few yards downstream from where Gore Slough emptied its clear water into the murky, tailings laden flow of the Uncompahgre River, he spied a fairly large rainbow trout, lazily fining its way along the bank, no more than fifteen inches from his feet. Since I was only a yard or two behind him I couldn't help being aware of it when he came to an abrupt halt and seemed to be getting ready to blow off one or the other of his feet.

Just at that moment though, I stepped on a dry twig and the resultant "SNAP" caused him to jerk his head around. Then he whispered "Whoa fer cryin' out loud, don'cha see that big trout right there by th' bank? He must be at least eighteen inches long! So if ya'll jist quit spookin' `im, I'm gonna see if I can blow `is head off."

So while I waited with baited breath, since that was about the closest thing I had in the way of fish-bait, I watched the barrel of Butch's single-shot move slowly back and forth, just an inch or so above the water's surface. Then, as the trout at last became stationary in the water, possibly hypnotized by the movement of the gun-barrel, I watched Butch lean just a little closer to his quarry, trying to make sure he didn't blow the body to bits, along with the head. I became so absorbed with watching him that for several seconds I didn't notice the end of his gun-barrel had now penetrated the water's surface.

But just as I yelled "Butch, fer cryin' out loud don't pull th' fool trigger, yer barrel's in th' water!", he did.

The best way I know to describe the commotion this produced is to relate Butch's words as closely I can. Because after he picked himself up off the ground, there were quite a few of them.

"Judas-jumpin'-up-priest, why'n hell didn'cha tell me th' stupid barrel was in th' water? Man-oh-man, talk'a bout'a slow-motion racket, did'ja hear th' way th' sucker jist kinda gargled b'fore it cut loose? Ah shit, would'ja jist lookit what it done t'th' end'a th' barrel? Looks jist like that dang trout bit an inch er two right off, don't it?"

And after running an inquisitive forefinger all the way around the somewhat ragged-looking muzzle, he asked "What happened t'that stupid fish anyhow, did I git'im? I couldn't see nothin' but that geyser'a muddy water comin' at my face. Then it felt like I was jist floatin' like'a bird. Why I bet my feet must'a bin off th' ground almost'a minute b'fore I lit on my butt."

So while he was replenishing his air supply, I said "Yeah Butch, ya sure a'nuff got `im. At least I think that's one of `is eyeballs on top'a yer hat. An' that looks like `is tail hangin' on that willow limb over there b'hind ya. An' all that mushy-lookin' yella foam floatin' along th' bank down there must be th' rest of `im. So I don't think yer gonna be eatin' fish fer supper, unless ya intend t'boil up that eyeball."

Then upon realizing that the front sight was missing from his gun-barrel, I said "If ya decide not t'eat it though, ya might try pastin' it on th' barrel. That ought'a help ya see where yer pokin' it next time, at least it should if th' sucker still works."

Grinning at the ribbing I was handing him, he replied "Jist don't worry about it smart-ass, all I gotta do is grind off th' end'a th' barrel'a little. An' once I drill'a hole in th' top, I'll be able t'rivet'a screw in it. It ain't all that big'a deal ya know, so it ought'a be as good as new in'a couple days."

Since there didn't seem to be much point in continuing our search for ducks, with Butch's shotgun in the shape it was, we decided we might as well head on back home.

But a couple of mornings later, I found Butch waiting for me outside the double-doors at the south end of the schoolhouse, looking more than a little down-in-the-mouth. So I asked "What gives, Ol' Buddy, Bonny kick ya outta th' house without yer breakfast, er somethin? Er did Art catch ya messin' with 'is blunderbuss agin?"

Eyeing me sourly, he replied "Naw, he didn't. But I might jist wind up havin' t'see how it'll work on ducks, since about all my twelve-guage is good fer now is pepperin' th' side'a th' barn. Er at least when I git up about ten feet from th' wall, it is."

Seeing the puzzled expression on my face, he explained "That inch'er so that got blowed off th' end'a th' barrel was jist about th' most important part'a th' gun, ya know, 'cause that's what's called th' choke. Ya can't hardly see it, but right there's where th' barrel squeezes down jist a'nuff t'make th' bee-bees stay in'a bunch 'til they git close a'nuff t'what yer shootin' at t'do some good."

After I nodded my head to show I understood what he'd said so far, he continued, "S'right now, unless ya can think'a some way I can git close a'nuff t'stick th' barrel up some goofy duck's behind, th' only way I'll prob'ly ever git more'n one beebee in 'im, is if he lands an' starts pickin' 'em up with 'is stupid beak."

When I broke out laughing at the picture this produced, he said "It ain't funny, ya know. I wasted six shells last night after I got th' screw riveted in place, jist tryin' t'git close a'nuff t'put more'n one hole in'a tincan. An' it was'a dang ol' coffee can, too! So I guess ya'll jist haf t'find somebody else t'hunt ducks with from now on. Since there sure ain't no way I'm gonna be able t'rustle up a'nuff money t'git another gun b'fore th' season ends."

So after letting him stew in his own juices for a minute or two, I said "If ya'll promise not t'shoot at anymore fish, we got an ol' double-barrel I can prob'ly loan ya. Somebody gave it t'Dad when they didn't have th' money t'pay fer some papers he fixed up fer 'em, but none of us has ever shot it. It's an old sucker an' both hammers're kinda loose, but when ya pull th' triggers, they sound like they ought'a still pop a cap. S'what'a ya say, since t'morrow's Saturday, how's about givin' it'a try?"

His grin was all the answer I needed, and it stayed pasted on his face for the rest of the day. Which was undoubtedly the reason our teacher was so sure we were planning some sort of mischief that she hardly took her eyes off us all day long. And since some of our earlier exploits had caused her to put two full rows of her better behaved students between Butch's and my desks, it's little short of a miracle she didn't wind up cross-eyed well before the final bell rang. Of course, once we'd been completely sure we had her attention, we'd made the most of it, winking and nodding at one another every time we got the chance. Just to keep her on her toes, you see.

But looking back from this point in time, it seems rather amazing that the poor woman didn't wind up with a bleeding ulcer, or at least something a little more serious than the case of fidgets she always seemed to suffer from whenever Butch and I were anywhere near her.

Of course Butch came home with me after school let out that afternoon, to take a look at the double-barrel, since I'd told him it would probably be best to keep it at our house. This was just because I knew that Dad had heard about enough of Butch's escapades so that I was sure he wouldn't have it any other way. So after throwing it to his shoulder a few times and trying the triggers to see how stiff they were, Butch said he thought it ought to do the job, or at least it should if we could find a way to get rid of some of the play between the stock and breech mechanism. But after wrapping nearly a full roll of friction-tape around where they joined, we decided it was probably as good as it was going to get.

Butch headed on home then, with the understanding that he was not to rock the boat the next morning by knocking on our door. Because even though I was pretty sure I could talk Dad into going along with my plan, I sure didn't want to give him the slightest chance to change his mind. Which was precisely what I was afraid might happen if Butch began pounding on the door before Dad was out of bed.

I'd barely made it into our outhouse the next morning when I heard Butch come through the back gate, just a few feet from where I sat. So I called "Hold up, I'll be right with ya. I don't think Dad's out'a bed yet, but he said last night that it'd prob'ly be okay fer ya t'use th' gun. Then he wanted t'know why we needed it an' I had t'tell 'im what'd happened t'yers. So even though he didn't say we couldn't, I'm pretty sure he's 'bout half scared ya might poke this'un in th' water too."

Just as I'd been sure was going to happen, when I exited the outhouse I could see that Butch had already just about decided that borrowing the gun was going to be more of a hassle than he wanted to contend with. So I said "Jist simmer down, Knucklehead, he ain't worried 'bout th' stupid gun ya know, he jist don't want'a be responsible fer yer gittin' hurt. He's got his own pump-gun, an' th' only reason we've even got th' double is b'cause he wanted th' guy that give it to 'im t'feel like he'd paid 'is bill. S'quit lookin' like ya bin suckin' on'a dang lemon an' let's git'a move on."

Looking straight at me, he said "Well I jist don't like havin' t'borrow stuff from other people, 'specially when it's b'cause'a doin' somethin' as stupid as what I done with my gun. So ya can jist go tell 'im he don't hafta worry 'bout me doin' it agin, 'cause it ain't even about t'happen!"

Since I hadn't yet had time to eat breakfast, I made two sandwiches while Butch waited outside, one to eat on the way and another for lunch. Then I hurried down to our root-cellar and grabbed several of our yellow-transparent apples, which were likewise stuffed into my knapsack. Re-entering the house as quietly as possible, I retrieved the shotguns and a box of shells from the closet where we kept all our hunting gear. And by the time I heard Dad closing his bedroom window, I was already headed out the back door. I couldn't help feeling that I wasn't doing right by him, but I still didn't want to take a chance on his changing his mind about letting Butch use the double.

Hurrying down the street to the arroyo at the south end of the block, we followed it down past the Rio Grande Southern's watertank. And from there we angled through the thick willow-jungle separating the tracks from the river, coming out right at the lower end of a long stretch of relatively shallow, gravel-riffles. Even so, the swiftly flowing water came almost halfway between our knees and the tops of our boots. And since we had no intention of getting wet any sooner than absolutely necessary, we took considerable care crossing to the other side.

So after hunting approximately a hundred yards up a small clear-water stream flowing from a drainage ditch between two hayfields, without jumping a single duck, we retraced our steps and once more waded the river. Then we headed straight up the other bank toward the slough we'd been intending to hunt the day Butch blew the end of the barrel off his single-shot.

But when he hardly even glanced at the little stretch of water where the incident had taken place, I couldn't help being aware of what was undoubtedly eating on him. So I asked "Ain'cha even gonna at least look? There might be another trout under th' bank, er maybe we can find th' end'a yer barrel. Then we can try tapin' it back on, th' same way we taped up th' double."

So when the only response that got was a dirty look, I decided to go for broke, by asking "Hey, d'ya think that if we took one'a th' shell-cases ya emptied th' other night, an' taped it t'yer gunbarrel backwards, that maybe it'd catch th' beebees b'fore they got spread out? Why I'll bet if we did it right, it'd wind up bein' ever' bit as good as one'a them fancy rifled-slugs we bin readin' about. Why somethin' like that'd prob'ly goose'a goose right outta th' air! At least if that new sight ya put on is in th' right place. An' are ya real sure th' whole problem with yer not bein' able t'hit th' coffee can wasn't jist b`cause ya went an' got th' screw in catty-wampus, er somethin'?"

That finally produced the grin I'd been digging for, and he snorted "Awright wiseguy, jist try this'un on fer size. How `bout th' first bunch'a geese we see flyin' over, ya jist hop up here on th' end'a this double an' let me pull both triggers at once. That way ya kin grab as many as ya want when ya pass `em, an' I won't hafta listen t'anymore'a yer smart ideas. An' if ya'll flap yer arms half as fast as ya bin flappin' yer dang mouth fer th' last ten minutes, ya kin prob'ly fly right on home with `em without hardly even workin' up'a sweat."

After punching his shoulder and telling him that was the kind of talk I'd been missing ever since he'd ruined his gun, I asked "What'a ya say we hike clear up t'Zadra's Lake this time? There's almost bound t'be some ducks there, an' we kin always cross th' river an' hunt down th' full length'a Gore Slough here, jist in case we ain't already got more'n we want'a carry."

As I'd been almost certain it would, this brought an immediate affirmative response, so we waded the river once more and headed straight across the meadows in the direction of the small man-made lake I'd mentioned, lying roughly a mile further south. But as we passed the first in a series of small ponds, Butch chuckled and asked "D'ya think it'sa good idea t'go hikin' along right in plain sight'a th' Orvis house, like this?"

So I said "Jist as long as he don't see us stop an' start messin' around like we're fishin', Ol' Corky ain't too likely t'bother us, ya know. It's jist when he thinks we're poachin' some'a th' trout they got left, that he gits all excited. Man, but that shotgun he was carryin' that day looked big, didn't it? An' when he yelled 'Drop them fish an' start hikin', b'fore I dust yer asses with birdshot!', I was scared ya was gonna hand 'im a mouthful'a static b'fore we could git out'a range."

Butch snorted and said "I ain't as dang dumb as I look, ya know. 'Specially when th' other guy's got'a gun an' I don't."

What we were both referring to was an escapade that had taken place a couple of summers earlier, when we'd been packing fishing poles rather than shotguns. And after getting so engrossed in our fishing that we'd not only forgotten to stay down out of sight, we also neglected to keep our eyes peeled for Corky. So the first we'd known there was anyone within a country-mile of us, was when an extremely belligerent-sounding voice barked out the orders previously noted. And we'd then turned around to find Corky standing no more than ten feet away, pointing his twelve-gauge at the air immediately over our heads.

So even though most of the dozen or so fish that we had in our sacks had been caught elsewhere, we decided it probably wouldn't be too bright an idea to make an issue of it. We didn't waste any time in carrying out the rest of his instructions, either, since we didn't slow down or even try to look back until we were a good hundred yards or more beyond the Orvis' property line.

Fully realizing that it's stuff like this that's usually responsible for my train of thought always jumping the track, I can't help but feel I'd be completely remiss if I didn't relate at least one of the other "Corky" anecdotes that are swimming around in my bucket of memories. Partly because we eventually became good friends, but mostly because of the fact that Corky's way of attacking even the most ordinary problems connected with day to day living was often so totally unexpected that I'd almost be willing to bet that even he found it hard to believe. At least once he'd had sufficient time to reflect on whatever had taken place.

I'm only relating the story as it was told to me by a mutual friend of Corky's and mine, so there's a possibility that someone else may remember the incident differently than I do.

This one year, probably in the late 1940's or early 50's, Corky had taken a contract that involved hauling the heavy bales of hay from a neighbor's field. This neighbor's name was Bryan Fisher, and he was the one who told me what I'll eventually get around to relating to you. So once Corky had hauled the bales out of the field, he was supposed to wrestle them into a pile that was probably close to fifteen feet high, twenty feet wide, and somewhere in the vicinity of forty feet long. And since it was Bryan that told me the story, I'm confident that it happened just as I'm telling it.

Anyhow, he said that even though he hadn't actually weighed any of the bales, he was sure they averaged at least one hundred and forty pounds apiece, perhaps a little more. Corky had insisted he could handle the job alone, even though Bryan was entertaining a fair amount of doubt about that. But after watching the other man pick one after another of the bales up and load them on the wagon, Bryan had to admit that it looked like Corky really wasn't in need of any help, so he went on home for the evening.

Some time after this occurred, but well before dark, Corky picked up a bale that had a jagged piece of sheet-metal imbedded in the underside of it, slashing one of his thighs in the process. The cut was fairly deep and long, and within the length of time it took him to hobble over to the tractor the wagon was attached to, his whole pant-leg was completely soaked with blood. Fully aware he'd still have another ten mile drive to the hospital, once he'd driven the tractor across the field to where his old Model-A was parked, Corky decided he might just as well see if he could find something in the tractor's toolbox to use for repairing the damage to his leg, at least partially.

You'd probably be more inclined to believe the rest of this if you'd been around Corky as long as Bryan and I were, and had seen some of the stuff he could jury-rig back together, but there's not too much I can do about that at this late date. Anyhow, after pawing around in the contents of the box awhile, he found a rusty sack-needle and several feet of equally unsanitary looking cotton twine. So after scraping most of the rust off the needle with a rock, and also honing the point to a satisfactory degree of sharpness, he then threaded the twine through the eye and hobbled over to the side of the tractor, where he removed the cap and dunked both needle and thread into the gas-tank. I guess he figured that if any germs lived through that, he'd just have to deal with them whenever they made their presence known.

Then he sat down on the wagon-tongue, gritted his teeth, and began stitching his leg back together. I seem to recall Bryan's telling me that shortly after punching that over-sized needle though both sides of the gash about half a dozen times, Corky decided to call it good. Then he climbed back on the tractor and proceeded to herd it across the field to where his Model-A waited. And even though Bryan tried to talk Corky out of working the next day, so that a bona fide surgeon could check his leg, Bryan said "Th' damn fool turned me down cold, just kept insistin' that he didn't hold with gittin' that penicillin junk shot in 'is carcass with'a needle. Claims he gits ever'thing his body needs, just drinkin' the damn hot water that comes outta that big mineral spring on their place."

Now whether you choose to believe it or not is entirely up to you, but that was Corky in a nutshell. Which is precisely what many of his neighbors would probably have told you he must have popped out of at some time or other.

Anyhow, Butch and I made it all the way across the Orvis place that day without seeing hide nor hair of Corky, even though we kept our eyes glued on their house right up until we were safely through the fence and once more on what could safely be considered public domain. But despite the fact that it would have been possible to detour around the Orvis place without adding much more than half or three-quarters of a mile to our journey, that would have meant admitting that Corky had us buffaloed, and we weren't even about to do that. Just because that would also have eliminated the element of danger most knuckle-headed kids seem to thrive on.

The water in Zadra Lake came entirely from several large and very cold springs, which bubbled to the surface no more than a few hundred yards from the hot-spring I mentioned a little bit ago. But to the best of my knowledge, the hot water all drained away from the lake, while the surplus water from the cold-springs flowed into a canal paralleling the length of the dam on the west side of the lake. And even though the surface of this canal was covered with a solid mass of water-cress, the canal itself was a good six feet deep and somewhere in the range of fifteen or twenty feet across. So unless a crafty duck-hunter's legs were close to seven feet long, he had no business trying to wade it.

And since Butch and I were about as crafty a couple of duck-hunters as the area boasted that day, we had no trouble at all in negotiating the forty-five degree slope of the dam, once a discreet peek at the lake's surface made it apparent that we needed to get to the little clump of willows growing almost halfway down the length of the dam. At least if we wanted to get within shooting range of the dozen or so mallards swimming near the willows. Apparently we weren't as quiet as we should have been while making the traverse, though, because when we poked our heads up high enough to see them, the ducks had all moved well out into the middle of the lake. And, of course, every beady eye in the flock seemed to be aimed right at where we were crouched.

So while we were involved in trying to figure out what to do next, since our quarry was completely out of range, they began quacking as though their lives depended upon it and then took to the air all at once. For some reason, after they'd gained enough altitude to convince them they were safe, they turned and headed straight toward us. I was pretty sure I'd just be wasting a shell if I took a shot at them, but Butch apparently decided it was at least worth a try.

So while I knelt there watching, he threw the double to his shoulder and followed their progress until the gun's barrels were pointed right straight at twelve o'clock high, and his back was bent almost to two-thirty. Then the barrels resumed their march until they'd passed one forty-five, just like they intended to head all the way to sundown. But for just a fraction of a second they became stationary, then an ear-splitting clap of thunder rolled off across the lake like a tidal wave. And almost as if it was happening in slow-motion, I saw Butch go cart-wheeling down the bank backwards.

It didn't take more than a split-second for him to prove that you couldn't make it across the canal on top of the water-cress, either. Because even with the double-barrel for a crutch, he didn't get any further than three feet from the bank before he sank completely out of sight. Feeling fairly sure he'd never be able to eat or drink his way back to the top, I scooted down the slope as fast as I dared, intending to see if I could reach him without getting anything other than one arm wet. Before reaching the water's edge, though, the barrels of the double popped into view. Then Butch's head just sort of erupted out of a pile of mangled water-cress, his eyes looking as big as saucers, while water was squirting from his mouth almost as if he was in some way connected to a fire-hose.

Not at all sure he hadn't somehow managed to reload while he was rooting around down in the watercress roots, I latched onto the barrels and got them pointed away from me first. Then I grabbed his arm with my free hand and started pulling him toward shore. And as soon as he'd discharged enough bilge-water so he could talk, he lost very little time in confirming what I'd already figured out for myself, by asking "Why'n hell didn'cha tell me both'a th' damn barrels'd go off at once on this lousy piece'a junk? I could jist as easy'a drowned down there, ya know!"

Then, suddenly remembering the cause of his ducking, he asked "How many did I git, anyhow. With that much lead t'fly through, at least'a couple ducks jist about had to'a come down, huh?"

By now he was most of the way out of the water, his elastic footwear looking more like ballons than boots, so I said "Butch, ya didn't even knock any feathers loose as far as I could see, so if there's any fish swimmin' around in them dang boots, ya sure better not let `em jump back in th' canal, er we won't be havin' nothin' fer supper but water-cress.", then I burst out laughing.

Giving me a disgusted look, he slammed the double-barrel down on the bank, rolled over onto his back and hoisted both feet toward the sky, not even bothering to look for fish as the water poured from them.

So just as the last few quarts flowed down the bank, I said "Guess I better try an' find me another huntin' buddy after all, ya not only missed th' ducks, now yer lettin' supper git away."

Bolting erect at this announcement, he was unable to resist looking to see if there actually had been a fish in one of his boots after all. But once he realized I was only pulling his leg, he grinned and said "If yer all that hungry fer meat, there's more'n a'nuff hellgramites in that damn water-cress t'fill up'a battleship, s'grab an armload an' let's git headed fer town b'fore I freeze t'death. That water down at th' bottom's jist like ice, an' I ain't kiddin'."

Doing my best to maintain a straight face, I said "Without even checkin' out Piedmont Slough? Fer cryin' out loud, that's where them ducks was all headed! An' if we jist hurry, it prob'ly won't take us more'n thirty minutes er so t'git over there."

Snorting as though he wasn't too sure whether I was serious this time or not, he said "Yer jist a reg'lar clown when it's me that's soaked, ain'cha?", then he got to his feet, picked up the double-barrel and started trotting down the dam toward town. Deciding I'd razzed him enough for one day, I fell in behind him, taking considerable care not to slip and fall into the canal as well. For the balance of that duck season, though, Butch always made sure he never again cocked more than one hammer at a time on the double-barrel. So even though we always had a blast whenever we went out, there was never another hunt quite like **'The Crack-up of Zadra Lake's Out-of-Control Duck-Bomber'**.

Buckeroooooooo Butch

There was one other hunt that Butch and I had that's worth telling about, although it wasn't for ducks and didn't involve our shotguns. And this one took place up on the northern edge of Miller Mesa, sometime between the latter half of December 1941, and the first of week or so of February 1942. We'd hiked up there with the idea of collecting a few cottontails, but after finding several fairly fresh sets of deer tracks in the four to six inches of snow covering the ground, Butch let his ambitions run away with him and said "If one'a them babies shows hisself, I'm gonna show ya how t'deck 'im with jist'a twenty-two. Ya gotta hit 'em right between th' base'a th' ear an' th' back corner'a th' eye, y'know, but it sure puts 'em down when ya do."

I frequently had a tendency to be somewhat skeptical of his exploits that I didn't actually participate in, so responded with "An' jist how many have ya shot like that, Deadeye? Yer always braggin' 'bout killin' deer all th' time, but I ain't never seen ya actually do it."

Having just endured the past two or three months of listening to my virtually non-stop bragging about shooting my first buck during the regular October deer season, he gave me a dirty look and shot back "Well yer gonna see it t'day wiseguy, at least if we jump one'a th' suckers that's bin makin' all these tracks."

Obviously rankled by my skepticism and unnecessary bluntness, he continued "An' jist 'cause ya managed t'git lucky an' shoot'a cripple that couldn't run fast a'nuff t'git away, ya don't hafta act s'dang smart about it. But if we do jump one, ya jist better not go trippin' over yer own feet th' way yer allus doin', an' spook 'im b'fore I git'a chance t'shoot!"

This got under my hide in a hurry, so I said "He wasn't no cripple, an' I don't make a dang bit more noise when we're huntin' than you do. But it'd prob'ly give both of us a better chance'a jumpin' one, if we spread out some anyhow. An' at least then ya won't be able t'blame me fer all th' racket yer makin'. S'which side d'ya want, right er left?"

Due to his already being on my left, and also following a set of deer tracks, he nodded his head in that direction without saying anymore. So I immediately began angling off toward my right and was still a good fifty yards from the crest of the slope we were climbing when he reached the top, where I saw him stop and slowly raise his rifle to his shoulder. Determined that I wasn't going to give him any excuse to blame me for noise, I stood there with all my weight on my right foot, doing my best to ease the left one back onto the ground without crunching the ice-crystals under the snow.

But before I'd much more than gotten the tip of my boot down on solid footing, I heard the crack of his rifle, followed immediately by "I got `im, an' he's a real doozy."

A second or so after he'd disappeared behind a clump of brush, I began trotting toward the place from which he'd shot, still concentrating on not making an excessive amount of noise.

Upon reaching the top of the slope, I stopped and tried to locate the most logical place for him to be, since he was nowhere in sight. Then, after several seconds of scanning the area in front of me without seeing any movement, I decided to just follow his tracks. I hadn't traveled much more than a hundred and fifty feet before coming to a shallow draw, where I found him straddling a nice four-point buck and getting ready to cut its throat. His coat was lying several feet away with his twenty-two on top of it and he'd already rolled his shirt-sleeves almost up to his elbows.

Before shoving the blade of his knife into the deer's jugular vein, he looked up and saw me standing there. Grinning from ear to ear, he said "See wiseguy, I told ya I'd show ya how t'git one with a twenty-two! There ain't nothin' to it when y'can hit where yer aimin', ya know. Man-oh-man, ya should'a seen `im go down when that little chunk'a lead"

At that instant the buck's head came up off the ground and, with a wild scrambling of his legs, he began struggling to get to his feet. Butch was so startled that the first thing he did was to wrap his arms around the buck's neck, somehow dropping his knife in the process. And while I stood there debating whether I dared try to get close enough to shoot the deer in the head, he managed to get all the way to his feet with Butch still on his back. Then he went charging out through the brush like a runaway bulldozer. And in the matter of just a few seconds both he and his rider were clear out of sight.

All I knew to do was to start following tracks again, so I began forcing my way through one clump of brush after another. Within the first fifty yards or so I found the cuff from one of Butch's shirt sleeves hanging on a limb that most assuredly wasn't one of his. A short way past that I picked his stocking cap off the ground, then a little later I found a small piece of cloth with blood on it. Fairly certain it had to be Butch's, since it didn't seem too likely that he could have clamped his teeth far enough into the buck's neck to draw blood, I now began tearing through the brush at an even faster pace. But when I made a wrong turn and had to circle around until I found the tracks again, I decided to try yelling for him, in hopes that he'd hear me and answer.

About the third time I yelled "Hey Butch, where th' heck are ya?", I got a faint answer of "Aw save yer breath fer cryin' out loud, I'm comin' as fast as I can.", and a minute or so later I caught sight of him limping in my direction.

And if you think he wasn't a sorry sight, you're sadly mistaken. The first thing I saw when he got a little closer, was the blood all over his face, since it was about all that showed above the brush. But when he finally reached where I was waiting, I could see that most of the blood had come from his nose. Which he soon informed me had gotten clobbered by a limb before the deer had covered the first hundred feet. Then he held his arms out toward me, grinning somewhat ruefully as he said "Jist take'a gander at all these dang scratches! They look jist like Texaco roadmaps, don't they? See, that big'un there could jist as easy be th' road from New York t'Chicago, an' that'un there prob'ly would'a made it clear t'Timbuctoo if it hadn't gone an' run clear off th' end'a my dang fool elbow. An' all these littler ones must go t'places like Cow Crick, an' Dallas, an' Pleasant Valley, an' Beaver Crick, an'"

Butting in at this point to say "An this un's th' one that takes us back t'where yer gun an' coat're layin', s'come on, Atlas, ya can tell me th'rest'a what happened while we're walkin'."

Both his shirt sleeves were little more than rags, with tatters rippling from them whenever he moved, and there were also at least three buttons missing from the front of his shirt. His hair was bristling with at least a dozen of the small reddish-brown leaves the wind hadn't managed to yank off the buckbrush during the past three months. And there was a four-inch sprig of scruboak stuck above one ear like an eagle-feather, its sole leaf fluttering every time he took a step.

But at least he was still able to grin, as he began filling me in on what had taken place. "Man, that sucker was really somethin' wasn't he? But when I dropped my dumb knife, all I could think of was that he was gonna git away if I didn't do somethin' fast. So I wrapped my arms around `is neck, figger'n on tryin' t'choke `im a'nuff to slow `im down 'til maybe you could take'a shot at `im. But I jist couldn't squeeze hard a'nuff t'do any good. An' about then I seen th' little nick my bullet'd made b'side `is right ear, so I knew th' sucker wasn't really even hurt. All I'd done was knock `im cuckoo fer'a couple minutes. Anyhow, I decided I'd better turn `im loose, just as quick as I got a chance to."

By now, despite how narrowly he'd missed really getting hurt, he was thoroughly enjoying the humorous aspect of his experience, and was almost giggling. "But th' hellov'it was, that sucker jist kept on tryin' t'ram them horns back over `is shoulders at me. An' I was scared that if I did let go, he'd turn around an' have at me jist as soon as I did. Judas Priest, but I don't know how he missed my head with them things, th' way he kept rakin' `em sideways. Then all of a sudden I seen we was headed straight fer that dropoff we climbed around before we jumped `im, so I let loose `bout two seconds b'fore he dove over th' edge. Thought fer'a minute I was gonna roll right on over b'hind `im, but I fin'ly got lucky an' didn't."

By now we'd reached the point where his ride had started, so he slipped into his jacket and zipped it clear to his chin, obviously chilled now that the flow of adrenalin had begun to slow down. A moment later he began raking around through the snow with one foot in a half-hearted attempt to locate his knife. So I dropped to my knees and started pawing around also. But after a good five minutes of searching, he said "Aw shit c'mon, let's git goin', we ain't gonna find it in this dang stuff. I'll come back in a couple months when th' snow's gone, an' see if I kin find it then."

Reaching the bottom of the hillside just as the sun dropped out of sight, when a cottontail hopped out from behind a clump of brush not thirty feet from us, I whispered "Go on an' take `im Butch, ya got it comin', `specially after what ya went through with th' buck!"

This time, after he'd retrieved the limp form, I was able to see that his bullet had flown straight and true, hitting right between the base of the ears and the corner of the left eye. I almost said "Well ya fin'ly got lucky.", but after thinking better of it I just said "Fat little bugger, ain't he?" And a few moments later we separated and headed for our respective homes, one more memory firmly locked between our own ears.

Flying Free My Love

There are times when I sit,
In the darkness of early Morn,
Alone and yet at peace,
For it's then my thoughts are born,
And as these shadows stroll,
So softly down memory street,
All comes dancing back,
In scenes now past, yet ever sweet,
Truly, I'm not forsaking you,
Al'tho I walk alone, you're there
In all that I do,
My love is strong, I care, Yet I'm bound, to heed,
The siren call, and try my wings,
Flying free, filled with the joy,
That this freedom brings,
Forever back to you I'll come,
What we have will stand the test,
So Please have faith in me,
For then will I be truly Blest.

The Highway

As you walk down Life's highway, you will find,
Much that you encounter, may seem less than kind'
The trail can be steep, troubles may await you,
But just keep on going, tho' dark be the view,
Storms may seem to follow, and fearsome they will sound,
Don't stop, wait, or hesitate, there's no other way around,
Lead out boldly, plant a smile upon your face,
Life may be just a gamble,
But we all get to race!

It's Your Bet

Life's but a game that we all play,
A game of chance, some might say,
Where risk is great and stakes are high,
When cards are dealt and hands don't lie,
So place your bet, just toss it in,
If you'll but try, you too can win.

Writing Machine

My typewriter goes
Like redhead bird with cold nose,
Pecks more when not froze.

`Tis Nought But Fate

Ah Wisdom, thou slovenly laggard
If indeed Wisdom truly be thy name
Why hast thou come calling at this ungodly hour
Surely t'would have been more fitting by far
Hads't thou but shown thy haggard old face
B'fore so many years had gone flitting by
And this pitiful, wayworn trav'ler
Had started down Life's last millrace
Ah yes thou late blooming flower
`Tis nought but thy shame now
That leads thee t'call
A'tall!

A
Poem
To Roast
Your Toes On

Oh thou twinkling speck of Infinity
If only thou coulds't see thy way free
To bestow upon me the gift of immortality
Oh how happy I would be!
But on the other hand
As I've now begun to understand
That would constitute somewhat of an annomaly
And more than likely I'd then come down with a nasty old allergy
And it would just last and last throughout all eternity
Then I'd have to spend all my time in the infirmary.
So if it's not already too late to cancel my other plea,
please promise you'll not get mad at me
Then help the operator find an open line to Schenectady.

R / \ P
E / \ L
B / \ E
M / \ A
U --/ \-- S
N -/ \- E

Tom

Of two differing schools were we
Yet shackled one to the other
By the bonds of our similar need
And though thou waged relentlessly
To instill thy waggish brothers
With that ever so elusive seed
Grown thru the umbilical of brevity
From the womb of Virgil's mother
By nature's extremely accidental deed
How, with naught but pleas for us to heed
Couldst thou in all reality hope to smother
The smoldering fires of our desires for levity?

But now that you've rid th' road
Our poor ol' buddy Arthur strode
When he throw'd `is book in th' pot
What I really just got t'know
Is what d'ya think took s'long
Fer yer's t'grow s'goshdarned short
B'cause unless I read it wrong I fear
Yer prob'ly gonna need at least'a year
T'start another'n like it, ya dad-blamed
Gray-haired, slow-motion, New England worry wart
But now that you too have braved th' bite'a birth
You've proved your worth. S'Godspeed ol' friend
Th' end!

Ode To My Poor Wife

With you my Love, I feel free just to be myself.
And altho' I'll admit even I may not always know
Just exactly who it is that I'd like to be,
Whenever I seem so prone to effect my tone
Of injured vanity, and then go thundering 'round
'Til your ears must virtually throb with the sound
All I can say is, just try to hang onto your sanity.
Because it would seem that you're really stuck
With the incredible luck of my just being me!
But for whatever it's worth, please accept the fact
That even tho' I'm so frequently lacking in tact
And my poor old head's so oft' in a muddle,
I sure do like these oh so cold Alaskan winters
And the way we've learned how to cuddle
On our expensive little plastic water puddle.
But Honey, I really think you also need t'know
That I positively, absolutely abhor the thought
That what all that big ol' pile'a money bought
Is s'dadblamed susceptible t'splinters!

It May'a Been Fate, But `Tain't Fair

An' by damn, gettin' all old an' ornery hasn't been easy either! For the fact'a the matter is, most of us old coots have to work our tails off, just doin' a halfway passable job of it. But even if I'd known I was gonna end up creakin' when I walk, squeakin' when I talk, an' sayin' stuff like "Hunh, what's that y'say?" at least ten times for every time I get t'say "Yep, I understand perfectly, an' what's more.", an' then havin' t'endure the way all you young duffers look at me like I'm non compost menace, just because my ears laid down on the job forty years before I'll ever get a chance to, I still don't know what in Hell ya think I could've done about it.

But, now that I've managed to make it look like I'm waggin' just another sad tale at ya, I might as well go for broke an' tell ya about the really goofy stunt I pulled a couple years back. For after forty-odd years (an' some of `em were a whole bunch odder'n others) of diggin' deep ditchs with dull shovels, wheelin' two-handled unicycles that were filled t'the brim with semi-congealed concrete (just because I was too macho an' dumb t'yell "That's full enough, dammit!"), drivin' soft drill-steel into hard rock, an' poundin' on my thumb instead'a the nail I was aimin' at, I finally decided the time had arrived for me t'acquire some knowledge via the college route.

But since my train hadn't quite reached the station in life that some idiots prefer t'refer to as "The Golden Years", an' I still had t'work ten or twelve hours a day t'make a livin', I was only able t'plunk down enough hard-earned cash t'get myself a ticket to a night-course in, of all things, "Creative Writing." Well Sir, by the time I found out it was poetry this nutty Professor intended t'help me create, it was too dang late t'get my money back, so I figured I might as well give it my best shot, an' hope it didn't turn out t'be just another dud.

But I'll tell ya right here an' now, if I'd known that dude couldn't speak nothin' but New Englandese, I sure would'a yelled "Ready, aim, fire!" before he had a chance t'open his mouth the second time. Man-oh-man but these electric ears'a mine put out a lot'a static, just tryin' t'sort some sense out'a what he had t'say. An' for that matter, he had somethin' to say practically every minute I was sittin' there, most'a which always seemed t'be aimed straight at me.

In all fairness though, I'll have t'admit that he really did have his work cut out for 'im, since about the only poetry I could ever remember readin' was "Hickery-dickery-dock." But I really did think ya had t'cram as many rhymes as ya could in your bucket, before you could even hope t'dump out a decent poem, an' that's a flat-out fact. (Just goes t'show how much trouble a lonnnnng memory an' a fat head can get ya into, don't it?) Night after night though, I'd sit there all red-faced an' smitten, while that sucker read and re-read whatever I'd written. Why by the time he'd get through renderin' out my hide, my face'd be white an' his jaws'd be tight, an' all I could do was wish the floor'd open up down under my chair, just so's I could slide right clean out'a sight, b'fore he singed off the rest'a my hair.

But you'd better believe that I'd do it all over again, just t're-achieve the one, solitary moment'a reprieve I got, the night he was poundin' on his desk, while expoundin' on somethin' I'd wrote. An' I quote, "Good Lord, Syd, would you really have us believe that people write and talk like that, wherever it is that you came from?"

Then all of a sudden, just like a breath'a fresh air, way back in the very last row, a hand shot up an' a voice shouted out, "Sir, I don't know where Syd came from either, but he sure sounds a lot like some folks I know, way down in Steamboat Springs, Colorado."

So even though he'd missed my point'a origin by a hundred miles or so, for the rest'a that night I sat there grinnin' like a fool, just baskin' away in the sweetest glow.

An' that's another thing, even though I fear it'll make me appear a mite vindictive, in spite'a what Ol' Prof was always yellin', there's lots worse things than pokin' a few 'postophes into what I write, even if it does make the readin' just a wee bit restrictive.

A Thirsty Business

Although I've always admired folks who had a college education, and have spent a good part of my first seven decades bemoaning the fact that I didn't, I've come to the conclusion that this college-minded society of ours may very well be the ruination of a whole crop of kids whose thirst for knowledge might better be satisfied by enrolling in the School of Hard Knocks a little sooner in life. Because after I went out and got my ears filled up with some of the latest electronic hearing marvels a few years ago, I also let my wife persuade me that it wasn't too late to get a seat on the Smart-train too, which was when I signed on for some night courses in the Halloween Halls of good ol' U.A.A., just to see if they could fill up some more of the space adjacent to the aforementioned ears.

Well Sir, even though it felt more than a little peculiar to be hobnobbing with a bunch of macho eggheads that were always spitting out words I'd never even heard of before, eyeballing all the cute little coeds was something I could handle with no pain at all. And since I was already smart enough to keep my mouth shut about such things, at least around Mama, I figured I was settled in for a real enjoyable time of it.

Then, right smack in the middle of the writing course I was taking, this one nut had to start spouting off about two old Greek geezers named Harry Stottle and Harry Cleetus, who he seemed to think were pretty smart turkeys. And even though those electric whiz-bangs in my ears were having a heck of a time ascertaining just what our New England-born professor thought about it, since they didn't seem to be tuned in quite right for deciphering foreign languages, I got a real bang out of hearing about how Ol' Cleetus's main claim to fame came from some words of wisdom he dreamt up one day while goofing off on the banks of the Meander River. What he said, more or less, was that over in Greece at least, it just wasn't possible to wade in the same river more than once. But since my power-cells were just a shade low on current right then, I didn't catch just why that was, so I decided they must have had some kind of law against it, or something.

Maybe it's only because I've always had a poetic streak, but just thinking about how fitting it was to name a river "Meander" sent the shivers shooting down the back of my neck like a herd of water-skippers. So I guess it's possible that I got just a little carried away when I wrote about what I'd picked up during that night's "critique" session. And by the time I finally got it all slicked up and ready to read at the next week's class, I was so exhausted I'd not only begun falling asleep at the keyboard of my word-processor, I was also dreaming that the fool thing had come to life just to help me create a genuine literary masterpiece.

The title I hung at the top of my little Greek odd-essay was "Gems of Wisdom", which had seemed fairly appropriate, at least while I was busily splashing around in my private little pool of creative ecstasy. As long as the subject's just sort of popped up this way, though, I guess you could say it was quite fortunate that I only had that class one night a week, since it took me at least that long to recover from all the holes our highbrowed professor poked in my balloon with that sharp tongue of his.

But due to the somewhat peculiar way the Three Goddesses of Fate sometimes have of balancing Justice's scales for her, when one of the students finally got through pointing out each and every fault he found in the piece the next fledgling read, by the time she'd burst into tears and announced that she'd had all she could take and was never, ever coming back, simply because it was quite apparent to the rest of us that the main reason she'd probably enrolled in the class to begin with, was just because she had a relatively severe case of the hots for the professor, she ended up alleviating just enough of my heat so I was not only able to come back the following week, but actually complete the fool course. So there!

My uncle Jimmy Cooper, my mother Mary Genevieve "Gene" Huffnagle, Jimmy's wife Mable, and their son Harlan in front.

Smoke Signals

I think that more than any other one thing, the Rio Grande Southern Railroad was the catalyst that held Ridgway's residents so closely together during my early years. For even though it almost always seemed to be floundering from one financial difficulty to another, there was hardly anyone among us who actually thought there would ever come a day when we'd no longer see its engines heading out of town, chuffing and puffing their proud gray-black plumes of coal-smoke as only steam-powered locomotives have ever done. And right up until it finally came to pass, few of us could contemplate a time when we'd never again have a chance to lie in our beds at night, listening to the oh so melodious sound those little singing teakettles made, as they sat at rest down in the yard beside the roundhouse. That soft ching-ching ching-ching was without doubt one of the sweetest and most reassuring lullabies I'd ever listened to.

And if there's anything on this earth more hauntingly beautiful than the notes coming from the whistle of a distant steam-locomotive, as it approaches yet another road-crossing, I've no idea what it might be. Filed away for all time with my more sacrosanct memories, is the ghostly image of one of those long-dead strings of cattle-cars and gondolas, as it rolls along through the twilight of a summer evening. And through the tears that somehow begin rolling down my cheeks, I can also see my small daughters, still standing there on the porch of the ramshackle old farmhouse we were then living in, as they take turns waving their flashlight at the men on the train. Few, if any, of those men are alive today.

The girls had first begun responding in this manner when Jay Phillips told them at our Christmas dinner get-together that if they'd just come out on the porch and wave whenever they heard his train coming, he'd do likewise from the platform of the caboose. So before many days had passed, virtually every man on each and every train had begun waving a bandana, brakeman's flag, or lantern, while the engineers would almost always give their whistle-lanyard two or three quick jerks. And if you think it wasn't comforting, on the days we happened to be gone as a train was returning from a run, to have our phone ring that evening and then hear a gruff voice asking "Them girls a'yers ain't sick are they Buzz? They didn't wave when we come by awhile ago, an' I jist wanted t'be sure they're okay.", then it's just because your personal train has jumped completely off the track somewhere back down the line.

Built during the late 1800's, the Southern's narrow-gauge rails linked Ridgway to Durango, as well as all the small mining communities in between. And due to the steepness of the terrain in that southwestern section of Colorado, the line possessed some rather unique features, such as trestles that looped completely back over themselves, as the rails climbed up out of the canyon depths to the high passes. During the winter, of course, the snow on those passes would frequently be in excess of ten feet deep, so there was the constant danger of avalanches thundering down from the surrounding peaks, thus burying the rails and anything on them several times ten feet deep.

From various vantage points along the route, such as miner's and rancher's cabins, it was more or less common during the dead of winter to see two, three, or four separate plumes of smoke erupting from what at first glance appeared to be an unbroken expanse of snow, since the plow-berm alongside the tracks very often would be piled higher than the tops of the cars. And due to the steeper than normal grade on so much of its route, the Southern was forced to use several locomotives whenever the length of its trains made it necessary. Which was actually most of the time, since the bulk of its freight consisted of ore from the mines, or cattle and sheep from the ranches.

But since the demand for passenger service between the communities it was serving so seldom justified the use of ordinary passenger cars on its trains, in 1931 the Southern modified two gasoline-powered Buick touring-cars, by equipping them with flanged wheels like those on the rest of its rolling-stock. Then they hooked shortened versions of a baggage-car to each of them, so they could haul the mail and also a fair amount of priority freight. These proved to be so successful, that by late 1936 the Southern's mechanics had added five more units to the fleet, most of which utilized Pierce-Arrow limousine bodies and engines.

Shortly after the first two busses began operating, it's my understanding that someone, upon observing the peculiar sideways rocking motion one of them made as it rolled down the tracks away from him, commented "That goofy lookin' sucker looks jist like th' damn ol' fat goose we usta have when I was'a kid! She was always a'gallopin' this way an' that too, jist like she couldn't wait t'git inta some kind'a trouble."

Regardless of how it actually came about, though, the name "Galloping Goose" was bestowed upon each member of the gaggle. And since the father of a friend of mine was driving one of them during the late-1930's, every now and then we'd be able to talk him into letting us ride from the round-house to the depot with him, a total distance of approximately three blocks. At least when you take into account the fact that it was always necessary to back out of the yard as far as the switch by the watertank, in order to proceed in the opposite direction toward the depot. And as long as we didn't get too carried away, Ted would generally allow us to take turns ringing the bell that was mounted beside the radiator, right behind the cow-catcher. I truly regret, though, that I didn't at some point in time get to ride at least as far as Placerville, while it was still possible.

And what would have made it even nicer, would have been if I'd done it while my uncle, Jimmy Cooper, was at the controls. But since he and Dad had had a falling-out right after Mom died in 1935, it wasn't until sometime around 1942 that their differences were eventually settled. Jimmy-da-Coop, as so many of his friends commonly referred to him, was a bonafide Irishman. And his hot-temper was every bit as legendary around our neck of the woods as his love of whiskey and beer.

Consequently, when I started sowing some wild oats of my own shortly after entering high school, Jimmy began taking far more notice of me than he'd done in a long time. And one night while a group of us kids were over in Telluride for a basketball game, I bumped into him after the game ended. For some reason I no longer recall, his `Goose' was laying-over there that night, and since neither one of us was feeling any pain at the moment, within a matter of minutes we were standing side by side, belting out an alcohol-induced accompaniment to whatever was blaring from the jukebox. And although I've no way of knowing whether it was this incident that actually broke the ice between Jimmy and my family, I've always felt it helped. Simply because from that point on he began crossing the street to say "Hi", where before he'd seldom done any more than grunt or nod. And every so often he'd invent some excuse to come by our house, most particularly after Dad and Doris Brown were married in May of 1944.

Having become a well-qualified butcher in his youth, while working in his father's meat-market, Jimmy had later worked at Wade Carmichael's little slaughterhouse, which was undoubtedly what helped bring about one of the more ridiculous stunts he pulled while he was herding one of the Southern's Geese. At that point in time it was rather commonplace for him to pull up to the Ridgway Depot and find a sizeable band of Navajo Indians waiting to take the Goose back to what was known locally as "the West End", since that was the term designating virtually all of the extreme southwestern corner of Colorado. And since a substantial number of them were quite frequently suffering from the after effects of too much firewater, it was left to Jimmy's discretion to designate which ones would get to ride up in the bus with him, and which ones had to ride in the adjoining baggage car. For some reason though, drunk or not, it was almost always the younger and more attractive Indian maidens who were picked to ride up front.

And since the season was then open for hunting four-legged deer, Jimmy had his 25-35 carbine propped in plain sight near the steering-wheel of the Goose. The only reason I know of for any of the Geese even having a steering-wheel, was to make it look as though the nut hanging on to it was actually in control of things, since it was impossible to turn the front wheels to either side. And in addition to a foot-pedal, there was also a hand-throttle that allowed the driver to set it at whatever speed he wanted, and then just sit back and enjoy the scenery. But even though he was fully expected to keep his eyes on the road ahead, with the rails in control of where the Goose could go, it was always quite possible for the driver to devote more attention to the scenery behind him than to that in front.

Be that as it may, several miles before reaching the station at Rico, as the Goose was waddling its merry way across the countryside, a fat buck deer decided to cross the tracks to see if the browse was any better on the other side. Quickly backing-off the hand-throttle, while easing the lever for the air-brakes to where he figured it would stop the Goose by the time it got to where the buck was now standing, Jimmy then grabbed his carbine, opened the door, took aim, and pulled the trigger. Of course when the sound of his shot caused all the two-legged bucks in the baggage-car to poke their heads out the already open door on that side, Jimmy was so pleased to see the deer collapse in its tracks that he immediately made up his mind to do something he was later going to regret.

For, as he would one day tell me, while we were in the process of cutting up an elk I'd killed a few days earlier, "I knew ever' damn one'a them Navvies was prob'ly kinda surprised at how easy I'd dropped that dang buck, so I jist d'cided t'give `em a little bit extra fer their money."

Wagging his head as though he could hardly believe it himself, he went on "So I jist propped th' carbine back against th' dash, jerked out my knife, shoved it b'tween m`teeth th' same way them movie heros is always doin', then I hit th' ground runnin'. An' since th' buck was jist breathin' `is last when I got to `im, I jammed m'damn knife clean t'th' hilt right b'low `is chin an' slit `is throat wide open."

But after waiting several seconds for him to continue his story, I finally asked "An' what did th' Navajos think'a that?", knowing full well that there had to be more coming, since Jimmy's stories almost always had an unexpected twist to them.

Grinning somewhat ruefully, or so it seemed to me, he said "I never did really git'a good chance t'ask `em, y'see, b'cause I'd no sooner bent down an' got'a big mouthful'a that hot blood, b'fore most of `em started pukin' all over my Goose! Even th' sober girls an' squaws up in th' cab! Judas Priest, you've never seen such'a mess as what I had t'clean up when we finally pulled inta Rico!"

Wrinkling his nose in disgust at the memory, he continued "An' if you think th' station agent wasn't some kinda pissed-off when he seen all'a that slop drippin' off'a his mail-bags an' packages, then you don't know nothin' a'tall about pissed-off! But jist t'prove what'a screw-up a'stupid Shanty-Irishman can be when he really works at it, I went an' told `im what'd caused it all, so there was no way in hell he was even about t'help me clean th' mess up then!"

By way of explanation though, since most of the people I've related the story to in the past have generally seemed more than a trifle skeptical of the part about Jimmy's drinking the deer's blood, there were still a substantial number of people during my childhood who considered a healthy animal's blood too valuable to waste, although most of them would catch the blood in some kind of container and then use it in blood-pudding or sausage. But since I knew for a fact that our family doctor had prescribed mixing still warm beef-blood with my younger brother's milk, to combat what he'd diagnosed as a severe case of rickets, I had no trouble at all in accepting Jimmy's tale as the truth. Of course I was also aware of his reputation for being one of the most sought-after lamb castrators in our locality, simply because once he'd snipped the bottom of their tiny scrotums off with his knife, he knew that the fastest way to get hold of their testicles was with his teeth, then they could be snipped loose with the aforementioned knife. This wasn't a chore your ordinary farmhand would try, but it never seemed to bother Jimmy.

Although the following incident was related to me by a mutual acquaintance of Jimmy's and mine, when I quizzed my esteemed Uncle about it one fall afternoon while we were once again involved in butchering an elk, he more or less admitted there was a pretty good chance that at least most of it had happened. But since it involved an un-married schoolmarm in one of the towns along his route, he refused to get very specific about what may or may not have taken place.

Apparently though, at some point along the route, since all his other passengers had disembarked at stations already passed, only Jimmy and the reportedly quite attractive schoolmarm were left aboard the Goose. And since he and his wife had reached a parting of the ways several years earlier, when she'd decided the grass just had to be greener out in sunny California and had headed there in the company of another man, Jimmy had ample reason for deciding to see if the schoolmarm was even the slightest bit susceptible to his Irish charm.

So after the passage of an appropriate amount of time, during which he made it readily apparent to her that his physical presence really wasn't all that necessary up in the driver's seat, he adjusted the hand-throttle to a considerably slower rate of speed, then he joined the lady on one of the much roomier bench seats normally reserved for the passengers. Consequently, after the passage of even more time, the first that either of them realized how quickly it had passed, was when they heard someone yelling rather loudly. And by the time Jimmy got in a position that allowed him to look out the window, the Goose was nearly a hundred yards past the wildly gesticulating agent of the station he'd been fully expected to stop at. But due to the necessity of rearranging certain items of their attire, he and his passenger travelled some distance further yet, before Jimmy was finally able to start backing the Goose toward its customary roost.

It's my understanding that the agent had seen enough of what was going on, though, so that it wasn't necessary for him to say much more than "Howdy Coop, sure is'a fine spell'a weather we bin havin', ain't it? Must be'a real comfort t'ya, not t'hafta worry `bout runnin' inta any mud-slides er washed out bridges!"

My future wife DeVon D. Johnson.

A Call In The Night

We've a friend, whose name is Bill.
He calls at times, just to tell us that
He's thinking of us as he sits there alone.
He called again last night, when it was still,
I guess it get's lonely down there, in Mexican Hat.
So we talked for over an hour, on the telephone,
And as he spoke about moonshine and whiskey stills,
It sure seemed awfully nice, to sit here gazing at
The bright, shining ball rolling thru our velvet sky.
For I knew that very likely, its powerful magnetic pull
Must be what had wrought this dear friend's poignant cry.
So at the returning tone, both my heart and the moon were full.
Thank you Bill, for caring enough and
sharing with us your phone.

Ain't Life Somethin'?

In spite'a how much we need it, love's pretty hard on'a man
Fer no matter how many times we say we won't do it ever again
We do, b'cause we jist can't seem t'help th' way we're made

But I ain't all that sure th' maid'ns fair really fare s'bad
As they're prone t'say they do, whenever we go t'bed at night
An' wind up in'a fight, jist cuz they say "No, turn off th'light"

Now how can'a guy hope t'win, 'thout havin' an identical twin
T'spell 'im off now'n then, so's he can slip off'n hoist'a brew'r
Two'r maybe four. But when we wind up
back at our own front door

Why d'girls haf'ta go makin' s'dang much noise 'bout how us boys
Always want'a cuddle then, 'til we're no more'n half'n inch apart
Why Hell's bells, what's s'awful 'bout needin' t'rip off'a little
Bitty ol' beer fart?

Miz Martin, Our Southern Belle

I'm fairly certain it was my own culinary efforts that helped bring this totally unexpected event all about, since both Dad and my little brother, Kayo, seemed to get pretty get tired of having fried potatoes and either ham or bacon for supper most every night. We did drink a lot of milk though, since all of us were crazy about dunking the gingersnaps Dad was always buying at Wade Carmichaels Grocery.

An authentic Georgia Peach, this rotund little lady came to us well after ripening on the tree, you see, via her daughter's household down in Montrose. Her son-in-law had been having a certain amount of difficulty in finding a job that paid enough to allow him to feed and house his wife and children, and he'd apparently been making it pretty obvious that he hadn't bargained on Miz Martin's being part of the overall package. Which was no doubt the reason he'd called our house one Saturday evening, to ask if the job he'd seen advertised in the Daily Press's classified section was still open.

Consequently, on Sunday afternoon the whole clan showed up on our doorstep, having only just barely made it, at least from the way Hubert's dilapidated old automobile sounded, as it sat there in the street wheezing and perspiring through its radiator. And after he'd deposited his mother-in-law's valises in the front bedroom (although they looked just like suitcases to Kayo and me) we all sat down in our living-room to get better acquainted. Both of the women were apparently quite jolly, otherwise they probably wouldn't have spent so much time laughing about almost everything the rest of us said. Actually, though, that was just as well, since it was really pretty difficult to understand a whole lot of what either one of them had to say. And as far as that goes, ol' Hubert wasn't too easy to keep abreast of either!

About the fifth time he looked over at Agnes, though, and said "We rilly outta be headin' back down th' trace, Sugar Buns, 'cause ya know th' Plymouth's headlamps ain't workin'." and she'd responded with "But Apple Dumplin' I jist wanna make sure Mama's not takin' on more'n she oughta, what with th' size'a these two boys an' th' house an' all.", it was fairly obvious to us that the main thing he was interested in was getting Mama out of his hair, while Agnes very definitely was not of the same frame of mind. But after their four older kids began whining about being hungry, and it became apparent to all of us that the unpleasant aroma assaulting our nostrils was coming from the baby's diaper, Hubert was finally able to head back down th' trace with all of the clan. Except for Miz Martin, of course.

Since we almost always had stewed chicken and noodles or dumplings for our Sunday supper, at least when Dad and us were batching it, I feel fairly safe in saying that one or the other of them would probably have been simmering away on the kitchen range by the time Miz Martin and her family had first arrived. So except for our breakfasts, which Dad invariably took care of, by setting a double-boiler of oatmeal and raisins on the back of the stove to steep overnight, we were now going to be at Miz Martin's mercy for the balance of however long she decided to stay.

Our toaster in those days was one of those folding wire-grill gizmos that a few of you may have seen in museums. But even though Miz Martin was perfectly familiar with its operation, it was quite apparent the next morning that she hadn't yet mastered the art of controlling our blue-enameled Banquet's cast-iron burners. Consequently, she wound up being pretty apologetic over the fact that most of the toast was almost paper thin, after its charcoal had been scraped into the coal bucket beneath the Banquet's chrome-plated draftdoor. Which was located just in front of our six-foot high, galvanized hot water tank.

And my primary reason for mentioning this handy arrangement is so that there will be no doubt in your mind as to Dad's only being interested in how well our new housekeeper could cook in the kitchen. Because with that big old water-tank to snuggle-up to on a cold winter morning, while the Banquet was chugging merrily along just about two feet to the right side of the tank, it would have been practically impossible to find a better place to get cozy.

So before leaving for his job at the Post Office that morning, Dad asked Miz Martin to make up a list of the things she'd be needing from Carmichael's Grocery, since he figured there would undoubtedly be certain spices and other things that we probably wouldn't have in our somewhat sparse assortment. And despite Kayo's and my combined protest of "Aw, gee whiz Dad, th' only place we keep stuff is in th' kitchen an' cellar.", we were given explicit instructions to devote the morning to showing Miz Martin where all our foodstuffs, dishes, and pans were stored.

But after spending about five minutes opening and closing all the cabinets in the kitchen, and at least that long just waiting for her to get her roly-poly figure out to the top of the stairs leading down into the dusky depths of our outdoor root-cellar, my brother and I were becoming resigned to the fact that we were probably going to have to waste the entire morning.

But after the two of us had preceded Miz Martin down the stairs, "Jist so's ya won't hafta crawl ovuh me, `case Ah rolls all'a way t'th' bottom.", she eventually announced "Well muh'sy me, wil'ya jist look'a all them cay'rots an' poe'tay'toes! Shuh wish ya had'a bin'a root'a'begguhs though, then we could have sum root'a'begguh pie. Oh'well, theahs'a bottle'a vinigah, s'awl jist fixum Vinagah D'liaht en'sted. An' Ah see's ya got'a lot'a ham'n bacon too, so's we'uhl jist fix sum'a thet fuh lunch. If'n yuh'll jist cay'ry a'tup t'th' kitchen fuh me?"

So when Kayo just looked at me and shrugged his shoulders, I said "Sure Miz Martin.", and unhooked the ham from its nail, since I seemed to remember fixing bacon on Friday, the day before Dad boiled up a pot of wieners and sauerkraut for Saturday.

But once she'd huffed and puffed her way back up those eight steps and out into the sunlight once more, she panted "Muh'sy me, but'uh puh'son cud ketch `is death dow'uhn they'uh! Jist go'a `hed an' lay thet ham'n th' kitchen'n go'a `hed'n do whut'evah yuh want, Ah got stuff undah cun'trol now.", I was beginning to think that maybe Miz Martin was going to work out alright after all. And when I came sneaking into the back porch for a clothespin around eleven-thirty, since Skinny McKinny and I needed it for the rubber-gun we were busy making out in Dad's workshop, what I figured must be the Vinegar Delight was sending some really scrumptious smells out of the Banquet's cavernous blue-fronted belly.

But when Dad came trotting home from the Post Office about five minutes past Noon, his mouth all cocked and primed for some real honest to goodness Down South chow, it came pretty close to misfiring when he saw we were having ham again. But at least Miz Martin's potatoes were boiled, rather than fried, even though we had to romp down on our forks pretty hard in order to smash them. Undoubtedly just because she still had quite a way to go in order to conquer high-elevation cooking. She'd also heated a can of green peas, though, which I almost never did when I was in charge of fixing lunch.

But since Dad was never one to jump on a conclusion too soon, at least as long as it didn't look like I might be goofing off down under it, when Miz Martin sort of patted his shoulder right after setting the platter of ham in front of him, and said "Y'all be shuh'n save pleny'a room fuh sum'a mah Vinagah D'liaht, yuh'rin fuh a'real treat.", his face brightened up considerably and he said "I was wondering what it was that smelled so good, Miz Martin."

Well let me tell you, we'd all have been a whole lot better off if we could just have kept right on enjoying the smell, without having to eat the source of it. The poor lady looked so apologetic when she came waltzing into the dining room with it, though, that when she said "It use'ly puffs up'a lil mo'uh than this, s'Ah gis Ah musn'ta got usta yuh stove yet, but Ah will in'a few mo'uh days, yuh jist waitun'see.", it just didn't seem right not to at least try it on for size.

She deserved at least a little credit for waiting to cut it until she set it down on the table, since the way she had to bear down on the knife made it pretty obvious that it was going to be slightly chewy. But right up until the moment she set it in front of us, we hadn't had the slightest idea whether Vinagah Delight was pudding, pie, or cake. So when it arrived in a pie-tin, looking like an overly sticky hot-pad, it was fairly easy to see that it was supposed to be pie.

In all fairness though, I really have to admit that it didn't taste as anemic as it looked, but it sure didn't come close to tasting as good as it smelled. The worst problem I can see that it had, but you've got to remember that it's been slightly over sixty-five years since my sole exposure to it, was that it was so difficult to reduce it to pieces that were small enough to slide down your gullet without hanging up on something en route.

I can still almost see my little brother sitting there at the table, right after he got tired of chewing and swallowed too big a chunk. Because when it lodged about halfway down, his eyes almost doubled in size, exactly the same as Alfalfa's always did, in the "Our Gang Comedies" at the movies. Then he even started trying to stretch his neck the same as Alfalfa did, just to see if maybe that would dislodge the lump inside. But when that didn't work either, he grabbed his glass of milk and just plain dumped it in on top of everything else.

And just as Dad started to jump up and go to the poor kid's rescue, Kayo stretched his neck another fraction of an inch. And down the tube it all went. Now whether you want to believe it or not, the grin of relief on his face looked half again as big as the one Alfalfa always got whenever he thought Darla liked him better than Spanky.

So that night, after the three of us were safely in our bedroom, I asked "Dad, are ya sure Miz Martin's th' kinda cook we need? I know some'a my stuff ain't so hot, but gee whiz, I ain't never pulled as sneaky a stunt on you guys as that Vinegar Delight stuff'a hers."

And Kayo said "Yeah, Dad, if my milk hadn't washed it down when it did, I might not even be alive now."

But Dad just said "Now boys, we've got to try and be fair, you know. It just wouldn't be right not to let her have a few more days to get used to the altitude and the Banquet, just in case that's what's causing the problem. What do you say?"

And since he put it that way, what we said sure wasn't what we were thinking. But even though I've long since forgotten what Miz Martin cooked up for us during the next four days, I do remember that all three of us buried it under an awful lot of Wade Carmichael's ginger snaps and milk, since the lady saw fit to comment one evening "Muh'sy me, but yuh'all shuh' do like gin'ga snaps, don'yuh?"

But by Friday evening, Dad realized that the time to take remedial action had finally arrived. So he said "Miz Martin, I really appreciate how hard you've been trying to look after these boys of mine this week, but I'm afraid they're just going to be too big a job for you to handle."

Before he could say anymore, though, she replied "I bin thinkin' th' same thing fuh a'cup'la days now Mistuh Huffaniggle, s'if yuh'd be kin'da nuff t'cay'ry me back down t'Agnes's place'in th' mawnin', Ah'd rilly `preciate it."

Dad's mouth dropped open then, but it still took several tries before he managed to get out **"IF I'D WHAT?"**

Miz Martin looked pretty startled for several seconds, then she broke out laughing and said "What Ah mean Mistah Huffaniggle, is would yuh'all take me down t'Agnes's in yuh auty'mobile. Ah wouldn' ax yuh, but Ah'm puh'ty shuh thet Hubuht's gone off down t'Gran' Jungshun t'look'fuh wuhk, s'he cain't cum aftuh me."

Dad broke out laughing then and said "Miz Martin, I'll be more than happy to take you down to your daughter's in the morning, but quite frankly you really had me going for a minute there, wanting to know if I'd carry you."

So even though the lady was a positively lousy cook, she really was a good sport. And from the safety of my present position, I can honestly say that most of my memories of our Southern Belle are relatively pleasant ones. It undoubtedly helps a whole lot, though, not having to be concerned about eating any more of her cooking. But despite the impact that Miz Martin had on our lives, we managed to survive.

To My Pen

Exlax I call thee,
For much comes out,
When we're out and about,
My oh so precious pen
You and me.

An Odious Ode That's Truly Owed An' Long Overdue

Oh let's give'a jeer boys, but on second thought, one won't do

So I su'pose there's nothin' for it, but t'add another two

For who else in this great land'a th' Ol' Red, White, an' Blue

Comes anywhere near as close, as th' heroic blokes'a th' B-yoo-ro

A'th' ol' I. R. S. do, t'makin' our lives such'a clam'orus mess?

S'come on, sing out at th' top'a yer lungs, ain't no need t'bleed

Er act nervous, an' even tho' its'a fact th'glorious folks at th'

Ol' Revvynoo Service're tirelessly workin' an' never a'shirkin'

their sworn duty (at least until th' free coffee's hot) t'deprive

Us'a th' beauty that comes from thinkin' we've paid our share

an' can slump in'a chair an' spit at th' pot an' jist rest awhile.

Now I can't help but think (since I've no free coffee t'drink)

That things're startin' t'stink, when'a man's considered guilty

Until he can prove otherwise, er otherwise why're we always'a

gettin' their nasty form-letters that threaten t'place us in fetters

unless we send'm more loot with th' Postal galoot who's always

a'rootin an' tootin' around in his weird
lookin' truck with th' chains

that're still bangin' an' clangin' in th'
middle a'July. So why, oh why

do they always feel that we lie, after we've
already sent `em th' biggest

chunk'a th' pie? An' oh my how they howl
an' cuss when they eventually

discover that most've us would rather invite
these round-headed hounds

that insist it's their God-given right t'bite
th' hand that feeds `em, jist t'git

their hands out've our pocket an' ram their
rocket-like noses straight up our

collective **Bureau of Internal Rectal Sanctity!**

That which is obvious and generously given,

One Cold Sonovagun

Although most of us have a tendency to become somewhat cynical while we're stumbling from one so-called catastrophe to another, every so often we end up meeting someone who makes us realize that things could just as easily be a lot worse than they are. And since that's pretty much what old Moose Moore did for me, quite a few years ago, we might just as well see if he can do the same for you.

One of the things that Moose always enjoyed as much or more than anything else, was spinning a yarn while sharing a cup of coffee with his friends at the old Sourdough Roadhouse, several miles south of Paxon. And even though it was pretty hard to tell whether he was just making one up, I finally noticed the way his eyes would begin to twinkle when he was getting ready to dump another windy on us. Right up until he'd actually reached the end of it, though, and had sat there nursing his cup for a minute or two, if it had been the gospel truth, he'd always add "An' that's a bona fide fact!" But if it had been just another bucket of hot air, he'd slam one hand down on the table and yell "Got'cha again, didn't I?" And talk about cackle, it's a flat-out miracle that he didn't strangle before he came up for air!

I really enjoyed all of his stories, but my favorite was the one about how cold it got the first winter he spent at his placer-claim on the McClaren River. So I'll try and relate it just the way he told it the last time I heard it, or at least as close as I can come to it.

"Ya can talk about cold all ya want Sonny, but ya'd had to'a been with me that first winter up on the McClaren, in order t'really know what ya was talkin' about. I'd spent the biggest part'a the summer tryin' to git me a grubstake, ya see, jist workin' at a cannery down in Prince William Sound. An' by the time both me an' the dang fish was played out, I knew I was really gonna hafta hustle to git to my claim an' build a cabin before the weather jist plain got nasty. Knew there was no way I could beat the first few snows, mind ya, but I sure as the devil counted on beatin' the really bad stuff.

Well sir, by the time I got all my gear freighted from Paxon to the river, then built me a raft an' floated ever'thing down to the claim I'd staked the year before, most'a the leaves was off the brush an' the river was makin' shore-ice pert near ever' night. The main reason I'd staked that claim sure wasn't because I figgered I was gonna git rich neither, no sirree! That little valley perched there on that big bend in the river jist like a reg'lar Garden of Eden, an' I was more than willin' to swap my share'a Eve's apples fer the berries that was growin' all over the place.

The little crick runnin' down the middle of it had jist about the clearest an' sweetest water I'd ever drank anywhere, an' there was more'n enough of it to wash my gravel with, too. But the real clincher was all that spruce timber linin' both banks'a the crick. That jist had to be the purtiest stand'a timber I'd ever seen in all my trampin' around Alaska's hills. Why that valley must'a had at least half a jillion trees in it, an' most of 'em was all the same size. Jist plumb perfect fer cabin logs ya know, about thirty-five er forty feet tall, an' eight, maybe ten inches acrost the stump. So I jist knew that by the time I trimmed their tails, I'd wind up with a big enough pile'a twenty-footers to build me a reg'lar dream of a cabin with. Why man, them logs didn't hardly taper anymore'n a couple inches at the very most.

Well sir, I picked me a spot on a little bench that was maybe five feet higher'n the crick bed, an' about a hundred feet back from the edge. Always did enjoy bein' able to lay in the sack at night, listenin' to a crick sing its song. Ain't no sweeter music in the world, ya know, least'wise as far as I'm concerned. 'Specially when dang near ever' night'a the year some dog-wolf takes it in 'is head to yodel fer 'is sweetheart. Great Gawd-a-mighty, a man can git to feelin' like there ain't no point at all in tryin' to find the trail to paradise when he dies. Not when he's already bin there fer the best part of 'is life, there sure as heck ain't.

Well sir, after I got the spot fer the cabin swamped out, I left only an occasional tree between it an' the crick, then I cut a twenty-foot swath down the near side, t'where the crick hit the McClaren. Wasn't over a hundred an' twenty yards altogether, an' there was a long stretch'a marshy ground right there that had more'n enough sweet willows in it t'feed a dozen head'a moose. See what I mean about it's bein' such a plu-perfect paradise of a spot? Why after I cleared that swath, I could set right there on my door-stoop, with my rifle across my lap an' my coffee mug in one fist, an' pick out jist about any size bull I wanted. An' jist about any dang time I needed one, too.

I'd already made up my mind that there was no way I was gonna settle fer a dang dirt floor, ya see, long before I started droppin' trees. So countin' the fifty-five t'sixty logs I was gonna need fer the walls, I had t'figger on roughly another thirty er thirty-five fer the floor. An' at least two an' a half times that many fer the roof, since I wanted a good sized porch out in front.

But even with a three foot overhang on the sides, fer stackin' firewood under, the roof logs only had t'be about fifteen feet long. So a'course they was quite'a bit lighter than the wall logs when it come t'draggin' 'em outta the woods. But that give me the idea that I might jist as well use what was left'a the tails t'put a second layer on top'a the first one, jist in case the snow ever wound up gittin' deeper'n the four er five feet I was figgerin' on.

So, jist in case your 'rithmatic's a little rusty, that meant I had t'cut at least a hundred'n sixty-five trees, an' git 'em piled in the shape of'a cabin in slightly more'n a month's time. Believe you me, I might jist as well'a saved the time it took t'set my tent up when I first got there, because I sure as the devil spent dang little time in the raggedy sucker. I had all them logs cut in jist under a week, but by the time I got 'em all drug t'where they needed t'be, my behind was plowin' a deeper furrow than the off-end'a them logs. An' another whole week had slid through my fingers jist like so much dust.

Why I was s'gol'danged pooped the evenin' I drug that last log in, I wound up decidin' t'give this six-foot-four hunk'a hide'n hair a quick bath in the crick, an' then I crawled straight inta bed t'see if I couldn't grab a full six hours'a sleep fer once. Well sir, I dropped right off the edge'a the world almost as quick as I hit the sack, but I couldn't a'been there more'n a half-bucket's worth'a winks, when all hell broke loose in the willow-pasture down by the river. An' even though I didn't know fer absolute certain what was goin' on until the next mornin', I was purty sure from all the bawlin' an' bellerin' that a couple grizzlies must be havin' a free-fer-all over somethin'.

So I lay there in the dark fer the next two, maybe three hours, listenin' to 'em. But jist when I'd start thinkin' things was gonna git peaceable again, one'a them nasty suckers'd have another go at the other one, an' I'd fergit all about sleep fer the next twenty minutes er so. Fin'ly though, an' it must'a been somewhere close t'midnight by then, I jist plain passed out.

It was full daylight when I come to, a'course, so I grabbed my ol' Enfield an' headed fer the pasture t'see what all the fuss had been about. Man-oh-man, you talk about a battlefield, why there must'a been at least five hundred square-feet'a that ground that didn't hardly have a blade'a grass that was still standin'. An' there was s'much bear-hair spread around that there should'a been at least half a dozen bare-butted bears scattered up'n down the river someplace. But when I found what was left of a calf-moose carcass, I figgered out the rest'a the story by readin'a good thirty minutes worth'a tracks.

Apparently the calf an' its mama had crossed the river t'feed on the willows right at dark, right about the same time I'd sacked out. Well sir, one'a them dang bears must'a jist come out'a the timber below my camp, so he caught sight of 'em jist about the time they hit the willows. He didn't run no more'n a hundred feet before he nailed that calf tight t'the ground. Must'a broke its neck with the first slap, because as far as I could tell, the cow didn't waste any time in headin' fer other parts.

That bear prob'ly hadn't much more'n dug in, though, when the other one come chargin' in from across the river. He'd more'n likely caught wind'a that hot moose blood an' you can jist bet he figgered on grabbin' his share. Y'know, the more I see'a them mangy devils, the less use I got fer 'em. Why most of 'em er so gol'danged ornery it's a miracle their own mamas don't do 'em in before they're half grown. Remind me a whole lot'a some'a the two-legged varmints I've known, always wantin' what the other guy's got, an' not givin' a tinker's damn how they go about gittin' it!

The only thing on that calf that wasn't plumb tore t'smithereens was the head, so after I cut the tongue out, I threw ever' last scrap I could find in the river. I knew I was gonna have t'keep my eyes peeled fer bears fer several weeks anyhow, at least until some'a the fresh blood smell wore off. But I figgered all my choppin' an' bangin' on the cabin would prob'ly keep 'em outta my hair. Kind'a funny thinkin' about it now though, no more hair'n what's left on my poor ol' noggin. But boy howdy, if ya think that fresh tongue didn't slide down my chute easy that night, ya sure got another think comin'. Moose tongue's jist about the very best there is, ya know.

Well sir, it didn't take me hardly any time at all t'git the sill-logs in place. But since me'n a foot-adze ain't hardly ever been any more'n jist barely on speakin' terms, you'd be right on target thinkin' them thirty-odd floor logs took quite awhile t'whittle out. Took'a right fair batch'a hide off the palms'a my hands too, before them suckers was flat enough t'pass fer'a floor. If I could jist'a took my time with 'em it wouldn'ta been s'bad, but I flat-out didn't have any time t'give away. Once I fin'ly got done with 'em though, the walls seemed t'sprout right on up, almost like that Jack kid's fairy-tale beans.

It was a little different story with the roof beams though. Them suckers had t'be a good twenty-five feet long t'give me the porch I wanted, an' I wound up havin' t'use seven instead'a five, since they wasn't quite as big around as I figgered they ought'a be. But by the time I got them heavy dang things up where I wanted 'em, I was beginnin' t'think havin' a porch might not be such a hot idea after all. I didn't want no posts under the off-end y'see, because I knew that more'n likely I'd never be able t'keep the frost-heave from jackin' that end'a the roof up ever' winter. Well sir, the first six inches'a snow come the night I got them beam-logs up, which was real lucky, since that soggy stuff turned them fresh logs greasy in a hurry.

Took me all the next day jist t'get half the first layer of roof-logs on one side, but things went a whole lot better the next day. Because once I had that first section of roof t'work from, I got smart an' started cross-haulin' the rest'a the logs up on a couple gin-poles, with a doubled-up chunk'a rope. The same way loggers use'ta load their wagons. That first day I'd pulled 'em up endways with my block an' tackle, an' by dark I was sure as the devil wonderin' why Mama had wound up raisin' such a dumb jackass, instead of a perfessor, believe me.

The way I'd built that roof was the way you'd ord'narily do when you was gonna pile sod on it, but I'd had a streak'a luck before leavin' the cannery, an' had wound up with enough sheets'a corrugated iron t'cover my roof with, jist fer tearin' down an ol' shed they was wantin' t'git rid of. Took some real doin' t'git the dang stuff to the McClaren though, but it sure ended up bein' worth all the trouble. But since it was more'n a little on the rusty side, an' I didn't know how much load I could trust it t'carry, I played it safe an' made dang sure there was plenty'a wood underneath t'keep it from cavein' in on top'a me some night.

I'd been figgerin' on usin' a fifteen gallon oil drum fer a stove, but when I got t'Paxon, the guy I hired t'haul my stuff t'the river told me about an old wreck of a shack that had a real cast iron stove in it. It was one'a them oblong suckers that all the railroads use'ta put in their cabooses. Two'a the legs was busted off, but what the heck? A couple rocks would hold the fool thing off the floor jist as good, an' I already knew there was plenty'a them where I was headed. The packer told me that the old guy that'd owned the shack must'a went off 'is rocker a couple winters before, an' had jist blowed the whole top of his head off with a twelve-guage wad'a buckshot.

Man-oh-man! If you think I wasn't some kind'a proud the night I got moved outta that tent an' into the cabin, you jist ain't never seen proud. I'd stuck'a two foot-square hunk'a window glass on each side'a the door, an' it's a flat wonder I didn't wear the hinges out that night, I was in an' out so dang much. Ya see, up until then I never had no idea how purty a plain ol' lantern can look, when it's shinin' through the windows'a the cabin ya've jist busted yer butt buildin'!

The very next mornin' I looked out one'a them windows before I fired up the stove, an' whether ya want'a believe it er not, right at that very minute, a fat three year old bull was wadin' the crick jist above where it dumped inta the river. Why it was almost like some kind'a omen, or whatever you want'a call it, because I jist plain knew that Providence was grinnin' down on me fer some reason. An' when I eased the door open an' poked the business end'a that Enfield out, I could almost swear that sonovagun looked at me an' winked. It was a plumb eerie feelin', I tell ya! But I felt some better when he went down without hardly even twitchin' a muscle. Felt a whole bunch better yet, though, when I got `im opened up and seen how fat he was.

Since I hadn't had time t'build me a reg'lar cache yet, I had t'hang the meat from a pole I run between a couple trees right close t'the cabin. I knew the meat would freeze plumb through in a couple days, so even though I'd rather'a had it age awhile before it froze, I had t'be content with jist knowin' the martens an' camp-robbers wouldn't be makin' off with too much of it. Gittin' a heap'a dry wood cut an' drug t'the cabin was a whole bunch more important than buildin' a cache right then, so I spent the next few weeks skiddin' ten-foot lengths'a wood in on a little sled I rigged up. I didn't figger on buckin' `em inta chunks until I had a pile'a logs that I was purty sure would last me fer at least the biggest part'a the winter.

Up until I'd fin'ly got the cabin finished, ya see, it'd only snowed about a foot er fifteen inches. But after I started skiddin' that firewood, it seemed like ever' couple nights er so we'd git some more. So by the middle'a December there was a good three an' a half feet in the timber. Out on the open riverbank, though, where the wind could git at it, part'a the ground was dang near bare. But wherever there was a stand'a birch er willows, that the moose could feed on, the dang drifts was a good five er six feet deep. An' even though it hadn't got much more'n thirty below yet, I seen that the neighborhood mamas an' their kids was havin' a purty hard time'a findin' enough browse. So I started puttin' my webs on jist about ever' day, an' hikin' either up the river er down fer a ways. Until fin'ly it must've amounted t'four er five miles that I was goin'.

It was a fairly easy deal fer me t'git at the moose-grub with my webs on, but them poor critters was flat havin' a time bustin' trails through all that drifted snow, don't ya know. Wasn't hard enough t'hold `em up, a'course. That's why I started usin' my ax t'lop off birch-limbs an' willow-tops fer `em. I can tell you, it wasn't very long before I had a reg'lar herd'a the poor things waitin' fer me ever' mornin'. But when the wind's kickin' up its heels, even if it is only thirty below, it can git t'feelin' like it'd be real easy to frost yer fritters, believe me. Once I had `em countin' on me, though, I jist couldn't see lettin' `em down. So day after day ya could'a found us traipsin' up er down that riverbank. That is, ya could if ya was dang fool stupid enough t'come lookin' fer us.

Watchin' them calves stoke their furnaces on that easy grub made me feel purty warm inside, though. But up until I fin'ly made some mukluks out'a that bullhide I'd saved, my feet was sure as heck givin' me fits. An' as far as tannin' that hide'd went, since I didn't ak'shuly know tan from purple, all I'd done was give it a good soak in a salt-brine t'set the hair, then I rubbed a bunch'a the gizzard-lard inta the bald side after it dried out. I ain't exageratin' a dang bit when I tell ya I'd got a good two gallons'a lard outta that critter's lights alone. Why man, it's a flat-out wonder that goofy sucker hadn't starved t'death, jist from all that lard mashin' his guts shut.

Well sir, Christmas come an' went, then jist'a couple nights after New Year's I was riddin' up my supper dishes when all of a sudden the short-hair on my whole carcass started feelin' like it was fixin' t'march right out the door with me. I couldn't see any of it jumpin' off my arms, but jist about the time I started feelin' the long stuff on top'a my head come to attention, I glanced out one'a the windows an' it looked like the whole dang world must be on fire. Why the way the red light was bouncin' off the snow made me think the roof must be burnin' er somethin', so I grabbed the dishpan full'a water an' charged out the door t'see what I could do with that.

That was when I heard this kind'a sizzlin' sound, almost like when we use'ta render out hog cracklin's back in Iowa. I'd run into an ol' yayhoo up on th' Yukon one time, who'd told me about how the Northern Lights'd git s'fired up sometimes that they'd jist start singin', but I figgered he'd jist been out in the hills by hisself too long an' had drifted right on over th' edge. I know better now, though, because that was sure enough what was goin' on that night. Why it was jist s'gol-dang purty that I wound up standin' out there 'til I was almost froze, before I even thought about how I should'a put my parky on.

Some'a the time the sky looked jist like an angel must be up there shakin' coals out the grates'a Heaven's furnace, if ya can picture that. An' at other times it was almost like he was dumpin' all the gold, silver, an' emeralds out of 'is purse, jist so those of us down below could ketch our share of 'em. I'm tellin' ya, when I fin'ly froze completly out an' come back inside, I was sure enough wonderin' who'd been pullin' the strings on that show. Then, after I'd crawled into my sack an' blowed out the lantern, I must'a laid there fer a full two hours, jist watchin' those colors come squirtin' through my windows. I sure wouldn'ta traded places with any man on earth right then, an' by Jingo that's a sure enough fact.

But when my feet hit the deck the next mornin', it plumb felt like I'd plopped 'em down on a dang iceberg. I'd only thought it was cold on the floor, though, because when I opened the front'a the stove, the real cold started shootin' down the stovepipe an' spreadin' across the floor like it thought it owned the dang place. An' even after I shoved a wad'a dry boughs and fairy-hair inside, I had t'light four er five matches before I found one that'd do anymore'n jist glow a little bit. The fairy-hair caught right away, but by the time that fool stove quit hiccupin' an' belchin' smoke, I thought I was gonna choke fer sure. An' the way the sucker started bangin' an' clangin' reminded me fer all the world'a that little steam engine Mama use'ta tell me about when I was little. Sounded jist like it was tryin' t'say "I think I can, I think I can,

I think I can." But I sure wouldn'ta made any bets on its gettin' the job done fer at least ten more minutes.

When I fin'ly worked up enough nerve t'go outside an' see if I could find the mercury in the fool thermometer, at first I thought some varmint must'a swiped most of it durin' the night, because there wasn't one solitary speck in the tube. The fifty below mark was a good half inch above the ball, so I knew full well it was at least sixty below, er maybe even seventy. I'd got chilly durin' the night, ya see, but after I'd drug the feather-tick off the comp'ny bunk an' piled it on top'a me, I'd warmed right up an' gone back t'sleep.

Y'know, it sure is funny the way'a man's mind can git t'doin' 'im at times. I knew gol-dang well there was jist no way I dared t'go out an' chop feed fer the critters when it was that cold, so I stayed there in the cabin that whole day, jist hustlin' out fer another armload'a wood whenever the last one had turned t'smoke. Why I must'a made the trip back an' forth t'the woodpile a dozen times all told, but ever' time it was over so quick that I never even noticed what was takin' place around the cabin. A couple times I'd thought I could feel the floor quiver a little. An' two, maybe three times I thought I heard somethin' go thump. But I jist passed it off as the ice on the river, crackin' an' settlin'.

Y'see, when it gits really cold like that, the water starts freezin' off upstream. An' before ya know it, there'll be whole big sections'a ice with nothin' between 'em an' what little water's left, but maybe two er three feet'a air. The ice keeps shrinkin', an' gettin' brittler an' brittler then, until all of a sudden, a whole big chunk'll bust loose with'a "ka-boom." A'course if it's big enough when it hits bottom, ya can usually feel the ground shake fer quite a ways.

So that's what I thought was goin' on that whole dang afternoon, ya see. Then jist at dark I headed out the door fer another load'a wood an' dang near tripped over a calf moose. His mama was pressed tight against 'im on the far side, almost like she was tryin' t'hold him right up snug against the wall. Then I heard a grunt right around the corner'a the cabin, an' I thought I saw somethin' movin' toward me. Well sir, I grabbed two, three more chunks'a wood an' hightailed it back through the door jist like some dumb kid that's scared of 'is own shadow.

After a few minutes, though, I realized that all the dang grizzlies had denned up a long time before, so I grabbed the lantern an' eased the door open again. That calf tried t'git to 'is feet, a'course, but 'is mama jist plain wasn't about t'let 'im do it. Jist then the snow crunched around the corner an' there was another soft grunt, so I eased the lantern around t'where I could see what the devil was goin' on. Well sir, I know good an' well ya ain't gonna believe this, but there was six sets'a eyeballs lined up in a double row that went plumb t'the back end'a the cabin. Then, when I caught sight'a what looked like a couple more noses pokin' around that corner, I decided t'ease on back there an' check 'em out. Why fer cryin' out loud, I knew by then that it jist about had t'be some kind'a goofy dream, an' that I was bound t'wake up before long. S'why not find out jist how crazy it really was.

An' by the time I made it all the way around the cabin, I'd counted eleven cows an' thirteen calves layin' jist as close t'the walls as they could git, so there was two sets'a twins in the bunch. The youngsters was all more'n jist'a little skittish, mind you, but them mamas jist laid there battin' their eyes at me like ever'thing was A-okay as far as they was concerned. I realized then, that even though I hadn't noticed it before, the temperature must'a been easin' lower an' lower all that whole day, so I'm purty sure it had t'be at least seventy-five below.

A'course, since I was still halfway convinced I must be dreamin', after I got back inside by the stove, I sat there fer dang near an hour, pinchin' ever'thing I could think of that might wake me up. The longer I sat there, though, the more I started thinkin' it really must be happenin', an' it wasn't no dream. All I could figger, was that after I'd fed 'em fer s'long, those cows'd decided they could trust me. An' whether they could smell it er what, I'll never know, but somehow they knew there was enough heat seepin' through the walls'a the cabin t'keep them kids'a their's from freezin' t'death. So I done what had t'be done a'course, an' kept that stove pumpin' out all the heat it would fer the next three days. I never got much more'n an hour's sleep at any one spell, because I took t'layin' down on my bunk with nothin' over me, jist so's I'd wake up as soon as the fire started gittin' low. An' even though I wasn't too awful worried about runnin' myself out'a wood, it was a real big relief when it fin'ly started warmin' back up on the evenin'a the third day.

The next mornin' it was all the way back up t'twenty below, so I got out my webs an' ax, an' headed straight fer the willow pantry. Man-oh-man but them critters ate a mess'a brush that day.

I s'pose ya prob'ly thought I got the name Moose tacked onto me because'a my size, er on account'a this flat nose'a mine. But when I ran into my packer friend the next summer an' happened t'mention what had took place durin' that cold snap, he started callin' me Moose. An' it wasn't too long before ever'body else was doin' it too. That three day spell was flat-out one cold sonovagun, an' I jist don't give diddly-squat about ever seein' another one like it. An' that'sa fact.

The last time I heard Moose tell this story, there were three or four other guys sitting around the barrel-stove in the old Sourdogh Roadhouse, between Gulkana and Paxon. They all broke out laughing when he finished, of course, and when they went out the door to climb into their pickups, they were still shaking their heads as though it was the most ridiculous thing they'd ever heard. Moose was getting pretty frail by then, and the walking-stick he'd begun using a few years earlier was lying on the floor beside his chair.

After the others had driven off down the highway, he looked over at me and winked, then he slapped both legs the way he always had when he'd finished one of his windies, and his chair hit the floor just as loud as it ever had. He didn't start cackling this time, though, and I could almost swear there were tears in his eyes when he whispered, just barely loud enough so I could hear him, "An' that's a bona fide fact, whether ya want'a believe it er not."

There were tears in my eyes too, a few months later. And they weren't caused by the slip-stream coming through the open window of the Super Cub I was in, either. They were there solely because I'd just sent my old friend's ashes streaming toward where a small spot of rusty, red roof was barely visible, down among what was still the prettiest stand of spruce on the McClaren River. So when I finally released the urn, and watched it tumble end over end toward the ground, I couldn't help wondering whether Moose had indeed been telling just another windy, about those cows and calves crowding around his cabin that night.

But right at that precise moment, a large bull came trotting out of the timber on the west side of the McClaren and began wading straight toward the willow-pasture, his heavy antlers rocking from side to side. I suppose it was probably only my imagination, but for just a second or two I could almost swear I heard Moose chuckling again. On the way back to the airstrip at Gulkana, though, where I'd left my pickup when I'd chartered the Cub, I couldn't help wondering if maybe what had taken place the night it got so cold, had happened solely because the Old Guy in charge of things felt that a little something extra was called for. It really would be nice to actually know that for sure, now wouldn't it?

With Visions Of Grandeur or Sugar Plums, anyhow

It happened again just this mornin', don't ya see
Precisely at four o'clock it was, or almost, I think
At least accordin' to the clock on the stand beside the bed
But since I'd been dreamin' I was standin' right on the brink
Of finally achievin' the greatness that I still seek
I decided I might as well get up and go take a leak
And then of course, tho' her voice sounded purty hoarse
And I really couldn't be sure of what all she'd said
I thought my ol' woman asked if I'd bring `er a drink
And since water was what I brought, that's what she got
Honest injun tho', I really didn't mean to dump it on `er head
But man-oh-man if you'd only seen how quick she turned red
I swear, you'da swore that dang water must've been hot
So since things wasn't goin' as good as I'd hoped they would
At least as far as me and the little woman was concerned
I decided they prob'ly wouldn't get no worse
If I tried my hand at stirrin' up some verse
So that's what I done and oh oh, I gotta run
Because that was my phone that rang

Hunh, what's that yer babblin' about Harriet?
Well now Holy cow, that'd prob'ly suit my ol' lady just fine
But if that goofy coffee house gang down at Latitude 59
Actually was able to swing a big enough loop
To rope in yer whole dang literary group
I ain't too awful sure I wanta become Homer's only nominee
HunhNow just hold on a dang minute gal, don't go gittin' sore
And say a buncha things we're both gonna be sorry for
Harriet I didn't flat-out say IHarriet?
Aww Criminy, she went and hung up!
But I guess if she feels that strong about it
Maybe I really oughta let `em try to see
If they can fix it up for me to be Alaska's next Poet Lariet!
Or at least the one after
So maybe it'd be a good idea for me to go see
If I can find where I put my Rhymin' Dictionary
Because there's only so many times
A feller can get away with usin' the same ol' rhymes
At least if he
Aww, Judas Priest, now someone's poundin' on the stupid door
It sure would be nice if Harriet's already over `er mad
One thing's for sure tho', it can't be Mister Opportunity
Since some dunce once said he hardly ever knocks twice.
**HOLD ON DADBLAME IT, I'M COMIN'
JUST AS FAST AS I CAN!**

Hey Doc, What's Up

"Ya know", he said, "th' main trouble with bein' born good-lookin', as well as stupid an' naked, is that ya gotta waste so damn much time jist puttin' beans in yer belly an' rags on yer butt. But if I hadn't wound up bein' so damn handsome, ol' Kay back there prob'ly wouldn'ta gave me a second glance, an' then where do ya think I'd be?"

Before I could think of an appropriate answer to that one, the lanky, grizzled character standing behind the bar slapped his huge hand down on its glossy surface and yelled "Well I'll jist tell ya where th' hell I'd prob'ly be. Back there in that gawddam hot ol' kitchen, is where! Jista slingin' slop an' soapsuds all over th' place, an' most likely wishin' that one'a you dang moneybags'd buy me a cold beer. Hell's fire, don't none'a you goofy suckers have any idea what that bell hangin' up there over yer heads is s'posed t'be for?"

Since there were only two of us sitting on the stools, he reached up and jangled it loud enough to wake the dead, saying "Well, I guess it's up t'me again! Man oh man, but I sure have been gittin' more than my share a'dang cheapskates in this here joint lately."

Just as he was reaching into the cooler for three more cans of beer, his wife, Kay, came out of the kitchen with a big grin on her face and sat down on the stool beside me. There were smudges of flour on her cheeks, extending all the way up into her hairline, which her left hand began dabbing at with one corner of her apron. But before any of us had the slightest idea as to what she had in mind, her right hand shot across the bar and deposited at least a tablespoon of flour all through Doc's beard. Then she said "Now you look like you've actually been earning your keep, instead of just bumping your gums, you homely old bag of hot air."

Squirming around on the top of the stool as though she was trying to change the location of some seams or wrinkles in her under-pants, she now said "And unless you want another shot of the same thing, that third beer had damn well better be for me."

Seeing the exaggerated look of dismay that immediately washed over his face, she then added "Oh alright, go on and pull another one out. One of these guys'll probably buy a piece of hot blueberry pie before they get sick of listening to you, then we should at least break even for today."

Reaching over and laying her hand on top of mine, she looked straight at Doc before continuing "And who knows, maybe you'll wind up passing out and I'll get an offer from one of these guys that'll be just too good to pass up?"

It was just this kind of give and take banter that had made Kay and Doc Pease so well-liked by all of us who frequented the Lake Louise area of Alaska, when they were still operating their lodge there. And while you could generally count on a fair percentage of Doc's yarns being little more than figments of his ever-agile imagination, there was almost always one or two tidbits of worthwhile information buried in them somewhere. Even if it did take quite a while for them to swim to the surface.

One sunny day back in the mid-1960's, my wife and I had gone into K-Doc Lodge to have a cool one and see if we could pry the location of some good lake-trout fishing out of Doc. Feeling that it might tend to bring him down out of the clouds and into the realm of realty a little quicker, I'd also bought him a beer. So after we'd tipped our cans at one another and offered up a prayer for the coming year's bountiful hop and barley harvest, I hit him smack between the eyes with the most pitiful and woebegone look you ever saw. Then I opened with "Man oh man, Doc, where in hell can a guy find any lakers around this gawdfersaken puddle? Me an' th' ol' lady here has been from one end of it to th' other, an' we ain't had even one lousy bite."

He sat there staring at me for what seemed like an eternity, his right forefinger beating out a tattoo on his can of suds, and just about the time I was beginning to think I'd fired off a dud, he said "Can't understand why everyone's so damn hooked on them spotted vultures, not when there's some really choice grub swimmin' around in th' same water."

Seeing the look on my face change into one of befuddlement, he said "I'm talkin' about lingcod, man. Er to be more precise, burbot. Most of us all call 'em lingcod though, er freshwater ling. Now there's some'a th' best eatin' th' Almighty ever invented. Leastwise th' way my gal Kay fixes it, it is."

After the passage of several second's of silence, my wife, Dee, asked "And just how does she fix it, Doc?"

The tip of his tongue made at least three full trips around his mouth, stopping occasionally to probe at some unseen object in its wooly perimeter, then his eyes rolled about halfway back over the top and he said "Oh, I don't know, 'bout three er four differ'nt ways I guess."

When Dee gave him her best "I don't know why I even try talking to you" look, he burst out laughing and said "There ain't really no wrong way'a fixin' it, ya know. Why I'll bet that woman could boil up a mess of it in gasoline, an' ya'd still swear it was manna from heaven. But I guess if I actually had t'pick th' way I like it best, I'd hafta say it was her beer-batter, deep-fried way."

About that time he slid off his perch behind the bar, pitched his now empty can into a box underneath, then he jerked the cooler open and hauled out two more beers for him and me, plus a coke for Dee. Then, after taking a long pull from his can, he said "There jist ain't no way I can talk about lingcod without'a beer to wash down my slobbers, ya know. Anyhow, when ol' Kay sets a bowl'a them crispy gold nuggets down in front'a me, it's jist like free popcorn night at th' movies. Because I can stuff my face 'til I'm plumb ready t'pop, but if th' platter ain't run dry by then, before I know what's happenin', my hand'll shoot out an' grab another chunk. Why there jist couldn't be no better way to die, ya know, than t'bust yer gut open with fresh lingcod."

After we'd all chuckled over that thought for awhile, he continued with "But let me tell ya, when it's boiled jist long enough so it turns white, which ain't hardly any time at all, then dipped in butter th' same way as lobster, it's damn near as good as deep-fried. An' it flat beats th' hell outta clams, fer makin' chowder. Aw hell, I guess there really ain't no way I don't like it best."

Realizing that the entire day could very easily pass before Doc ran out of gas, I turned to Dee and said "Come on Babe, drink up. It looks like we asked the wrong guy about lake-trout."

Looking more or less like he thought I'd thrown a low blow, Doc now said "Hey ol' buddy, I didn't come right out an' say I didn't know where t'catch'a trout. See that long white cliff over there on th' far side'a th' lake?", and he pointed a bony finger at the window in a generally northeast direction. "Well sir, if yer so all fired set on wastin' yer time, ya might jist as well do it over in front'a them sand cliffs."

So after put-putting our way across what was probably right at four miles of open-water, fifteen minutes after we'd begun trolling, we were in the process of netting our first laker. If I remember correctly, though, we trolled for at least another hour to get the next one. Then a stiffening breeze began breeding whitecaps on the lake's surface and we decided we'd probably caught enough fish for one day.

Somewhere close to five miles across at its widest point, and twice that much in length, Lake Louise is connected at its north end to Lake Susitna, via what is now a narrow, man-modified channel. Some twelve or fifteen miles further north, Lake Susitna turns into a third, relatively small lake, called Tyone. So depending upon whether a boater gets confused by the numerous channels and arms in Susitna, and runs out of gas, or chugs out into the middle of a deceptively calm Louise, there's more than enough cool, clear water to dampen any weekend admiral's hackles.

There are places in both of the larger lakes where it's completely possible to step out of your boat into water that's less than waist deep, right out in the so-called middle. But there are also any number of spots where the water may be two hundred feet or more deep. And every bit of it is usually cold enough to set your teeth to chattering in only a few minutes. But since the main thing that has an appreciable effect on a lake's surface is wind, it's never too smart to hang around out in the middle of Louise or Susitna when a breeze begins to blow. Because the longer a lake is, the more chance the waves have to grow into genuine trouble-makers.

Even though I tried to make it a regular practice to swing by Doc and Kay's lodge whenever I had time to spare at the lakes, I always kept my boat moored at another lodge, located about half a mile south of K-Doc, or Evergreen, as it eventually came to be called. Started by Ruth and Earl Moats, Lake Louise Lodge was the one I happened to go to the first time I visited the lake in the fall of 1963. And since I didn't meet Kay and Doc until after I'd gotten to know Ruth and Earl, I had no real reason to change roosts.

Back then, it was a common occurrence for the owners of the various lodges to swing by one of the other establishments every so often, just to say 'Hi' and have a beer or cup of coffee. And whenever one of them headed out to the highway to pick up their own mail, they'd always bring their neighbor's back with them. Because, when you're making a thirty-plus mile roundtrip, on a rough, gravel road, it'd be damned un-neighborly to do otherwise. And you just never know when a good neighbor's going to make the difference in whether you live or die, in a place where the temperature drops into the minus fifties or lower every winter. Which is plenty cold enough to turn heating oil into a thick goo that just plain refuses to flow through the line from the tank to your stove. And if you've never seen 86 proof whiskey turn into a chunk of ice, then it's only because you've never been where the temperature drops lower than forty-five below.

Consequently, several stories about Doc came to me via Ruth and Earl. And even though I can't guarantee that I remember them exactly as they were related, I should be able to come close enough so it won't make a whole lot of difference one way or the other. You see, Doc was one of those nuts that always seemed to feel he had as much right to fly as any other duck, and if the facts were only known, he probably walked away from as many crashes as any pilot that ever splashed down on Lake Louise.

According to Ruth, one day Doc flew out to the highway to pick up the mail, more than likely in his Super-cub, since that was the make of plane he usually flew. The main reason I said "more than likely", is simply because I can't help seeing images of that helmet and roller-skate clad bird in the comic-strip, Shoe, whenever I think of Doc's flying anywhere at all. I'm reasonably sure Ruth said he was wearing his airplane instead of roller-skates, though, when he buzzed their place that day.

By the time she got outside to see where their bundle of mail was going to land, it already had. Right up on top of the roof. Seeing what had happened, Doc made a tight turn, which to be completely truthful about it, could have been said about most of his turns, since tight was a fairly common condition for him. As he came back over the lodge, the bottom of his floats were barely thirty feet above the roof, and just as he leaned his head out the window to yell "Sorry about that, Rrruuuthhhh", he saw a tree-top sprout directly in front of him.

There were still quite a few trees around the lodge in those days, but this one just happened to be a good six feet taller than all the others. Despite some instantaneous maneuvering and even quicker cussing, the plane's prop now began squirting spruce needles all over the windshield. And by the time Doc realized he was probably going to crash, he was doing just that. As luck would have it, though, when all the water settled back in place, the plane was still right side up, squatting semi-serenely on its floats.

Since the engine was still running (although I seem to recall Ruth's saying it was always more of a lope than a run), as soon as Doc's knees stopped knocking, he headed across the lake toward his place, with the Cub sounding like half its pistons had fallen out of their cages. But that was pretty much the way Doc himself actually sounded, the biggest part of the time.

He used his plane quite a bit in the winter too, for running his trap-line. And according to a relatively reliable associate of his, who was also a good friend of mine, he and Doc had more or less teamed up one winter, just to save gas, as well as wear and tear on their planes.

Theoretically at least, two can fly almost as cheaply as one, as long if they're both doing it in the same airplane. The trouble with theory though, is that it's fairly easy to overlook various important factors until you actually come face to face with them. Which, if I remember correctly, is precisely what happened to Doc and Virgil. But even if I don't have the facts exactly straight, there's just no way it could hurt either nut's goofball-reputation one iota.

Before consolidating their equipment, Doc had set one of his traps beside a small pothole lake that lay no more than six or eight feet from yet another pothole, which was nearly identical in size. The barely perceptible ridge of grass and mud separating them was adorned with somewhere close to a dozen small spruce trees. And since Doc had apparently forgotten how he'd had to squinch up the pucker-muscles in his rump, just to get his plane back in the air after setting the trap, Virg claimed that before he was able to figure out what Doc was trying to do, the prop of that little rag-bucket looked like it was going to make tossed salad out of the tree branches before they were able to stop.

So after checking the trap and administering the coup de grace to the fat fox it contained, an additional twenty pounds or more was added to the little plane's cargo manifest. I can't say whether Destiny actually played a part in the circus that followed, but after Doc played several games of ring-around-the-rosy with the plane, it became fairly evident that the plane's skies weren't going to let go of the snow.

For those of you not familiar with the peculiarities of flying in Alaska, a plane can sometimes be coaxed into the air by taxiing round and round a lake or clearing that's too short for a normal takeoff. Not that I'm trying to imply that anything Doc was ever involved in could really be considered normal.

Faced with the choice of plucking his bird out of its nest with a helicopter, since Doc didn't have any close friends who had one (In this case, 'close' meant within yelling, or at the very most, snowshoe-distance.), they had only one viable alternative. Which just happened to involve cutting the evergreen umbilical cord between the twin pot-holes, then piling several tons of snow over the scar. Every flaky grain of which, quite naturally, had to be scraped up and carried to the spot by utilizing the aforementioned snowshoes for shovels.

Consequently, since daylight is always a skimpy commodity at that time of year around Lake Louise, it took the intrepid trappers until the middle of the following day to get the deed done. Of course this meant that they'd not only had to coax enough heat out of their campfire to keep from freezing to death, during their unscheduled sojourn on the ground, they'd also had to use a substantial amount of it to keep their mechanical bird's lifeblood from solidifying. And this invariably means draining the oil into a bucket, while it's still in a liquid condition, then getting it almost to the boiling point before pouring it back into the engine, just before you're ready to see if there's the slightest chance it's going to start.

So even though my version of this fiasco has omitted an abundance of smoke, sweat, and screaming (and believe me, its entirely possible to work up a sweat when you're trying to find enough firewood to keep from freezing), we've now arrived at the starting line of yet another fun-filled Alaskan game. I could probably call it Hop-scotch, or even Musical-chairs. But just because Virg said he yelled "Holy-shit-Doc-look-out-fer-that-stupid-gawddam-stump!" while it was taking place, that seems like a much more appropriate title. It should also make it a whole lot more realistic if you'll just try to imagine it's being uttered at least one and a half full octaves above high-C.

Because once they'd gotten their bird fired-up and had taxied clear to the appropriate end of the pothole, when Doc cranked the throttle open and aimed the nose at the snow-bridge they'd worked so hard to construct, he somehow failed to notice the tip of the stump until Virg screamed. By that time the right-hand ski had just barely missed the only remaining evidence of the trees they'd cut, and they were once again airborne. At least they were for the first couple of seconds.

Then they slammed back down on the surface of the second pothole and went streaking for the far side. Luckily, since it really wasn't all that far, Virg said his and Doc's pucker-muscles had gotten synchronized enough by then to pry the skies loose from the snow. And even though they just barely nipped the top of one tree with a ski, they were once more back in the trapping business.

Before he goes winging clear off over the horizon, though, I might as well tell you about another stunt Virg related one April afternoon when a couple of friends and I stopped by his cabin on our snow-machines, as we were returning from Dog Lake. Just to help you get oriented, his cabin isn't much more than a stone's-throw from the white cliffs Doc had sent my wife and I to, the day we caught the two lake-trout.

We'd just come from checking our burbot lines over on Dog Lake and it was just too nice an afternoon to waste by going right on past Virg's without stopping to shoot the breeze. We also figured there was a good chance he'd have some coffee left in the pot, which as it so happens, he did.

Anyhow, once we'd gotten comfortable and I'd introduced my companions to Virg and his wife, Jan, the wild stories started crawling out of the woodwork like so many hungry termites. It doesn't take a whole lot to get Virg cranked up, you understand, and since my friend Ed also owns an airplane, within a matter of minutes they were both winging around the cabin like a couple of bats, at least verbally. Ed's no slouch in the wind-tunnel either, so he was pretty well holding his own as far as telling us about some of the weird things that happened to him while he was flying.

For some reason, though, Jan decided to get even with Virg for something or other, the way women are always doing when they're outnumbered, and she said "Why don't you tell them about your Gas-barrel Incident, Honey."

A pained expression spread across Virg's face then, much the same way a wet stain so often appears on a guy's pants when he's got to turn around and face a packed restroom, then waltz back to his table through an equally crowded restaurant, and he groaned "Aw fer cryin' out loud, Jan, what'd ya hafta go an' bring that up for, anyway?"

If Virg can be accused of anything at all, it certainly isn't not being able to make the best of a bad situation, so he scraped up a grin from somewhere and said "Her an' me'd been checkin' traps all day long, ya see, an' was clean down near where th' McClaren River dumps inta th' Big Su, but still up close to th' top'a th' ridge leadin' over t'Brush Mountain. We'd seen quite'a bit'a wolf sign th' last time we'd been over there, an' I decided it was worth settin'a few traps."

After shuffling over to the stove and making sure the coffeepot was going to start perking before too much longer, the second one since we'd arrived, he resumed his tale. "Well sir, I'da been one whole hellova lot better off if I'd jist stayed in th' sack that mornin', believe me. Because even though it was easy enough t'see there wasn't nothin' in th' traps, from up in th' air, it didn't make sense t'fly all that way an' not make sure a dang fool camp-robber hadn't sprung 'em, er somethin'. A'course that mean't settin' down in th' only flat spot on th' ridge, then puttin' th' webs on an' hikin' t'each set."

Chuckling then, as though he could hardly believe it himself, he said "But th' dumbest part of it all, was in not pullin' th' damn things up right then an' there. So while we're sloggin' back t'where we left th' plane, I looked around an' finally realized that if we didn't start bustin' our butts purty damn quick, we was gonna wind up smack in th' middle of'a lousy white-out. Why Hell's-fire, by then I could jist barely make out th' plane, an' it wasn't a bit more than two hun'ert yards away."

By now he was fully immersed in his story and mimicking the way they'd begun running on their snowshoes toward the plane, stomping and tromping around the room with his tongue hanging out the whole time. Then just a second or so later his arms were fully extended and he was gunning his imaginary engine for all it was worth. Airborne at last, he said "So there we was, zoomin' along like we had good sense, with me lookin' fer what might jist as well'a been a damn pearl in'a bucket a'milk. But since most'a th' ridge was pokin' up through th' slop, I was able t'follow it 'til we got clear'a Tyone Mountain, without too awful much trouble. So I took a bead on th' compass an' flew jist long a'nuff so I figgered we oughta be real close t'home. "

Heaving a sigh of relief, almost as though he was still up in the air, Virg wagged his head from side to side a couple of times before continuing, "Then I made a couple circles, an' all of a sudden there my windsock was, hangin' there jist as purty as ya please, dead ahead an' only'a hair off t'th' left. So I'd already chopped th' throttle before I remembered th' lousy, stinkin' fuel-barrel I'd hauled out from shore jist'a day er so before, t'help me locate th' pole that goofy sock was hung on. But by th' time I yanked th' dang throttle out again, an' swung th' nose hard t'th' right, we was already on th' ground. Fer a second or two, I thought we was gonna miss th' barrel, but then th' tip'a th' wing give it jist enough of a clip t'knock it over."

After sitting there and staring at each of us in succession for thirty seconds or so, he laughed a little ruefully and said "It really didn't put much of'a ding in th' wing-tip, but that sucker sure shot one hellova humongous hole in my self-esteem. 'Cause whether ya believe it er not, that was th' very first scratch I ever put on one'a my damn planes."

Remembering the way he'd once gotten a little carried away, while excavating for the foundation of an apartment house we'd both been involved in the construction of, and had completely filled the bed of my half-ton pickup with some of the beautiful pea-gravel he was digging out, I said "After that load'a gravel ya saddled me with that night on Fireweed Lane, Wise-guy, it just serves ya right. It's a damn good thing there weren't any blue an' whites hangin' around while I was tryin' t'git home with it, because I'd'a done a whole lot more than clip their wings, th' way that fool thing was waddlin' all over th' road."

Of course that brought on a virtual gale of laughter from Virg, followed immediately by "Well hell, ya said ya wanted a load, didn't ya? An' ya sure couldn't kick about th' damn price."

By this time the sun was getting awfully close to the horizon, so a temporary halt was called to the gas-war and Ed and Craig and I headed back out to our snow-machines. We still had a day's catch of burbot to clean, you see, which brings us right back to where this tale started wagging awhile ago. Before we hang it out to dry, though, there's another Doc story you might enjoy. I heard this one from Ruth Moats too.

It seems that shortly after they'd started Lake Louise Lodge, Ruth and Earl had gone over to the Air Force Recreation Camp for an evening of pinochle, where Kay and Doc were working as caretakers for the winter. And since it's relatively easy to become dehydrated in cold weather, it's my understanding that a substantial amount of liquid refreshments were consumed during the course of the evening. Which was no doubt responsible for Doc's calling several spontaneous time-outs. But even though it was completely obvious to the others that he was never gone long enough to get as far as the outhouse, this one time he'd hardly even shut the door behind him before he came rushing back inside, babbling "Ya gotta come see this, er ya jist ain't gonna believe it. It looks like th' whole damn world's plumb bleedin' t'death out there!"

Since they all figured it was just another of his goofy stunts, they continued to sit there until he yelled "Gawddam it, I ain't kiddin', it's th' damnedest thing I ever seen. Now come on!"

Still fairly convinced he was up to something that would soon become obvious, Ruth said they all followed him back out the door. Once they got outside, though, it did indeed look as if the world was bleeding to death, or at least in the process of being consumed by some heavenly firestorm. All three times that I heard her tell the story, Ruth's voice would drop almost to a whisper and she'd say "My God, when I think of how close we came to missing out on seeing it, just because we thought the old fool was up to another one of his tricks, I could almost cry."

And by the time she'd finish telling how even the trees and snow seemed to glow with a soft, luminous red hue, her eyes would be brimming with tears. It had all been brought about, of course, by one of the relatively rare, totally red displays of the Aurora Borealis, or Northern Lights.

My wife and I were fortunate enough to witness another such display during the late 1980s, while we were still living on Skyline Drive, high above Eagle River. And even though the street lights down below had a tendency to diminish the effect of the Aurora somewhat, it was nevertheless a truly beautiful thing to see. It was probably only my imagination, but while Dee and I were standing out in our driveway looking up at the sky, I could almost swear I heard Ruth whispering "Now you know what I meant don't you? Now you know!"

Make Use Of All That You Possess

Frequently has not the worth of that which is hidden,
But search for it with diligence,
For it is a must,
And when your steps begin to falter,
Offer upward your trust
For when you fell beaten, broken and bended,
With no place to turn, Then HIS hand is extended,
So grasp it—Clasp it—With all that you possess.

Stealin' Out Th' Door

What's the matter Honey, why are you getting up?
Can't sleep Babe, so I might jist as well.
What time is it? It's still awfully dark.
4:30, but don't you fret none, I think I'll drink me a cup,
n' jist set fer'a spell. There must'a bin'a moose messin'
around out in th' yard, leastwise somethin' made ol' Pard
growl. You go on back t'sleep now, n' I'll be all right,
cause it's really kind'a nice, jist loafin' in th' easy chair listnin'
T' my Willy tapes, n' watchin th' Anchorage light,
a'glistnin off th' Inlet ice. Th' shadow shapes a'th' trees
up on Skyline Ridge are purty too, n' oh yeah, I meant t'ask
you, are those purple grapes still in th' fridge?

Cabin Fever

After Jim, my electrical-hunting-buddy, and I shelled out six hundred bucks apiece for slightly less than five acres of beach-front property on Lake Susitna in early 1969, we flipped a coin to see which one of us would end up owning either the north-half, or the south one. Although I was more or less hoping I'd get the one on the north, since it supposedly had a tree-covered knoll whose elevation should provide a better overall view of the lake, once some of its trees were cut down, I ended up with the other one.

But just because there's a chance you might've missed that "supposedly" in the preceding paragraph, I'd probably better go ahead and admit that what we'd actually done was cough up all that hard-earned money for what's sometimes referred to as "Buying a pig-in-a-poke!", since neither one of us had as yet laid eyes on the property. Which, if I could ever get that contrary dang Jim to own up to it, was the main reason I'd held off as long as I did, after him an' my wife started yelling at me about how we were going to miss the fool boat if we didn't get busy and buy the dang ground before someone else beat us to it!

Consequently, after handing over all that money to the gal that owned the ground, she gave us an itty-bitty slip of paper that said she'd been paid in full for Lot # so and so in U.S. Survey # so and so on April 30, 1969. So just because Jim and I didn't know diddly-squat about what we should have gotten, the lake had already thawed out three times and froze up twice before our dang fool Warranty Deed was finally filed on October 19th, 1971. All of which just goes to show that buying pigs in a poke is about as good a way to go broke as there is, unless you're really lucky, mainly because I never did own anything else that gave me anywhere near as much downright pleasure as that place did!

But I'll tell you for definite and dang sure, by the time Dee and I'd towed the lumber we'd bought in Anchorage, all the way to the old Army dock at Lake Louise, on the good for nothing, tail-heavy-whip-sawing-tandem-axel monstrosity of a so-called boat-trailer I'd cobbled together a few years earlier, then piled all of said lumber on the fifty-man-surplus-life-raft I'd borrowed from a guy by the name of Del, who was keeping it over at his cabin half a mile east of Lake Louise Lodge, it was the next thing to dark-thirty when we finally started towing it across the lake toward the channel, sometime around the middle of August, 1969, followed by our oldest daughter's Air Force husband, Ron, who was supposed to be on the lookout for any stray boards that had somehow managed to fall off the raft we'd had to pump-up with the teeny-weeny air-compressor Del used for putting enough air in it to keep it afloat!

If you had a little difficulty wallowing your way through that last sentence, you just should've been with us that night, trying to find the channel we needed to go through to get into Lake Susitna. But just because I always was so gosh-darn lucky, we only had to tow that humongous rubber-ducky back and forth past the mouth of the channel two times before we were finally able to make out the dinky little white stake they were using for a marker that summer. And despite the fact that fairly close to thirteen gazillion blood-thirsty mosquitoes followed us all the way from the channel to the cabin just north of our property, we were lucky enough to find barely sufficient room to roll our sleeping bags out on the dirt floor of the little screened-in meat-house, adjacent to the path leading to the cabin. Since it was already a little after 3:00 A.M. before I decided to release the trigger on the can of "Off" we'd found just inside the door, I still wasn't able to smell anything else when I finally slithered out of my bag shortly after 6:30.

As a staunch advocate of the age-old Alaskan adage as to the quickest way of jump-starting a group of bleary-eyed travelers being by way of the ambrosial vapors spewing from the spout of a percolator, I now yelled "If you dang deadbeats ain't out'a them sacks by the time I git back here with a bucket'a water, I'm prob'ly gonna dump at least half of it on each one'a ya!"

Needless to say, by the time I'd rummaged around in the pasteboard box I seemed to recall having put the two and a half gallon galvanized pail I'd purchased at McKay's Hardware a few days earlier, and had dumped its assortment of metallic utensils into the dinged-up old enameled washbasin I'd hauled to and from my Colorado hunting-camps for nearly twenty years, at least fifteen or twenty magpies and camp robbers were flitting from tree to tree in the immediate vicinity of our airy little aerie.

Although my two companions weren't exactly flitting around when I came back from filling the pail a few minutes later, once I'd informed them that I'd seen the tracks of a fairly good-sized grizzly bear approximately fifty yards west of our sleeping quarters, for the balance of the next week it was all but impossible to get Ron to venture any further from Dee and myself than the first spruce tree that was bushy enough to provide the 'bearest' semblance of privacy.

Consequently, despite pitching the little two-man GI tent I'd brought for him, barely ten feet from Dee's and my 9x9 umbrella-variety, he was so ill at ease during the next two or three days, I couldn't help wishing I'd kept quiet about the bear tracks. Anyhow, since Dee and I had made a quick trip up to the lake as soon as the ice had gone out in early June, we'd already located the brass survey cap at the northwest corner of our property. But due to the meandering shoreline of the lake, as well as my only having a one hundred foot tape with which to measure the approximate three hundred and forty-five foot distance to where the northeast corner was supposed to be, Ron and I still hadn't been able to find any evidence of either a metal or wooden stake when I finally growled "Aw, t'hell with the damn thing! We'll jist hang a ribbon where it's s'posed t'be, an' I'll call that dang Jim an' tell 'im he can look for it whenever he takes the notion! It don't make a hellova lot'a diff'ernce anyhow, since Ozzie said they was jist gonna be subdividin' it on paper fer us!"

Due to there still being a fairly visible slash-line along the west side of the property, we soon found several partially decayed survey stakes that had been driven into the ground approximately a hundred feet apart as we worked our way up the gentle slope that first afternoon. And since a thoroughly rusty 8-penny finish-nail was protruding from the top of each stake, I was reasonably sure every one of them was close enough to where they needed to be to satisfy almost anyone. For simply because I had no intention of shelling out anymore of my hard-earned money than was absolutely necessary, despite my good friend Ozzie Oswald's having assured me that the people at the Borough Recorder's office wouldn't be requiring an actual on-site survey in order to approve the subdividing of Jim's and my property, I still wasn't totally convinced that some trouble-making eager-beaver-bureaucrat wouldn't eventually end up deciding to come snooping around someday. All of which just goes to show that some of us 'Pig-in-a-poke-buyers' aren't necessarily as smart as we probably ought to be!

In any event, shortly before 5:00 that evening, Dee asked me whether I wanted her to continue fixing our meals down where the boats were tied up, or in our tent. So just because doing it in there would require carrying several boxes of food up from the boats, and would more than likely end up giving that dang fool bear the idea that he was welcome to come calling whenever he got hungry, I said "I don't think that's too good an idea, Babe, since Ron's s'dang spooky now, if one of us even passes gas er belches when he ain't lookin', he's liable t'rip a hole straight through the side'a the dang tent!"

The main reason I'd brought it to her attention, of course, was to make sure she was as fully aware of Ron's present state of mind as I was. So as a firm believer in humor's ability to alleviate so many of society's ills, after winking at her as I nodded in our momentarily preoccupied companion's direction, I literally pulled out all the stops by saying "Even though I didn't have any intention of ownin' up to it at first, roughly an hour after I ate that lousy baloney san'wich ya gave me fer lunch, I let loose of a louder'n ordinary rumble-seat rattler that was ripe enough t'jist about send our buddy right straight inta orbit. An' even after I said "Sorry 'bout that Pard.", if I even s'much as cleared my throat er snorted a'bug out'a my nose fer the next couple hours, the goofy sucker'd pert near jump right out of `is dang boots!"

The thoroughly incredulous look on Ron's face made it quite obvious that my more than somewhat exaggerated version of what had actually occurred was doing an even better job than I'd hoped, so I now continued with "I know the main reason ya went an' bought the dang stuff, was jist because'a his sayin' how much he likes it. But if it's all the same t'you, once that big jar'a Skippy goes dry, I'd jist as soon settle fer Moose-nugget san'witches after that! As long as ya'll put mayonnaise on `em instead'a mus'turd, anyway!"

Consequently, while Ron and I were erecting a `visqueen' lean-to down on our so-called beach a few minutes later, when Dee came back from what I'd mistakenly assumed was a trip to the shallow latrine-pit we'd dug that morning, bearing approximately a dozen sun-bleached `nuggets' on one of the paper-plates left from lunch, and ever so sweetly asked whether I wanted her to add them to my portion of the hamburger and onion gravy she intended to fix for supper, well after we'd called it a night and crawled into our bags once again, it was still possible to hear our son-in-law's periodic fits of laughter over in his tent for quite awhile.

Oh yeah, in spite of the fact that the statute of limitations has long since expired, you can bet your sweet bippy I'd made dang sure that fool latrine was dug well over on my side of the line, instead of the U. S. Government or State of Alaska side! For simply because so many of the provisions that were <u>supposedly</u> settled by the establishment of the Alaska Native Land Claims Act over thirty years ago are still being challenged on a fairly regular basis, very few of Alaska's present citizens have the slightest idea as to when, where, or why some heretofore unknown band of `Seminal' Aborigines' from over in Gadzookistan or Thumsucksoopy might suddenly decide to file claim on the land we've worked our butts off to acquire. But that's the way it goes I guess, way down in the sold-out Halls of our good old Bureau of-craps-ville!

Be that as it may, once we'd gotten all the way to the bottom of the ten to fifteen inch blanket of moss, lichens, and decayed vegetable matter in the spot where it looked as if there was adequate room for the A-frame cabin I'd foolishly hoped to commence construction thereof the previous day, it now became necessary for us to spend the entire balance of the second day, along with the first half of the following one, picking, shoveling, and raking as much of the (as far as we were able to determine at that point in time) all but bottomless layer of permafrost that had almost immediately begun melting all over the damn place.

Consequently, by the time we eventually chopped down enough of my less than bountiful supply of suitably-sized spruce trees to construct four two foot by six foot log-cribs, which would (hopefully, at least) provide adequate clearance between the greasy, semi-solidified layer of formerly rock-hard material and the as yet to be fabricated triple two by twelve beams on which the cabin's floor-joists would eventually be placed, I'd long since begun to wonder whether there was the slightest chance in hell of our actually getting the sheet-aluminum roofing installed before my `Texas Troop'ador' had to report back to duty at Elmendorf Air Force Base.

But by dint of a vast amount of positively profane screaming and yelling by yours truly, as well as a thoroughly copious quantity of perspiration from both Ron and myself, when he at last threw Dee and me a left-handed Adios, while hanging onto the tiller of the first plywood and fiber-glass john-boat I'd ever turned out, I at least, had to blink several times in order to keep from making a silly, sentimental fool of myself.

And even though Dee and I managed to get the two end walls framed and sheeted before we too headed for home a few days later, it was necessary for us to make several more trips to the lake that Fall, in order to haul and install the five small windows, one door, fiber-glass insulation, and enough inexpensive mahogany paneling to make the cabin more or less livable. On one of those trips, although I no longer recall just which one, we brought the first and very best combination-barrelstove-hotcake-griddle-hotwater-heater-hand-warmer-contraption I ever cranked out, bar none! Because if it hadn't been for that little jewel, it's hard telling just how long it might have taken us to discover how positively delicious a quart of fresh-picked blueberries stirred into a couple cups of hotcake batter really is. Man-oh-man, if there's anything that tastes any better than those things do, I sure don't know what in heck it could be!

Clancy Fleetwood.

Jist Minin' My Ghosts

There was once a time, not so awful long ago,
When shiny yellow buses groaned back an' forth,
Haulin' as rowdy a crew as ya could possibly find.
Jist one'a th' bunch, I had a small part in th' show,
Settin' there in all that stinkin' stogie smoke,
Headin' South at th' start, an' later on, returnin' North,
Jist goin' to an' from that black ol' hole where we mined.

There was Clancy an' Willie, Les an' Little
Joe, along with Spider an' Vic,
Ray too, an' that clown'a th' bunch, Ol' Bunkhouse Benny.
Why I worked with'em all, tho' there was still'a lot more,
All fellers ya could count on, thru th' thin an' th' thick.
Aw, I know some of `em was losers, but not really very many,
Out'a fifty er so, I doubt there'da been much more than four.

An' far as I know, er th' last that I heard, none ever got rich,
Er hit it big, though some sure as hell got hit,
Hurt bad, an' even smashed, when a slab'd come crashin' down.

Fred "Spider" Stollstiemer and Ike Flor.

An' all of us wondered at times, when
a widow makin' sonovabitch

Might have our name wrote on th' top of it,

T'send us feet first outside, on our ride in th' basket t'town.

Ever' now an' then, some clown might tell
ya he never worried about it,

but he was either'a fool, er a damn liar.

Why I remember one shift in a dirty rotten stope,

Where ol' Hal Kernudson an' me had t'crawl on our gut,

Jist t'git in, an' when we seen what was hangin' over our backs,

we damn near lost our cool.

Why ya couldn'ta drug us back under that mess with'a rope.

Because our door under th' ore was hangin' by only'a thread,

jist waitin' t'slam shut.

So Nipper Phil tied five loadin' sticks end t'end
an'shoved us some powder an' fuse,

An' even tho it took `im awhile,

He saved us a trip we sure as hell wasn't about t'make.

Six red sticks'a dynamite, but one was all we had t'use,

A single bang, a big KAWHOOSH, an'
down come that Gawd awful pile,

Chunks th' size of a truck, all muck we'd
soon be jackhammerin' t'break.

S'Phil sent word down t'little Polack Joe,
tellin' `im t'pull pocket number one,

An' each time it run, why t'come up an' take a peek

Gene Orr.

At our doghole in th' raise, an' jist wait'a minute t'listen

Fer our yell, an' then, if he didn't hear none,

T'go drop'er again, an' maybe again, even if it took all week.

But then at last, from our side'a th' hole,

we seen `is lamp's teeny pinpoint glisten.

An'a week er so later, Kernudson up an'
blew his wad on'a five day binge

an' a damn ol' two dollar haircut.

Sick of hisself, as well as booze, an' claimin'
he'd never go near another dang barber,

He headed on over th' hill, an' I never seen `im again.

Fer he was one'a them guys that jist couldn't handle 'is rotgut.

I sure hope tho', that him'n ol' Clancy's found'a good fishin' hole,

somewhere close to that so-called eternal harbor,

An' that Ray's put on some weight, since jist
before he died he got awful thin.

Even now tho', whenever I shut my eyes, I can still see `em all,

Ever' last grinnin' an' grimy face,

Of th' whole dang gang, from up there on th' hill.

They're most all ghosts now y'know, gone.

But I sure wish that jist fer'a little bit I could bring `em back

from that big ol' stope in outer space.

Can'cha hear `em too? Well by damn, ya could if ya'd listen!

Clancy, ya deaf ol' galoot! Is that you on th' drill?

An' Aw fer cryin' out loud, is that you with `im, Will?

Ron's Green Monster

Two or three weeks after Dee and I got home from burying my stepmother in Colorado, Ron called to tell me he'd gotten a really good deal on a used Evinrude snow-machine from one of the guys he worked with, who was being transferred to another base in the lower 48. And since someone else had told him he'd gone up to some fairly large lake near the old Sourdough roadhouse with several of his buddies, where most of the guys had managed to bag two or three caribou apiece, Ron wanted to know if there was any chance I could get a couple of extra days off that weekend, just in case we needed the extra time to track down a 'bou or two of our own, while trying out his new toy.

Needless to say, due to my still being more than a little down in the dumps over losing Doris, I said"There sure as hell is Ol' Buddy, that's the best news I've heard in quite awhile! But jist because it don't make any sense t'take that no-account Ford'a yers up too, I'll come over t'morrow night as soon as I git off work an' we can see whether it looks like there's gonna be enough room on my trailer fer yer machine an' my big Puddy-tat too. An' if it does, we prob'ly better throw yer rig in the back'a the Chevy tonight. So as long as ya ain't figgerin' on checkin' out anywhere near as many'a them humongous flight-suits the goofy U-nutty States Bird-herders loaned ya while yer folks was here last month, we sure as the devil ought'a be able t'high-tail it up t'Ruth an' Earl's an' drag yer 'Rudy-tooter from the truck t'the trailer without losin' too much time."

Consequently, despite the sense of foreboding I felt the following evening, after seeing how heavy and awkward Ron's machine proved to be, simply because he was so tickled about finally having a snow-machine of his own, I somehow managed to keep my big mouth shut for once. But due to the fact that neither one of us felt like spending the money it would have cost to spend the balance of Friday night at the Sourdough Roadhouse when we arrived shortly after 1:00 A.M., we drove another quarter-mile up the road to an old gravel-pit, where we were eventually able to spread a canvas-tarp on the lee-side of the Chevy and crawl into our surplus GI mummy-bags before they were either covered or filled with the snow that was so busily swirling all-round-about for most of the next four hours. Which was roughly how long it had taken the slight amount of warmth emanating from my poor ol' posterior to thaw enough of the snow both above and beneath the tarp to soak through both it and the underside of my double-(take yer pick)dummy or mummy-bag!

    I've no idea just how cold it actually was when I finally got my two-burner Coleman camp-stove fired up, but I was sure as hell glad I'd had enough sense to fill it's tank before leaving home. Because once we'd thawed enough snow t'perk-part'of a-pot'a coffee, it was flat-out what ol' Doc Syd an' `is misplaced Texas Troop'ador had ordered, an' that's fer definite an' dang sure! I seem to recall gnawing on one of the well-preserved sandwiches one or the other of our wives had made for us the day before, just long enough to prevent sending my digestive-system into a state of complete hypothermic shut-down.

    Which condition, if I remember correctly, was what ol' Doc Pease claimed had very nearly happened to him one winter, when the thermometer took an over-night nosedive to somewhere between forty and forty-five below. And unfortunately, for both himself and Kay, his long-suffering wife, that had been all that was necessary to turn the oil in their heating-stove's fuel line into jelly. Which, even though she had a considerable amount of difficulty in maintaining her composure, Kay more or less verified by saying "An' that's when the crazy damn fool decided to take a big slug out of the bottle he'd nearly killed before finally crawling into bed shortly before midnight. Which was the main reason I'd had such a hard time waking him up, after I finally realized why it was so damn cold in that dinky little one-room cabin we were living in. Anyhow, once he finally remembered where he'd left his blowtorch the last time he'd used it, and had managed to get the stove's fuel-line hot enough to make him think it might be a good idea to throw a match or piece of paper in the stove before he turned the blowtorch off, THE STUPID JACKASS STILL DOESN'T KNOW HOW LUCKY HE WAS THAT I DIDN'T SHOVE IT STRAIGHT UP HIS YOU KNOW WHAT, RIGHT AFTER I HEARD ALL THE FLAMES ROARING UP THE CHIMNEY! By that time of course, that super-cold whiskey had him bent over double, grunting and groaning for all he was worth, which, simply because I'd gotten pretty attached to him by that state of affairs, was actually quite a bit!

    Now that poor ol' Kay's fin'ly had `er say, I guess we might jist as well pick up where we left off Once Ron and I had more or less pulled out of our outdoor bedroom and driven roughly a hundred yards back past the Sourdough Roadhouse to yet another old gravel-pit, this one on the lower side of the highway, we parked the truck fifty or seventy-five feet from where a well-defined trail crossed the mostly frozen surface of the Gulkana River. For approximately ten or fifteen feet on either side of the trail, as well as several other places even further away, the swiftly flowing water made it readily apparent that it wasn't too good an idea to venture any further from the beaten path than absolutely an' positootly necessary.

Due to already having spent a good deal of time and effort in getting this far up the creek, so to speak, when we heard what sounded like one or more snow-machine engines in the general vicinity of the Roadhouse, I said "Fer cryin' out loud Ron, lets git the hell out'a here before them guys show up. If we can jist make it inta the brush an' trees before they git here, there's a good chance they'll turn around when they see the truck, an' go somewhere else! Anyhow, since Ewan Lake's the biggest one this side'a Crosswind, its jist about gotta be the one yer buddy was talkin' about!"

Luckily, even though I wouldn't have bet a plugged nickel on his chances of doing so, once we'd dragged both machines off the trailer and shouldered our packs and rifles, Ron had his pride and joy purring like an overgrown green dinosaur, several lonnnng seconds before my black puddy-tat finally hiccupped its way to life. And by the time I eventually managed to catch up with him, it was no longer possible to even see the little road we'd driven down from the highway on, let alone my truck and trailer. Which needless to say, flat suited the hell out'a me!

Since neither one of our machines were equipped with odometers, I've no idea just how far we'd come when we saw the first reasonably fresh caribou tracks and droppings, but I'm fairly sure it must have been at least five miles. Covering the next mile or two took us nearly as long as the preceding ones had, for simply because I'd long since learned that the quickest way to spook a band of caribou was either to turn off your machine's engine and start walking, or speed up and try to overtake them, so I told Ron to just slow down and keep his eyes open for any sign of movement or variation in the color of the surrounding brush and trees.

But when we finally came to a fairly good-sized clearing without encountering anymore fresh caribou sign, and saw what I assumed was a local trapper's cabin, I leaned as closely as possible toward him and whispered "Idle along as slow as ya can without stallin' out, down through that little swale runnin' from the cabin toward that other clearing ya see through the trees. I kinda think we've either got t'the lake or some pot-hole fairly close to it. An' I'm purty sure yer prob'ly gonna find there's a slough runnin' down the middle'a that swale, so whatever ya do, don't drive off into it! Anyhow, once ya've made it t'the swale, I'll keep goin' on the main trail fer a little longer, okay?"

He hadn't much more than headed for the swale though, before I realized I should have made sure he not only had plenty of extra ammunition in one of his coat-pockets, but had also remembered to load his rifle's magazine before we left the truck. Which had been the main reason it had taken me so long catch up with him after crossing the river.

Consequently, when all hell seemed to break loose by the time I'd driven another hundred yards or so along the main trail, I soon discovered that even though Ron had most assuredly loaded his rifle, he'd neglected to take any of the shells from the one and a half boxes he had in his day-pack, and put them in his coat pocket, simply because he was so afraid they'd `clink' loudly enough to spook the animals we were after.

Due to his dropping one caribou in its tracks, after the second one he hit began running in circles, he kept right on shooting and missing until his rifle was empty. By this time I'd put two down, and was just pulling the trigger on my third one, when I finally realized why Ron wasn't shooting at the one he'd wounded. Since I'd apparently jerked the trigger on my third shot, and had managed to make mincemeat of the upper ten or fifteen percent of both hind-quarters, due to its being totally obvious that this animal wasn't going anywhere, just because Ron still hadn't managed to find the shells he was so frantically pawing through his pack for, I managed to empty my rifle and was forced to reload before I was finally able to put his second caribou down for the count. Needless to say, it was a real relief when the next shot put my third caribou out of its misery.

Although I'm well aware this sort of thing has probably happened to every hunter from time to time, and will undoubtedly continue doing so for however long mankind continues to feel the need for meat to eat, all I can say is "It flat bugs the hell out'a me whenever I'm the guy that causes needless pain to one'a the critters I've always counted on to keep my family well-fed, and that's the gospel truth!

In any event, once we'd dressed the five animals out, rather than take a chance on the sharply-ridged surface of the long trail back to the river stripping the hide off the caribou's backs, and thereby ruining even more meat, I said "Well ol' Buddy, now we're gonna find out jist how good a pack-horse yer machine is. I already know I can prob'ly git away with tyin' the two smallest ones a'mine on the Cat's back, as long as we whack the heads off an' I take it slow an' easy, anyhow. But there ain't any way in hell it'll handle three! So jist on accounta my bein' too damn stupid t'realize this might happen, as well as yer bein' dumb enough t'let me git away with it, we went an' left both'a my sleds back at Ruth an' Earl's, where they're doin' ever' bit as much good AS THE TITS ON A DANG BOAR HOG!"

Barely able to keep a straight face when I finally realized the relatively simple solution to our dilemma, particularly in light of Ron's somewhat doubtful grin, I growled "Well don't jist stand there, gimme a hand with yer two, so's we can see if Ol' Rudy-tootie's gonna hold still fer haulin them an' you too, fer cryin' out loud!"

After tying the animals across the rear two-thirds of the seat, though, and starting the truly smooth-running engine, when Ron sat down on the front caribou's back and began squeezing the throttle harder and harder, before the machine finally began moving, well before it had gone a hundred feet it was totally obvious that something was haywire with the suspension-system. Unfortunately, once we'd untied and removed both caribou, then rolled the machine over on its side, the super abundance of baling-wire wound around almost everything visible made it fairly apparent that Ron's 'really good deal' was nowhere near as good as he'd originally thought.

But once we discovered that so long as he sat as far forward on the seat as possible and took it easy on the throttle, there was just enough room between Rudy-tootie's track and chassis to allow for the hauling of a single caribou. Which needless to say, made it necessary to cobble together a somewhat larger travois than what I'd originally intended. And despite the necessity for one of us to grab hold of Cat's skis while the other one jerked the rear of the travois in the opposite direction whenever we got to a fairly sharp turn in the trail, you jist better believe it was one hellova relief to yer's truly when we made it all the way back to the Chevy with only eight or ten broken cleats on Cat's track!

Consequently, due almost as much to 'hunter-euphoria', as to the desire to get our so-called 'free meat' hung up in my little work-shop before it froze, we pretty much burned the candle at both ends for the second night in a row. Which, now that I stop to think about it, was awful dang close to the way most'a my hunts always went. Back when I still had the git-up an' go to git-up an' go, anyhow!

Rustic Refuge

You know, when you stop to consider some of the things a man does, it truly is amazing how little it takes to bring him contentment. The difference that even the smallest things make is to me a vast and wondrous part of everyday living. For I've found that so often they possess an almost limitless capacity to comfort, heal, and renew.

At times all of us need a word of encouragement, the touch of a hand, and just so we can get our lives back in order, a private retreat. A place to relax and unwind, and perhaps even to hide. With time enough to meet, alone with ourselves once more, so that we can sort things out, dream awhile, and once again discover what life's all about. I've a place such as this, that just meets my needs, and Gee but it's grand.

It is but it isn't, if you know what I mean. For even though it's only a simple little cabin, I think it's especially nice. Because you see, it sits beside a lake, which in winter is covered by ice. Some folks might find it cold, but to me it's ever so warm. Others might think it dreary, but I see only it's very special charm. I suppose though, it all depends upon the eyes from which it's seen.

I love it there in the summer of course, but the winters are the very best of all. For then, as I race the descending sun and the bitter cold that always follows close behind, it looks almost like a picture of Heaven, with it's windows all framed in shimmering gold. Returning from off and across those ice-bound waters, there's never a chance of missing those shining beacons, for they literally dance, as though cheering me on. Yet invariably I'll stop and listen, yes listen, to the silence of their sweet call.

At times it can become lonely there, but far more often it's not. For within moments of my arrival, most any time of the year or day, there'll be a flutter of sound, as in drops a friendly Jay. He'll perch there on the porch awhile, just letting me know he's not forgot that I fed him before, and will again before I go. You see, it's not so much what I give him that he likes, it's the thought.

On some winter days, small bands of caribou will drift slowly by. Single file they march, as they always have and more than likely always will. Often they'll trot for a while, then they'll stop, serene and still. Then a small shadow will sail by, and as though on cue, they raise their heads toward the sky, where high above an eagle wheels. From my little window I can see it all, and Oh God, how good it feels, to watch those graceful circles and hear that piercing cry of purest ecstacy.

So as the hours slide swiftly by, becoming days, I slowly mend. And the cares I brought with me seem to fade and disappear. Then at last, so too does my fear. Now, when I look in the mirror, I seem to have shed a full ten years. For my eyes are bright, my thoughts as well. Oh surely it was more than just a scant few days ago, when seemingly, I walked alone thru hell, afraid I'd surely break, or at least begin to bend?

And then I finally realize, each of these things are only a part of the whole. Just your normal, everyday sort of life. But the difference is, now that I've regained my perspective, I can grin. I'm still not ready to leave though, for I know way down deep within, it will be far, far too long before I can return once again. And quite possibly by then, I'll have forgotten that Life is really nothing but a balancing act, more or less like eating peas with your knife!

Things That Go Bump In The Night

Not that it really makes much difference, it was probably mid-September of 1968 when I first became aware of how terrified my oldest son-in-law, Ron, was of bears, primarily the huge, horrible, and hairy variety sometimes referred to as Ursus horribilis, but more commonly called a Grizzly. Which is more or less described, at least in my ragged old Second College Edition of Webster's New World Dictionary, as being a large, ferocious, brownish, grayish, or yellowish hump-shouldered bear with long front claws, that's generally found in western North America. And if that isn't enough to give a guy a full blown fit of screaming-meemies, I don't know what in heck would be!

But just because three other nuts and I had spent slightly over a week a couple of years earlier, just about as far up Slana creek as I had any intention of driving my four-wheel-drive-three-quarter-ton-Chevy-pickup, without coming even halfway close to seeing, at least as far as we knew, any critters that looked as downright awful as that, I decided I might just as well take my youngest and oldest girls' Sweetie-pies up there to see if I could get them out of my hair by helping them find a moose apiece! It's kind of funny at times the way some things work out, particularly with some of my dang sentences, which if you want to know the flat-out fact of the matter, was beginning to look like the one I had going right then was probably going to be for life, without even the tiniest chance of parole. Unless, of course, I managed to find each of them a big enough moose so they'd quit sponging off me and Mama at least once every other month or two! I mean for crying out loud, if they hadn't gone and signed up with Uncle Sammy's Buzzard Brigade right after getting out of school, they might have stood a chance of finding a job just like mine, working out in the fresh air most every winter, when it's either slicker than spit, or thirty beloby golly now that I stop and think about it, those goofy suckers were a whole lot smarter than I gave them credit for!

So now that I've more or less compensated for a few of the less than complimentary remarks I always made a practice of feeding them, mainly just to make sure they didn't become so emotionally-attached to me as to think they might be able to get away with actually moving in with Dee and me, we might just as well start with the day I first became aware of Ron's dislike for bears. For even though I can practically guarantee that he hadn't so much as even been introduced to one at that particular point in time, either formally or informally, when I made it a point to point at a fairly well-defined set of indentations a few feet from where he, Roger, and myself were then standing, and said "As brushy as this dang bench seems t'be, I kinda think it'll be a good idea if we make it a point not t'git much farther apart than seventy-five or a hundred feet, since the size'a that sucker's feet makes it purty plain we better keep our eye's peeled for any sign of `im!", the diameter of Ron's eyes seemed to increase to the point where if either Roger or I had even so much as sneezed, both of them would more than likely have rolled right out of their sockets and onto the ground.

In so much as we'd already spent most of the morning crisscrossing the large, open area I'd now begun referring to as `The Moose Pasture', without seeing hide nor hair of a single bull or cow, I decided that simply because I'd fulfilled my obligations to each of my companions by alerting them to the somewhat questionable possibility of seeing a bear, everything would probably work out in the same manner it <u>usually</u> does, <u>most</u> of the time. For as a general rule, whenever a bear becomes aware of your presence, he's <u>probably</u> going to be heading somewhere else in short order. Unless of course, <u>he</u> happens to be a <u>she</u> with cubs, or is guarding the site of a recent kill. But in any case, since I've had only one face to face encounter with one of the usually cranky critters, which took place during my first hunt on Afognak Island, the only sure-fire way of avoiding problems with bears is just to keep the hell out of their domain! Which here in Alaska at least, means missing out on dang near everything most of us came up here for.

The most logical way of keeping track of both my companions whereabouts was by having each of them stay approximately a hundred feet to either side of me, and for the first fifteen minutes or so, as we worked our way toward the low ridge lying along the far side of the bench, everything seemed to be working just as smoothly as I'd hoped it would. But when the next ten minutes passed without my seeing anything whatsoever of Ron, I motioned for Roger to come on over to where I'd now come to a complete halt, stuck approximately halfway between the first pangs of anxiety, and those of "Aw fer cryin' out loud, Roger, the sorry sucker's went an' got `isself lost!"

Needless to say, when this outburst was immediately followed by a much louder, and highly belligerent bellow of "Dammit Ron, where'n hell are ya?", which generated absolutely no response whatsoever, it in turn was followed by an extremely tentative "Judas Priest, Roger, what'n hell am I gonna tell Sharon, if the goofy clown really has got `isself clobbered by that dang fool bear?"

Anyhow, after due consideration, during which both of us eventually reached the same conclusion as to the best means of either locating our missing partner, or enlisting the help of some of the hunters in one or more of the half-dozen or so camps we were aware of, being by way of high-tailing it back to where we'd left my pickup barely a short hour before, which I'm sorry to say, left me so out of breath that, after seeing how much trouble Ron was having in lining up the match in his trembling right hand with the cigarette in his equally nervous lips, while perched right square on top of the Chevy's cab, all I could croak was "You stupid jerk, if you ever pull another stunt like this, I swear t'gawd I'm gonna kick yer butt all the way from hell t`breakfast, right after I've blowed what few brains ya got t'smithereens! An' if ya ain't real awful lucky, I jist might cram `em right back in that thing ya call a head an' do it all over again!"

Looking over at Roger then, only to see him fumbling for one of his own cigarettes, while the barest hint of a grin twinkled in his eyes, I growled "Aw hell, ya dang idiots, if ya ain't smart enough t'know them things're gonna end up killin' ya one'a these days, `specially when ya know good an' well I always got a can'a snoose right here in my pocket, I guess I might jist as well stick another dip in my lip."

Once I'd done so and had dropped the little Copenhagen cannister back in my left breast-pocket, I glared at Ron and said "I'm gonna say it one more time, Ol' Buddy, if you ever git me this wound up again, I ain't never ever gonna take ya huntin' again", I paused momentarily before adding "until the next time, anyway!"

Approximately forty-five minutes later, as the three of us sat side by side on the Chevy's tailgait, I lowered the lukewarm can of Budweiser from my mouth to Ron's knee and said "I know how much it had to've bugged ya to admit how scared ya was up there awhile ago, but jist so's ya'll know some'a the rest of us've been there too, a couple months before Dee an' us moved up here, I came within a gnat's eyelash a'gittin' buried alive one Saturday, more'n two miles back in the damn mine my partner, Leo, an' me was workin' in. So if you think I wasn't scared spitless when I looked up an' seen a big gob'a muck an' rocks come shootin' straight at us, jist try an' imagine how it felt when I was layin' there in the bottom'a that lousy ore-car a split-second later, while all them rocks was poundin' holy-hell out'a my back an' legs, not knowin' if Leo was already dead er not! But ya know what, jist because most'a that crap turned out t'be mud an' water, after Leo'd got washed clean out'a the car, I was fin'ly able t'grab hold'a the rim an' haul myself up an' over the edge, where I fell down between that car an' the next one. But jist because my cap-light'd got smashed t'smithereens by one'a them rocks, I couldn't see nothin' but black! An' I'll tell ya fer definite an' damn sure, you don't know diddly-squat about how black black really is, until ya've been as as far back in one'a them filthy holes as I was, without a damn light!"

Since neither Ron or Roger uttered a sound as they sat there staring at the ground, after taking a long drag of beer and setting the nearly empty can down between us, I lay my right hand on Ron's arm and continued with "But I'll tell ya Ol' Buddy, if even one'a the guys I worked with back then had ever took off without so much as sayin' a word, the way you did awhile ago, I'da done ever'thing I could jist t'make damn sure they never worked with me again, an' that's a flat-out fact!"

His voice barely audible as he struggled with his emotions, Ron finally said "I knew I should'a told ya how I felt after ya showed us them tracks, but since I didn't really know how to, I jist decided I prob'ly better do like ya said. But even though it went alright fer a little while, when I heard a stick pop jist a little ways ahead'a me I—II jist plain freaked out an' took off fer the truck as fast as I could go. An' even after I got inside an' locked the doors, when I still couldn't quit shakin', I'd already stuck a cigarette in my mouth before I even thought about how much ya've always hated the smell'a the dang things. So that's how come I was sittin' on the roof when you guys showed up. Anyhow, all I can say is, I'm really sorry."

As might be expected, during the next couple of days, while we continued combing the Moose Pasture from one end to the other, I spent a great deal of that time thinking about and wondering what I might have done to alleviate his fear after it became so apparent. But since I've always felt, and will no doubt continue doing so for the rest of my days, that it's far better to make someone aware of any potential for danger than it is to let them blunder headlong into it, that's pretty much what took place sometime around the middle of the second afternoon. For, as has happened so many times in the past fifty-odd years, quite a few of which have been even odder than what passes for relatively normal with me, I almost blew the only chance I would probably get at shooting the bull that was so preoccupied with his purely copulative pursuit of the cow he was doing his damndest to talk into letting him have his way with her, I couldn't help feeling a little guilty when I put him out of his misery, as well as hers, with a neck-shot immediately behind his bone-hard head.

But even though the ungrateful wench took off for the toolies without so much as a `Thank you, kind Sir', now that we finally had some meat for the proverbial pot, I came as close to being just as pleased as punch over my highly debatable prowess as I probably ever will be! Not t'mention a whole hellova lot more'n I had any right t'be, jist on account'a how close I came t'plowin' right on through the big clump of brush the young bull and his reluctant sweetie were right on the other side of.

So when Roger showed up less than ten minutes later, by the time Ron arrived on the scene approximately twenty minutes after that, we'd already gutted the bull out and begun peeling the hide off. Despite the fact that he was slightly out of breath after having misjudged how close I actually was when he heard my shot, Ron had gone at least a quarter-mile on past us before deciding to turn around. So I tossed him the keys and asked him to go get the Chevy while Roger and I finished skinning the bull.

Once we'd hauled the quarters back to camp and hung them on the meatpole, barely thirty feet from where we'd pitched the somewhat faded blue umbrella tent that had been brand new in 1963, when Dee and I set it up in the little grove of trees on the Homer Spit with the help of our three girls, I ended up spending the next half hour or so, telling the guys how much we'd enjoyed sitting around our campfire without having to smear bug-goop all over our arms, faces, and necks, simply because the mosquitoes didn't seem to care for the Spit's salty atmosphere. Which all three of us were totally convinced would have made it a whole lot more pleasant that particular evening, if only we'd been able to transport enough salt that far up the creek to get the dang job done!

As things frequently work out for me, particularly when I start feeling a little too smug about the manner in which I've taken care of all the various chores involved with the somewhat primitive, and totally tedious life of a hunter, once we'd spread the bull's hide out on a large upended tree-stump just across the Mankomen Lake road from our tent, stuck the freshly-washed liver in a meat-sack that had then been tied to the smaller pole above the heavy-duty one the four quarters and rib-cage were suspended from, the heart I fully intended to fry at least half of for breakfast, was duly placed in the largest kettle contained in the handy-dandy aluminum cook-kit I'd purchased with part of the proceeds I'd received from the only medical-insurance policy I would probably ever have, after having an upper-gastric hernia operation a full two years before I'd gotten so thoroughly fed up with living right smack in the middle of what was probably one of the biggest sand-dunes in the entire Navajo Indian Reservation, I finally said "Aw t'hell with it!" and wound up moving lock-stock and rifle-barrel to the good ol' U. S. of Alaska in midJuly of 1962, which I'd subsequently filled with ice-cold Slana River crick water and added a heapin' handful of salt to the whole works thereof before setting it right outside our little blue umbrella-tent's screen-door, yanking the zipper closed, and crawling into the sack! But just in case you bogged down in that cold crick water a minute ago, yer jist gonna hafta waller yer way out of it yer ownself!

As I undoubtedly should have expected, though, I'd barely dropped off to sleep before some clowns in a noisy Dodge Suburban came splashing across the relatively shallow river-crossing and parked roughly a hundred feet up the road from us, at least from the way it sounded. But after crawling back out of my bag and unsipping the door, just so I could see what in hell they were up to, when I heard one of them say "See what I told ya, Bob, this's where the dang moose're at!", I'm not even about t'tell ya what I felt like doin' right then, since ever' dang bit of it was jist about as obscene an' illegal as it's possible to get!

Anyhow, after muttering "Aw t'hell with the lousy!@#$%^&* S.O.B's! If they're low-down enough t'pull a filthy stunt like that, there ain't any point in even talkin' to 'em!", I re-zipped the door and my bag and had probably been asleep for somewhere close to thirty or forty-five minutes when a loud gulping sound just outside the tent jacked me straight out of bed once again, this time yelling "Them dirty, rotten so an' sos must'a turned a worthless, good fer nothin' dog loose, jist so's he could snarf our breakfast down when we wasn't lookin'!"

Naturally, by the time I'd once more unzipped the zipper and had pointed my flashlight at the kettle, the only thing left in it was about a gallon of bloody water. So when Ron picked that particular moment to pipe up with "I don't really think that was a dog out there Dad.", I growled "Aw fer cryin out loud Ron, all ya ever seem t'think about is bears, so will ya jist shut up an' go back t'sleep!"

So even though I lay there fussing and fuming for a good ten minutes after once again sliding into my considerably less comfy bag, I was just dropping off to sleep when a relatively moist sounding "Snuff-snuff, snuffing" seeped through the canvas wall immediately adjacent to my right ear, followed a split-second later by the fairly audible "Keruuunnchkeruuunchkeruuunnch" sound of the increasingly more ominous sounding footsteps of something that sounded a whole hellova lot heavier than any dog I'd ever seen or heard. So when this was immediately followed by a resounding "TWAAANNNG", as whatever the hell it was banged into one of the guy-wires attached to the green-spruce pole supporting the chimney of my little airtight wood-stove, I whispered "Fer once in yer life, Ron, I kinda think yer right about that's prob'ly bein' a bear out there! So jist keep quiet 'til I can shove a shell in my cannon and find where in hell I set that lousy 9-volt search-light'a mine." By now, of course, our stealthy intruder had made it around to the kettle again, and was even then "SLUP-SLUUP-SLUPPING" the last few spoonfuls of bloody saltwater from the kettle.

Due for the most part to this considerably more precarious turn of events, when Ron now whispered "Jist hold up 'til I can load mine too, Dad, there ain't any sense in yer goin' out there alone.", for once in his life I was more than willing to take his advice. But as might be expected, by the time I'd once more unzipped that ridiculous zipper, our caller had long since disappeared.

Before firing up the two-burner Coleman stove shortly after daylight the next morning, though, I headed outside to see what sign I could find of the bear, accompanied by both of my hunting partners. Due to the fairly heavy growth of short shrubbery and grass, we didn't find more than three or four footprints, but judging from the twelve or thirteen inch length of the ones that were obviously made by the bear's rear feet, as well as the fifteen inch diameter of the huge pile of scat that had been deposited 'bearly' seventy-five feet from the door of our tent, I was fairly well convinced that it was fortunate for all concerned when this bear chose to follow the same path *most* of them do, *most* of the time.

Once we discovered how efficiently it had rolled up my moose-hide, though, and stuffed it beneath the overturned stump we'd spread it on the previous evening, all without alerting either us or our new neighbors, you can bet your sweet-bippy that I truly enjoyed walking the forty or fifty feet on up the road to where their still somnolent forms were still snugly encased in their sleeping-bags, within the fully visible confines of that noisy dang Suburban, no more than four or five inches beyond the hinges of its wide open rear doors. Once one of the two guys opened his eyes far enough to see the three of us standing there, and had asked "What're you guys up to, anyway?", when I then filled him and his partner in on virtually every last detail of what had taken place while they'd been sleeping so soundly, in barely more time than it's taken to write this, both them and their hoopie were right on the verge of bouncing out of sight, roughly half a mile on down the quarter-mile width of the gravel bar on the far side'a the crick! Needless to say, neither I or my companions were even close to shedding so much as a single tear.

I'm fairly sure this was the morning that my old buddy, Louie, drove up from his and his partner's cabin about three-quarters of a mile downstream, wanting to know whether we'd been having any problems with bears lately. When all three of us burst out laughing, and he'd asked "What's so dang funny, anyhow?", I said "Well Louie, since I'm purty sure ya must've had a fairly good reason fer drivin' that humongous moose-wagon a'Bob an yers this far up the crick, if ya think ya can climb all the way down here without gittin' too out'a breath, it'll be a lot more fun showin' ya, than jist tellin' ya!"

Due to his and Bob's having laid cement-block foundations on several of the construction jobs I'd been involved in, we'd long since gotten used to one another's penchant for sarcasm, both the good and ill-humoured variety, depending of course, on what either had or hadn't gone wrong that particular day. Anyhow, when he'd no more than gotten to the ground before heading straight for the tarp-covered pile of canned and bottled goods sitting on the shady-side of our tent, simply because I had no doubt whatsoever as to what he was after, I said "Hey ol' Buddy, ain't it kind'a early in the day t'be hittin' that stuff?", he bellowed "You sure as hell wouldn't think so, if it'd been you that set up most'a the night, jist waitin' fer the hairy Sonovabitch that made off with half'a the caribou ya'd worked yer sorry ass off haulin' in from the top'a that high ridge over there day before yesterday, t'come back after the rest of it!"

Since he'd already removed the cap from the half-gallon jug he'd had good reason to think would more than likely be there, just before lifting it to his mouth he growled "If I'd had any idea how long it'll be before that dang partner'a mine makes it back with a fresh batch'a this stuff, I prob'ly would'a drank ever' damn bit we had left last night, `cept fer the fact I sure as the devil didn't want'a be sound asleep er passed-out when that mangy-low-down-growly-grizzly-sucker showed up! Which, when ya git all the way down t'the bare-bones a'the matter, is the only damn reason I set there in the doorway fer over eight solid hours without drinkin' anything that had any more kick than a cold pot'a left-over coffee, fer cryin' out loud!"

Winking in the general direction of my hunting-partners then, he took another long pull on our jug, before adding "So if that don't give ya a little clue as t'how ticked-off I was, it's jist on account'a yer bein' even dumber'n I always thought ya was! Anyhow, now that ya've went an' let me waste s'much a'my val-ya-bull time, how's about pullin' yer thumb out'a yer butt long enough t'show me whatever in hell it was ya wanted t'show me!"

Consequently, after being shown how neatly my bull's hide had been rolled up and stuffed under the stump, and we'd led him on past the scat-pile to where we'd found the few sets of track's, which he promptly proclaimed were considerably smaller than those of the bear that had stolen half of his caribou, on our way back to the partially glazed dark-brown surface of the scat, Louie stood there sniffing the air somewhat louder than necessary, before snorting "That crap don't smell like there's any fresh heart in it t'me, it smells a damn sight more like stale fart! If ya want my honest opinion, anyhow."

As we stood there on the bank of the Slana a few minutes later, watching that goofy World War II, Army surplus 6x6 rolling along on its huge airplane tires, down the same gravel-bar the Dodge Suburban had covered a couple of hours earlier, if I'd had the slightest idea that within the passage of a few more years, this really special guy would end up falling off a scaffold and breaking his neck, I truly hope I'd have had the courage to shake his hand and tell him how much I'd always enjoyed knowing him. But that's the way it usually goes, I guess, when a guy gets so wrapped up in his phony facade of male-macho'dom, he's too afraid the glint of tears in his eyes and the big lump in his throat will make him look and sound like a sentimental sissy.

Be that as it may, after one or the other of we Three Musketeers ended up shooting a large dry-cow a day or so later, and we'd packed the last of the meat to the furthest point it had seemed safe to drive my pickup along the boggy trail half a mile past Mankomen Lake Campground, when we came back early the following morning and discovered that sometime during the night a sow grizzly with fairly good-sized twin cubs had raked a huge mound of moss, dirt, and brush over the cow's head, hide and gut-pile, I can assure you that Ron wasn't the only one keeping a sharp lookout for any sign of that remarkably industrious trio for the balance of the day.

I've no recollection whatsoever of whether I had a camera with me, or not. But if I did, I truly screwed-up by not having one of the guys stand as close to the pile as possible, just to provide photographic evidence of what the animal that's generally considered to be one of the most powerful on the entire North American continent is capable of. While I'm fully aware that most people probably wouldn't have any particular problem in believing that over a period of six or eight hours, such as these three bears certainly had at their disposal, they sure as the devil had plenty of time to pile up a heap'a dirt. But once those folks had gotten a look at the three an' four inch diameter of some'a those dang alders that had been ripped out of the ground by their roots, a hellova bunch of which were at least half as big around as the trunks, and were split from one end to the other, they'd more than likely stop thinking ol' Syd was just shooting another batch of B.S., or had flat flipped his lid, neither one of which was the case! Leastwise not this time.

Anyhow, just because the more or less dazed look in Ron's eyes kind of made me wonder whether he'd finally given up all hope of making it back to Elmendorf alive, especially after some fairly fresh moose sign somewhere close to a hundred and fifty yards up the bench from Three Bears Mountain, caused Roger and me to think we had a halfway decent chance of bagging our third (I dang near wrote `final' before realizing just how terminal it sounded) moose for that year, for some reason the third member of our threesome seemed to think so too. Which is the only halfway logical explanation I can offer as to why those contemptible Fate Triplets decided to send the junior (at least as far as age was concerned) member of our party straight into yet another encounter with none other than what in all likelihood was the same hard-working trio yours truly had been stupid enough to think would probably be hunkered down either in or real close to the dense alder-jungle a quarter of a mile or so below the boggy area from which the newly-named Three Bears Mountain had so miraculously sprouted forth during the last twelve hours!

In any event, despite Roger's somewhat `peculiar' penchant for audibly advising himself as to what he either should or shouldn't do in various and sundry situations, he'd somehow managed to keep his hyper-active lips from flapping just long enough to avoid provoking the (thus far, at least) slightly curious (and more than likely extremely short-tempered) sow into a headlong charge straight up the hill at him. And, quite possibly during one of their notoriously rare and short-lived periods of sympathetically induced indulgence, the highly fickle Goddesses of Fate, otherwise known as Clotho, Lachesis, and Atropos, allotted poor Roger just `bear'ly enough time to disappear in the scant few seconds the sow was distracted by one or the other of her adolescent offspring's more than likely futile pursuit of a mole, vole, mouse, or shrew, just to name a few of the poor little things the big bullies seem to get such a charge out of raising hell with!

Consequently, once the somewhat breathless junior member of the newly-formed Mankomen Lake Musketeers had duly apprized Ron and myself as to this altogether deplorable turn of events, we quickly decided it would probably be a real good idea just to get the hell out of there and spend the rest of the day hunting for our third moose, up close to the top of what I usually called Mankomen Mine Pass.

So just because one or the other of us lucked out again, by dropping a fairly small spike-bull with a neck-shot somewhere around 4:00 P.M., you can bet your britches that all three of us were just as pleased as punch when we finally got the last of that meat hung in my meat-shed on Fireball Street, there on the upper edge of beautiful downtown Eagle River. And once we got all that `free and easy' meat cut, wrapped, and stuck in our freezers, just because there was still enough room left for a caribou or two, it wasn't too long before we were trying to decide whether it'd be best to wait until March to go after them, or take a chance on enough of them having moved down from their summer range, to make it worth our time to drive up to Nabesna, Sourdough, Paxson, the Denali Cutoff, or maybe even all the way up to Northway or Forty-Mile, which just incidentally, were two of the places we never did get to hunt!

Singin' a Scrofulous Song

Ya know, when ya get right down to the nitty-gritty heart of the matter, in spite of what ya might've heard, there ain't a hellova lot of gold, or good, in gettin old. Unless maybe it's muckin' around thru the dust and cobwebs in your head, just rememberin' the places ya've been, and the folks ya've knowed. Which's why I spend so much time, doin' just that.

Why only last night I seen a guy on a T.V. show, who brought to mind a partner of mine, back when I was mining in the mountains of Colorado. Bunkhouse Benny was `is name, and he was a regular clown, just chasin' around all over the place, followin' rodeo shows. An' whenever I think of his freckled face and pointy beak, I can't help but grin, since that's what he done best of all.

For even tho' he couldn't ride worth half a hoot in hell, he didn't care, because he'd discovered there was always some purty gal just dyin' to wipe the manure off `is goofy face. And at times it seems I can hear `im yet, just whoopin' and hollerin' somewhere off down the street, with somethin' sweet tucked under `is arm, swoonin' away on account of `is manly charm.

And that's more or less what this is all about, for the amount of Benny's appeal truly was downright awesome. As ya could prob'ly verify for yourself, at least if ya ever come across one of `is sweet-smellin' little ex-rose blossoms.

Now the story I'm fixin' to tell just might win me a seat far below, in the darkest regions of Hell! At least if my ol' buddy gets a whiff of it, it prob'ly will. Because a long damn time ago, he made me swear on all that's fair, that I'd never, ever say one more word about the day our local womankind dang near come face to face with total dispair.

We was way down deep in the mine ya see, and doin' just fine, when Benny tried to cross over a ragged ol' rock he'da been a whole lot better off goin' around. And even now, in the dark of night, I sometimes think I can hear it yet, that strangled sound as he rolled off that stone, just givin' birth to moans and groans, while holdin' `is crotch fer all he was worth. So it was for sure and certain, the poor little bugger was really hurtin'.

But bad as it was, it got even worse! For at that very minute, our shift boss comes cruisin' by. And judgin' from my chum's pain-filled cry, Bill figured sure as Hell ol' Bunkhouse was about to croak, or at least that somethin' purty damn vital was broke. So he told `im to drop `is pants and knock off `is knock-kneed dance, and the sight we seen made us feel Benny'd prob'ly heard `is last girly squeal, unless he beat it right away, just to get some minor surgery from the miner's Doc. It was kind of hard tho', tellin' how bad it was, what with all the swellin'. But there really wasn't all that much blood.

Now ya oughta know, that even tho' a guy was barely scratched, whenever an accident form got filed, a report was always attached to ever single check the mine's payroll gal dished out. And when she gave poor Benny his, along with some words of sympathy and a couple pats on the hand, all those birds standin' in line could hardly wait to see what it was all about. So there was just one Gawd awful shout, when Ol' Electrical Fred read those revealin' words danglin' from poor Benny's name.

And from that day on, those dad-blame clowns hardly ever gave `im a moment's peace. For just when ya'd think the razzin' was gonna cease, some joker would stir up the fire with another pointy word poker. Then poor ol' Benny would stand and glare straight down `is beak, like some dang Indian totem, while a quivery falsetto voice would howl "OOOOOOOh Dear me but that smarts, as you'd surely know, if <u>youuuuuuuu</u> ever had a bruised an' lacerated scrotum." And if that gaff failed to receive enough of a laugh, then the knock-kneed stance and tippy-toed dance was plumb bound to succeed.

And even after all the years that've passed, I think of him quite a lot, and more often than not, he's still right there, in that same hunkered-up squat, with tears of pain rollin' down `is grimy cheeks, while both `is fists are clenched down there, in front of his fatter backward pair.

But then I remember the way he grinned at my hoppin' and howlin', the day he accidently mashed my finger with a damn ol' drillin' steel. And if that wasn't bad enough, no more than three seconds after he done it, my ol' buddy just had to up and ask "How does it feel?"

But just in case the rest of ya are still tryin' to figure out why I went and wrote all this junk, you're about to find out. BUNKHOUSE, YA DADBLAME MANGY OL' GALOOT, I know yer out there somewhere, so ya can finally consider us even. Because with what's writ right here in black and white, we're square at last! And if ya still wanta know the fact of the matter, IT REALLY DOES FEEL AWFUL DAMN GOOD!

An Ear For Music

The year was probably about 1970, and I was camped far up the Slana River with two young men who each, in moments of extreme vulnerability, had relieved me of responsibility for the care and feeding of both my eldest and youngest female offspring. Being fully aware of the magnitude of their undertaking, I felt it my duty to at least try and make amends by assisting each of them in tracking down as large a moose as possible.

Our camp was situated beside a fork in the trail, with the right-hand arm heading on up the river past a grove of dense spruce, which was commonly referred to as `The Island'. We'd set our tent just a few yards up the left-hand arm, which eventually ended a short distance beyond Mankomen Lake, after passing through a large basin that was filled to overflowing with the sweet-willow thickets all moose love to browse on. The basin itself was called `The Moose Pasture' by most of the hunters who regularly hunted this part of Alaska.

I think we'd already managed to shoot one young bull, and were fully involved in trying to find two more on the day I decided to climb straight up the side of the small mountain we were camped at the base of. Because with its being situated right between the two forks of the trail, I figured there was an excellent chance there would be moose lying on its numerous benches. And even if I didn't actually get a shot at one, I'd probably succeed in driving it down to my two highly enthusiastic companions. I'd climbed to the upper limits of the timber in roughly an hour's time, and from there I got a panoramic view not only of the Moose Pasture and Island, but several thousand additional acres of gorgeous scenery.

Through the lenses of my binoculars I was able to make out several of the other hunting camps. At each location the frequent flash of sunlight bouncing off the wings of camp-robbers and magpies supplied ample proof of well-stocked meat-poles. I was also able to hear the faint sound of country-western music coming from a radio in one of the larger camps at The Island.

But as I began working back and forth across the face of the mountain, in a gradual descent, the sound of music became even louder. And since I was seeing plenty of evidence of game, but no actual animals, it wasn't very long before I began entertaining some highly uncomplimentary thoughts about the owners of that infernal radio. They apparently already had their moose, so loud noises wouldn't have an adverse effect on their efforts. But I soon became completely convinced that they were flat-out raising hell with mine.

I was already up the mountain, though, and since it didn't make any sense to just give up, I continued my slow descent. Suddenly, a movement in the dense brush caught my attention, no more than seventy-five feet away. Unable to make out what had caused it, I eased slowly to the right, and gradually, two large ears came into focus, then the head of the cow moose they were attached to materialized. It looked for all the world as though both of those ears were involved in a mating-dance with the clown playing that radio, and her whole head seemed to be bobbing up and down in time to the beat. You can talk about syncopation until you're blue in the face, but you've never seen anything to compare to that babe. She was just wound for sound and wired to the max, and I do mean really!

I got so tickled from watching her that I couldn't keep from laughing, and when she heard me, all she did was look back over her shoulder and blink her eyes. After a second or two, though, and a couple of haughty sniffs, she turned back around and resumed listening to the music. But each time my laughter would get a little too loud to suit her, she'd shoot me a quick dirty look, then her ears would start dancing again.

After what had to be almost ten minutes, I decided there was no point in disturbing her matinee any longer, so I slipped back away from her as quietly as possible, and continued hunting toward camp. I think we ended up getting one more bull that year, although I wouldn't swear to it. But I can guarantee that the memory of that homely old sister is as sharp and clear today as it was that afternoon, almost thirty-five years ago.

So many times, you know, it's not the major events in a person's life that stick in his mind, it's the small, seemingly insignificant things. Just like the time I went up to my Lake Susitna cabin one March day. Because even though I much preferred having my wife along, when she said she had other plans, I'd decided I really needed to get away from the so-called rat-race for a few days, and had driven up the highway alone.

After leaving my pickup at Lake Louise Lodge, I headed off across the lake on my ancient Arctic-Cat snow-machine, pulling a loaded sled behind it. And since I've never been what could be called mechanically inclined (unless the time my truck broke down on a steep hill and I crawled beneath it to pound on its belly with a crescent-wrench qualifies me for that dubious distinction), the thought of going anywhere but to my cabin, on a snow-machine all by myself, would more than likely have been enough to turn my knees to jelly.

But I somehow managed to herd that contrary bucket of junk all the way to the cabin by the time the sun started trying to make up its mind whether to go on and go to bed, or turn back around and see how much chance there was of making fools out of the roosters. So as soon as I'd fired up my gasoline-powered ice-auger and drilled a hole out in front of the cabin for drinking water, carried in a bucket and five-gallon screw-top jug of said water, then built a fire in the barrel-stove, I got back in the saddle just as the sun muttered "to hell with the goofy roosters" and rolled on over the edge of the horizon.

By the time I'd nursed my un-trusty steed a mile or so across the lake and had scraped the sixteen inch layer of snow off a dozen or so six-foot circles of ice with my shovel, daylight was fast becoming little more than a pleasant memory. The circles were laid out in the form of a much larger circle, and had lacked approximately forty feet of meeting when I decided to quit shoveling and start drilling holes. As I hustled across this gap toward where I'd first begun scraping circles, I saw what looked like a pile of moose-droppings lying in a small depression in the snow, so I jabbed an inquisitive shovel at them.

Even though I'd long been aware of what curiosity had done to that poor old cat, I wasn't really prepared for the trap it had set for my shovel. Because if I hadn't let go of the handle when I did, I'd undoubtedly have followed it right on down to the bottom of the lake. So as soon as my heart quit trying to hammer a hole through my ribs, I got down on my knees and began searching for the point where solid ice left off and the Black-hole of Susitna began. And by the time I finished, a three-foot circle of extremely cold water was reflecting my sky-lighted silhouette back at me.

Now even though I'd long known that bubbles of methane gas, from decaying vegetable matter and much deeper coal-seams, have a tendency to rise to the surface throughout the year, frequently causing holes to form in the ice, this was the first one of a significant size that I'd come across. What really spooked me, though, was how close I'd come to blundering straight into it, since the path I'd made through the snow ended up being no more than twelve or fifteen inches from the actual edge of the hole.

But since a miss is supposed to be good for a mile, once you find out where she's hiding, at least, I soon decided there was nothing to be gained by missing out on what I'd come to do. So I fired the auger up and drilled a hole in each of the circles I'd made. The ice averaged about thirty-six inches in thickness, more than enough to support a large truck or bulldozer, so that should give you some idea as to why that big hole came as such a shock.

After setting a fish-line in each of the small holes, I hiked over to the shore and broke off a large dead willow to use for setting three more lines in the big hole, just to see if Fate had been trying to clue me in on something when she steered me around it. That done, I got on my snow-machine and headed back to the cabin to cook supper.

For those of you who've never been exposed to a winter's night in Alaska, you need to be aware that when there's snow all around you, even the slight amount of light emanating from the stars seems to be magnified, and it's truly amazing how light the night can be. Which is pretty fortunate in the Lake Louise area, where a mid-winter night is usually as much as sixteen hours long. Consequently, when I left the cabin again, just shortly after 9:00 P.M., I didn't bother turning my machine's headlight on.

My earlier trail was almost as well-defined and easy to follow as though I was travelling in the middle of the day, and with the temperature a very mild thirty degrees above zero, I hadn't bothered to wear a jacket inside my insulated coveralls. It was really pleasant to be out and about, especially after I'd pulled three fat burbot from my holes. Having felt at least two more let go of the hook as I was pulling the lines up, I decided to sit out there awhile and see if they'd bite again.

And sure enough, after another fifteen or twenty minutes had elapsed, I had three more fish lying on the ice. Then all of a sudden I seemed to hear just a whisper of sound, and it felt almost as though someone, or something, was watching me. I've never been one to go around telling folks how brave I am, solely because it would be a complete waste of time. Why all they'd have to do would be to look back over my shoulder, yell "Shoo, git the hell out'a here.", and I'd more than likely run right over the top of them.

Anyhow, I did as swift an about-face as any gung-ho recruit ever did, and smack-dab behind me was the damndest sight I'd ever seen. Looking almost as though some totally invisible being was shaking the stardust out of a huge, dark-blue, velvet blanket, the southern hemisphere of the sky was virtually writhing with shafts of iridescent light. Most of them were greenish-white, but there were also pale shades of pink, amber, and blue. And whether you care to believe it or not, there was also a soft, rustling sound, very similar to what a sheet of cellophane makes when it's removed from a package. After awhile, though, it began seeming more like I was feeling it, rather than actually hearing it.

All thoughts of fishing were forgotten for the next twenty or thirty minutes, while I sat there on the seat of my machine and watched those lights come sliding toward me in one rippling wave after another. And by the time the display finally ended, I felt almost as if I'd been floating clear up among the stars. It was an extremely profound and humbling experience, believe me, and I've never had another one quite like it.

For some reason the fish stopped biting altogether during the time all this was going on, but I couldn't have cared less right then, since I'd seen something that most people never get a chance to see. And except for what I'd spent driving up to the cabin, the only cost involved had been that of sitting out there on the ice in the middle of the night. Man-oh-man, if I could just strike a bargain like that a little more often, I'd flat-out have it made in the shade!

Am I Too Profound?

OH! I suffer so, but not you see, from plain ordinary pain,

for whenever I quest for a touch of literary excitement,

I almost always discover those around me
are in need of enlightenment.

Now am I really and truly so extraordinary?
Do I actually seek in vain?

Why? Oh please, when I merely petition
Pretty Kitty to sit upon my knee,

oh why must I endure your suspicion?

Can there possibly be such a hopeless generation gap, that when
I entreat sweet little Kitty to park her lovely charms within
my encircling arms, I have to receive all this awful degenerate
crap about "Oh, how pornie, he gets horny over a cat."

Now why can't you admit, it would be far more kinky if I
slipped into something dinky and skipped out there to watch
our Binky Polar Bear slip into her snowy Anchorage lair.

And who's to say that dang old Zoo's not just really stinky?

Is it truly so hard for you egg-headed whiz-kids to perceive,
since we've all shared this dreary high-brow space with
Karen C.'s cheery face for all this while, and when her
last name's the very same, still you cannot conceive that
I might actually achieve reprieve while I cleave that
ever so witty Kitty Carlisle between my sleeves?

So please be kind, if nothing else, and relieve my
mind by letting me believe you're no longer deceived.
'Cause I really am pretty peeved, you know! An' hurry
up for cryin' out loud, 'cause I really gotta go.

Bottoms Up, My Friend

One of the most enjoyable things about living in Alaska, at least for me, is the opportunity it offers one to observe the various creatures we share the land with. And one of the critters I get the most pleasure out of watching is the Trumpeter swan. For something so regal appearing though, they frequently come as close to acting like complete dodoes as the real ones probably did.

One April, twenty-five or thirty years ago, my wife, Dee, and I had gone up to spend a few days at our cabin on Lake Susitna. And even though the road ended somewhere close to five miles short of the cabin, or eight whenever we parked our pickup at the Lake Louise Lodge, we'd decided to drive across the ice to the cabin. This was just because the owner of the Tyone Mountain Lodge, some fifteen miles or so further down the chain of lakes from our place, had plowed a trail all the way to his establishment. And even though I had to chain my four-wheel drive rig up, after turning off the trail, the remaining three-quarters of a mile was a breeze.

So after spending several glorious days, just put-putting all over the lakes on our snow-machine, setting out fishing lines and hauling in the burbot that took our bait, it eventually came time to load up and head back to civilization. We'd hardly even gotten back to the plowed trail that morning, before stopping. Approximately one hundred and fifty feet off to the left of us, a flock of at least twenty swans was hopping around on the ice and squawking like mad.

For the next twenty minutes or more, we sat there laughing at those goofy birds until the tears were running down our cheeks. They sounded and looked just like what I've always imagined rush-hour in New York City probably does, non-stop honking while everyone's running in circles and flapping their arms (wings in this case) and mouths at the poor dumb bird that had led them north before the ice left the lake. But at least when we finally grew tired of watching them tuck first one foot up under a wing to get it warm, then the other, and we'd resumed our homeward journey, I could empathize somewhat with the traffic cops and other officials who usually end up bearing the brunt of so much of humanity's less than civilized ire. Authority may be for the birds, but there was one hen-pecked sucker standing there on the ice that day, who was more than likely wishing it belonged to anyone but him.

Almost as though each of them was attached to an unseen axel, one bird's black-beaked head would swap places with his feet for several seconds, while he was undoubtedly probing the depths for succulent morsels, then when that head reappeared, the other one would go under. Each time one of them turned upside down, of course, it was to the accompaniment of a wild flailing of wings. In no way, shape, nor form did it even come close to resembling the so-called swan-dives I'd seen on T.V.'s Wide World of Sports. But I thoroughly enjoyed watching their performance, nevertheless.

During the forty or more years that have passed since I saw my first Trumpeters flying overhead, these magnificent birds have come to represent for me all that's right and good about Alaska. Surely, if they have such a need to return to it year after year, just to ensure that their kind endures, it must truly be the place that dreams are made of. And every time my soul weeps at the sight of them heading south on their annual Fall migration, it also rejoices in the knowledge that, come Spring, they'll once again return.

I'll grant you that birds such as the Arctic Tern fly much further and they're certainly no less beautiful, but when something as stately as those `flying fortresses' comes winging through the air, it's just got to mean something special.

A very dear, but long-departed lady once said to me "You know, Kiddo, the more I see some of the things that people do, the better I like dogs.", and we both laughed at the irony in what she'd said. For Doris probably had as many two-legged friends (and I'm not talking about birds this time) as anyone who's ever walked the face of this earth. Yet I knew instinctively that what she was saying was simply that, despite its so-called superiority, mankind has become entirely too complicated for its own good. But when you gain a dog's trust, it's almost always forever, and it's all so totally obvious that it can't be mistaken. It's a really nice feeling, and it was the way I always felt around that special lady.

Who Gives A Stinkin' Damn?

You know, when you really take the time to think about it,
Most of us get so wrapped up in our own trivial pursuits
That ever so frequently, or at least once in'a while,
We sort'a lose track'a good old reality!
So three dings of the alarm puts us in such a hell of a snit,
That we waste the rest of the day, glarin' down our snoots
And subsequently, we'll just walk a country mile
T'thumb our cold old noses at congeniality!
Just puttin' on'a show, and actin' like we wouldn't give'a whit,
If the folks we passed was nothin' but dust b'neath our boots.
And consequently, we almost never put on a smile
Or take a swig from that blessed jug, called Conviviality!
But if you haven't figured it out by this time,
The answer to the name of this cussed little rhyme
Is just, That I do!

Loon's Legacy

One mid-September afternoon as I was coming back down the Parks Highway, after spending ten less than productive days in moose-hunting camp, I rounded a bend in the road and saw my old friend Loon Loudermilk hot-footing it along the right-hand shoulder like he thought he was late for Happy-hour at the Montana Creek Bar. I was clipping along at least a notch and a half faster than I should have been, considering the fact that it was raining just hard enough so that I didn't see his slightly stooped figure until I was almost on top of him. But as soon as I saw that seagull feather sticking out the top of his droopy old southwester, I was certain it had to be Loon.

Because about the only time he doesn't wear the fool thing is when the sun is beating straight down and it's hotter than the hubs of Hades. And since that doesn't happen all that often in our neck of the woods, you can safely assume that it's perched on his head a good 99.9 percent of the time that he's up and about. Which is the main reason I've come to think of it as his Ivory Soap hat, although it sure isn't because of its purity, just in case you're one of those poor unfortunate souls who's inclined to jump on the first conclusion you come to. Why I can practically guarantee that the only washing that thing's ever gotten has been from the rain, since Loon would never waste anything as valuable as soap on it. But that's the way his cookies are assembled, so there's not too much to be gained by gumming them any longer than necessary.

Now it may only be because quite a few of Loon's stories border right on the fuzzy fringe of highly unlikely, but I've always had kind of a hard time swallowing the one about him taking that hat off a dead Indian he found down on the Knik mud-flats several years ago. But since that's an altogether different story, I guess I'd better just stick to the one I was figuring on when this kettle of chowder started bubbling.

Anyhow, I tromped down on the brakes just a little too hard, and if ol' Loon hadn't been real quick on the trigger and jumped when he did, I just might have tailgated him with my pickup's rear-end. Because that fool 4x4 swapped ends so fast I wasn't too sure whether I was coming home from camp, or just heading out to it. But by the time poor ol' Loon got all my slipstream wiped off and had cranked his jaws open to yell some of his more profound obscenities at me, he saw who it was and decided to just grin and let it go. I felt really bad about dousing him like that, needless to say, so I waited for him to come around the truck and get in before I turned it back in the direction we both wanted to go. Then I said "Sorry about that Loon, but all this dang rain seems to have Ol' Betsy feeling a trifle feisty."

That's when he said "Hell Kid that's okay, I prob'ly needed a bath anyhow. But ya ain't never seen no real rain, er ya sure wouldn't be callin' this little drizzle rain. Why did I ever tell ya the story about how Mt. McKinley really happened?"

I'd gotten used to him calling me "Kid" a long time before, even though he can't be much more than a couple of years further down the trail than I am, and I just turned sixty-eight the last time the little woman fired up a cake for me. So when I said "Naw, I'm purty sure ya haven't Loon.", I figured I was in for a long siege of it. Then I eased back in Betsy's saddle to get as comfortable as I could, and if you've got any smarts at all, you'll be hunting up a soft spot of your own along about now.

Before we go too much further, you really ought to be aware that Loon's always claimed to be the only living descendant of the Talneetka tribe's greatest chief, Wah-den-ah-li. And since Loon's mama, Wa-tah-da-li, was supposedly a direct descendant of Wah-den-ah-li, and also the last full-blooded member of the tribe when she died a few years back, you can see that this makes the Talneetkas pretty darn close to extinct. And that in itself should help you understand why I'd have felt so downright awful if I'd run over Loon that day. Why I'd probably have had to spend all the rest of my days, just being pointed out to the school kids and compared to those short-sighted clowns who wiped out the last of the carrier-pigeons and dodo-birds, whatever their names were.

There's not too much sense in sweating out a bunch of what-if's, though, so maybe we'd better get on with the story before one of us winds up with a saddle-sore or something.

This is pretty much the way Loon told it to me that day, so if it's alright with you I'll just call it "Loon's Legacy." I suppose some of you are probably wondering how an Indian named Loon ended up with a name like Loudermilk, so we'd better try to straighten that out first.

You see, by the time Wa-tah-da-li was fourteen and of marrying age, the last eligible buck in the tribe had gotten himself all hopped-up on happy-juice one day and had decided the best way to prove his manhood was to do battle with one of the Alaska Railroad's newest fire-breathing monsters. Back in those days they were still running steam rigs, just in case you get to wondering about that one too, Stanley. Sorry about that, but sometimes I just can't seem to help myself when the door more or less pops open the way it did this time.

Anyhow, he figured the best place to catch the monster by surprise would be just as it got halfway across the bridge up at Hurricane Gulch, so a day or two later he was waiting there behind the middle "Fire" barrel when that day's monster started across. And as luck would have it, the engineer was a big Swede by the name of Carlquist, who had a bet going with the fireman on who could shoot the biggest blob of tobacco juice into that very same barrel.

So just as soon as they started out across the bridge, they both ran back to the little platform between the locomotive and tender and got ready to let their wads fly. Consequently, the first they knew that anything was amiss was when that goofy redskin cut loose with a warwhoop and jumped smack between the rails, right square in front of the engine. The poor clown had apparently figured the element of surprise would bring the monster to a halt just long enough so he could plant his spear right in the center of its eye, you see.

As you've no doubt guessed by now, he'd figured dead wrong, real dead. Why ol' Loon swears up and down that the half-buck that went off the uphill side of the bridge made a bigger splash than the one on the downhill side. But since the creek must come awfully close to being three hundred feet below the rails, and neither the engineer nor the fireman would have been able to see both splashes, even if they'd each been where they were supposed to be, I've never been able to figure out where Loon got his information. It sure isn't in any record books that I've ever come across. But like I told you earlier, most of Loon's stuff slips in and out of the light about the same way a bat does when he's been nipping on moonbeams. But at least the train didn't jump the track, the way mine seems to keep right on doing.

Anyhow, the fireman's name was Lief Loudermilk, and when he finally heard about how poor little Wa-tah-da-li was still grieving over the dead buck a couple of months later, he quit his firing job and started courting her full time. Only partly because of the part he'd played in the buck's demise, you understand, since Loon claimed his mama was positively the prettiest thing he'd ever laid eyes on. At first her daddy wanted Lief to ante-up one of the railroad's locomotives for her hand. But when he found out how much it cost to feed one, he finally settled for half of however many beaver pelts Lief caught that winter, as well as all the tails. Loon said his grandad was really wild about beaver-tail soup, which is kind of pathetic in a way, since Lief fell through the ice and drowned just shortly after getting Wa-tah-da-li in the family way. But that's another story too, so here's "Loon's Legacy", just the way he told it to me.

"Way, way back, jist a short spell after Moon give birth to Sun's only child, Earth, the proud parents decided that if Earth was ever gonna live to a ripe old age, she was gonna need a full time nanny. So Moon took a little dab'a this, an' Sun tossed in a dab er two'a that, an' that's how they made the first two Talneetkas, Wah-den-ah-li an' his mate, Ah-mi-ga-li. Then they kept right on stirrin' the pot 'til all the rest'a Earth's two-legged an' four-legged critters had crawled out, an' the sky was plumb fulla birds, bees, an' butterflies. An' jist in case ya git t'wonderin', it wasn't 'til Moon tipped the pot over on its side t'see if it was empty yet, that all the rest'a the bugs popped out. But when she picked it up then t'shake out anything that was left inside, an' the dadburned snakes come slitherin' out, Sun yelled "That's enough ya goofy Ol' Broad." So he took it away from 'er an' crammed the snakes back in, then he flung it jist as hard as he could. Fact is, it got to goin' s'dang fast it jist flat-out exploded into a jillion pieces, an' that's how the stars happened. It's also the main reason snakes wound up with the idea they wasn't exac'ly welcome up here in Alaska, don'cha see?

Well sir, even though the sky did look kinda purty then, it really ticked Moon off that Sun had up an' busted 'er pot like that. So she jist went an' moved halfway around the sky from 'im, where she's been givin' 'im the cold shoulder ever since. An' ever time he's tried cozyin' up to 'er since then, she's up an' doused 'er light so's he couldn't find 'er. A'course this always gits 'im s'steamed up that the sky gits all fulla clouds. Then, when he can't see what's goin' on because'a all them fluffy things, he really gits fired up an' starts shootin' off sparks an' yellin' fit t'kill. An' that's why we still have so much lightnin' an' thunder when it's cloudy.

Bein' the flighty kind'a female she is, though, Moon never seems t'figger out that all she has t'do t'put an end t'all the foolishness is jist t'move back over beside Sun. So whata ya think she winds up doin'? Why she jist starts bawlin', a'course! An' that's where the rain comes from. So poor little Earth's jist been stuck right in the middle of 'er folks squabbles ever since. But once, way, way back, Moon got on such'a cryin' jag that 'er tears was jist about t'drown 'er only baby. Because somehow er other, she'd got it into 'er head that Sun was foolin' around with one'a the stars behind 'er back. An' let me tell ya, the tears flat come down by the bucketful when that happened.

By this stage'a the game, though, Wah-den-ah-li an' Ah-mi-ga-li had already begot themselves a whole passel'a little Talneetkas, an' poor Ah-mi-ga-li was havin' one devil of a time keepin' 'em away from the edge'a this big lake that Moon's tears was makin'. An' even though poor ol' Wah-den-ah-li was gittin' sick an' tired'a havin' t'help move their lodge t'higher ground ever' couple days er so, he was hard put t'come up with a cure fer the fix they was in. But fer several days runnin', he started gittin' up earlier ever' mornin', an' jist hikin' up t'the top'a this little hill they was camped by, t'see if a little peace an' quiet would help 'im dream somethin' up. An' from up there he could see that before too many more days went by, Moon's tears was prob'ly gonna completely cover the last'a the high ground.

Then fin'ly, one day way out on the horizon, he seen a whole herd'a critters swimmin' toward 'im. Why ever' direction he turned, it seemed like the water was plumb full of 'em, an' when he fin'ly figgered out that the ones out in front was Beavers, he knew what he had to do. Now back in those days, all'a Earth's critters still spoke the same lingo, ya see. So jist as soon as the chiefs of all the diff'ernt critters had made it t'shore, Wah-den-ah-li called fer a pow-wow an' told 'em what they was gonna have t'do t'save theirselves.

An' before very long the Bears was pilin' mud an' rocks onto the Moose's horns jist as fast as the Caribous could shovel it outta the lake, then the Moose would run up t'the top'a this little hill t'dump their load. All the other critters was doin' their share too, even the bugs an' birds. The Ants was chinkin' in the cracks b'tween all the loose rocks with sand, then the mud-dauber Bees an' the Swallows would plaster ever'thing up tight with the mud that the Gophers an' Shrews was ferryin' up from the shore on their noses. Like I said, ever'body was jist doin' 'is part. They had to ya see, er ever' last one of 'em was sure enough gonna drown.

Well sir, that pile jist kept gittin' higher an' higher, until it finally reached the bottom clouds. But ol' Wah-den-ah-li still wouldn't let the critters stop, since he knew they had t'reach the top'a the cloud-heap before the Beavers could ever hope t'dam the dang things up an' put an end t'all the rain that Moon's tears was makin'. So he jist kept 'em humpin' night an' day, until the top'a their heap was up there even with the highest clouds. It was real purty up there I guess, so after ever'one had took a peek at it, Wah-den-ah-li sent a band'a the biggest Beavers out t'have a look-see at the situation. They was s'posed t'report back on what they found by nightfall, but night come an' went an' it was purty easy t'see that the first buncha beavers had jist plain went. So Wah-den-a-li sent out another bunch an' the same dang thing happened.

Well sir, he jist wasn't about t'git snookered the third time, not with the fate of Ah-mi-ga-li an' the whole Talneetka clan hangin' in the balance. So on the third day he sent a couple Ravens out with the Beavers, jist t'keep an eye on things. But before they was much more'n outta sight, the Ravens had ran low on wind an' had set down on a star t'rest fer a minute er two. The Beavers jist kept right on goin' though, an' by the time them lazy birds decided they'd better go see what the Beavers was up to, they couldn't find hide ner hair of 'em.

Now you can jist bet that ol' Wah-den-ah-li was flat steamed when the Ravens come back an' told 'im what'd happened, so the next day he sent two

Eagles out jist t'keep an eye on the Ravens, who was still s'posed t'be keepin' an eye on the Beavers, jist in case yer havin' trouble stayin' on top'a all this.

Well sir, more er less the same dang thing kept on happenin', until Ol' Wah-den-ah-li fin'ly got smart an' sent a couple Loons out t'keep an eye on ever'one else. Them Loons're real honest-t'golly watchdogs, as ya'd know if ya'd ever tried sneakin' up on one. An' that night they brought ever'body back t'camp t'report t'Wah-den-ah-li. So jist as soon as he heard that most'a Moon's tears was pourin' through a great big hole in the biggest cloud'a the bunch, he sent all the critters back out t'git that there cloud.

An' even though it turned out t'be a real doozy of a job, by the time Sun went t'bed the next night, all the critters'd managed t'tow that fool cloud t'where it was floatin' right smack over the top'a the big mound they'd worked s'hard t'build. So Wah-den-ah-li told ever'one t'git a good night's sleep, because once they started pluggin' that hole up, they wouldn't dare stop 'til it was crammed jist as full as they could git it.

Well sir, even though they wound up workin' non-stop fer a solid week, they fin'ly got the sucker plugged. An' jist like that, the rain that was drippin' from all them bottom clouds jist flat-out dried up. Ol' Wah-den-ah-li was s'proud'a what they'd accomplished by workin' together, that he up an' invited all the critters to a potlatch at 'is lodge. An' that fool party might still'a been goin' on too, if that silly Moon had jist gotten 'er wits t'gether an' shut off 'er tears. Why that dam, that ever'body had worked s'hard t'build, was s'dang tight that Moon's tears fin'ly run all the way across the sky an' jist plumb soaked Ol' Sun's moccasins to a fare-thee-well.

An' jist let me tell you, that ol' boy threw a real dilly of a fit then, because he cut loose with a lightnin' bolt that jist dang near put an end to the whole shebang. Why after that sucker blew the dam t'smithereens, it ricocheted into the mound that Wah-den-ah-li an' the critters had made, an' jist knocked the top half of it plumb off. Then that bolt went t'zingin' around Earth like it had been all her fault that her Dad's moccasins had got wet, jist touchin' down ever' little bit an' flat raisin' holy heck. An' talk about rain, why by the time all them dammed up tears'a Moon's had drained out, dang near a month an' a half had gone by, an' about the only way poor Wah-den-ah-li an' the rest'a the clan could come up with t'git halfway dried out, was jist t'take a dang bath.

Apparently, that lightnin' bolt'a Sun's had scared the wits plumb out'a the other critters, ya see, an' from then on they all yabber-jabbered away in so many different lingos that Wah-den-ah-li an' his bunch couldn't make heads er tails out'a anything they said. Then, jist before the ol' guy fin'ly got too old t'run the show any longer, the rest of 'is bunch decided it was only right t'name what was left'a the dam-buildin' mound in his honor."

Loon looked over at me then and said "So they called it Den-ah-li, which jist incidentally sounds a whole damnsite better'n what you white-eyes all call it. Because what I'd jist really like t'know, is jist what in heck did President McKinley ever do that even come close t'what ol' Wah-den-ah-li done?"

All I could think of to say was "Beats me Loon, but we're almost to Willow, so what do you say to stoppin' off fer a cold beer?"

Loon grinned and slapped his leg before saying "I was kinda scared I wasn't gonna make it to the end in time, so I left out the part about why Mama named me after the Loon. But it shouldn't take much more'n a couple brews t'fill ya in on that part."

It didn't either, but rather than wag this tale any longer, let's just suffice it to say that Loon's mama felt there was a good chance both he and Earth might derive a certain amount of benefit, if he felt he was needed to look after the other critters. Because, just in case you're still interested, the Talneetkas always placed a Loon at the top of their totems. Or at least that's what Loon told me as we were leaving the Willow Roadhouse, a good long hour later.

Now that I stop to think about it, though, I don't remember ever reading anything about the Interior Indians carving totem poles. Maybe that's why the goofy sucker was snickering when I dropped him off at the trail leading to his cabin. Oh well, what the heck, I've anteed up a lot more than a couple of beers for worse balls of yarn than that in the past. And I'll more than likely be doing so at some point in the future, too.

Just In Case Someone Wants To Know

At first it seemed more than just a trifle odd to me
That such a quiet, dinky little ol' broad could possibly be
The kingpin of Homer's more famous, high-browed literary crowd
But after learning better, I decided to write this here letter
Just so she'll know that even tho' I've seldom got a lot to say
I'm convinced today's the day for this little doll to realize
That even if she's not quite what a feller might call regal-size
She's just flat-out the Queen of Hearts down around these parts
Because we all just really love our Dear, Sweet Caroline!

It Sure Ain't Th' Paint

Some folks git real tuned in, t'th' way a fella's dressed,
an' that can be pretty important, I'll not attempt t'deny.

`Cause neatly pressed pants, an' a slicked up pair a'shoes
sure do look nice with combed down hair, an' a spiffy tie.

But then again, `tain't really th' clothes that make a man.

An' those folks think too, that unless a'guy talks jist so,
an' sounds real smart, he ain't even worth listenin' to.

`Cause they claim th' trail t'fame, fortune, an' glory will
prove t'be way too rough, if a man ain't got th' stuff
a'gentlemen in `is bones, an' can't talk in hi'falutin' tones.

But I don't pay `em too much mind, b`cause I
can't help but b`lieve they're half blind.

Fer t'me th' whole secret of'a guy's story is easy t'perceive.
At least if ya`ve got th' nerve t'look in `is eyes.

B'cause eyes're really nothin' but windows that look right thru
t'th' very soul of'a worthwhile man!

Rat Reagan's Ace In The Hole

For whatever it may be worth, the first time I laid eyes on the rancid little renegade this particular story is about, I wasn't smelling too much like a fresh bouquet of petunias myself. Not that I ever do, mind you, but this time I'd gotten a little too enthusiastic about potting a moose for my winter's meat. And after a full week of beating all the brush within reasonable packing distance of my Lake Susitna cabin, I'd ventured several miles further than I'd intended to, roughly due west from the south end of the lake.

At least it started out to be mostly in that direction. But then I'd cut some really fresh sign, and after zigging this way and that for a good hour and a half, I'd spotted a moose rump just as it was disappearing behind the crest of a hill. I wasn't real sure there were any horns on the other end, but based entirely on the size of what I'd seen, I figured there was a pretty darn good chance there were.

I knew I could probably make it back to the boat in close to an hour, at least if I eliminated most of the zigs and zags of my out-bound route. But when it's been several years since you've had to shoulder more than your everyday amount of bull for any further than three or four hundred yards, you somehow manage to forget how heavy a fully loaded pack-board can be. So before common-sense had the slightest chance of wiping out the fantasy of filling my freezer with fresh moose-chops, I'd passed completely through the realm of reality and entered the never-never land of sheer stupidity. In short, I eventually ended up crossing not just one, but three more ridges.

There's a fifty-fifty chance that I'd have headed over a couple more too, if I hadn't caught a faint whiff of smoke about the time I began trying to figure out whether I'd be better off detouring to the right, or the left, in order to get around the fairly good-sized body of water I now found myself staring at. It would actually have been shorter to go to the left, but since the slender column of smoke was coming from a stand of fairly decent spruce trees, a quarter mile or so to the right, I was soon headed in that direction.

By now I'd been riding Shank's mare just long enough to wonder why I'd been dumb enough to leave the cabin with nothing but one sandwich, a candy-bar, and a couple of half-shriveled apples in my pack. And as was usual for me, I'd polished all of them off before I'd much more than gotten beyond spitting-distance of the lake. Susitna Lake that is, not the semi-stagnant, weed-choked expanse of mud and water I was now traversing.

Stumbling along within a few feet of the water's edge, I crossed numerous muddy slots in the shore-grass that had been created by the back and forth passage of countless generations of muskrats, as they ventured ashore in search of the succulent willow-shoots they always seem to crave. And together with the large number of push-up mounds that dotted the more shallow, shoreline areas of the little lake, more or less like warts on a toad, it was completely evident that I'd blundered into a virtual muskrat Utopia. Two or three times during the fifteen minutes it took for me to reach the stand of timber the smoke was issuing from, I narrowly missed stepping on one of little rodents as it went racing toward the safety of the water.

Just as I reached the first of the trees, though, I heard a raspy "Awk-awwk-awk" and jerked my gaze skyward just as a large, glossy-black raven deposited itself onto the uppermost branch of the tree right beside me. Then, as it perched there flapping its wings and squawking as though its very life depended upon how much racket it could generate, a man's voice said "Awright Edgar, he don't look all that danger'us t'me, jist simmer down while I find out what he's up to."

Standing no more than twenty feet away, almost completely hidden by the overlapping limbs of two bushy-butted spruce, the source of the voice proved to be all of five and a half feet in height, give or take an inch one way or the other. And except for a long, pointed nose and the whites of his eyes, it was all but impossible to tell where the hair on his head left off and that on his face took over. I mean, that joker was hairier than anything I'd ever even had nightmares about. And back during the days when I was still susceptible to trying to cure what ailed me with a little shot of morning-after, hair-of-the-dog-that-bit-me tonic, I'd long since become well acquainted with my share of wild-looking critters.

Then, almost as though he'd begun an instantaneous molt, a section of hair an inch below the speaker's nose dropped down about two inches, to reveal a set of the yellowest teeth I'd ever seen. I swear, when he started cackling the way he did at that moment, I wouldn't have been the least bit surprised to see a forked tongue come darting out of his mouth. Right about then he said

"Name's Reagan, Rat Reagan t'my friends. An' since ya look friendly enough, that's what ya might jist as well call me."

Heaving a sigh of relief, I started toward him, right hand extended and my rifle still slung over my left shoulder. But I hadn't managed to complete the second step before that bundle of ebony-hued feathers, which I'd last seen sitting twenty feet above my head, had launched itself on a collision course with my hat, squawking loud enough to wake the dead. So while I'm spending six or eight of the longest seconds I ever hope to put in, this Reagan character comes charging at me, waving a six-foot hunk of peeled spruce in the air and yelling "Dad-blame it Mister Poe, I said simmer down. Because if ya don't, yer gonna find yerself swimmin' in our cookpot before too much longer, minus all them purty feathers."

Then he thumped the ground with the lower end of his stick a couple of times, held out his other arm, and just like that's what he'd been waiting for, that crazy bird lit on it. While I'm trying to get my wits back into some semblance of order, and also locate where my hat had disappeared to, the fool thing took a couple of sideways hops and wound up roosting on Reagan's shoulder, where he proceeded to give me the once-over with those beady eyes. Then his beak popped open and a halfway sociable sounding "Awwk, awww-wk" squirted out of the reddest looking gullet I could ever remember seeing.

It may only have been because of the sharp contrast to the blackness of his feathers, but the throat on that bird looked like it was all of six inches deep and at least half that much in diameter. When another "Awwwk" came rolling out of it, though, I couldn't keep from laughing. Then Reagan said "He ain't exackly whatcha might call well-versed, but there ain't hardly anything that comes around our place, without his lettin' me know about it. An' since he don't eat anywhere near as much as a dang fool dog would, I figger that's worth makin' a few allowances for. This far out in the sticks at least. Well c'mon, let's go see if the water's still hot enough fer a cup'a tea. I'm plumb outta coffee, though, jist in case that's what ya prefer."

Following along approximately five feet behind him, I quickly reached the conclusion that it had been more than a few days since either he or his clothing had come into contact with soap, so I dropped back even further. But when he turned around and saw me lagging behind, Reagan said "Hells-bells man, there ain't no need t'be bashful, ol' Edgar'll behave hisself now. An' I wouldn'ta asked ya in fer tea, if I didn't figger on feedin' ya a little bite'a somethin' too."

Casting caution to the winds, I mentally rotated the sensitivity nob on my smeller about three full turns as I closed the gap between us. Once we got inside his ramshackle little one-room cabin, though, there was more than enough wood-smoke aroma to put a damper on its owner's personal aura. This was due entirely to the so-called stove that sat in the left rear corner of the cabin. It consisted of nothing more than what had once been a fifty-five gallon oil-drum, which had been hammered just flat enough on one side so that a skillet or kettle would sit on it without sliding off.

At the rear of this flattened area, an X-shaped cut had been made with a chisel, then the resulting points of metal had been bent up at right angles, so they'd fit inside a length of six inch stovepipe and thus hold it in place. A square hole had been cut in the opposite end of the barrel from the pipe, so that full lengths of firewood could be inserted. And over this hole a piece of flat metal, which looked as though it had once been the end of a smaller barrel, now hung from two nails that had been bent in the form of hooks. The whole assembly rested on several hundred pounds of small rocks, which were contained in a framework of peeled spruce-poles.

So due to the loose fitting door, as well as the base of the stovepipe, a pretty fair amount of smoke tended to seep into the cabin, rather than out of it. But as far as I was concerned, at that moment at least, the smoke was very definitely an asset. All of which brings us to the construction of the cabin itself.

Approximately ten feet wide and twelve or fourteen feet in length, the walls consisted of logs that probably averaged six inches in diameter. The dirt floor wasn't quite what I'd call hard-packed, although the heavy layer of sand on top of it seemed to keep an excessive amount of dust from rising when you walked across it. There were also two small windows, one in the sidewall adjacent to the stove, and the other in the end containing the door.

The gabled roof was constructed of poles which were supported in the center by a ridge-beam that was roughly a foot in diameter, making it the largest log in the entire structure. Most of the metal on the exterior of the roof appeared to have been salvaged from five-gallon fuel cans, although there were a good many smaller pieces that probably came from coffee cans. But at least the pitch was steep enough so that it should have been relatively watertight. Although the slight amount of light that managed to get through the two smoked-glass windows (just a little play on words there) made it rather difficult to recognize any evidence of recent water leakage.

The door was made from two layers of hand-hewn boards, one that was horizontal and nailed to the outer, vertical one. The hinge-system was one of the most ingenious I've ever encountered, for it consisted of nothing more than the extended ends of the vertical board on that side. Roughly twice the thickness of its neighbors, the ends of this board had been whittled into round pivot-points that were fitted into the upper and lower logs of the door frame.

The stop on that side was placed so that the outer face of the door came up against it in the closed position, while the one on the latch-side was secured to the inner edge of the frame. Consequently, it would have been all but impossible for a marauding bear to swat it open. Although I doubt that this had anything to do with the reason it had been built as it was. Strips of caribou hide were tacked all around the inner perimeter of the door itself, providing what appeared to be a fairly efficient form of weather-proofing.

And except for a two-foot length of twelve-inch log, which served as the only chair, the rest of the cabin's furnishings consisted entirely of shelves of various sizes, which were supported by however many braces as the builder had deemed necessary. The narrow sleeping bunk occupied the corner opposite the stove, and since it was secured to two of the cabin-walls, a single block of log was all that was needed for support of the remaining corner. The three-foot by two-foot table-shelf was directly under the window next to the stove, so it was completely obvious that all thought of entertaining guests had been cast to the winds by its owner.

So when Rat, as he'd said I was free to call him, said "Take yer pick'a seats, the bunk er the stump.", I quickly rolled the stump to a spot halfway between the door and the table and plopped down with my back against the wall.

This was solely because (as I'm sure you can understand) I wasn't exactly anxious to encounter anymore of his pets, by sitting on the bunk. Most especially after Edgar, or Mister Poe, if that's what tickles your fancy, dropped off Rat's shoulder like a bomb and began pecking at random all around the rumpled assortment of bedding on top of it. Mind you, I'm not saying my host was actually buggy, but from what I'd thus far seen, I figured there was a pretty fair chance of it.

So while I sat there with my eyelids cranked as far toward full-open as they'd go, Rat lifted the lid from the soot-encrusted teakettle sitting on top of the stove, and tested the temperature of its contents with the terminal-knob of his left forefinger. I'd already noticed that the original end of it had parted company with the rest of him quite some time in the past, you see, so I consoled myself with the realization that at least there wouldn't be anything washing out from under a fingernail.

Mumbling "She's not quite hot a'nuff, but a little bear hair ought'a take care'a that.", he hustled back outside.

After hearing several second's worth of snap, crack and pop, I was pretty sure of what he'd have in his hands when he came back inside, but I just hadn't heard it referred to as 'bear hair' before. And sure enough, both hands were filled with several of the dead lower branches he'd pulled from a nearby spruce, all of which were well covered with a wooly layer of the dry, black moss that seems to thrive on all the spruce trees in this part of Alaska.

Within just a few seconds of his jamming them into its black gullet, the stove came to life once more, roaring fiercely and puffing smoke all around the door and stovepipe, like some totally demented dragon. This chore taken care of, Rat rummaged through the conglomeration on a shelf near the ceiling and came up with two tin-cans that looked as though they may originally have contained beans or soup. And just to make sure they didn't still hold anything more substantial than aromatic memories, he turned them upside down and rapped them sharply on the table. Then he reached into a large can at the back of the table and extracted a pinch of material that rattled softly as he dribbled some of it into each of the small cans.

Winking at me, the hair under his nose parted company with that on his chin once again, and with his yellow fangs glowing in the soft light provided by the window, he said "Hope ya like Lab'adore tea, because it's all I got. But I can guarantee it's fresh, since I jist picked it a couple days ago."

So while I was saying "It's been a long time since I've had any, Rat, but I always thought it was real tasty.", he picked up the kettle and dumped some of the now steaming contents into each can. Then he shoved one toward me, picked the other one up and said "Here's mud in yer eye."

Bracing myself for the possibility that there'd also be some rolling down my throat in a second, I took a tentative sip. But even though I had to lower the container back to the table almost immediately, since it was uncomfortably hot on my fingers, I was pleasantly surprised to find the contents completely palatable. Then, sensing Rat's eyes following my every move, I extracted the handkerchief from my hip-pocket and folded it several times before wrapping it around the can, which was soon hoisted to my lips once more.

Satisfied that I found his beverage acceptable, he said "Ain't no need to be bashful, there's plenty more where that come from. All I gotta do is pick s'more whenever I run out."

Once that first cupful was safely down the chute, I had no qualms about accepting his offer of a second one. But after we sat there visiting for the better part of an hour, and my insides began making some highly audible comments about the length of time that had elapsed since they'd last been stoked with something solid, Rat's next offer took just a little more consideration.

Apparently triggered by a loud "Awwwk" from Edgar, my host slapped his leg with one hand and exclaimed "Don't know what's the matter with my manners, unless it's on account of it's bein' so long since me an' Edgar's had comp'ny. But I jist bet yer gittin' hungry."

Winking slyly, he then added "Leastwise when my gizzard growls that way, that's what the trouble usually is. Anyhow, I boiled up four swamp-rabbits yesterday an' there's plenty left, so how 'bout I stir up some dumplin's t'go with 'em an' we have us a bite t'eat? I'd boil some spuds, but I been outta them fer quite a spell too."

Having trapped muskrats for spending money during my youth, I was already familiar with the term 'swamp-rabbit'. But due to the amount of time that usually elapsed before I got around to skinning my catch, the little animals generally smelled a bit too ripe for my palate. Consequently, I'd always felt somewhat guilty about wasting their meat, since I was well aware that if they were just handled properly, there was no reason they shouldn't be every bit as tasty as cottontail rabbits.

So after completing a quick mental footrace back to where my skiff was waiting, an equally hurried glance at my watch made it all too plain that there was no way I'd be able to reach my own cabin until well after dark. And since I'd begun carrying a set of long-johns and a chunk of canvas in my pack just shortly after I'd last had to shiver my way through a night out in the open, I decided to take a chance on Rat's culinary abilities, and worry about where I was going to hole up for the night after my grumbling stomach had something in it besides Labrador tea and fond memories.

So I grinned and said "As long as you're sure Edgar won't mind, Rat, I'm half starved. What can I do to give you a hand?"

After commenting that Edgar could either hold his peace, or expect a prolonged bath in the stewpot, Rat said "Well, if ya don't mind hikin' down the trail to the head'a the lake, ya kin fetch back some fresh water."

Then, after dumping approximately a quart of water into the teakettle, he handed me the well dented galvanized pail and I headed out the door. Mistakenly assuming that the most heavily traveled of two trails was the one to take, I soon found my route blocked by a length of peeled sapling that was supported at each end by the bottom limbs of two very bushy spruce trees. It didn't require an abnormally high IQ to figure out what the pole was for, because the open pit on the other side of it made its purpose all too plain. Although there was no sign whatsoever of toilet tissue in the muck at the bottom.

So once I'd backtracked to the correct trail and then hiked roughly a hundred and fifty yards to where a small trickle of water entered the lake, at least ten minutes had elapsed. And by the time I'd filled the bucket and hiked back to where the trail reentered the grove of spruce trees, roughly halfway to the cabin, the sound of splashing water behind me caused an instantaneous about-face.

And there, not fifty feet from where I'd just filled the bucket, stood a bull moose. The tips of his antlers must have been somewhere close to sixty inches apart at the widest point, very definitely a respectable-sized bull. But he seemed to be so intent upon the raft of water-lilies a few yards out in the lake, that he'd missed seeing me.

Moving slowly, and as quietly as possible, I slipped into the spruce grove and then proceeded to hot-foot it the rest of the distance to the cabin. Easing the door open, I quickly informed Rat of what I'd seen, adding "If you'd like me to, Rat, I'll shoot him and help you butcher him. He should give you enough meat to."

Before I could finish, though, Rat yelled "You jist ain't even about t'shoot Bruce, Mister. Not unless ya wanta have me breathin' down yer collar from now on. He's my ace in the hole ya know, because if the pickin's ever git really tough around here, I always got that ol' fool t'fall back on. So jist plunk yer dang butt back down on this here stump an' fergit about 'im."

After I'd done what he said, he began spooning a spongy looking mass of dough, which had all but outgrown the skillet he'd mixed it up in, into the steaming contents of a large aluminum kettle. Then he inverted the skillet and placed it on top of the kettle. This done, he sat back down on the edge of his bunk and proceeded to fill me in on all the many reasons about why "Bruce the Moose" shouldn't be molested.

A lot of hunting seasons have come and gone since that evening, and Rat's been dead for at least half of them, but if I squint my eyes just right at times, I can almost still see him sitting there in front of me. For in the dim light of that little cabin, his raspy, sing-song voice seemed to pick up a rhythm similar to that of a crosscut saw, with its rusty teeth biting its way through a log. It certainly wasn't what you might call melodious, but it most definitely had a pleasant, hypnotic effect on me that afternoon. And for whatever it's worth, I'd give quite a bit for the chance to hear it again.

He told me how Bruce had been just a yearling calf when he first ran into him, the fall he built his cabin. Bruce's mother had apparently died earlier in the summer, for he was quite thin. Apparently he was every bit as lonely, because he started hanging around Rat's camp, and even took to coming almost up to him when he was called. And before very many weeks had passed, he'd begun nibbling on the sourdough pancakes Rat would set out for him, shaking his head from side to side and mouthing each piece as though he wasn't too sure whether he liked the taste or not.

But somehow Bruce made it through this, his second winter, undoubtedly because Rat began breaking trails from one stand of birch trees to another, falling just enough of them so the calf could browse on the small limbs. Then with the advent of spring, Bruce disappeared and Rat was afraid he might have been killed by a grizzly. But one mid-October afternoon Bruce showed up again, following a young cow that was just coming into the first stages of estrus. Bruce's antlers didn't amount to much then, but each year after that they'd grown progressively larger, until they'd finally reached their present size.

The dumplings had gotten done well before Rat finished telling me Bruce's story, but as soon as we'd loaded up the only two tin-plates in the cabin, he filled me in on the rest of it while we ate. It seems that every spring Bruce would pull his vanishing act, then shortly before the first snow began falling, he'd return to the lake and stay in its general vicinity all winter. Rat said he'd nearly shot the animal once, when he got sick and tired of eating muskrats and smoked fish several weeks before the annual caribou migration provided another source of meat.

So even though it may surprise you, I wound up spending the night in Rat's cabin, spreading my canvas out on a caribou pelt he'd rustled up for me.

Somehow or other I'd missed noticing his cache, which was located several yards out behind the cabin, and he'd gotten the pelt out of it. He also brought down a pan-full of pinto-beans that he said he'd boil up the next day, if I wanted to hang around and shoot the breeze a little longer. I told him I really needed to head back to my place as soon after daylight as possible, which was precisely what happened.

Oh yeah, I almost forgot, muskrat meat beats the heck out of porcupine. And it's even better than most of the snowshoe rabbits I've eaten. The meat's fairly dark and sweet, so the only reason I can think of that might keep most folks from enjoying it, is its name.

That night at Rat's, though, I learned that it's hardly ever very smart to judge another critter solely by the way it looks, or by what it's called. Because if you do, there's a real good chance you're probably going to wind up pretty darn hungry at some point in your life, or downright lonely for company.

Straight Out Of The Blue

The original version of the following story was printed in We Alaskans on April 8, 1990.

Despite the heavier than normal snowfall that Skyline Hill has been blessed (or cursed) with this winter, it's been really pleasant to once again observe fairly large flocks of feeding snow-buntings and chickadees. And there have even been a substantial number of waxwings darting about among the trees here, high above downtown Eagle River. For several years though, the most commonly seen feathered inhabitants of our alpine neighborhood have been the extremely loudmouthed black and white comedians, the common magpie. And while their antics are amusing to watch from behind the safety of my kitchen window, they do very little for the peace of mind of a certain hyper-active squirrel that shares the outside of my property with me.

It really has been quite entertaining watching both species of the long-tailed clowns chase one another up, down, in, out, and all around the countryside. For even though he's at something of a disadvantage, since Mother Nature decided he wouldn't require wings in order to survive, Squirrel appears to spend almost as much time airborne as he does on the ground or in the limbs of our numerous spruce trees. And whether he's the chaser or the chasee doesn't really seem to matter, for at times he seems to be attached, either fore or aft, to one or another of his feather-duster playmates, dragging or being dragged through the atmosphere by a very short and totally invisible link.

It wasn't always thus, though, for only three or four years ago a plague almost wiped out our local squirrel and small bird population. In fact, I guess you could say it was a pair of plagues that more or less descended right straight out of the blue. At least the air was blue within a few seconds after I retrieved my cap from where it had landed in the driveway, right after I'd suddenly ducked out from under it while returning from collecting my morning paper.

You see, about the same time my peripheral vision had picked up this misguided missile that was headed straight for my head, both of the electronic marvels that help me hear what in Hades is going on about me had begun screaming an extremely shrill "KI-KI-KI-KI-KI", and I'd hit the deck as quickly as my arthritic old bones would allow. So by the time I'd gotten my cap in a position to protect what hair I still had left, there was a beady-eyed bundle of feathers glaring down at me from the top of a nearby spruce. Then within a matter of milliseconds I heard a whooooshing sound as a second bundle swooped past my head doing at least 900 miles an hour. After it had deposited itself on the limb beside the other one, it began giving me the evil-eye also.

So once I'd made it into the house and located my "Field Guide to Western Birds", a full five minute's worth of rapid-eye maneuvering soon convinced me that I'd just had a close encounter with a pair of Pigeon Hawks or Merlin's, one of the smaller members of the Falcon family. And despite what their earlier activities would indicate, that dang fool book claimed they didn't ordinarily feed upon itinerant members of the clan known as Homo sapiens.

Well Sir, within the matter of the next day or so, those malevolent suckers had taken up residence in one of my spruce trees and for the balance of the next two or three months they seemed to think they owned the whole mountain. And about the second time she got dive-bombed, the woman I've been trying to keep pacified for the last forty years or so began yelling at me to do something about it. So what I did was get out my long extension-ladder and prop it against the nest-tree, after which I informed her the rest was up to her. But as soon as she saw the way one of the nasty suckers was either sitting on the nest or sitting on ready in the next tree, only a few feet away, she soon decided she wasn't cut out to be a home-wrecker after all and went back in the house to see if she could conjure up a stray lightning-bolt or something.

Anyhow, during the course of the next few weeks and months we began finding bits and pieces of fur and feather all over the place, as those ravenous raiders wiped out most of the local birds and squirrels in order to feed the lone chick they hatched. And by the time the three of them finally headed off into the wild-blue somewhere else, I halfway expected to wake up some morning and find out they'd slaughtered a bull moose right in my front yard, or at least one of the stray mutts the neighborhood had such an abundance of.

Silent Soliloquy

I stood this morning, in the dark stillness of my hillside home, gazing out the window at the ghostly shapes of surrounding trees which seemed to come and go. They stole ever so softly thru the silken mists, yet were standing so still, as they drifted in and out of my view. The faint sound of the gentle rain that fell, likewise faded, and then returned, like the notes of some sweet melody. And as the mists continued to swirl all roundabout, I too, continued to stand, alone and still, yet not alone, nor even still, for I now drifted thru the mists of memory.

Cat-Scanning The Neighborhood

Shortly after I began building my house here in Homer, in May of 1992, I was startled one sunny afternoon by a sound I hadn't heard in far too many years. And, after swiveling my head quickly toward where it seemed to have come from, my eyes soon verified that it was what I'd felt it just about had to be, the cry of a ring-necked rooster pheasant.

Standing no more than a foot from the base of the new transformer that supplied the life-blood my saws and drills depended on, the bird made it very plain he was upset about something. Moving only my eyes, so as not to agitate him even more than he already was, I eventually made out a crouching form that was a deeper yellow than the matted jungle of the previous summer's once lush grasses. And that was my first introduction, albeit an informal one, to the tiger-striped tomcat who still continues to think he owns the whole dang neighborhood. And is thus free to do just about anything, wherever and whenever he chooses.

As that first summer wore on, though, and I became aware that at least one member of the rooster's harem had succeeded in hatching a brood of chicks, I began entertaining some serious thoughts as to whether something drastic needed to be done about that fool cat. But since I too have been a hunter virtually my entire life, I just couldn't seem to ignore the fact that all he was guilty of in the first place, was following his natural instincts. Which was precisely what he was born to do.

Consequently, in the intervening months I've begun addressing him simply as "Cat." And our entirely one-sided conversations are pretty much limited to "Hey you, knock it off!", or just plain "Get away from there!", whenever I see him searching for someplace that will allow him to crawl under the chain-link fence I put up just last fall. Which was done mostly to prevent the dad-blamed moose from gobbling up my little woman's flowers and shrubs. As well as my four apple trees and two May-day trees.

Due to the fact that Mama's not exactly what you might call real wild about finding kitty-poop buried in her flower beds, though, I've more or less been forced into trying to make sure Cat stays on the other side of the fence too. But despite my having to yell at him all the time, as well as to chunk an occasional rock just close enough to let him know I mean business, the goofy sucker apparently decided to try a totally new approach to our common problem early this summer.

Because even though I first thought it had somehow gotten stepped on, or had died of natural causes, the first mouse carcass I found lying just outside our garage door proved to be only the first of the many that were soon to follow. Although most of the others have actually been the same variety of long-nosed little shrews that made such a mess of our yard every winter, while the little woman and me were still living in Eagle River.

But close examination of the dang things, as well as actually seeing him pussy-footing to and from our driveway just shortly after daybreak on several different mornings, has made it obvious that Cat's the critter behind these dad-ratted peace offerings. So I just hope he's shrewd enough to realize before too much longer, that even though I truly appreciate his concern for my well-being, I much prefer bagging my own meat.

Thanks A Lot, Doc

Since this was the third piece I sold to Kathleen McCoy at We Alaskans, I can't help thinking she was more than a little relieved to find she had less editing to do on it than had been the case with the other two. In any event, since very few of us ever reach the point where we're satisfied to let sleeping dogs lay, this particular version is slightly different than the one she purchased.

One April afternoon several years ago, I headed up the highway to my cabin at Lake Susitna alone, intent on restocking my freezer with burbot. For downright ugly and slimy, burbot (or fresh-water ling-cod, as they're commonly called) deserve an award. But since they also win honors, hands down, as delectable table fare, I wasn't about to let the season end without having a good supply in the aforementioned freezer.

Quite a few years earlier, you see, my better half and I were sitting in ol' Doc Pease's lodge one day, trying to get some straight answers on where to find some lunker lake trout. But since all he wanted to talk about was burbot, and what fine eating they were, when his wife, Kay, stood there grinning and nodding her head as he carried on about how the dang things had to be just about the best grub ever invented, I was fairly sure she must think so too. So when he claimed she could deep-fry a batch that had been dipped in beer-batter, that mortal man was powerless to resist, and that you could get so stuffed on it you'd have to shove the platter away in order to keep from busting your gussets, and that before you knew what was happening, you'd be dragging it right back again, just like popcorn, I took him at his word.

The goofy ol' Windbag's dead and gone now, but I can flat-out guarantee that he'll be raising a bona fide ruckus if they don't serve burbot in whichever one of the places he went to. On second thought, though, if they're not serving burbot, he's bound to have gone straight to Hell!

Anyway, it was almost dark by the time I got all my plunder unloaded from the freight-sled, and had headed away from the cabin on my Arctic Cat to set some holes. Going all the way across to the other side of the lake, I was soon scooping the snow off the ice in order to drill my holes. So once I'd cleaned off a dozen sets, as I was heading back to the sled for my gas-powered auger, I noticed what appeared to be a pile of moose-droppings right smack in the middle of all the different sets. But since it was dark enough by then so it was hard telling what it actually was, I took a poke at it with my shovel. And if I hadn't let go when I did, I'd more than likely have followed the fool thing all the way to the bottom of the lake, which I eventually discovered was almost twenty feet beneath the surface of the three and a half foot layer of ice.

Methane gas bubbles up all over the lake, where it's usually trapped under the ice until such time as the spring sunshine melts its way through to the bubble, which may be several yards in diameter when this finally occurs. Once I'd ever so cautiously brushed the snow away from the edge of this hole, though, when I realized it was slightly over three feet across, it took several minutes for my knees to stop knocking long enough so I could fire up the Arctic Cat and run over to the shore to cut some brush to lay across it.

But after setting a couple of lines in the big hole, then drilling and setting the other twelve, I headed back to the cabin to cook supper and goof off until about 9 or 9:30, when I climbed back on my Cat and putted on over to see what luck I'd had. And since the sky was completely full of stars, with the thermometer just outside the cabin registering a balmy 34 degrees, once I'd taken 3 or four fish off the lines and re-baited the hooks, I could hardly have asked for anything better than just sitting there in the stillness of the night.

At least until this really weird sensation caused the short hair on the back of my neck to stand right straight up. Never having been particularly brave, I'd barely turned halfway around before discovering that the entire southeastern portion of the sky was literally pulsating with an eerie green incandescence. And every few seconds a burst of multi-hued light would begin cascading across the heavens all the way to the northwest horizon. Predominantly yellow-green, there were tints of rose and blue as well.

Forgetting all about fishing for the next thirty or forty minutes, I was thoroughly engrossed in watching what seemed to be a special presentation for my eyes alone. Witnessing that kind of beauty has a way of making one aware of his own insignificance, so even though the fish had stopped biting when the display began, I was too overwhelmed by what I'd seen, to care.

But just to keep a goofy ol' hot-air merchant from getting the idea that I've forgotten who it was that helped make it all possible, thanks once again Doc, for telling me about some really special grub!

A Wee Bit'a Doggerel

I had'a dog once
That I named Laddy
But Laddy wouldn't learn
T'lift up `is leg
Like other dogs did
S'fin'ly I jist changed `is name t'Lady

Bits Of Fluff And Stuff

Like ships of old they sail the endless sky,
And `tho they hardly ever seem to tarry
So that I can swiftly scamper on board
From here in this soft and sunny glen where I lie
I can't help but wonder at the cargo they carry
Perhaps they're filled with Blackbeard's hoard

And no matter how loud I'm hailing them,
They never seem to hear my call at all.
So I have come to believe now, that they
Are nothing more than vaporous figments
Of some fool's deteriorating mind.
So dream your time away if you aspire,
Just watching fluffy bits of white pigments.
I've something better to do with my hours
Than getting soaked while standing there beneath
The cold old showers of some nut's desire.

Two For The Price Of One

I'd already picked up the phone and begun dialing by the time I happened to glance out the window. And what I saw coming out of the lush growth of fireweed-jungle bordering our recently mown (but already overdue for a repeat performance) lawn, caused me to slam down the receiver and bellow "Babe, c'mere quick!"

And for quite possibly the first time in the past forty-five years, she did just that, without bothering to reply "Say purty please.", or something equally as ridiculous. But when she saw what I was looking at, her indrawn breath and drawn out "Ahhhh" echoed my sentiments to a tee.

For bouncing along beside their long-legged mama were two moose calves that couldn't have been much more than a few days old, their lustrous brown eyes and twitching noses pointed on what amounted to a collision course with some of our shrubs and flowers. The shrubs would have been May Day trees by now, were it not for their all too frequent encounters with numerous relatives of these three new arrivals. So after making a mad dash to get my camera, which just happened to be where I remembered leaving it when we'd returned from a recent trip to Homer, I quietly eased out onto the small balcony off our dining-room and began snapping the shutter.

Although our visitors took only slight notice of the soft clicking sounds coming from the camera, the sudden booming of thunder got their attention in a hurry. And they immediately began running around the yard in ever widening circles. After several minutes of this frantic activity though, they stopped for a drink of water at our birdbath, then meandered slowly off up the trail toward the low rise bordering Meadow Creek Canyon. By this time my camera was out of film and I was half soaked, so I came back inside.

And as luck would have it, when the trio underwent an unexpected change of heart and returned a few minutes later, to have a look-see at the motor-home in our driveway, I finally remembered that there was another role of film sitting on the breakfast-bar. Consequently, I wound up having to wind my camera with what seemed to be ten thumbs, all of them working in total opposition to one another. So I didn't get pictures of the cow each time she decided the twins had ventured far enough in one direction. At which time she'd paw at the air alongside their heads in order to get them turned toward where she wanted them to go. But I could almost hear her demanding "Awright ya little buggers, yer gonna wind up with lumps on yer noggin's if ya don't do what I say!"

When they left the yard this time I mistakenly assumed it was safe to go to bed, so I didn't get to see them partaking of a midnight snack of my May Day branches. But at least I got a few more pictures when they arrived for breakfast shortly after I got up the following morning. About then though, it seemed advisable to step out on the balcony and bellow "Fer cryin' out loud, don'cha think it might be'a good idea t'leave'a little fer next year?"

So now the cow's mad at me and the twins are probably wondering what could possibly have caused me to be so goshdarn cranky.

Same Song, Second Verse
(At Least)

Oh 'twas amateur night in at th' Ol' Northern Lights Coliseum
An' I'm tellin' ya, th' program was s'cluttered up with names
It looked like one more would prob'ly a'sent it up in flames
Why whilst I was'a settin' there jist tryin' t'read'm
My eyeballs got s'dadblame hot they plumb went t'steamin'
An' th' more that I read, it seemed I sure must be a'dreamin'
Why there was jist talent galore an' right at th' top'a th' list
Was Arlis, sort of'a so-so-soprano, who thumped her own pie-ano
Then come Mr. McSteve, a'Piney Woods
kid who was a real hypnotist
But Ol' Railroader Jim's main claim t'fame came from th' way
He could hammer out'a tune on a bell as was cast in pure brass
An' little Softshoe Bill jist scurried on an' off th' stage
Whilst carryin' a'bird in'a big ol' gilded cage, jist'a twirlin'
N' whirlin' s'fast, I was downright worried he might slip n' fall
Right flat On'a sliver er'a sharp ol' chunk'a glass!
Then Rack-em-up Rick, assisted by'a downright cute little dolly
Rolled out from b'hind th' curtain his felt-covered table
An' let me tell ya', when he took'a poke with that ol' cue-stick
Golly gee, but it was slick th' way them balls'd jump around

But when Slight-a-hand Tony waltzed
out t' do his usual Magic act

Y'could hardly hear yerself think, cuz
th' wimmin plumb went wild

An' he grin'd s'dang big I was certain he had lights in `is mouth

Why even if it took `im a while t'git
warmed up, Man when he did

It was flat-out eerie th' way he could pull money outta thin air

T'wasn't no chore a'tall, fer `im t'poke it right back there too

An' I sure don't mind tellin ya Dearie, a'fore he got done with

Shiftin' that ol' money around, my head felt like it was swimmin'

Then th' lights begun dimmin, an' all I could think of was t'jam

M'fists in m'pockets, a'fore what money I had left went up in'a

PAC'a smoke too, er somethin' ever' dang bit as capricious.

But now tho', even if it does wind up soundin' sort'a malicious

I jist couldn't help bein' purty suspicious when I up an' read

Where th' ambitous clown still has his sights set on'a new act

Way off down in Ol' Juneau town, which
fer some unknown reason,

At least fer this ol' waste-`is-vote-goat, is still our Capitol

But since that place has always been s'dadblame repiticious

`Bout makin' capital disappear, it jist really seems like it'd

Be awful inauspicious fer us t'take'a chance on maybe havin'

T'dance thru th' end result'a yet another ol' insult season

Playin'strip-yer-pockets-poker with that officious-actin' joker,

Whose reputation seems t'come s'doggone close t'bein' downright

Meretricious! Nope, I jist don't b'lieve it'd be all that propitious.
Not even t'git rid'a that gherkin that's presently lurkin' in that big
ol' house up there on th' hill! Why Holy
Moly, I'm still'a waitin' fer
that ol' sucker t'start perkin'Altho'maybe if we was jist
t'write in th' name'a that eeny-meeny
feller with th' big ears an' loud
mouthAw you know th' one I mean,
that dried-up carrot, ol' what's
`is name from that little bitty ol' state way off down south

Dadblame Birds

It all began with the strawberry stealing robin that came back to life, sometime during the summer of 1938. Because when it flew off before I could grab it, I was thus cheated out of the final penny I needed for the five-cent "Oh Henry!" candy bar I craved so badly I could almost taste it. For when a guy's only ten years old and his livelihood more or less depends on how much bounty he's able to collect with his BB gun, a bird in the bush just doesn't hold a candle to one in his hand. At least it didn't with the lady who'd offered to pay a penny for every poacher I potted.

For the next dozen years or so, I was pretty much willing to live and let live, at least as far as the birds went. Then one day a dang ol' chicken-stealing chicken hawk got the best of me and I wound up shooting him out of a big cottonwood tree on the little farm my wife and I were living on. But since history has a way of repeating itself, I'd no more than picked him up and started back to the house, just to show my wife what a Dead-eye Dick I was, before two of the talons on one of his feet were buried so deep in the palm of my right hand, it looked like so much raw hamburger by the time I managed to rip them out.

Consequently, since it was fairly apparent that some changes needed to be made, after moving to Alaska a few years later I actually began baking a few extra pancakes to feed the camp-robbers that hung out at our cabin on Lake Susitna. So it was quite a thrill to have one land on my head one April afternoon, while I was down by the lake cleaning and filleting burbot. But just because he shoved my new down-filled Eddie Bauer hunting cap a little bit cockeyed when he flew off, it wasn't until I reached up to set it straight again, that I discovered the soggy little pile of gray goop he'd deposited on its once bright red bill!.

Then just a few years later, I made the mistake of building us a new house up on Skyline Drive, overlooking beautiful downtown Eagle River. Which just happened to be right where two of the most ill-tempered falcons in all of Alaska were then hanging out. So for one whole summer, or at least until their stupid chicks finally got smart enough to leave the nest, Mama and I had to put up with getting dive-bombed practically every time we set foot outside the house.

And even though it took me at least six more years to think of it, I finally wound up selling that place and moving down here to Homer. Which, as most of you probably know by now, is precisely where most of the bald eagles in the world are presently hanging out, thanks to the efforts of the goofy ol' broad that figured out just about the neatest scheme for getting rid of dead fish, while also getting on television at the same time, that I ever heard of.

And even though Jean lives at least five miles from where I do, hardly a day goes by when there aren't four or five of her danged eagles, circling right over the top of my house, just like so many vultures waiting for me to kick the bucket. So in spite of the fact that I haven't been able to prove it yet, I'm almost positive those white-headed suckers were responsible for my almost having a heart-attack just the other morning. Because when I opened the door on our wood-stove to toss in some wastepaper, just in case it turned cold enough to start a fire later on, out pops one of the sootiest and scaredest-looking swallows I'd ever seen.

So by the time I finally managed to herd the little turkey back outside where he belonged, my ol' ticker'd had about all the excitement it could handle for one day. But since it was just barely five A.M., and I knew Mama wouldn't be getting up for at least two more hours, I nuked myself a cup of day-old coffee before sitting down to contemplate how much soot would have gotten smeared on the walls if it had been a swallow that chased an eagle down the chimney, instead'a the other way around.

That's Th' Way Th' Ball Bounces

T'be perfec'ly frank, even though Frank sure ain't my name,
I git t'wonderin' at times what I ever seen in'a certain dame.
Leastwise I do when she starts naggin' an' bossin' me around.
Cuz'a man jist don't never git treated that way, by `is hound.
    No sirree he sure as shootin' don't, not by'a long shot!
    A'course th' little lady may smell'a heap better'n ol' Spot,
    but she sure wouldn't amount t'much at tree'n a`coon.
An' `tho I've never had'ta whup `er fer yowlin' at th' moon,
    `bout th' only dang thing she's ever found with er nose,
was'a stupid cold that wound up turnin' it redder'n a rose.
    An' so-what if I said it looked like'a bouquet'a flowers?
I was sick an' tired'a gittin' sent t'th' showers jist `cuz she said she had another one of `er dang headaches whenever I wanted t'git cozy. But I guess that's th' way th' cookie breaks.
Anyhow, I ain't really got'a whole lot'a choice in th' matter,
    not after seein' what she jist piled on our big ol' platter.
Cuz there's hardly anythin' half as good as her pot-roasted hog.
S'go on'n quit grinnin' that way Spot, ya goofy dad-blame ol' dog!

Proceed With Caution, My Love

The original version of this piece appeared in the "We Alaskans" section of the "Anchorage Daily News" on October 14, 1990.

    While backing out my front door one rainy morning a few years ago, resigned to yet another ten hour siege of climbing the walls and rafters of my latest house-building project, all the while encased in what was left of my rubber pants and jacket, it suddenly occurred to me that it had been about this same time the previous Fall when a shrill shriek from my little woman had brought me running to the front window one Sunday evening, just to see what in Hades had gotten her so excited.
    Barely avoiding tripping over the coffee-table, which would no doubt have resulted in my ramming my head straight through the window, I'd reached her side just as she started going "Ooooh is it a bear, is it a bear?", all the while jumping up and down and waving her arms round and round like a runaway windmill.
    Well sir, by the time I'd shoved her sideways far enough so I could see out the fool window too, whatever it was was just disappearing behind one of the big spruce trees in our yard. Consequently, once I'd spent the biggest part of the next few seconds gulping down as much oxygen as possible, just about the time my gulps had diminished to somewhere in the neighborhood of three per second, out from behind the spruce waddled the weirdest looking apparition I'd ever laid eyes on, bar none.
    For a little while I was almost as mixed up as Mama, more than likely just because I was at least a year and a half late in getting my trifocals realigned. But when this big hairy brown blob seemed to separate into two somewhat

smaller hairy brown blobs, I was at last able to figure out what they were—nothing more exotic than a pair of amorous porcupines.

And simply because I've always had a fairly inquisitive mind, as well as a healthy interest in what it seems to take to keep the world going around, I came awfully close to acquiring a double hernia then, by making a sudden detour to the closet for my camera while still trying to get out to the yard in time to record the event for future generations of Nature Lovers.

Before you wind up writing me off as just another danged ol' pervert, though, please stop to consider the anatomical armament that Porkies are equipped with. And if you still can't understand the poor little boar's dilemma, and my interest in how he went about handling it, you're in a hell of a lot worse shape than I am. Because every time little Guinevere batted her lashes at him and raised that pin-cushion tail of hers, Lancelot was fully expected to perform. And despite the fact that he'd earlier managed to imbed a big bracelet of her quills in his left wrist, perform he did.

But since the rapidly waning daylight, coupled with my almost total lack of photographic expertise, caused my pictures to turn out so under-exposed that you couldn't tell right side up from inside out, you'll just have to settle for trying to imagine a short, fat and furry Fred Astaire, doing a syncopated soft-shoe shuffle, while singing "Look Ma, no hands."

Finally, just before the poor little devil would more than likely have collapsed from sheer exhaustion, their capers brought them up beside a fairly succulent stand of alder shoots that were growing along one edge of the yard. But even though Guinevere continued to moan in her most provocative tone of voice, it was plain to see that ol' Lance already had his mind set on a mouthful of salad. Several mouthfuls actually, but in the darkness I lost count of just how many he eventually consumed.

It was right about then that Guinevere apparently remembered having seen me hovering in the background, so when she started in my direction, still singing her seductive little song, just to keep Lancelot from getting the idea that I might pose a threat to his domestic tranquility, I took off for the house in a bona-fide hurry. Because when a guy's got the kind of stamina that little dude had already proven he did, I sure as the devil didn't intend to provide him with any additional reason for being sore at me!

Take Jessica Please

They say they will
Then they say they must
Go to one and all
I say it's a crock

Why, you have to ask?
I thought it was you
That gave me that jive
On how they need out

To wade thru the snow
And look at a star
This has gone too far
You know, and even tho'

It's not nice to pout
From now on at five
You try out the view
For now it's your task

To give her her walk
When she hears the call
Oh yes, it's very just
It's your turn

To stand in the chill
Till the dumb dog Pees

Around And Around She Goes

The original version of the above story appeared in Anchorage Daily News' We Alaskans magazine on May 26, 1991. And the next day a lady called from Anchorage to tell me how much she'd enjoyed it, and wanted to know if it would be alright if her husband brought her out to see the tree and watch the squirrels for awhile, which I quickly assured her it would be. So when they came out a short time later and I saw how difficult it was for her to get around, I was doubly glad I'd been able to provide her with the enjoyment she so obviously derived from seeing the tree and watching all the squirrels' antics.

Back around the first of March, my wife and I were eating lunch at our breakfast-bar when one of us noticed some rather frantic carryings-on taking place a short distance beyond our window. Two of our more squirrelly neighbors seemed to be taking turns at chasing one another all over the yard, shooting up one tree after another, just to jump several feet through the air and go racing down another tree. At least half the time though, before they'd reach terra firma once again, they'd do an abrupt about-face and the chasee would then become the chaser.

Such strenuous activities seemed to call for frequent pit-stops, but just as soon as they'd refueled themselves on a spruce-cone or two, the game would continue. Before very long a couple of magpies decided to join in the fun, but each time they'd land on a limb, both squirrels would go charging at them as though they were bent on birdicide, and the black and whites would take to the air once more. I eventually decided I'd better head back down to the job again, since my hammer and saw never seem to accomplish anything unless I'm hanging on to them, so I missed out on the balance of what was going on.

Apparently though, my participation wasn't required, for within a few weeks time I noticed that some serious re-modeling was taking place in Squirrel-haven, the name I've given to the modest little apartment that's situated about fifteen feet up the side of one of my birch trees. I've never actually seen the inside of the apartment, you understand, since the doorway is barely large enough to poke my thumb through. And since I've always been able to mangle my thumb with just a hammer, I've never tried to collect any rent from them. But at least the Municipality's nosy assessor has so far failed to notice this particular improvement to my property, otherwise my taxes would undoubtedly be even more ridiculous than they already are.

Anyhow, for the next ten days or so, one of the squirrels spent a considerable amount of time shopping for bedding, judging by the number of trips it made in and out of the apartment. And since I'm only too well aware of how things work in my own household, I quite naturally came to the conclusion that this was the female of the species, getting ready for company. Then for several days, I saw no activity at all in the immediate vicinity of the little apartment. What I took to be the male member of the duo seemed to steer clear of the place, coming no closer than one of his cone-caches beneath a stack of my fireplace wood, some forty feet from the base of the birch.

But one day while my wife and I were again eating lunch, we watched him climb up to the front porch limb and poke his nose through the doorway. In less time than it takes to tell, his little woman was out the door and in hot pursuit, chasing him all the way up the hillside and into the territory of their nearest neighbor. And when the neighbor came running up to see what was going on, he ended up getting chased also. But once she was sure they'd gotten her message, the female came back to the apartment, carrying a cone that she dismantled while sitting on the front porch. Then she went inside, and for the next week or so we'd only see her come out long enough to make a quick trip down to the aforementioned cone-cache.

Finally, on the morning of April 21st, my wife and I were eating breakfast when we saw a smaller version of Madame Squirrel exit the apartment and head cautiously toward the ground. But before she reached it, if indeed she was a she, there were three other seemingly identical editions following close behind. Since that day though, all four of them have tossed caution to the winds, and are now leaping from tree to tree with almost as much abandon as their parents. Just yesterday I saw one of them hanging upside down, a good thirty feet above the ground, munching birch-buds. An' ya know what? It really made me glad I hadn't decided to evict his folks for falling behind with the rent!

Hardrock Hill

There once was a time, oh so very long ago, in'a faraway place
'Twas back when I was young an' healthy, 'stead'a old an' ill
An' I was strong as an ox, taller then, with a smilin' face
I like t'rock an' r'member, th' way it was, I can see it still
That ragged ol' shack we called home, ah what a hellova place
Sat at th' end'a th' road it did, way up there on Hardrock Hill

At th' time we'd been wed fer a spell, my missus an' me
Man, but I'd found me a real life doll, an' I can see 'er still
Jist th' way she looked, way back then, young an' s'fancy free
But then our babes, they come along, an' Oh God, what'a thrill
Girls they was, an' I was really glad too, t'take all three
Out t'that shack, at th' end'a th' road, there on Hardrock Hill

An' even with money s'goldang scarce, an' times s'really rough
We had each other, an' love was there, more'n a'nough t'fill
Our hearts with joy, an' our souls with peace, fer we was tough
An' we got by, best we could, why we even paid th' Doctor's bill
'Tho he had t'wait quite'a spell, but we finally found a'nough
Jist by diggin' really deep, way back there, on Hardrock Hill

An' when I shut my eyes, I still see it now, 'twasn't s'bad
Ah Lord, some'a th' things I tried t'do, like build'n that mill
T'saw th' ties I'd already sold up at th' mine, Man but I got mad
With th' road s'steep m'truck wouldn't go, I sure got my fill
I was scared y'see, a'that icy ol' trail, but I sure was glad
T'get back on level ground, an' head out there, t'Hardrock Hill

An' then there was th' day, late one fall, all warm an' sunny
Th' birds was singin' an' soundin' nice, Th' breeze was still
An' bees was flyin' about, jist buzzin' 'round makin' up honey
So I follered one home, right t'th' tree he was tryin' t'fill
He had in mind th' storin' a'grub, but I was needin' money
He'd built that cache y'see, right on top'a Hardrock Hill

So I marked it well, then run like hell, I gotta confess
But I come back, jist totin' th' bucket I wanted t'fill
An' I robbed them poor bees that day, Oh Lord! What'a mess
Th' pine was rotten t'th' core, an' they was mad, fit t'kill
Chased me 'round, wavin' n'swattin', but I knew neverth'less
I had it comin', way up there, on Ol' Hardrock Hill

Why if there was jist a'way, I'd go back t'day, You bet I would
Sure, our walls was ragged an' holey, an' let in th' chill
There was lots that was bad I know, but a'bunch more was good
Th' dreams we shared, way back then, they still bring a'thrill
An' even tho' I'm old an' gray now, I'd return if I could
All th' way, back up there t'Hardrock Hill!

Go Ahead Sucker, Jist Make My Day

If I've learned anything at all in the past 68 years, it's just that if a feller <u>isn't</u> completely stupid, and <u>isn't</u> ready, willing, and able to start dukeing it out, the way ol' Clint

Eastwood's characters are forever doing, he sure as heck needs to be pretty dang choosy about when and where he says stuff like the title hanging at the top of this thing. But if he's fairly sure his Nikes are faster than the other guy's, and is positively positive their laces are securely tied, he <u>might</u> get away with shooting his mouth off once in awhile. But if he's let his dad-blamed dentist talk him into investing as much hard earned loot in his teeth as what I was crazy enough to let mine do, he really ought to keep quiet. Since he's probably going to wind up eating a few of those same teeth with his words.

But when a guy's spent most of his life just getting as much mileage as possible out of what little cash he's been able to latch onto, if there was ever enough sporting blood in his veins to let him take a chance that he's tough enough to hold his own in an impromptu round of jist-have-at-`im, by the time he's reached my age, it's probably grown so damn sluggish that all he's fit to fight is the desire to take another fool nap.

Which is the main reason most of my ire for the past few years has been vented on inanimate stuff, like telephones and newspapers. But'cha know what? Almost every time I get my mind made up to cancel my subscription, or yank the ding-a-ling phone off the wall, it seems like something just has to go and roll my wagon all the way over.

That's precisely what happened this past week, too! Because after spending a lot more time than I like to think about during the last few months, having to pry my rump loose from my recliner only a few seconds after I've plunked it there, just to have the clown at the other end of the line ask if I'd care to donate some money to whatever it was that he just happened to be pushing, I'd about run out of the more polite obscenities in my normally adequate epithet repertoire.

Which really was a pretty fortunate thing to have happen, because by the time I finally realized the voice coming through the receiver was that of a very special friend back in Colorado, I could just as easily have already said something I'd truly have been sorry for. I've no way of knowing how many of the rest of you have reached the point where your inability to hear certain tones makes it difficult to catch what others say, but I've long since gotten in the habit of replying "Just a minute, I think you need to talk to my wife.", as soon as I hear a soft, female voice on the other end of the line.

In this case though, the lady just happened to be the girlfriend of the very best elk-hunting buddy this old fool has ever had. And since one of Shirley's daughters has been married to one of Bud's boys for quite a few years now, just because she and Bud were due to arrive at our house for a visit on the 9th day of July, when she asked if I thought it might be possible for Dee and me to help them turn their little trip into a bona fide honeymoon, I didn't feel like it was the least bit out of line to yell **"YOU JIST DANG-WELL BETTER BELIEVE IT, YOU GOOFY OL' BROAD!"**

I'll tell you this much, though, if either one of `em shows the slightest indication of backing out on me after they get here, Homer's gonna be the location of a sure enough shotgun wedding, and that's for dang sure!

Our daughter, Sue Ann, in her highchair. Dee's brother, Delbert Johnson, me fixing "hot cakes," Jerry Aasen facing away from camera. Photo was taken by Dee's older sister, Dorcas Assen.

Here's T'fanny

Once, a'long, long time ago, in'a land a'snow, an' jist sittin' way up high in th' mountains of ol' Colorado, there was'a purty special lady that lived in'a rickety ol' shack in Silverton town.

Now, I know there's some as might argue m'point, fer she ran a joint where a shiny red light was jist hangin' over th' door. Yup! Ya got it right, Ol' Fanny was runnin' sort of'a sportin' goods store.

An' she jist got more'n 'er share'a dispute, runnin' that house'a ill repute, fer'a lot'a strong minded dames made one awful fuss in that little ol' town, where minin' was 'bout all that fueled th' fires'a trade.

Fer they was allus all cocked, primed, an' ready t'discuss some way jist t'shut 'er down. Why they was never ever willin' t'consider that it was mostly them a'fannin' th' flames'a their menfolk's desire.

Fer they jist couldn't see, that by withholdin' their charms, they was only drivin their men,

time an' time agin, right straight inta sweet Fanny's enfoldin' arms.

So t'was them stingy witches an' their connivin' that kept 'er Hustlin' at rustlin' 'er riches right down t'th' Bank. S'by damn I say "Here's t'Fanny", fer there weren't none better around!

Now, I'll grant ya, there was plenty as called 'er a whore, but she opened up'a whole
lot more'n 'er door t'th' lonesome miners in that gawdfersaken little ol' town.

An' them wives, with their tongues s'sharp an' jist slicin' away
like knives, would'a bin wise t'heed th' size of `er heart. Fer
that's what really set `er apart, not th' shape of `er b'hind.

Now it didn't often git told, by those s'busy carpin' 'bout what
she sold, but she took'a
whole lot'a her gold jist t'raise a poor little orphan gal.

Th' way it happened, ya see, ol' Fanny snuck
`er right out'a some damn place in

Denver town, er that's what I heard, fer
Fanny sure never spread it around.

Why, she took care'a her somethin' grand. An' tho she never
hid from what she did, she never let that little gal come around,
`cept to'a special door, jist so's she'd know it was little Nell.

An' when that little doll went off an' b'come'a fine teacher lady
at some big ol' east coast institute, that gang'a harpies didn't
waste no time at all, hoppin' right up on t'th' bandwagon,

Where they spent most'a their time braggin' on
ol' Silverton's pride an' glory. But Fanny,

Lord bless `er great big ol' heart, She jist didn't seem
t'give'a hoot. An' that's th' end'a m'story!

Afognak Sojourn

    I experienced an almost naked feeling as the big white Goose went roaring past us, throwing steadily diminishing geysers of spray from each side of its fuselage as it picked up speed. And when one of our recent neighbors began waving his hand behind one of the plane's small windows just as the right-hand wing float broke free of the water, I turned toward Bill, my son-in-law, and said "That goofy clown'll hafta flap `is arms a whole lot faster than that if he figger's on helpin' the pilot pry that sucker loose from the water before they git to Kodiak!"

    He just grinned and nodded his head as the craft finally struggled into the air. With the weight of five hunters and their camping gear, as well as the un-skinned carcasses of several Sitka Black-tails aboard, it was well out over the wider part of Izhut Bay before it leveled off. It was Thursday, November 13th, 1986, and for the third time in the past four years of hunting deer on Afognak Island, we were once more faced with the prospect of spending an extra week in camp, possibly even longer.

    Before leaving Kodiak in Peninsula Air's wheel-float equipped Cessna 206 on Wednesday, November 5th, we'd made arrangements with the company's dispatcher to have Bill's friend Steve pick us up with his Widgeon the following Tuesday afternoon, just so we'd have time to load all our gear and meat in my pickup and be ready to drive it aboard the ferry for Homer late that night. But in the event that weather conditions prevented this, he was to come back again the following afternoon, which would give us more than adequate time to catch the boat to Seward on Thursday morning.

    The Kodiak to Seward leg of Alaska's Marine Highway system almost always left port by noon on Thursdays, so when the Goose had shown up shortly after 11:00 to get the other hunters, with word that the Widgeon ought to be arriving at any moment, it was readily apparent to all of us that unless something totally unforeseen delayed the ferry's departure, Bill and I would be forced to stay in Kodiak until the following Tuesday. Which was the main reason we'd asked the Goose's pilot get on the radio as quickly as possible, just to tell Steve to forget about coming after us until Monday or Tuesday.

This somewhat unlikely sounding scenario had all begun at 2:30 in the morning, nine days earlier, when I'd picked Bill up and we'd headed for Seward, roughly 140 miles from our hillside homes in Eagle River. We made good time until we got halfway down the other side of Turnagain Pass, then we ran into a snow-shower that quickly turned to rain. And from Granite Creek to the far side of Moose Pass the road was so slick it was all I could do to keep my pickup pointed in the right direction.

After shifting into 4-wheel drive and slowing to about ten miles per hour, we'd barely gotten past the sign at Drygulch Creek before coming to another pickup that had skidded sideways for over a hundred feet before completely swapping directions. I managed to stop just in time to avoid hitting it, despite sliding up to within just a few inches of its front bumper. So when the driver and his three hunting buddies told us that even though they intended to drive back to where it was safe to turn around, they still had hopes of making it to Seward in time to catch the ferry, we said we'd make sure the load-master knew they were on their way. Providing we got there ourselves, of course.

Simply because there was such a line of trucks, cars, and pickups waiting to board when we got to the terminal a little after 6:00, the fool boat didn't pull away from the dock until 9:10. And since the slow-motion sucker took a full thirteen and a half hours to get to Kodiak, by the time Bill and I finally crawled into our sleeping-bags at Fred and Mylar Almendinger's house that night, it was already one-thirty in the morning!

In any event, after getting up barely five hours later, we were able to drive out to the airport in time to load all our stuff into the 206 and take off by 9:30, splashing down into the breeze-dappled waters of Izhut Bay approximately twenty-five minutes later. After taxiing as close to shore as he thought advisable, our pilot asked me to step out onto the right-hand float and jump off with the mooring-line while he attempted to keep the breeze from blowing us close enough to some protruding rocks to scrape or puncture the floats. So just because I'd neglected to exchange my knee-high "Ketchikan Sneakers" for my hip-boots before taking off, I ended up getting soaked halfway to my crotch by jumping a little sooner than I really needed to. But at least I managed to guide the floats in between the rocks without transferring any paint from one to the other.

Although it's entirely possible to pitch a tent at the base of the steep hillside at this spot, Bill and I had long since learned it was a whole lot safer to carry everything up what comes real close to being a 60 degree slope to the top of the hill, roughly a 150 yard climb. Because in addition to avoiding the possibility of having an onshore wind drive the surf high enough to flood the tent, the trees on up the hill are sufficiently tall and dense to more or less prevent the even less desirable aspect of having your cozy little nook blown down while you're out hunting, or even worse, while you're inside.

Despite having to make at least six trips apiece, to and from the so-called beach, we'd pitched the tent and sawn enough dry firewood to last four or five days by 12:30. So with approximately four hours of daylight left, we grabbed our rifles and headed out to see how many deer we could find. All I saw during the next few hours were three or four eagles and at least five times that many ravens, all of which were either swooping down to see if there was any chance I might be giving up the ghost in the near future, or were perched in the tops of the tallest trees they could find. Somewhere around 3:00 I thought I heard a shot, but it was so faint and far away I couldn't be sure that's what it actually was.

In any event, I hadn't anymore than gotten back to camp before Bill came puffing back up the hill from the beach, carrying the plastic bag filled with the odds and ends of polypropylene rope we'd brought along for hanging meat. Since there were also some stains on his pant-legs that looked more like blood than mud, I said "Okay, Hotshot, how big is he, she, it, or whatever it is? I thought I heard a shot quite awhile ago, but it sounded so dang far away I didn't see how it could'a been you!"

Grinning as he wagged his head at me, he replied "It probably wasn't, although I'll be the first to admit it might have been, at least if you somehow managed to hike past the first clear-cut without sitting down under a tree and taking a nap! But just to answer that ridiculous compound question as best I can, he she it's not much larger that most of the button-bucks around here. Although I can't really be sure since I'm pretty sure the only available scales are the ones on the trees, not to mention those on all the itty-bitty fishies swimming around in the altogether frigid depths of the briny-deep!"

Glaring as menacingly as possible, I snarled "Jist fer that, Smart-ass, yer gonna hafta start the fire ever' dang morning this trip. Because if ya don't, I'll tell Sue she don't need t'worry about my askin' 'er t'let ya come along next year! So jist stuff that in yeruhwell, any dang place it'll fit!"

Which, as I'd thought it probably would, caused my sparring partner to say "Well if that's the way ya feel about it, ya crotchety ol' Fart, it must be just about time to get out a couple cans of Rainier! Do ya want me to open yours for ya, or do ya still remember how to do it yourself?"

So by the time we finally realized we probably ought to head up to the waterhole and fill the two five gallon buckets that our cook-kit, lantern, and various other essentials were still packed in, it was already dark enough to make it just a little difficult to find the big flashlight both of us distinctly remembered seeing while it was still light enough to be aware of its whereabouts. But simply because it felt so darn good just to know we had almost a week left in which to wander around looking for enough venison to justify at least part of the expense of doing what both of us enjoyed so much, the evening eventually ended somewhere around ten o'clock, when we crawled into our sleeping-bags once more.

Friday, November 7. Heading out of camp together shortly before 8:30, we followed the barely perceptible outline of a game trail we were reasonably certain would take us to what the partially exposed remnants of a long discarded plastic container had prompted us to name "Blue Bucket Clear-cut." While angling along opposite sides of the same ridge some forty-five minutes later, one of us spooked a two-point buck that Bill managed to drop just before it could disappear over the top of yet another hill.

After making sure he didn't need my assistance, I headed for what we'd begun calling "The Planter's Cabin" the first year we'd hunted on Afognak together. Built to provide living-quarters for the men involved in planting the countless thousands of fir and spruce seedlings that were intended to replace the trees harvested by the logging company Bill and his dad once worked for, it was located near the junction of several different "haul-roads."

Resembling, at least as much as anything else, the moldering remains of a somewhat grotesque and box-like tarantula, with its now muddy and potholed limbs extending every which way out into the surrounding countryside, the little cabin still contained a stove, several bed-frames, a table and benches, along with a vast and varied assortment of plain old junk. But just because someone had already deemed it necessary to pry the padlocked hasp loose from the doorjamb, I eventually found a piece of wire that was long enough to reach between the hasp and a protruding nail-head, and was thus able to make things more or less secure once again.

In any event, I hadn't travelled much over a quarter of a mile along one of the roads leaving the compound, before realizing the distant drone of an airplane seemed to be drawing closer by the second. But due to having entered the upper end of a winding and extremely brushy swale, I was unable to see the plane until it suddenly burst into view, barely two hundred yards away and no more than half that far above the tops of the nearest trees. And even though I had no way of knowing at that moment just what impact it and its passengers would ultimately have on Bill's and my activities during the next few days, that was my first glimpse of the "Great White Goose." Which, just for the record, most assuredly wasn't intended to be the least bit complimentary.

Consequently, after spending the balance of the day without seeing anything that even came close to resembling a deer, when I finally staggered into camp that evening, just to have Bill say "Guess what, ol' Buddy, that crummy white goony bird flat raised hell with things around here today!", I wasn't exactly in the best of moods. So when he went on to inform me that we now had five neighbors camped less than a hundred yards from our meat-pole, I yelled "What the gawddam hell're ya talkin' about, Man? If that's what that lousy good fer nothin' plane was up to, how come the stupid clowns didn't make the pilot take `em somewhere else when they seen them deer'a yers hangin' right in plain sight? There ain't no way in hell they could'a missed seein' `em, fer cryin' out loud!"

Despite all the ranting and raving that took place in the next twenty minutes or so, when one of the other hunters stopped by as he was heading down to their camp shortly before dark, and told us that even though they'd seen the deer hanging on the pole, they'd assumed they probably belonged to the people on the boat that was anchored over in Saposa Bay, which was separated from Izhut by a short, narrow peninsula less than half a mile across the water from where we were camped, I was pretty much forced to let it go at that.

The wind and rain were downright nasty when we left camp the following morning, more or less staying just far enough apart to keep track of one another's whereabouts. But by the time I eventually came out on the road near Blue Bucket Clear-cut, I'd long since lost track of Bill. Just because the rain had let up, and I hadn't yet been to what we called Elk Knob Clear-cut, I now began angling in that direction.

After picking my way from one swamp-bottom to the next for most of the next hour, as I was utilizing the trunk of a huge, uprooted tree in order to get across yet another swamp, a limb that should have been strong enough to support my weight suddenly snapped and sent me crashing toward the ground. Twisting as I fell, I lit flat on my back on the only patch of solid terra firma in sight, which just for the sake of enlightenment, was more than firm enough to launch somewhere in the vicinity of several dozen shooting stars, asteroids, comets, and countless dead spruce needles, while thoroughly scrambling what few brains I had.

Once the celestial display ended, I decided it would probably be a good idea to avoid using anymore deadfall gangplanks for awhile. But after due consideration, during which I discovered that the bog I hadn't yet reached the other side of seemed to be several inches deeper than my boots allowed for, I was soon forced to abandon my earlier decision and crawl back aboard the damn tree, where I ever so cautiously made my way a couple of feet above the slimy surface of what it now seemed appropriate to name either "Soggy Bottom Swamp" or "Black and Blue Lagoon."

Nevertheless, when the sun finally burst through the clouds shortly after noon, I was perched on a large ledge of rock on the west flank of Elk Knob, munching a peanut butter and jelly sandwich while scanning the partially denuded slopes below me. Situated as I was, no more than a hundred feet below the knob's summit, the view was truly spectacular.

For simply because my vantage point was located near the center of a relatively narrow and approximately two mile long peninsula, the entire western half of Izhut Bay was literally blazing with the reflected fire of what appeared to be millions upon millions of virtually every gemstone imaginable. And even though clouds of varying shapes and sizes were continually sliding between the sun and the surface of the water, rather than detracting from this "Dance of the Universe", it only served to enhance it.

Just because Who, or Whatever it was that was responsible for this display seemed to realize that too much of anything usually has a tendency to cause we foolish mortals to take things for granted, no more than ten minutes after the curtains had first parted, they closed again, this time for the duration of the afternoon. There didn't seem to be much point in waiting around for an encore, so I headed down off the knob toward the western tip of the little peninsula.

But by the time I'd worked my way across the last clear-cut, without seeing hide nor hair of a single deer, I now decided to ease on down through the slender fringe of timber separating the clearing from the shoreline, just to see what the waters of the restless sea might have left for nuts like me. This time, though, rather than the normal conglomeration of plastic bottles, shopping-bags, rubber gloves and bits of rope, I found a welded aluminum fishing-float that was nearly a foot in diameter, plus two smaller plastic ones that were imprinted with what I took to be the name of their Korean manufacturer, all three of which I managed to find room for in the day-pack strapped to my shoulders, and eventually carry back to camp.

I'd almost reached the fork where the main branch of the road veered uphill to the left and the short branch leading to what had once been a log-yard or loading area, when a fairly good sized fishing trawler moved out from behind a scraggly thicket of trees and brush lying between me and the bay, apparently for the purpose of finding a safe haven for the night. And sure enough, after watching through my binoculars for several minutes, I saw it circle back on itself and a moment later its anchor splashed into the water.

I hadn't been back in camp long enough to consume much over half the can of Rainier that Bill dug out of the case as soon as he saw me coming down the trail, before we heard the chugging of a small outboard motor approaching the little strip of gravel near our meat-pole. And by the time we'd gotten down there, the short aluminum skiff the motor was mounted on had already nosed into shore. Despite the fact that I neglected to record the name of the man operating it in the journal I'd begun keeping a few months earlier, the trawler it came from was called "Laura", and was 95 feet in length.

Sunday, November 9. After a fairly warm night, Bill and I headed for Elk Knob together. Then, after glassing as much of the area as we could see from that elevation, we dropped down into a small creek bottom that eventually led us to the Planter's Cabin. We hadn't been there more than a few minutes though, before the sound of several rapid shots made it totally obvious that our neighbors had apparently arrived well before we did, and either had meat on the ground, or most assuredly should have.

This pretty much put a damper on our plans for hunting in that direction, so when Bill said he intended to cut across country to Blue Bucket, I decided to hike down the swale I'd been following when the White Goose had first shown up two days earlier. I'd only gone about 200 yards when what eventually proved to be a "button-buck" ran across the road some distance in front of me, stopping in a clump of brush that shielded everything but his head and ears. After firing twice and missing, I aimed just enough lower and further back to drop the animal in his tracks.

Having thus far elected to leave my surplus GI pack-board in camp, rather than hiking back after it now, I decided it made more sense to rig the little buck up for what's usually called an "over the shoulder, satchel-carry." So once I'd removed all the viscera but the heart and liver, and cut off the head, I made slits in the lower part of all four legs and slipped the rear hooves just far enough through the frontal slits to secure them with two short sticks shoved through the rear ones. I probably would have substituted rope for the sticks, if not for the fact that I'd left the chunk I usually keep in my daypack, back in camp, while I was making sure my lunch and "nearly" everything else was where it needed to be.

Despite the necessity of stopping to change shoulders every fifteen minutes or so, I made it back to our meat-pole in slightly over an hour. But since I'd followed the road all the way to the previously mentioned log-yard, then taken our usual trail down to camp, I hadn't seen anything of Bill. So when I later found out he'd begun working his way up the ridge between Blue Bucket and where he figured I probably had at least two deer on the ground, "Almost as soon as I heard ya shoot!", I snorted "Yeah, I jist bet ya did, after settin' down an waitin' long enough so I could git all the dirty work done before ya got there! Otherwise, ya sure as hell could'a caught up with me in plenty of time to at least help me hang `im on the dang meat-pole!"

His reply to this, of course, was his usual "Mama didn't raise any idiots in our family, ya know!"

Monday, November 8. It had gotten so warm during the night that I'd finally removed the inner half of my GI mummy bag and crawled back into the outer one, which I eventually ended up zipping part way down. So after fixing hotcakes, bacon, and eggs for breakfast, I headed straight up the ridge toward where I'd gotten the little buck the day before. Coming out on the road slightly east of where the gut-pile was located, I turned to the right and followed it to what the well weathered face of a crudely lettered sign still proclaimed to be the intersection of the "210 Road."

Having hunted along it several times in the past two years, I was well aware that it ended in a relatively small clear-cut at the end of the little peninsula separating Izhut Bay from Saposa, where our neighbors had seen the fishing boat anchored a few days earlier. Consequently, rather than taking a chance on running into one or more of its hunters, I continued following the main road for another quarter-mile before turning uphill toward a ridge that was now visible through the trees.

After climbing to the top of it and discovering an even higher one approximately three hundred yards further on, I hadn't gone more than another fifty yards before a buck jumped to his feet and began trying to locate whatever it was that had just interrupted his nap, turning his head from side to side and sniffing loudly enough for me to actually hear him. Easing my rifle ever so slowly to my shoulder, just as he turned and looked straight at me, I squeezed the trigger.

And simply because the .375 H & H Magnum has long been considered to be as good a weapon as there is for hunting where you're just as apt to come face to face with a charging grizzly as not, when that 270 grain soft-point plowed straight through the buck's forehead, it seems safe to say he never knew what hit him. But since Fate frequently finds a way of putting us in our place, after I finished dressing the deer out and had begun dragging him back down to the road, a particularly steep and brushy stretch of hillside caused me to lose what little control I had of the situation.

And by the time all the dust settled, I was much relieved to find that despite the necessity of having to extract one fork of the buck's antlers from the seat of my brand spanking new GI surplus pants, he hadn't managed to draw any of my blood. Even though more than enough of his had found its way into my Fruit-a the Looms to make it somewhat difficult to "ascertain" just which one of us it had come from!

When I finally made it to the road, my clothes were so saturated with sweat I decided to take my shirt off and hang it on a limb to dry. And simply because the angle of the sun was just right to cast the shadow of my upper torso and head across the large flat rock I was sitting on, it was actually possible to see what in all probability was the faint shadow of vapor rising from my wet tee-shirt. I'd already taken at least two swallows from the can of Rainier I'd had in my daypack, so even though there's a slight chance my eyes were playing tricks on me, I don't really think that was the case.

In any event, by the time I'd washed down the last of my sandwich, the sun had slid behind a huge, fork-topped spruce in back of me, thus putting an end to yet another of the somewhat peculiar incidents I've experienced on Afognak Island. Not the least of which had occurred four years earlier, during my first hunting trip with Bill.

That time, after following the fresh tracks of a small band of elk through the snow for over an hour, I'd decided it might be a good idea to turn around and head back to the road while it was still light enough to see where I was going. And just because it eventually became apparent that I'd gone quite a bit further than I realized, I was soon picking them up and laying them back down with ever increasing speed, albeit not by way of my initial route.

One of the more aggravating aspects associated with getting in too big a hurry during the winter months in Alaska, most particularly for those of us who find it difficult to find much of anything without the help of the corrective lenses straddling our nose, is the necessity of stopping to wipe the fog off their surface fairly often. So the simple fact that I'd completed this odious task for what was fairly close to the umpteenth time barely a second or two earlier, and was still in the process of stuffing a thoroughly soggy bandana back in my hip pocket when what to my incredulous eyes did appear, but the ever so fresh tracks of "HOLY, JUMPIN' UP JUDAS PRIEST, THERE'S A DADBLAME BEAR AROUND HERE SOMEPLACE, I BETTER SLOW DOWN BEFORE I RUN PLUMB OVER THE TOP OF `IM!"

Anyhow, once a closer inspection of the tracks made it quite obvious that the animal almost had to be an `ER rather than an `IM, since it was accompanied by at least two very young cubs, this goofy ol' coot quickly began making a complete revolution after every five or six tippy-toed steps, all the while searching ever so diligently for a glimpse of anything that even looked like it might have hair on it!

But by the time I zeroed in on what I was looking for, I was smack-dab in the middle of a small clearing where all the nearest trees were at least two and a half feet in diameter, and not a single one of them had any limbs that were close enough to the ground for me to reach! So when that dang fool hairball turned and looked straight at me, from a total distance of what I knew damn well wasn't an inch over forty yards, I slid straight into a state of suspended animation. Except for my poor ol' ticker, that is, which was going "WHUMPITY WHUMP, WHUMPITY WHUMP, WHUMPITY WHUMP" fast enough to make me wonder just how much longer it could keep it up!

When the first cub eased out from behind its mama's rump, though, and actually took two or three inquisitive steps in my direction, I figured my goose was practically cooked. But just as I was raising my rifle to my shoulder, a loud "WOOF" put an end to Junior's plans, as well as my most immediate dilemma. And the last I saw of the "Three Bears", the two cubs were right on their mother's heels as she headed in pretty much the same direction she'd been going a few exceedingly long moments before.

In retrospect, due to the fact that the cubs were "barely" as large as a medium sized cocker-spaniel, I'm reasonably sure they were probably the first ones the sow had given birth to, which would indicate that she probably wasn't more than three or four years old herself. But simply because she almost had to have weighed at least three times as much as I did, and possessed teeth and toenails that were one hellova lot longer and sharper than mine, I'm absolutely positive she did the right thing for all of us, by calling that cub back when she did!

Due to the necessity of getting me and my buck to camp, I now put my still damp shirt back on and proceeded to separate the hind-quarters from the front ones by chopping through the backbone just below the lower ribs with my hatchet. For even though I would have preferred splitting the carcass lengthwise, I was already too pooped to try doing it with my little twelve-inch saw. Then after hanging the hindquarters as far up a nearby tree as I could manage, I chopped the buck's head off and put my rubber pants and jacket on before hoisting the front-quarters onto my back and starting up the road.

I hadn't gone much over 200 hundred yards though, before a red Honda three-wheeler came putt-putting around a bend in the road and stopped directly in front of me. So when the driver said "Howdy, friend, if ya wanta lay that load on this little rack in front'a the handlebars an' climb on behind me, I'm purty sure I can git ya where yer headed a lot quicker an' easier than walkin'!

Scarcely daring to believe I wasn't hallucinating, I groaned "If its all the same t'you ol' buddy, I'd a hellova lot rather run back down the road a little ways an' git the rest'a this sucker first. Then I can trot along behind 'til ya git t'the Planter's Cabin, or wherever yer goin."

Snorting "Hell's bells, I should'a knew ya hadn't had time t'carry all of it in yet, it ain't been much over an hour since I heard ya shoot, fer cryin' out loud! Throw that thing on here anyway, an' we'll jist go back after the rest of it. Ya can prob'ly sit on the hams, that way nobody'll hafta walk!"

By the time we'd done precisely what he'd suggested and had started back up the road toward where he first showed up, I'd learned that his name was Dennis Thomas, and that he and a couple of friends were staying on the boat anchored in Saposa Bay. But even though he lived in Palmer and had wired houses for several of the building contactors I knew in Eagle River, we'd never run into one another before. And as it just so happened, despite my building houses in and around Eagle River for another five or six years, after he dropped me off at the log-yard near Bill's and my camp, I never ran into him again.

After hanging the meat on the pole with the other three deer, I hiked over to Elk Knob, where the only thing I saw was a beautiful silver fox. but since it started sprinkling a short time later, I headed back to camp, arriving just in time to help Bill hang the second of two nice does he'd killed that afternoon.

Tuesday, November 11. The weather had been positively nasty all night long, with the wind whipping the sides of the tent every which way, while the rain pelted down horizontally, the way it seems to fall on Afognak the biggest share of the time. Nevertheless, since Steve was supposed to be picking us up in a few hours, after crawling out of our bags at six-thirty to fix and eat breakfast, we got all our gear ready to pack down to the beach, and left it in the tent.

But when the entire day passed without sight or sound of a single airplane, we were forced to set the wood-stove back up, blow our air-mattresses full again, and fill both the lantern and two-burner stove with white gas, just so we could fry some fresh liver and onions to smother in enough "Son of a gun Gravy" to satisfy our appetites for one more night. After accomplishing all that, then unrolling our bags again, we lay there bumping our gums until nearly ten o'clock, trying to figure out what in the world could have kept Steve from coming to get us.

Wednesday, November 12. It was still raining when we got out of bed at 6:30 again, got everything but the damn tent ready to go again, then hiked back and forth between the beach and tent at least six times again, during which time we probably hiked over to our neighbor's camp at least that many times, just to try and get warm around the big bonfire they'd started shortly after it got light enough to find enough dry wood to build the damn thing! But since the day finally ended without the arrival of either their plane or ours, by the time Bill and I crawled into bed at last, we'd pretty much run out of things to discuss.

And simply because I've already covered most of what took place the following day, way back in the beginning of this soggy little saga, it seems just a little pointless to tell you that the main reason Steve hadn't come after us when he was originally supposed to, was just because he'd been weathered in for three full days, at some bay with a ridiculous sounding name, all the way over on the far side of Kodiak Island!

Friday, November 14. After lying in bed until 5:00, when I stepped outside the tent just barely in time to avoid peeing all over its canvas floor, it was somewhat disheartening to discover that the entire sky was literally overflowing with winkly twinkly little stars, quite a few of which appeared to be somewhat larger than itty bitty. Once I'd built the fire though, and Bill still hadn't crawled out of his bag, I lay back down on mine and ended up falling asleep until almost 7:00. Anyway, by the time I finally got away from camp and had managed to hike all the way over to where I'd killed Ol' Pants-ripper, I hadn't gone much more than another hundred yards before jumping another nice buck. Which, luckily for him, resulted in my blasting a big chunk of wood loose from one of the trees he'd already passed.

After losing his tracks in a large mossy clearing, I'd just started back across it the second time when a doe and a 2-pointer came charging out from behind a little clump of trees no more than fifty yards away. I missed him completely with my first shot, but my second one plowed a shallow furrow across the top of his shoulders, slowing him down just enough so that my third shot broke his neck.

I'd worn my pack-board this time, but just because this buck was at least thirty pounds heavier than the last one, by the time I finally got all four quarters lashed on the board, it was so heavy, the only way I could get back up after slipping my arms through the straps was to roll over far enough to get it on my back, then crawl to where it was possible to pull myself erect by grabbing hold of one limb after another on a conveniently bushy spruce tree.

Despite knowing I really ought to take half the meat back off the board and make a second trip, I was too stubborn, not to mention stupid, to do so. Consequently, when it took me over an hour just to make it back off the hill to the road, by staggering from one stump or fallen tree to another just to ease my load down long enough to rest for a few minutes, I managed to carry the damn thing all the way to our meat-pole by shortly after 4:00.

But just because I was too pooped to hang it up by myself, I left it lying on the ground and headed for the little lake we got our drinking water from, stopping at the tent just long enough to grab my bar of soap and a set of my cleanest dirty underwear, along with some dry socks.

Wading out into the water well down the shore from where we usually filled our buckets, I shivered and shook my way through what turned out to be the coldest, but most satisfying bath I've ever taken, bar none! And even though my legs were so stiff by the time I'd waded back ashore, that I very nearly fell in again while trying to get dry enough to put my clothes on, it sure felt fantastic when I finally succeeded! Some of us seem to do quite a few things that just don't make any sense at all, and that was sure enough one of them. I'm pretty sure, though, that I probably won't be trying it again, very soon at least!

Saturday, November 15. Made it out of bed by 6:45, to find the sky clear and close to a quarter inch of ice on most of the puddles around the tent. Bill accompanied me back to the 210 area this time, hiking a little further down the road after I headed up toward where I'd shot the buck the previous day. Upon jumping two fork-horns barely a hundred yards from the cold gut-pile, I managed to drop one of them with my second shot. But when I got up to it and discovered that my first bullet had nearly cut its throat, while the next one had actually broken its neck, it was more than just a little reassuring to find I'd come that close to where I was aiming.

Of course when Bill showed up while I was still dressing the buck out, and I just happened to mention the fact that both shots had hit a running target within barely three or four inches of one another, he couldn't resist saying "It seems to me that you could probably save at least enough money to buy an extra case of Rainier next year, if you'd just take time for a little target practice before we come!"

So when he went on to inform me that "Just because it takes at least two shots for you to get any meat around here, the really big buck I jumped no more than five seconds after your second shot, was already running so fast I didn't even get a chance to aim at him! And just as if that wasn't bad enough, the doe and spike I ran into not more than five minutes later, were only hitting the ground every six or eight feet, so does that tell you anything?", I came right back with "It sure as hell does! It makes it pretty plain that you'd better either learn how to keep from making so dang much noise while you walk, or just sit down and wait for some deer that's stupid enough to wait around long enough so you can take a shot at him! Or maybe even walk up to where your standing, and lay his head right up against the end of your dang barrel!"

Which, as I was reasonably sure it probably would, prompted him to say "Well if that's the way you're going to be, I just might decide to let you pack that scrawny little thing out all by yourself! So how does that grab ya?"

Due to the fact that I didn't really need any assistance, but mostly just because I truly hated to give him the opportunity to go back and tell the whole family "If I hadn't had to waste so much time helping this crotchety old fart of ours carry his deer back to camp, I probably would've had more than enough to shoot all of mine as well the rest of his!" All of which, needless to say, is the main reason I enjoyed hunting with the Smart-aleck Sucker as much as I did!

Since I was able to get the buck all the way to our meat-pole by shortly after 2:30, all by myself, I ended up spending the rest of the afternoon boiling a pot-full of potatoes to add to the bean and sausage concoction I'd cranked out the previous evening, while recovering from my bath. Consequently, when Ol' S-A-S eased into camp shortly after 5:00, with his nose wriggling like a rabid rabbit's, we managed to finish eating approximately ten minutes before a middle-aged native couple motored over from their camp in Saposa Bay, more or less just because they'd heard me shoot and were curious as to how much luck we'd thus far had.

Although their welded aluminum skiff didn't really look big enough to have come all the way from Kodiak, where they told us they lived, when I said "Judas Priest, after seeing how rough the dang water was just a couple of days ago, the only way you ever could've talked me into coming with you, would have been with a really big club!", both of them burst out laughing. Then they spent the next twenty minutes or so telling us about all the different times they'd barely made it to shore after an especially big wave had either drowned-out their outboard engine, or dumped enough water in the boat to soak most of their belongings.

But after finding out that neither one of them could swim, when I said "You guys're either completely crazy, or you're the luckiest two nuts I ever met!" he winked at her and said "Oh I don' know 'bout dat, she plenty fat she not sink, so if boat ever do, I jus' crawl on top of 'er an' paddle to shore!"

As might be expected, by the time they finally decided to head back to their camp, I truly hated to see them go. Back in 1961 I'd spent slightly over five months falling in love with virtually the entire population of Savoonga and the little village at Northeast Cape, on Saint Lawrence Island. I'm fairly sure this couple was Aleut, rather than Eskimo, but they were sure as the devil cut from the same fabric as the folks I'd known that long ago summer!

Sunday, November 16. There were no stars visible when we crawled out of bed at 6:45, and since the breeze was light enough to make me think it probably wouldn't rain, I decided to hike back to the 210 area once again. This time though, after spending almost four hours without seeing anything that even looked like a deer, I headed all the way over to the end of Elk Knob Peninsula, as it just so happened, for no other reason than to take a few pictures and make sure I hadn't overlooked any stray fishing floats the last time.

It was nearly dark when I finally made it back to camp, and when Bill told me he'd gotten another small button-buck around the middle of the afternoon, which meant that he'd now filled all his tags, while I still had one to go, I knew I'd be hearing about that for a long time to come. But simply because the sausage slumgullion was almost hot, and our last two beers were as cool as they needed to be, I'd have had to be crazy to ask for anything more!

Monday, November 17. Out of bed by 6:45 again, and even though the sky was mostly cloudy, there was barely enough breeze to ripple the surface of the bay. Consequently, by the time Steve's Widgeon splashed down slightly over three hours later, we had all our meat and gear ready to load, and were back in the air by 11:15.

After piling everything in the back of my pickup and checking in at the Ferry Terminal, to discover that we were #5 on the waiting list, we headed over to Almendinger's. Fred was still at work, of course, but when Mylar insisted on our spending the night with them again, Bill said "Ya got a deal, ya raunchy ol' Batt, as least as long as ya think ya can fry up a big mess of fresh heart and liver without burning the Billy Bejabbers out of it, the way ya did over on Afognak that time! That stuff sure stuck with ya though, at least one chunk of it did! Man oh man, by the time I finally got rid of the fool thing, I'd already ate enough chocolate Ex-lax to coat a whole herd of turdles!"-

Consequently, by the time Mylar eventually stopped spouting off long enough to suck in a fresh supply of air, Fred had gotten home. And simply because he insisted that the folks who'd invited him and Mylar over for spaghetti and meatballs always made enough to feed an army, I soon discovered that as long as you were a friend of the Almendinger's, you were pretty much welcome anywhere you went in Kodiak.

Tuesday, November 18. After crawling out of our bags at 6:15, when Fred started fixing breakfast for the three of us, Bill and I wound up spending most of the day reading and gabbing with Mylar, once she finally got up, anyhow. We drove down to the terminal around the middle of the afternoon and learned that we were now #3 on the list. Then when we went back at 8:00 to find we'd moved up to #2, we were still in that position when we drove aboard at 10:10. Twenty minutes later, we were in what passes for a two-person stateroom on the Tustamena Ferry.

This time I'd had enough sense not to leave my fool mummy-bag down in the pickup. For even though I was fully aware I wouldn't need it for warmth, just because there was no way of predicting (with any degree of accuracy, at least) just how rough the water would get before we made it to Homer, I had absolutely no intention of sliding from one end of my bunk to the other, every time the boat rolled far enough to make me think it was going all the way, as had been the case two years earlier!

For unless a guy's at least six feet three inches tall, there's no way in hell the skimpy little pillow they give you is going to be thick enough to keep you from ramming your head against the hull every few seconds, for what I can pretty well guarantee will be the longest night you'll ever spend. Even if you're not barfing up your socks in the dinky little commode beside the door!

In any event, since the crossing turned out to be the smoothest Bill and I had yet made, by the time we drove onto the dock at Homer at 9:20 Wednesday morning, even the greasy sausage and hash browns we'd had with our scrambled eggs were riding on a relatively even keel. But just because we couldn't help feeling a trifle sorry for the four guys who'd shown up at the dock in Kodiak just late enough so that we'd been allowed to park my pickup where theirs would otherwise have been, I hauled them on over to the ferry terminal so they could make sure everything was as it needed to be, in order for the fifth member of their party to load their pickup full of meat and camping equipment on the boat the following week.

So even though we still had to make the 240 some mile drive to Eagle River, then spend two or three days cutting, wrapping, and freezing all of our venison, by the time we'd passed over the top of the hill on our way out of Homer, we were already making plans for the following year's hunt!

There'sa Hare In My Stew, Dang It!

A jackrabbit died, way back in th' Fall'a 1947, er purty close to it,

An' his soul, at least if he had one, should'a
drifted right on up t'Bugs' Bunny Heaven.

But th' balance'a him was took home t'my bonny sweet bride.

So she stuffed 'im in'a shiny new pot that
was jist flat-out her joy an' pride.

Then as th' pressure begun t'rise, an' th' aromas they flew,

Fer an' hour er so, that long-legged bugger did stew.

Why our Thanksgivin' table was jist s'lovin'ly set,

By this Wifechild, my Darlin' an' purty little Pet.

But while she was'a flittin' an' flutterin' s'busily about,

Her smile'a triumph soon got erased by'a look'a doubt.

An' 'er sweet song'a love turned right into'a howl a'rage,

When outta th' pot she lifted my darn ol' King'a th'sage.

Fer th' smell comin' from 'is carcass was downright convulsive,

An' th' sight'a that shriveled up beast was jist plumb repulsive

So th' Calm, Peace, an' Tranquility sure did git shattered,

When that bomb, that thing, that foul critter was plattered.

Fer y'see, t'was then that I knew my gift had truly been fumbled,

An' since my joy'd been swiped, I wound up wishin' I'd stumbled,

Th' evenin' I'd got that dumb ol' bunny that flew
Off'n th' hill an' right straight out'a th' blue.
Ah s'swiftly he'd run, inspite of 'is great age,

Jist leapin' an' boundin' down thru that smelly ol' sage,
Dartin' an' dancin' all over th' place, then s'quickly I shot.
Aw if only I'd missed, er not bought th'
missus that dadblamed ol' pot.
So th' plans fer our meal sure wound up gittin' thwarted,
Tho' Skippy, our speckled mutt, was so
delirious she jist wildly cavorted.
Why what I dumped in 'er bowl jist flat
made 'er rapture supreme,
B'cause that low down beast'd now turned
inta her Thanksgivin' dream.
But it's greatful I was, an' thankful I still am
Fer th' spuds that we had, along with that damn ol' can'a Spam!

P.S.

Ya might think Ol' Snakespear gave me a hand with
that, but I really did it all by myself. Honest!

In Search Of Glory

    Despite what the gal that shares my little love-nest keeps telling me, I can't help thinking there almost has to be at least one other joker that saves things nearly everyone else tosses in the garbage-can without so much as batting an eye. But almost every time she browbeats me into throwing some of my stuff away, barely a week goes by before I wind up wishing I still had it.

    Consequently, whenever there's some little keepsake I just can't bear to part with, it's become necessary to stash it where I'm fairly sure she won't find it, like down in the pockets of the various coats, shirts and pants I hardly ever wear anymore. And whenever it's too big to fit in one of the pockets, I've got to go to all the trouble of remembering which one I stuffed my ball of string and bag of safety pins in, just so I can hang whatever it is in one of the sleeves or legs. Boy howdy, the stuff I have to put up with in order to maintain a state of sanity and solvency is almost too much to bear. Why if I was just a dog or cat, there's no way the S.P.C.A. would ever allow her to keep me hopping through the hoop the way she does.

    Just the other day, while I was mulling over some of the goofy stuff that's happened since I first came to Alaska back in the spring of 1961, I suddenly realized that this coming February will be the 37th anniversary of the first Talkeetna to Anchorage 200 Mile Cross-country Snowmachine Race. And since this required some really heavy-duty reminiscing about which pocket I'd stuck my Pepsi-Cola racing bib in, before I could do a dang thing about it I'd worked myself into a regular frenzy, jist tryin' t'remember what pantleg I'd poked my completion plaque up. That last part'll prob'ly come clear if ya think about it awhile an' use jist a little imagination, the way I had to before I fin'ly found the fool thing.

It didn't take too much ingenuity t'come up with the bib, though, since it was in the pocket I'd put the bronzed baby shoe I'd saved from the pair'a cheapies we'd got suckered inta buyin' the year after our first kid was born. Baby shoes an' bibs jist sort'a go together, ya see, in case ya was wonderin' how that come about.

But ya'd jist better believe it took a buncha creative agility t'find my plaque in the pair'a Hawaii shorts with the busted zipper. Because even after I'd pondered on it fer a whole half hour, all I could come up with was that jist because I knew how much Mama always hated replacin' a zipper, even a short one, I musta figgered it'd be safe there. I purty much needed t'rest up after all that, a'course, so I leaned back in my Lazy Boy an' flat out let the memories start unwindin'.

An' all of a sudden there I was, jist settin' on the startin' line in a reg'lar blizzard of blue smoke an' snowy white flakes, even though most of us drivers prob'ly wasn't a dang bit flakier'n the nuts that'd showed up t'see us take off. It kinda rubbed me wrong, though, when a couple'a beered-up bystanders started snickerin' at the way my legs kept jerkin' an' jumpin' all over the place. Then the flag come down an' away we went, straight outta town t'the skinny little ice-bridge we couldn't help hopin' was thick enough t'keep us from fallin' through inta the Big Su, which even if it ain't as big as the dang Yukon, is still a fairly nasty stretch'a muddy water.

Things purty much went t'hell after we got across, though, with the trail windin' ever' which way through all the brush that was tall enough t'poke through the four er five feet'a powder snow. An' ever' time one of us got tired'a playin' follow-the-leader an' tried t'pass the idiot in front, our motor would suck up so much powder that by the time we was able t'git back in line again, we'd lost at least ten spaces. There was one long ol' hill where we fin'ly climbed away from the Su, an' unless you jist happened t'peek through my window while I was huntin' my plaque, you never seen such a mess, let alone heard so much screamin' and cussin'!

But after we made it back across the Su t'the Montana Creek checkpoint, the trail ran alongside the highway fer several miles. Then all of a sudden it jumped up on the roadbed, where jist because the Race Marshall'd said we'd git disqualified fer ridin' it any longer'n it took t'git across, I started huntin' fer someplace t'git over the berm on the far side. An' even though it was close t'five feet straight up, as quick as I seen some clown wavin' 'is flag at me, I romped down on the gas an' away we went, jist like a dang Saturn Rocket.

Cat's vertical thrusters must not'a been hittin' quite up t'snuff I guess, since we only shot about three vertical feet an' fifteen horizontal ones before nose-divin' right back down in 6 feet'a the coldest crap you ever seen. An' in spite'a the fact that I'd gone t'all the trouble'a paintin' "Cool Cat" on 'er cowling before the race, the poor 'ol thing jist plain shivered 'erself t'death right there between my knees!

What really torqued my toupee though, was when the fool with the flag poked 'is head over the berm an' asked "How come ya left the damn road anyway? All I was wavin' my flag for was jist so's ya'd know ya was s'posed t'keep on comin'!"

But if ya've never tried flingin' a fistful'a feathers at anybody, ya prob'ly ain't gonna 'preciate how frustrated I felt at that pertic'lar moment. It was more'n likely lucky fer both of us that I couldn't reach a rock, since he was nearly twice my size an' there wasn't no way in hell I could've outrun him in all that dang snow. He must'a started feelin' a little guilty about then, though, since he tried t'cheer me up by sayin' "Ya don't need t'feel too bad about bein' down there, ya know, since at least six other knotheads done the same thing in the last thirty minutes er so, even though none'a them done it quite as quick as you did!"

It wound up takin' over a half hour's worth'a swimmin' around on my belly before I finally wallowed out a good enough trail t'convince Cat t'climb back up on the road, where she purred along fer all of two hundred yards before the trail jumped straight back in the damn ditch. Nevertheless, things was really startin' t'look up fer the next minute er so, then I did too, jist as one'a the State's snowplows whizzed past, headin' the other way an' doin' somewhere close t'three zillion miles an hour.

So by the time I found my way out of 'is blizzard, I could probably've made it inta the big time as the only Abdominal snowman that'd ever managed t'make it t' that part of Alaska without a seein'-eye dog. But jist when I decided I prob'ly oughta stop an' dig some'a the junk out from between my eyeballs an' glasses, a little hunk'a frozen slop jammed Cat's throttle wide open. As luck would have it though, I managed t'scrape a small glacier off one lens jist as the trail took off through the toolies, straight away from the lousy road.

Since I was doin' a pretty decent job'a dodgin' the trees with my head twisted at a forty-five degree angle, rather'n stoppin' t'scrape the gunk off my other lens, I decided I might as well keep on goin'. Roughly three milliseconds later, though, we shot around a sharp bend an' all the trees an' brush jist flat out evaporated. What would've really helped the situation, a'course, would've been fer the 16 inches'a water an' slush we'd managed t'git clean out in the middle of could jist've evaporated too. Consequently, Cat cooled off so dang fast this time that even with 'er engine runnin' wide open, she couldn't so much as turn 'er track a solitary inch.

So fer the next 45 minutes all I was able t'do was try t'roll 'er on 'er side an' flag ever'body else around the hole I was knee deep in. I prob'ly should'a let 'em come on in with me, but since I was too damn pooped t'fight, it seemed like I prob'ly better wait fer a Good Samaritan t'show up.

By the time the simple sucker finally did though, we was both so far behind the rest'a the pack that he must've figgered it didn't make a whole hellova lot'a differnce anyhow. I still can't help wishin' I'd thought'a smearin' the blood from my skinned knuckles on my face a little sooner, but that's the way it goes at times. Anyhow, within another thirty minutes er so we was both ready t'head down the trail t'Big Lake once more, which was where we was s'posed t'stop fer the night.

Due t'the fact that my canvas mukluks and Carhartt pants was plumb soaked, when I finally chugged across the line an' tried t'stand up, jist on accounta ever'thing from my rump down bein' glued t'Cat's carcass with a quarter inch'a ice, I didn't quite git the job done. An' if Mama hadn't drove up when she did, t'help chip me loose, I don't know what in hell I'da done. But if yer one'a them clowns that's really big on physical sensations, jist jam yer legs into a couple thirty gallon garbage bags filled with cracked ice, then squat in a deep-knee-bend an' hold it fer a solid hour an' a half. An' by the time ya fin'ly hobble inta the lousy restroom, ya'll be so damn good at holdin' it ya'll wind up wonderin' if it's even remotely possible t'git an ice-jam in yer personal plumbin', the same as I did.

After that first day, though, the second one was purty much anti-climatic, unless ya consider runnin' 5 miles down a dead-end, mis-marked trail, then beatin' yer butt black an' blue fer another ten miles, climatic. Because by the time we got t'the mud-flats at Knik, it was purty dang apparent why Talkeetna had so damn much snow, since there wasn't over half an inch on the trail now. So as machines with as many as fifteen horses under their hoods began sheddin' gas tanks, skis, engine cowlings, an' even a few drivers, those of us as managed t'keep goin' really had our hands full, dodgin' all that loose livestock.

Once I crossed the new Matanuska-Knik bridges an' started down the Alaska Railroad tracks, I figgered I had it made, which jist goes t'show how simple a guy can git after 'is brains has been shook from hell t'breakfast an' back fer as long as mine had. Because all of a sudden the trail took off t'the right an' the next thing I knew, Cat an' me was headin' straight down an eighty-degree precipice. A whole bunch'a odds an' ends was partin' comp'ny all the way t'the bottom, but by the time my eyeballs stopped spinnin', it looked like a few of us'd made it relatively unscathed. An' since I'd only scathed about six square inches'a skin off my shins an' knees, bloodied my fool nose an' split my lip when I sailed over the windshield, I headed on down the trail, jist grittin' my teeth and wonderin' how long it'd be 'til some smart-aleck noticed all the yellow slush that was now sloshin' around on Cat's runnin'-boards.

At the Clunie Lake gas-stop I managed t'scrounge up enough bailin' wire t'convince Cat t'go in the same direction I turned 'er handlebars. Then almost before it seemed possible, we'd limped right on past Fort Rich an' dropped inta the Ship Creek bottoms. So as soon as I seen a buncha folks up ahead, wavin' an' cheerin' us on, I opened Cat's throttle all the way, an' she grabbed the bit s'dang quick I was still tryin' t'ketch up with 'er saddle when I noticed that the road seemed to've sunk at least ten feet. Then we slammed down like a ruptured seagull an' spun around at least four times before we got pointed in the right direction again. But if I live t'be a hunderd an' ten an' two-thirds, I'll never, ever trust any'a them sneaky Mountain View clowns again.

So jist because we'd parted company with Cat's muffler on that lousy ski jump, when we headed up the final hill t'the finish line, she was roarin' loud enough t'give MGM's lion an inferiority complex. Then when I rared back on the handlebars t'help lift 'er across the line, they said "Adios" t'the rest of 'er carcass an' I ended up flat on my back in the snow. So it was more'n jist'a little humiliatin' t'hafta drag 'er the rest'a the way with 'er skis.

A couple minutes later, though, a great big sonovagun come up the hill on a Skidoo that only had one ski left. But when he pulled the same stunt I did, jist on account of 'is bein' too tuckered out t'git up, the crowd pitched in and drug 'is rig across fer 'im, while somebody else latched onto 'is feet an' skidded 'im over the line on 'is back. Along about then he blinked 'is eyes a couple times an' croaked "Gawd but that was fun! What'a ya say we turn around an' head on back t'Talkeetna jist as soon as we ketch our breath?"

Before he got violent enough t'really hurt 'isself though, somebody that knew 'im drug 'im on over t'their car an' stuffed 'im in the back seat.

So if ya think I'm even about t'let Mama git 'er hooks on my completion plaque an' greasy old #9 bib, yer ever' bit as goofy as that silly sucker was!

A Stammerin' Man

Whistlin' Willie was `is name, an' timberin' was `is game.
Tho t'wasn't th' kind that's done out in th' woods
An' sun, jist in amongst th' trees.

Ah no, fer this little guy plied `is trade an' did `is deed
Way down deep, within th' bowels'a this here Earth,
At'a gory black hole called th' Pride a'th' West.

S' tho' ya prob'ly don't know, th' ground `round ol' Silverton
Town is made'a rock that lays more up than down
Why it's s'steep even strong men weep.

Cuz that burg sets s'high that th' snow ever winter
Jist squirts straight up an' piles s'goldang deep
That th' miners haf t'tunnel down, jist t'see th' sun.

But if ya think I'm jist shootin' th' breeze,
Place yer bet an' then head up there

Cuz I know ya'll find there's plenty t'spare.

But in spite'a that, it ain't really s'bad
Tho it's kinda rough on trees an' stuff t'sow their seed,
Since things don't grow a'damn bit good in cold ol' snow.

An' even when it ain't a'snowin', tho it might
In most ever' season, th' reason th' miners all like it
Is cuz'a all th' fun stuff that goes on at night

Fer right down most any street, yer apt t'meet
A'shady lady a'ill repute. But jist heed m'words a'warnin'
An' don't go messin' 'round with that ol' Fanny doll.

Cuz she's all Will's, 'least when he's in town, an' Gawd
It jist chills m'bones t'think'a th' dispute yer gonna face
If ya don't fill yer needs some other place.

Cuz that little guy's really got'a problem,
An' it's jist th' curse, er even worse,
A'that whole damn goofy town.

Why th' pore little bird can't give birth t'nary'a word,
'Thout spittin' an' sputterin' an' whistlin' an' mutterin'
An' jist carryin' on like some poor halfpint canary.

But I'm'a tellin' ya, don't go off half-cocked
Cuz by th' time ya've d'ciphered `is notes a'warnin',
It'll be way too late, er at least t'morra mornin'.

S'jist trust what I say an' go look fer'a `nother gal.
Leave Fanny alone with `er little pal, it'll damn well pay
Cuz then at least, ya'll live t'love another day

An' b'sides it's awful nice, in that land'a ice, jist watchin'
Th' happy pair, visitin' th' bars b'neath th' stars,
An' perchin' on th' hard ol' stools a'settin' there.

Fer it's plain t'see they truly care, an' tho' she'll never
Mother a'child a'his, only fools could ever b'lieve
There's any other that means near as much t'her.

Fer when she's with `er little ol' whistlin' man,
There ain't no way ya kin help but see
Th' better part at least, a'Life's natch'ral plan.

Fer jist as soon as he starts gittin' weary,
She'll smile an' softly whisper
"Are ya ready t'go home now, Dearie?"

With Eyes That Shine

From high above, and standing still, here on Skyline Hill,
I see much that passes by, far down below my dark window sill.
It's so very quiet and truly peaceful way up here,
That at times, as I peer thru passing clouds, I sometimes wonder,
Are my loved ones and the friends I know in dreadful danger?
The innocent victims of progress, or something even stranger?
Can it be that it's already too late to sound the alarm?
But if I don't cry out, might they not experience harm?
Or perhaps I only imagine that long red, morning's line,
Leading from GOD knows where, and stretched so fine?
But then, once again, from out of the shadows of early night,
The serpent-like image returns, tho' now it's glowing white.

Is it some monstrous, prehistoric being, this everyday thing?
And if it's writhings persist, will they eventually bring,
The wanton weeds of ruin, death and destruction,
Or, just possibly, once more the sweet seeds of construction?
Could it be that those shining and shimmering trails,
Are heralding a coming season of snugly driven nails?
Oh please let me believe, if you will, that it is so,
For tho' I'll weary of running, 'tis better far than going slow.
So, mighty, wriggling and sinuous snakes, just shake your tails,
And bring to this land that so often jiggles and quakes,
Something more than horns, curses, and the smog we all dread.
Send me some customers too, for I know a builder so dear
Whose pocket is runnin' awful low on Bread!

Riding The Red-Eye Special

If I've learned a solitary thing on this long ol' trail I've been following, it's the importance of planning ahead. But just because clairvoyance was washed completely out of my genes long before I ever slipped into them, I've always had a considerable amount of difficulty in determining just where the rest of the pack was headed. Consequently, I've pretty much grown accustomed to tagging along behind the front runners. But, as another of Murphy's victims once told me, being accustomed to something doesn't necessarily mean ya gotta be satisfied with it.

So that, at least as much as anything else, is probably responsible for some of the hairy deals I've managed to poke my thick head into. Take the Sunday morning back in early February of 1969 for instance. I'd jumped out of bed and raced for the bathroom just like most of the other red-blooded inhabitants of Anchorage's then abundant mobile home parks. For even if your kidneys aren't hyper-active, you soon learn it's not too good an idea to leave your bare feet on the linoleum for an extended period of time in Alaska. My wife had tried putting a throw-rug on that icy stretch of hallway, but the first time it dumped me I ended up throwing the fool thing out in the homemade camper we'd brought up the Alcan with us seven years earlier.

Once the important details had been attended to and I'd successfully undergone the first coffee transfusion of the day, I asked Mama how she'd like to take in the Willow Winter Carnival. One thing led to another, the way it almost always does, and before too many more hours passed, we'd unloaded my old Arctic Cat snowmachine as close to Willow's Community Hall as we could get, roughly 70 miles up the highway from Anchorage, and I'd soon entered the fool thing in the race to Sheep Creek and back. I'd had to do it as quickly as possible, you see, because I was fairly sure that if the little woman ever got a look at the thermometer hanging beside the hall's main door, she'd end up wanting to head right back home. But with all the other nuts wandering around, and the sunshine just flat pouring from a clear blue sky, it really did seem a whole lot warmer than 20 below!

Ol' Cool Cat, my faithful steed, had recently undergone an enginectomy, since she'd blown her old power plant in the 1968 running of the Talkeetna to Anchorage 200 Mile Cross-Country Race. A few modifications had been necessary to install 15 horses in the same stall that 8 had earlier occupied, but she looked real sweet, even with the hole in her bonnet where the spark plug stuck through. And the baling-wire garter on her muffler didn't even show with the hood down.

The idiot with the starting flag finally waved us away and within another few seconds we'd crossed the highway and were bouncing up the bar-ditch like we had good sense. The excitement and strenuous activity of herding all those horses soon had my glasses iced up, so I jerked my goggles off and let the breeze take care of the defrosting for me, all without having to relinquish my position by stopping. With my helmet pulled snug about my ears and all the noise coming from the other racer's machines, I didn't notice the decibel level increase when Cat's muffler came unglued. The 20 miles to Sheep Creek Lodge went by almost as swiftly as sliding down a 40 foot barbed-wire bannister would, and we were soon reversing our course back down the other side of the road.

Every now and then somebody'd go roarin' around me and I finally got so tired of looking at red taillights I decided to turn mine on and see if that'd speed things up. But since the trail up ahead was just as murky as before, and Cool Cat's tail-end was still black, I raised the hood without stopping and discovered that the hot muffler'd melted just enough wires to keep me in the dark the rest of the way to Willow. So that's when I started prayin' for people to pass me, just so I could ride their tail as long as possible. The closer I got to Willow, though, the fog just seemed to get thicker'n thicker. But after dang near running over a crossing guard, I stopped and asked how come he was standing there in the dark without a light. Acting like he thought I'd lost my mind, he pert near shoved his flashlight up my nose as he snarled "I don't know what the hell yer talkin' about, Buddy, it's clear as a bell out!"

Another machine zipped past right at that moment, so I latched onto the red-glow again and went all of a hundred feet before Cat rolled off the big clump of alder brush I'd tried to coax her over, and she wound up on top of me. The guard realized something was definitely wrong by now, so once he'd pulled me out from under Cat, he said "You must be snow-blind, Buddy, yer gonna hafta wait here with me 'til the last'a the slowpokes show up."

So as I sat there in his idling pickup and started thawing out, my eyes began feeling like two red-hot coals and it seemed like the last racer never would show up.

Somebody from the Community Hall finally drove up after a while and said "All the nuts but one's already made it in, so if that's him in there with ya, ya damn well better git a move on before they decide t'lock the joint up an' go on home!"

There wasn't enough room in the guard's pickup bed for Cat, so we left her on the side of the road and followed the other guy back to the Hall. By the time we got there, though, my eyes felt like twin blow-torches, so as quick as I got checked in with the race commission, I asked someone where I might be able to find some grated raw-potato to pack on my eyes, which was an old home remedy I'd learned from the welders in the New Mexico gas-patch a few years earlier. So once Mama drove me over to the little beer and burger joint across the highway, in just a few minutes time the cook had mashed a big potato to a pulp with his meat-hammer, and a couple of the customers had headed back up the road to get poor ol' Cool Cat for me.

Anyhow, once they'd loaded `er in the back of our pickup, one of `em said "There was a hellova bunch'a moose between here an' the Knik bridges when I came up awhile ago, so jist watch out fer `em uh Mam!"

Consequently, for the next for the next two or three hours, it seemed like Mama would barely get back up to speed before she'd have to stomp on the brakes again, while I shoved my feet a little deeper into the floor-mat and jammed the top of my head a little harder against the roof of the cab, gritting my teeth and grunting every foot of the way. At that time of night back in those days, the only drugstore we knew of that stayed open until midnight was Carr's Payless at 13th and Gamble. Up until she went running in and asked the pharmacist to call our family doctor for her, neither one of us had the slightest idea what time it actually was. But after griping about it's being almost midnight, Doc Hale laughed and said "Just tell the crazy fool to keep his eyes bandaged after you put this stuff in them, otherwise he's liable to end up with some really major damage."

Thanks to his ointment and a large bottle of aspirin, a new day finally dawned and Mama led me into the examining room of my regular Eye, Ear, Nose and Throat man, Mahlon Shoff. He chuckled and clucked away like a banty hen while I filled him in on my latest exploits, then he peeled away the bandanna and peered deep into my baby-blues. The sudden sucking sound of his breath and a loud "I don't believe this" soon had me wondering how I was going to get along with a white cane and a dog for the rest of my life. But once I screwed up enough courage to ask just how badly I'd screwed-up this time, he said "Well, once all the shredded outer layer peels off each one of your eyes, provided the damage hasn't gone beyond that, you'll probably be able to see as well as you did before, but we'll just have to wait and see. In any event, other than for taking the pads off to administer the drops I'll order for you, don't you dare even think about removing the bandages until you come back to see me this coming Friday! Understand?"

After explaining that the icy blast of moving air I'd faced into when I'd removed my goggles had apparently freeze-dried the outer membrane of both eyes, and the wind had then proceeded to rip strips of it off, he hesitated for several seconds before adding "The only thing I can think of that even comes close to looking the way you eyes do right now, is one of the ragged old baseballs some of the kids in my neighborhood are always throwing around."

Needless to say, the next three days were the longest I'd ever spent, but even though the faint light in his darkened examining room nearly lifted me straight through the ceiling Friday, I could still see. I'd never worn sunglasses before, but for the rest of that spring I wore them almost constantly. And for several years after that, whenever the sun reached a certain point on the horizon, both in the Spring and Fall, the tears just seemed to flow all day long.

It seems more than a little ironic that almost another thirty-five years would pass before anyone else pulled the same stunt. Because when you stop to consider how many dog-mushers and sno-machine addicts either live in Alaska now, or spend the biggest share of the winter here, I can't help feeling there really should have been a lot more than just two of us.

Ain't That Jist Ducky

When I first arrived in Anchorage almost fifty years ago, it seemed as if virtually every goofy sucker I talked to considered himself to be an authority on what someone with extremely limited leisure time needed in order to stand a prayer of catching a few fish on a weekend. Right at the top of the list, of course, was either a Cessna 180 or a Super-Cub, both of which positively had to be mounted on floats.

But since the likelihood of my being able to float a loan of that magnitude at one of the two or three banks then in operation was somewhat remote, particularly in light of the fact that I was already several thousand dollars in hock to one of them for the well-used trailer-house my wife and I had managed to scrape up an acceptable down-payment on, the consensus of opinion was that I'd better try and find myself a boat that was seaworthy enough to make it across Cook Inlet to the mouth of the Little Susitna. Then, as long as the tide was in my favor and I didn't get hung up on one of the countless sandbars and half-submerged logs in the first five miles of river, I might conceivably make it far enough upstream to catch at least one of the three or four varieties of salmon that came back each summer to spawn.

But since the small non-union construction outfit I worked for wasn't exactly notorious for paying high wages, it wasn't until mid-summer of 1963 that I finally found a listing in the Anchorage Times' "Boats for Sale" section that I might be able to afford. By this time several of the more simple-minded members of our crew had already donated a considerable number of after-work hours in helping our foreman, Jack, shovel at least five tons of Ship Creek mud out of the flat-bottom skiff he seemed to think he'd gotten a real bargain on. So even though we'd eventually hauled the damn thing out to his house and spent innumerable evenings sanding, fiber-glassing, and painting, I was still gullible enough to consider paying six hundred bucks for a duck-billed monstrosity that was nearly half-full of the Kashwitna River's extremely muddy water.

Back then, you see, the only way to get to that particular stream by road was to drive all the way to Palmer, then over to Wasilla. And if what would someday become the Parks Highway had been graded more than once since break-up, there was a fairly remote possibility of making it all the way to the Kashwitna in as little as another hour. Providing that is, the tires and springs on whatever mechanical marvel you were herding were in reasonably good condition.

Anyhow, since I certainly couldn't afford to waste that much money on what might turn out to be a pig in a poke, I told my wife that if she'd just fix enough sandwiches and Kool-aid to take the place of supper for us and the three girls, we'd hit the road as soon as I got home from work that evening. So even though we'd already eaten most of our bread and baloney when we sailed off the blacktop onto the gravel, we'd have been a hellova lot better off if Dee just hadn't been in the process of passing the kool-aid jar back to the kids right at that moment. Because by the time I'd zigged around the next four or five potholes and eventually got slowed down enough to pull over and stop, all five of us looked like we'd been standing too close to the vat at an old-fashioned grape-stomping jubilee. Particularly after the dump-truck I'd passed a couple of minutes earlier went by, blowing it's horn and dragging a cloud of dust as long as a dang freight train.

So even though it didn't take me over five minutes to scrape most of the purple mud off her and the girls with my pocketknife, Dee was in nowhere near as good a mood as she'd been a few miles back down the road. But once I'd explained that the main reason I'd been driving as fast as I had, was so we'd have plenty of time to check the boat out and still get home by midnight, and that I probably would have seen the "End of Pavement" sign in time to slow down, if the dump-truck just hadn't been cranking out quite as much smoke from its exhaust-pipe, she finally admitted she'd been hoping I'd pass it pretty soon anyhow.

In any event, after stopping at a cabin a short way from the Kashwitna bridge, we were told that although there was a "tractor-trail" leading down to the river just a short distance from where the boat was, it would probably be quicker to park on the shoulder of the so-called highway and walk the rest of the way. So after dousing all four of my females with nearly half a can of bug-goop, we eventually made it down to the sandbar where "Ducky" was sitting. In retrospect though, squatting comes a lot closer to what she was actually doing.

But since the eight or ten inches of slimy-green-slop inside her hull made it fairly plain that she probably didn't leak, I finally convinced Dee that we'd better buy it before someone beat us to the punch. For after determining that all the ribs and crosspieces were solid oak, and that the somewhat greasy-looking six-cylinder Chevy engine was probably capable of turning the two-stage Hamilton jet-drive fast enough to send us flying across the water at somewhere close to the speed of "Hot Diggity-Dog", I was every bit as hooked as it's possible to get.

Consequently, after all but wiping out our checking account the following evening, we hit the road yet again on Sunday morning. This time of course, since it was fairly obvious some extra help was required, I'd conned one of my co-workers and his wife into coming along. So with Dee, Anita White, and the three girls leading the way in our '54 Chevy two-door, Charlie and I were bringing up the rear in my six-cylinder '56 Jeep pickup, towing a flatbed trailer I'd rented for twenty bucks a day. So I was sure as heck hoping it wouldn't take more than one day to do what had to be done.

But even if I live to be a hundred and sixty-six and two-thirds, I will never forget what an ordeal that turned out to be. Because even though we made pretty good time all the way to where the blacktop ended, from that point on that miserable excuse of a trailer jerked Charlie and me every way but loose. Dee was trying to gauge her speed so that she could keep track of us in her mirror and still stay far enough ahead so most of her dust would have time to settle, but we'd inhaled enough of it by the time we finally got to the river to make me wonder how much likelihood there was of Charlie's deciding to sue me for causing him to come down with consumption. Or at the very least, whiplash and a severely chafed hemorrhoid!

Anyhow, when the lousy tractor trail turned out to be so overgrown with brush and grass I couldn't see where I was going, I asked him to get out and lead the way on foot. But during the few seconds it took the women to boost the girls into the back of the Jeep, then crawl in beside me, the goofy sucker just flat out disappeared. Consequently, since I was pretty sure Anita might get sore if I wound up running over him, I decided I'd better shift the transfer-case into the low-range, four-wheel drive position. Before I could do that, of course, since she'd crawled in ahead of Dee and was now straddling the transmission console, it seemed like a good idea to ask if she'd mind spreading her legs just a little more.

Which was precisely when that knot-headed Charlie yelled "Want in hell's goin' on in there anyhow? It'd help a whole bunch ya know, if ya'd quit messin' around with my wife an' come help me turn these damn things!"

For simply because I'd completely forgotten about getting out to engage the front-wheel-drive hubs while the women were getting in, I hadn't seen him drop to his knees by the right front wheel after he got out. Needless to say, when Anita more or less cooed "Can you reach it now, Syd, or do I need to spread them a little further?", my face was red as a beet by the time everyone else quit laughing.

As luck would have it, after plowing our way through nearly three hundred yards of four foot high grass and alder shoots, we came out on a sandbar that was so cotton-picking narrow we had to unhook the trailer in order to turn around. Once we'd done that, and I'd gotten the Jeep pointed back in the direction we'd just come from, it was necessary for me to help Charlie lift the trailer-tongue while Dee backed the truck up.

Now even though I learned a long time ago that it doesn't take hardly any time at all to say too much about her driving, by the time she finally got the damn thing where it needed to be, my arms felt like they were three limes as long as my legs and poor ol' Charlie was groaning like his hemorrhoid had already popped out again, or was right on the verge of doing so.

I'm fairly sure we'd just plunked the hitch back on the ball when the first few million raindrops began falling. And since I sure didn't want to take a chance on its raining long enough to wash out the sandbar, after telling Charlie to let me know when I'd backed the trailer far enough into the river to float the boat aboard without too much trouble, I jumped right back in the driver's seat. That's the whole problem with getting in a hurry, you know, particularly when there's a bunch of smart-aleck females hanging around!

Because when Charlie finally started yelling, the wheels had already dropped off the edge of the sandbar and were still going down when the current grabbed hold of the rest of the trailer and swung the whole works just far enough downstream so that it's a miracle it didn't drag me and the Jeep in with it. It just might have too, if the rear-end hadn't grounded itself on a fairly long stretch of hard-packed gravel.

Since the Jeep's hand-brake didn't work, I didn't dare take my foot of the brake-pedal until I'd cranked the steering-wheel as far to the right as it'd go, then I shifted my foot just far enough to romp down on the gas with my heel. And even though it sounded like I was dragging a dumpster-load of alley-cats across seventeen sets of rails at one of the Union Pacific's main switchyards, when Charlie finally yelled "That's far enough!", it's a dang good thing there wasn't anyone standing between me and the brush on the other side of the sandbar. Because they'd sure as the devil have gotten run over or drowned, or maybe both!

As unlikely as it still seems, once we'd bailed all the slop and several hundred pounds of glacial silt out of that pathetic excuse for a boat, it turned out to be relatively easy to slide back into the river and float down to where we were able to pull it far enough onto the trailer so the women and girls could hold it while Charlie and I hunted up a couple pieces of driftwood to use for rollers. And despite having to re-hook his come-along at least twice before we got Ducky far enough forward so the trailer wasn't tail-heavy, it was just a few minutes after four-thirty when we started back down the highway.

I've a vague recollection of stopping to get some potato chips and candy-bars somewhere, but since Dee and Anita had brought plenty of sandwiches and kool-aid to satisfy our lunch and supper needs, the two jerry-cans of gasoline I'd put in the back of the Jeep made it possible to get back to Anchorage without any further expense. It was nearly eleven o'clock when we pulled up behind our place in the Forest Park Trailer-court, but just because Charlie knew I wanted to take the trailer back before I went to work the next morning, he helped unload the boat before heading on over to their house.

During the next couple of months, in addition to flushing the boat's engine out with fuel oil a couple of times, I also crawled under our trailer-house and removed both sets of axles and wheels. These were then hauled out to Jack's, where I'd gotten permission to use his cutting-torch and arc-welder while I was converting an old grease-rack into a tandem axle boat trailer. But despite setting my clothes on fire at least three times before I finally finished the fool thing, the simple fact that I got it done in time to haul the boat to Lake Louise when Jack and some of the guys headed up there for the Labor Day weekend, more than made up for all the hassle. Which just goes to show how simple I really was!

I was so anxious to get up there and try my boat out, that Dee and I pulled out of town a full three hours ahead of Jack, who'd taken his boat up several weeks earlier. But after missing the turnoff and driving ten miles further than necessary, I turned around and drove right on past the dang thing the second time. By now it was pretty close to 2:00 A.M., so when I flashed my lights at an on-coming semi just in time to get the driver to stop, he said if I could turn around in time to catch up with him before he went past it, he'd flash his lights four or five times when we got to where I needed to turn.

Anyhow, since I'd barely caught up with him when he blinked his lights, I soon found out that the main reason we'd missed the turnoff the first two times was just because some construction outfit had parked two dump-trucks and a grader in front of the sign. There wasn't a whole lot I could do about it at that time of night, so I just kept right on rolling along. Albeit, barely over ten miles an hour.

So when I pulled up in front of Lake Louise Lodge and saw Jack's truck parked in front of one of the little cabins, it didn't take too high an IQ to figure out he probably hadn't been more that a couple of miles behind us when we missed the turnoff the first time. Which he pretty much verified when he pounded on the Jeep's window approximately three hours later and bawled me out for not having enough sense to look for the note he'd left on the dash of his truck, telling me the cabin next to theirs was still empty when they went to bed shortly after three o'clock.

In any event, once we'd loaded up on some of the lodge's hotcakes and eggs, then unloaded my boat and headed down the lake, we zipped along at somewhere close to the speed of a paraplegic turtle for nearly twenty minutes, during which time we covered a total distance of slightly over a mile and I filled the air with more than enough foul language to scare most of the seagulls away. By now of course, the silt that had still been caked in the crankcase had eaten up the bearings and the engine was knocking worse than one of the first John Deere diesels.

So even though things hadn't gone quite as well as I'd hoped they would, while Jack and the guys were towing us back to the lodge, I told Dee " One'a these days I'll git this thing goin' again, Babe! An' when I do, we're gonna have s'dang much fun in it, you'll fergit all about this, jist wait an see if ya don't!"

Ballad Of Mean Mouth Mack

While hikin' along down th' trail of Life,
I've run inta some strange an' curious folks,
Most was easy t'know, but some was extra peculiar blokes,
Some of 'em's been funny, an' there's those that was sad,
An' ever so often, once in awhile, there's one that's mad,
An' one'a them had a mouth that was sharp as a knife.
A paradox he was, fer down under it all, lay a heart'a gold,
Mack was his name, an,' carpenterin' was 'is game,
As boss of a crew, he'd earned a fair amount a'fame,
He was big an' husky, but lots younger'n me,
He claimed I couldn't stand th' gaff, don't'cha see,
But I needed th' work, so I decided t'play it bold.
Mister, say's I t'he, yer big like'a bull,
But ya've never seen th' day ya can work me under,
He give me a funny look, an' said in a voice like thunder,
Alright Ol' Man, we'll find out if it's brag or bluff,
Show up t'morrow, an' we'll let ya do yer stuff,
Maybe ya'll make it, but ya talk more like some kind'a nut.
At seven th' next mornin', they was there, all three,

Little Jim, Laughin' Ronnie, an' Mack, just waitin' an' ready,
Th' poundin' an' houndin' started then, an' continued steady,
Before th' day was done, I was pooped, an' ready t'drop,
Th' yellin' was awful, went on an' on an' wouldn't stop,
But I'd learned long before, that'a guy's lunch is hardly ever free.
At last, th' day was done, Mack'd had his fun, so I did'a dance
Just t'show 'em all, there was still a'little left,
Tossed my hammer high, three spins, An' then caught it deft,
Ronnie laughed, a jolly sound. An Little Jim, he winked,
But Mack just snorted, then swore, an' never even blinked,
I didn't care, I'd gambled an' took my chance.
Th' days drug by, an' the houses went up,
tho' Mack was always mad,
Foundations went in, an' was hardly dry, before they was decked,
Th' yellin' an' screamin' hardly ever stopped,
but slowly I gained respect,
An' now an' then Mack'd call'a halt in th' afternoon,
An we'd all mess around, havin' fun, but it ended soon.
He had'a soft spot at times, an' it was really sad.
Fer he could never see all that he missed, just by bein' tough,
Maybe we wasn't so smart, but sure as Hell, we was good,
Given just'a little time, we could build
damn near anything, in wood,
An' we did, too. Even in winter, all over Anchorage town,
But no matter how much we done, Mack
was hardly ever up, only down,
Men came an' went, but some of us stayed, just callin' 'is bluff.

Fer that's all that it was, as some of us'd learned,

That day I fell when I slipped on th' ice, but I heard 'im yell,

Down thru th' joists I went, hittin' then hurtin' like Hell,

Mack come'a flyin', Lord, I couldn't breathe, thought I was dyin',

He held me there, yellin' like always, but I seen the Bastard cryin',

Then I was in 'is Rambler, an' down th'
road we went, then turned,

I tried t'yell then too, but couldn't, 'cause my chest was on fire,

At Emergency he braked to a'halt, I bit hard
an' tasted salt, tho' t'wasn't his fault,

Th' least little jolt was like a lightnin' bolt, I
knew then that he cared, an' was scared,

Later on I tried t'say Thanks, an' I'd a'hugged 'im if I'd dared,

By then tho' , he was back in control, tongue
sharp an' pointed, like'a briar.

I'd busted four ribs, a couple of 'em in two places,

They kept me there fer nearly three days, just t'be safe,

Taped an' wrapped like a dang fool mummy,
OH DAMN did it ever chafe,

Was only there fer three nights, an' after work they'd all come by,

Mack an' th' rest'a th' guys, Stoppin' in just t'say Hi!

I'd get all choked up, an' with tears in my
eyes I could barely see their faces.

Fer three weeks I laid around home, but my
Babe found a job an' went t'work,

'Cause we needed th' money, an' that's fer
sure, but I was just as certain,

My job was waitin', since Mack'd call t'see how bad I was hurtin',

Then late one afternoon, he rang an' said be here t'morrow,

We got somethin' fer ya t'do, so's ya won't hafta borrow,

    Sharp again, like before, it'd come back
    again, that damnable quirk.

    I went back, too, grittin' my teeth an' still
    hurtin, but now I knew he was human,

    He didn't crowd me or push, but I still
    sweated, an' Damn it was rough,

    I could stop t'rest, but if I even tried t'quit,
    He'd yell "It ain't enough!"

    We both stuck it out, an' finally it was
    over, I was on the mend at last,

    Before long he went back t'bein' his usual self,
    Rantin', Ravin', Screamin', Fumin',

    Things had seemed really right fer a spell,
    an' then they plumb went t'HELL,

Oh we kept busy, went right on buildin' fer several more years,

He let me run th' crew, but he run me, just 'cause I'd seen 'is tears,

    An' just maybe a few a'his fears. But it
    sure would'a been awful nice,

    If he just could'a stayed thawed, back when
    my busted ribs broke th' ice,

It's been a long time since I've seen 'im, but I really wish 'im well!

If You Knew Su Like I Knew Su

Having already spent far more than I could afford by trying to prove I'd known what I was doing when I bought my very first boat, I was eventually forced to admit that hauling my wife and two youngest girls back and forth across the highly unpredictable water of Cook Inlet wasn't too smart a thing to do. So just because I'd already bought a fourteen foot fiberglass runabout that had sustained a substantial amount of damage when its owner's trailer-house had been destroyed by fire a year or two earlier, once I'd re-glassed the starboard side of the hull and given the entire thing two coats of bright yellow paint, we loaded it back on its trailer and headed for the Little Susitna river once again, this time via what was known as the Goosebay Homestead Road.

So even though it took almost twice as many hours to cover the last three and a half miles of road, as it had to drive the first sixty-five or seventy, the simple fact that I made it without being forced to put the chains on at least two wheels left me feeling more than a little euphoric. Now whether you're aware of it or not, euphoria is a condition that virtually every died in the wool four-wheel-drive Alaskan experiences whenever he's able to get where he wants to go without having to chain-up, particularly when he's too cheap to buy a winch for his rig.

Anyhow, just to show how easily success can go to your head at times, I'd barely backed the trailer far enough into the water to unload the boat before remembering I'd forgotten to put the fancy adjustable rubber cork in the drain-hole at the back. But since the bank I'd just backed down was a lot steeper than it had looked, I'd no more than shifted the transmission into low gear and hit the gas-pedal, before both rear wheels were buried so far down in the mud the differential was high-centered on something that was a dang sight harder than the goop the wheels were now buried in.

By this time of course, despite the fact that the boat's little bunghole was barely three-quarters of an inch in diameter, at least fifty gallons of water had already passed through it. And just to make matters worse, once I'd waded out into the river far enough to more or less slither aboard, I discovered that the bucket of stuff I'd put the cork in had upset when I'd backed down the bank, and all the heavier junk was now under a foot of water, smackdab against the bottom of the transom.

Since the only thing I could think of that might fit in the bunghole turned out to be the middle finger of my right hand, I rammed the fool thing in just far enough to make me think I could probably get it back out. But since there'd been at least as much flotsam as jetsam in the stupid bucket, it wasn't until I'd shoved a little plastic bag out of the way for the third or fourth time that I finally remembered sticking the cork in it, just so it'd be easy to find. Which, simply because it'd been floating around under my nose the whole time, didn't do a whole hellova lot for my self esteem.

In any event, once I'd finally yanked my finger loose, it didn't take hardly any time at all to shove the cork where it belonged. And since it was fairly obvious that it would be a lot easier to get the truck back where it belonged if I finished launching the boat first, that's what we wound up trying to do. But just because the rope on the trailer's winder-upper doohickey wasn't anywhere near as long as it sure enough should've been, I wound up having to wind our pretty little yellow canary all the way back to where I could reach the hook and unhook it. Of course if Dee had just been willing to get half as wet as I was by then, she could have saved me a bunch of time and trouble by wading out and unhooking the dumb thing as quick as we found out the rope wasn't long enough. Which only goes to show how unreasonable some women can be at times!

So once I'd spent at least forty-five minutes jacking each front wheel of the pickup high enough to put the chains on, when the differential still wouldn't come off whatever it was hung up on, I decided to hook the chains for the rear wheels to the big log-chain that had been in the back of the truck, just to see if that would make it long enough to reach a tree stump and use my handy-dandy Handyman jack for a winch. Which, even though I ended up having to use the boat's ten-foot anchor chain to anchor the jack to the stump, eventually made it necessary to use a rope in place of the chain when we finally got far enough down the river to start fishing, roughly two hours and eight zillion gravel-bars later.

But since I'd been smart enough not to do that until after we'd gotten the truck pulled back to what passes for solid ground on the bonny, bonny banks of the Little Su, it didn't make a whole lot of difference to anyone but me, that my now eleven-foot anchor-chain was nearly stiff enough to stab sharks with by the time the stupid differential came loose from the buried log it had been hung-up on!

But as luck would have it, once we'd loaded the boat down with eighteen fat Silver-salmon, it was just stern-heavy enough so I was able to bail out almost half of the water that had still been trapped between the deck and the hull when we'd started downstream. For even though you're supposed to be able to get rid of the water by taking your cork out as soon as the boat's going fast enough to get up on what's called the "Step", the dang fool gravel-bars had been so close together that I'd no more than yell "Pull out th' plug, Babe!", before it was time to cut back on the throttle, just to avoid grinding off anymore of our old 40-horse outboard's propeller than we could afford to lose.

Anyhow, just because it was nearly midnight by then, and the lousy mosquitoes were so thick you had to squint your eyes really tight just to keep them from sucking you blind, we finally decided to head back up to the truck and pitch our tent while there was still enough light to see where we were going. Which, despite its hardly ever getting very dark on the Little Su on Saturday, the 6th of July, in the year of "Oh LORD, why was I ever stupid enough to come all the way down here without stopping to think about having to go back the way we came?", turned out to be a real ordeal!

Because by the time I'd dragged that yellow monstrosity far enough across another gravel-bar so Dee could throw out the anchor again, I'd crawl back in and lower the motor back in the water again, yank on the starter-rope long enough to start the engine so she could haul in the anchor again, and if I was just real awful lucky for once, there was a really, really remote chance of my getting to ride for as much a minute or so before shifting into neutral again, jumping back in the water again, splashing back to where I could hold the boat and help tilt the outboard back up again, there was one hellova buncha time after time stuff that took place during the four or five hours it took to get back to the truck.

So even though we still lacked six fish of having our limit, it just seemed like we couldn't load that boat back on the trailer and head for home fast enough. And if you think I was ever stupid enough to haul that fool thing back to the Little Su again, you're long overdue for a brain transplant! Once I'd built my third and fourth boats though, we hauled them back and forth from the river too dang many times to keep track of. Because in spite of all the mud and misery you had to go through to get there, it was flat-out fantastic when you finally did!

Th' Ol' Tin Bucket

Ya know, when ya get right down t'th' nitty-gritty a'things, there's hardly a'gadget that was ever invented that even comes close t'holdin' a'candle t'th' ol' tin bucket, no sir, not even one that's old an' dented. B'cause, as goofy as it might sound, I'm flat-out convinced we'd all be extinct if th' guy that rinky-tink-tinked that first one t'gether hadn't been born.

An' in spite'a their dang susceptibility fer spillability, buckets jist can't hardly be beat fer plain ol' versatility. Why what if that clown had hung'a handle on'a box, er somethin' jist as ridiculous? Can't ya jist see yerself, luggin' slop fer th' hogs, an' water out t'th' chickens an' dogs, in'a dumb ol' box? I thought not.

An' what about late at night, when it's rainin' out, an' ya know fer'a fact that ya'll sink plumb out'a sight, if ya even try t'get t'th' dang outhouse? B'cause when ya git right down to it, an' it ain't too smart not to, a slop-jar's nothin' but'a bucket that's bin dolled up'a little, leastwise on th' outside.

An' no matter how ya feel 'bout buckets yerself, why d'ya think folks allus hang on t'th' ones they got? B'cause even when they start t'leak, they're still good fer lots'a things, is why. Don't make any sense a'tall, ya know, havin' stuff scattered all over'a shelf, not when an ol' bucket'll keep it nice'n organized.

Why if I could jist'a gone t'college fer awhile, an' got'a little more knowledge an' style, I'll bet I could'a learned a'nough highfalutin phrases t'jist sing'a bucket's praises fer at least six more verses, maybe more.

But since I'd hate t'make ya sore, b'fore I go I better let ya know, th' main reason I wrote this here little poem was jist b'cause two bucketheaded buddies'a mine bet me five whole bucks I couldn't. An' I figger this sucker sure ought'a show'em!

Just Another Day In Paradise

I'm sure you've all noticed how some folks tend to age gracefully and seem to mellow with the passing of each successive season. But then, of course, there are those who adapt to the passing of youth with all the dignity and grace you'd expect to witness when lancing a boil on a bear's butt. And unfortunately, at least for my long-suffering spouse and the handful of progeny (both lawful and in-lawful) that we've somehow managed to acquire during our time together, I seem to lean more toward the latter of the two categories, bellowing my displeasure at unexpected (or at least unaccepted) deterrents to my daily existence with all the grace and aplomb of a rampaging rhinoceros.

But there's a reason for this (as you've undoubtedly deduced there would be), and at least part of it stems from spending all but a few months of the last twenty-nine years here in the Greater Anchorage area, just trying to inflict my will upon the natural order of things. And since banging crooked-boards into salable shelters for my fellow man is what my warped mentality seems best suited for, getting said shelters erected and closed-in before the advent of winter has always been almost as desirable as that certain look in my wife's eyes (which you'll just have to figure out for yourself).

Now although I haven't actually kept a written record of my wins, I'm relatively certain my earned-run average probably runs just a fraction under one in twenty-eight (because of a near miss the year a wall hit me over the head and broke my dumb leg). No fooling, I don't think there's been a single year that I haven't swatted enough snowballs with my hammer to at least win an Honorable Mention in the Homebuilder's Hall of Infamy.

Consequently, whenever I've stumbled out of bed in the pre-dawn blackness of my hillside haven, longing to hear the chirp of the bluebird of happiness just once more before my hearing-aids give up the ghost, all it takes to get me started off on the wrong foot is for some stupid radio announcer to inform me that there's a ninety percent chance of rain, accompanied by gale-force winds. Just like what we've been getting for the last three hundred or so days of this month. Man-o-man, I've had more plywood ripped out of my grasp, or had to find an alternate route down from the roof, after a playful zephyr sent my ladder splooshing into the mud, more times this Fall than I can ever remember.

So I think that by now you can probably appreciate the fact that my demeanor couldn't have been much meaner when my little woman came down to check on how I was getting along the other day. But just when I was all set to snarl that the only way things could be any worse, would be for a major earthquake to knock down everything I'd been busting my butt to build, she cocks her head to one side, then looks up at the clouds. Luckily for her, the damn downpour had let up a short time before (no doubt marshalling it's forces for another go at me).

So I think "what the hell have I got to lose" and crank my neck back as far as it will go. And, just like they'd been pasted up there with all-weather glue, seven cranes were flapping their wings like crazy and going absolutely nowhere at all. But even though I couldn't hear them, since my electric ears had been left in the pickup to keep them dry, Mama said they were whooping it up like kids on a merry-go-round. Then in a few minutes another flight of seven appeared out of thin air and they all began making a little headway against the wind. And by the time they finally evaporated into the distance, Alaska had its hooks firmly imbedded in my mangy ol' hide once more. It felt pretty dang good too!

The Ballad Of Big Bold Benny

Big Bold Benny, yes that was his name,
A man of th' sea he was, a man of th' sea was he,
Or that's what I was told, by this feller I'd gone to see.
Th' gang with which I worked, they all wanted a goat,
An' we decided to hunt, figgerin' on goin' by boat.
So th' feller rented us his, an' said it'd be a terrible shame,

If Cap'n Benny we didn't retain, for ever so great was his fame.
Th' messages they flew, an agreement was reached over th' phone,
An' great was our glee as plans fell in place, with nary a moan.
Mountains of gear piled so high, 'cause little was weeded out,
For all was deemed essential an' needed for our glorious bout.
Riches was spent, just rushin' an' searchin', preparin' our game.

Th' hours passed slow but sure, till th'
day of departure finally came,
An' th' caravan assembled in th' snowy cold of our meetin' place.
Drivers up, head'em out, with spirits so high, brisk was our pace,
Laughin' an' singin' filled up th' air, as th' miles rolled swiftly by,
An' th' stars twinkled an' glimmered, way up high in th' sky.
Th' trail was covered with frost, an' th' cold bore th' blame,

Tho' at last we came to a halt along side
th' dock, where we saw th' name,

San Ce Don II, her hull all trimmed in
heavenly blue, but great was our shock,

For th' windows was dark, an' th' door
was tight, secured with a lock.

We ranted an' raved, then headed right straight for town,
Gone was th' laughter, an' th' smiles was replaced with a frown,
But Benny's abode was darkened too, as tho' standin' in shame.

We rattled an' pounded, an' eventually
hounded that Cap'n of fame,

A window went up, an' a groan come down from out of th' black,
Th' voice that we heard was raspin' an' slurred, an' seemed to crack

"Whadda ya want?" Oh, so hoarsely it croaked,
Why th' bugger was stoned, Lord a'mighty,
our skipper was soaked.

Then an apparition appeared, starin' down an' askin' our game.

Cap'n Benny we called, it's us, th' goat hunters, an' we've came,
Th' tide has too, so rattle your bones, we're real anxious to go.

Cursin' was heard, an' vile was his word,
but it now came from below.

Th' door swung open at last, an' th' pore
critter come tumblin' out,

Shakin' an' shiverin', bloodshot eyes peerin' from over his snout,
Boose was his problem, but his missus was handed all th' blame.

So down th' street we headed, as he tried to remember th' name
Of th' fisherman he'd badgered for th' loan of a skiff,

An' we was leery he'd spoil all our chances,
if th' gent got even a whiff

Of our glorious Cap'n, but our worries was
needless, for they was two of a kind,
Th' feller proved to be heedless, to Benny's faults he was blind.
His little boat set out back, sound but
neglected, Ah what a shame.

Th' motor that pushed it was a Johnson, an engine of some fame,
Twas pitted n' rusty tho', an' all covered with mud an' grease,
But Benny was joyous an' happy, thought it a marvelous piece.
Finally we got headed, once again, for our little ship,
An' tho' th' tide'd long since turned, an'
th' wind was startin' to whip,
We boarded an' started, thru water that
churned, at last in search of our game.

With Cap'n Benny at th' helm, we all
wondered if our time'd came
As th' swells turned to rollers an' grew,
just chillin' our landlubber crew.
Plungin' into valleys, groanin' an' shakin',
oh but th' spray then flew,
An' strong men grew weak, an' some was soon forced to seek,
That little throne of a seat, gaggin' an'
groanin' an' green of th' cheek,
Cursin their luck an' our Cap'n, hurlin' at him all of th' blame.

But Benny, big Bold Benny, was just livin' right up to his fame,
Fearless he was, brave as th' best, an' tho'
th' San Ce Don II wasn't his,
He was bound an' determined to prove hisself a bonafide whiz.
He twisted at th' wheel, givin' us all a
spiel, on how we'd doubtless win

A trophy so grand, each an' every one. Then Fate softly stole in,
    Th' motors went dead, an' th' silence was
        loud, Oh great was his shame.

For he'd not checked both of our tanks, in spite of his fame,
    Now one was dry as a bone, how much
        in th' other, we couldn't guess.
    We searched an' hunted, an' tore all around,
        just makin' one hellova mess,
Then we split off a chunk, from a slat down under a bunk,
    Crawled out onto th' bow, that was bobbin'
        about, an' shoved in th' stick, ker-thunk,
    Shieldin' th' spout th' best we could, keepin'
        out water became th' name of th' game.

Th' inches of fuel was fairly easy to see, but th' distance we'd came
    Made us believe we was far short of what we needed,
    For th' return of our little band, so some of us pleaded
With Benny to call, askin' for help, an' just blabbin' to all,
    Th' story of our plight. But he went right into
        a stall, looked plumb ready to bawl,
    He ended up sayin he'd think of a way, without
        havin' to swallow near all of th' blame.

    Th' engines they stuttered an' sputtered, an'
        Benny spit out a terrible name,
Then one gave a cough, an' th' other one sort of a wheeze,
An' they started to purr then, just as purty as you please.
Now we needed a haven, some little nook, for spendin' th' night,
    Then someone said "Look, down there Benny,
        at th' end of th' bay, is that a light?"
    His grin was huge, for he was rescued
        at last, an' freed of his shame,

So he opened 'em up, just headin' for glory,
once more proud of his fame.
Then we tied for th' night, snug an' secure, to a neat double ender,
Whose skipper gave us some fuel, then loaned us his fender.
Rockin' an' creakin', we listened to Benny most all of th' night,
Why th' sound of his snores rattled th'
doors, an' we prayed for th' sight
Of th' mornin' sun, so's we'd have some light, to look for th' game.

But th' racket only increased, then finally, over it all there came
A shout from th' deck,"Rise an' shine, way up there is a speck.
I swear, it moved, an' we've a ways to go, for its higher'n heck,
So come on Benny, rustle your bones, an' get 'em fired up,
When you get us on shore, then you can finish your cup.
Oh no, now th Johnson won't run, an' your buddy's to blame,
Tho' I don't seem to recall, ever hearin' his name.
C'mon Jack, c'mon Jim, grab a couple of slats, so we can paddle,
Just a little closer now Benny, then we'll all skidaddle.
WHOA! Oh for cryin' out loud man, don't
take all day, swing'er around,
Ah Hell Cap'n, now you gone an' done it, you run us aground.
Th' screws'er bent, can't you feel'em
shake? Oh Lord, what a shame.

Well, your goose is done for now, it's th' end of your fame,
So you might just as well get on th' mike, an' call for a tow,
Th' hunts now over, without a hike, tis sure th' end of th' show.
Well don't just stand there man, wishin'
for luck, 'cause there ain't any,
You cost us th' game, but by Golly, you won a new name,
OLE BAD LUCK BENNY!

Eleanor, taken in 1927 when my parents were on their way to Alaska. Eleanor later married Harry Trimble.

Love's Not Really Blind You Know

Although my father's first marriage undoubtedly brought him a fair amount of happiness, at least in the beginning, the one thing it didn't bring him was the children he so desperately longed for. So it's little wonder that, after hearing about how some folks he'd known for several years were looking for someone with whom to leave their small daughter, he told them he'd be more than happy to look after little Eleanore in their absence. It was understood by all concerned, you see, that it would only be while they went further west to see if they could somehow manage to get their affairs back on an even keel in Oregon or California. And even though his wife wound up agreeing to the arrangement, it was always my understanding that it was with considerable reluctance.

And thus began a relationship between a man and a little girl that would endure for each of them throughout the balance of their natural lives. I can well imagine how heartbroken Eleanore must have been during her first few hours under Dad's roof, after having to watch the two people she'd always loved and trusted more than anyone else, drive off in a cloud of dust. For since kids have always been able to sense when someone really doesn't want them around, I rather imagine she instinctively knew that Dad's wife much preferred not to have her cluttering up the scenery she'd grown so accustomed to, during the years she and Dad had been married.

But due to the fact that all of what I know about this period in Dad's life came to me via things he himself found reason to tell me about, at different times during my childhood, and since all of them actually occurred well before I was born, it would be grossly unfair to deny his wife the possibility that there existed a second stanza to the song. And that hers had every bit as much right to be heard, as did Dad's.

Yet, since both Dad and his ex-wife continued living in Ridgway for the balance of their lives, during which time her subsequent marriage to another man produced no offspring, it was relatively natural for me to assume that this was probably because neither party wanted them. So I just about had to believe that what Dad told me about his situation was what actually happened. Especially in light of the way he constantly emphasized how important it was to treat others the way we ourselves want to be treated. And for as long as I live, I'll never be able to forget the look in his eyes when he'd begin entreating me once again with "Buzz, whatever a man does in this life, and I don't care if it's just shoveling out a barn, or being president of the whole country, if his word's no good, he just plain and simple isn't either!"

And simply because of things that have happened in my own lifetime, I can just as readily understand his need of someone on whom to lavish affection. For when any of us are denied something by circumstances beyond our control, it almost invariably makes us desire it all that much more. Consequently, once I'd entered the picture and had learned who the beautiful girl in the picture that would forever sit on Dad's chest of drawers was, I could often be found gazing at it, just hoping that there would someday come a time when I'd get to meet my `almost' sister.

But long before this would ever occur, Dad's love for his wife slowly but surely began dissolving. For although I never once heard him say that she ever mistreated Eleanore openly in any manner, I always got the impression that it was what she withheld from the little girl that eventually caused Dad to realize his marriage was doomed.

And even though it managed to limp along for some time after Eleanore's parents did indeed get their affairs in enough order so that they were able to come back after her, I can almost still hear Dad's voice break when he first told me what had happened on that day. But since it should hold more meaning if I relate it as best I remember his words, this is a pretty close approximation of what he had to say about it.

"Buzz, when I first got the letter from Eleanore's folks, letting me know they'd finally been able to start getting their feet on the ground again, and that unless something unforeseen happened, they'd be back to get her before many more weeks passed, I came real close to hoping something actually would happen, just so I wouldn't have to give her up. Because with all the problems Selma and I were having, that little girl's need of me had begun seeming like the only thing I could really count on. And there wasn't the slightest doubt in my mind that she felt the same way about me."

He'd have tears in his eyes by now, and it was very apparent that he was having a great deal of difficulty in going on, but he eventually continued, "Because there just isn't any mistaking the look in a person's eyes, at least a little person's, when the first thing they do upon coming home from school, or wherever they've been, is to come running up and throw their arms about your neck, yelling `Daddy, Daddy, just wait `til you hear what happened t'day. And while she's busy telling you all about how her teacher's going to let her do this or that, or how she just knows that she'll probably be getting an A for the arithmetic test she took an hour or so ago, because it was so easy that she finished it at least five minutes before any of her classmates Well, Buzz, if you're ever lucky enough to have a child of your own come to you that way, you'll know what I'm talking about."

Then, after staring off into space awhile longer, he said "Anyhow, by the time Eleanore's folks finally did show up, I'd managed to convince myself that it was probably best for all concerned. Especially since there was just no way I could deny that they had first claim on her, and that I'd never have gotten to have her in the first place if it hadn't been for all their tough luck. So somehow I was able help her get all her things together and out to the car that was going to take her away. And II even got through saying goodbye to her, without breaking down altogether."

By now, though, he looked as if he was in danger of doing just that. But then, almost as if he still found it completely beyond comprehension, his voice hardened and rose considerably in volume. "But, as God is my witness, when Selma turned and smiled at me for the first time in ages, before the dust from that car's driving off down the street had even had time to settle And as if that wasn't bad enough, when she even started humming Well, I knew right then and there that there was just no way we'd be able to stay together much longer!"

After a final pause, he went on "But I'll give her credit for this much, though, she tried a damn sight harder than I ever did after that day, to make a go of our marriage! But by then I'd turned to the bottle instead of her, so I sure didn't leave her much to work with."

And so began one of those long-distance relationships that so frequently fizzle out and die. But for some reason or other, this one wasn't destined to do that. For as the years wore on, during which time neither party managed to find a way to visit the other, except through their letters, their faith in one another's continuing love remained constant. And even though I wouldn't discover it until after Dad's death, some forty-seven years after it had first been put away for safekeeping, a February 19th, 1921 copy of the Ridgway Sun, the weekly newspaper then being published every Saturday by one John J. McCarthy, Editor, Manager, and Member of the Colorado Editorial Association, began taking up space with other odds and ends of paper memorabilia that my father refused to part with.

When I first found the age-yellowed issue among his things, and saw his business ad at the bottom left corner of the eighth, which was also the final page, I thought that perhaps he'd saved it because of that. But after scanning each brittle page, and noting several references to certain functions that had been attended by Mr. and Mrs. G. C. Huffnagle during the preceding week, I began wondering whether Dad might not actually have kept it because of these. Then at last, near the center of that final page, I discovered the real reason behind that little paper's existence. And with your permission, I'd like to quote it in its entirety.

The standard in the third and fourth grades for headmarks in arithmetic and spelling, has not been so good this month as last, on account of new and more difficult work being carried on in both subjects. Dorothy Janet Moshisky, Earl Edwards, and Eleanore Huffnagle have the most headmarks in arithmetic. Clara Fisher leads the class in spelling. The interest in both grades seems very good and all are putting forth their best efforts in order to accomplish the highest standard in their work.

I don't have the slightest idea whether Eleanore was in the third or fourth grade when this little article first appeared, but this much I'll believe for as long as I live, that article and that one alone was Dad's sole reason for hanging on to that newspaper. And I'm equally as certain of how proud it must have made him, just to have her wear his name.

So when my future mother's first husband died shortly before the death of their only child, and Mom then had to spend several months in a California tuberculosis sanitarium before she was diagnosed as being free of the disease she'd apparently gotten from her husband, she came back to Ridgway in the summer of 1926. So Dad's marriage was already well beyond salvaging, at least as far as he was concerned.

Mom's family had lived there when she was just a tiny girl, during the time her parents own marriage was falling apart. And since one of her older brothers, Jimmy Cooper, still lived there with his wife and son, Mom moved in with them, just to try and pick up the pieces of her life. She'd been taken in by an aunt right after the divorce of her parents, you see, while her older sister and five brothers had either been left to shift for themselves, or been adopted. So because of her tender age, it was several years before she even learned her mother had died and that her father had reportedly abandoned all of them by moving off to Alaska.

Anyhow, since Jimmy and Dad had been deer-hunting buddies for several years already, it wasn't very long before Dad began courting the girl who would soon become his second wife, as well as my mother. And even though I wasn't destined to learn of it until quite some time after Dad's death in 1968, on December 24th, 1926 the final decree of his divorce from his first wife was issued by one Judge Norpel. And then, within what was undoubtedly only a matter of minutes, this same judge united my future parents in the bonds of Holy Matrimony.

But due to the fact that it didn't seem especially sensible to contemplate making a mid-winter honeymoon voyage to far off Alaska, since Dad had already made it plain to Mom that she ought to give her father a chance to make his side of the story known to her, their wedding trip was delayed until early the following summer. And even though there's more than a slight chance that I may actually have been conceived on that voyage, that was as close as I ever came to meeting my mother's father.

Shortly after my birth though, I was taken back to Ohio to meet Dad's folks. But despite my ability to remember most of the things I've ever been involved in, I have no more recollection of that than I do of that long ago journey up the Inland Passage to Wrangell. Although you'd have one hell of a time convincing me I didn't somehow manage to catch the Alaska Bug from Grandad, either through osmosis, hypnosis, or just a plain old case of gnosis. Which I'll save you the problem of looking up, by explaining that that's supposed to be a knowledge of spiritual things. At least according to my handy-dandy little rhyming dictionary.

But just in case that seems to be coming in from left field for you, finally being able to move to Alaska more than forty-five years ago came just about as close to being a religious happening with me as anything I ever managed to do. So will the completion of this book, though, if indeed that too ever comes to pass. But the real reason behind these last few sentences, has been solely to get us headed toward Oregon, where Mom got to meet Dad's little girl before resuming her trip to meet her father. Eleanore was no longer a little girl in that long ago spring of 1927, though. For in the pictures taken of the occasion, she looks enough like my mother to have been her younger sister, at least to me.

And even though Eleanore's physical appearance had been altered substantially by age, when I at last got to visit overnight with her in April of 1961, her eyes were still filled with the warmth and beauty so evident in the picture I'd spent so much time staring at, back when I was just another kid, lonely for someone I'd never really known. But nevertheless someone to whom I was bound by my father's love.

And it was during this solitary visit that I also met the son she'd named after her husband's uncle as well as me, in tribute to the man both she and I loved so much. The following day brought about the realization of yet another dream for me, though. For after being taken to Sea-Tac International by my `almost' sister and her husband, I spent the next six hours flying high above the Inland Passage to Alaska, re-tracing by air the route taken so many years earlier, first by my grandfather, then by my parents. And even though I had every intention of coming back to spend more time just getting to know Eleanore better, I didn't get to. Because unknown to either of us at the time, Fate had already scheduled her to die of cancer before I could return.

Alaskan Storms

Like Lions of the sky, with flashing talons so bright,
Their wildly flowing manes billowing all roundabout,
Just lunging forth in wild bursts of searing light,
Raging and rearing, harsh voices thundering out,
Feinting first to the left, then to the right,
With muscles rippling, they pound thru the sky,
Sinews of steel flaunting an all but limitless might,
Ah such magnificent giants are they, and yet slowly,
Oh so slowly, they sink to the horizon and die.

Clairvoyance, Or Dementia

A few days back, just about the time I began wondering whether anyone but me had noticed the abundance of seed-cones that our local spruce had set this year, it became very apparent that my nearest neighbor, Dr. Livelystone, had indeed noticed. And it's barely short of a miracle that the little nut-noodler hasn't busted a gusset since then, just trying to harvest what he seems to consider his own personal bounty.

The good Doctor, as you may already have guessed, is one of my more squirrelly neighbors, so the bushy tail that's tied to his carriage looks fairly appropriate as he goes rushing about his task. And although his antics can seem more than a little peculiar at times, close observation over the past few seasons has led me to believe that he may actually be more psychic than psycho. One thing's for certain though, acrophobia's not his problem, for he'll dash right out to the very tip of the smallest and highest limbs on the trees, just to retrieve cones that I can't even see from forty or fifty feet below. And most of the time he'll then hang upside down, anchored in place by only his rear feet, and just looking for all the world like a hair-ball that's about to go into orbit, while he snips cones loose with his teeth or pulls them free with his front feet.

Several days before the snow arrived this past week, my wife and I were eating lunch at our breakfast-bar when we caught sight of the Doctor bouncing along through the still-standing jungle of dried grass and fireweed that separates our place from the vacant lot to the south. And although she denies doing it, I'm almost positive that Mama must pour several bags of fertilizer on this chunk of our property every summer. But at least the lush four foot growth keeps my horde of firewood hidden from public view during the short few weeks when the same depth of drifted snow isn't making the procurement of fuel a virtual nightmare for whichever one of us decides that a blazing fireplace would add a little romance, if not actual warmth, to our lives. (And if you think that last sentence was a tough sucker to wade through, you just ought'a try wading out to my woodpile sometime, winter or summer.)

Anyhow, once the Doctor's kangaroo gait had finally deposited him at the base of the tree he was searching for, he shoots up it like a soapsuds-enema, clean to the top. Then, just like he's got bubbles in his brain, he hangs himself right smack in the middle of a cluster of at least thirty or more cones, somewhere in the vicinity of forty-five feet above the ground. And although we couldn't hear anything but our own laughter from where we sat, it didn't take much imagination to dub in some "phtt-phtt-pttooey, phtt-phtt-pttooey" to accompany the cascade of cones that he began spitting at the ground.

With the sun highlighting each one of them, so that they looked like burnished gold, it was easy to understand why the little miser was in such a frenzy, and I half expected to see him sink his teeth into one of his stern-anchors by mistake and come tumbling down also. Apparently, he'd decided his earlier method of taking each and every cone to one of his numerous caches as soon as he harvested it, just wouldn't do this year, at least not if he hoped to collect the roughly three trillion cones (give or take a few) that are now decorating the trees of his bailiwick.

And it's a flat-out wonder that the enamel on his teeth didn't melt, because for the next ten or fifteen minutes he went through those upper cone-clusters like a Kansas Wildfire. Finally, though, he must have realized that it was going to take him until dark-thirty at least, to get all the loot rounded up and stashed. So he came down to earth just as I decided I'd better go get my snowblower tuned up and ready for another long, hard winter.

Moonhead

Way back in th' spring'a "45", up in th'
soarin' San Juan peaks'a Colorado,

I served some time in'a hell hole of'a mine that ya

might have t'search fer quite'a spell t'find.

That hole where I worked was known as
th' Green Mountain, an' was

leased by th' Pride'a th' West, which'd long
been ranked with some'a th' best.

Now the road's fairly wide as ya head up ol' Animas Crick,

Out'a Silverton town. An' if ya go about four
miles, ya'll come to a dusty little spot

alongside th' trail. At one time there was'a log
cabin where th' miners got their mail.

I doubt that you'll find even a trace of it now tho',
fer there was only a shack or two in Howardsville
way back then, when it was still alive.

Here ya forked t'the right, on'a road that was narrow enough
so even'a sparrow had trouble findin'a safe place t'light.
Ya wound on up Cunningham Gulch fer'a few miles, an'
there on th' left sprouted th' flower'a Green Mountain,
from as scrawny an'thin'a mulch as I ever seen.

I stayed with th' folks of 'a chum'a mine by th' name'a Baird,

    down at Howardsville, an' fer'a spell I
was kind'a scared of 'is ol' Dad.

"Moonhead", he was sometimes called, 'cause he was bald

    except fer'a fringe above 'is ears jist tinged all
silver gray. But if ya weren'ta friend'a his,

ya were apt t'come to'a sorry end, unless ya called 'im Walt.

He was one tough ol' galoot, but he talked an' walked real soft
in 'is high heel boots, around'a nice lookin' woman he always
called Darlin, but that was 'er name. Back before she got
tangled up in 'is act she was Darlin Frame, an' that's'a fact.

Once in awhile he'd start snarlin' at her but it was only a careful
game, for he was one Gawd awful tease. Why, when he was
playin'a joke, he rode ya til' ya almost broke, never by degrees.

I had me a gal, down in Silverton town, by the name'a
Maxine, an'some'a th' stuff ol' Moonhead said t'me was jist
plumb obscene. I'd set there at the table, jist tryin' t'eat,

an' then meet 'is eyes an' realize I was in fer it, again.

Th' damn ol' fart thought he was smart when he'd git me t'turn
all red, but he'd fast come to'a halt, when Darlin yelled, "WALT!
That's enough, th' kid's gonna choke on one'a yer raw ol' jokes
if ya don't leave 'im alone. Now I mean it, jist knock it off."

Then he'd jist sort'a groan, an' say all meek an' mild, "O.K.

Darlin, honey child." An' then he'd cast ya a wink, jist so's ya

wouldn't think he was knucklin' under, the damn old phony.

No Siree! Ya never stole Ol' Moonhead's thunder.

One Saturday mornin', on'a day'a rest from our job at th' mine,

we were settin' there at the table when he said "Syd, if ya kinda

think ya kin git by without Maxine fer awhile,
why don't ya come along with me,

an' maybe ya'll see somethin damn few folks has ever seen.
Fer ole Kit Taylor's got'a bronc that's strong an'mean, an'he
wants'im broke. So ya might git t'see th' Moon go down.

Darlin gave out with one hellova shout, "Dammit all Walt, ya

crazy ol' fool, ya ain't some dumb school kid no more, but I know

I'm jist'a wastin my breath, s'go on now,
an' have yer fun, fergit I spoke.

But by damn yer goin' t'be th' death'a me yet."

In a little while, we parked th' truck at Taylor's corral in th'
heart'a town, an' walked across th' turdy muck just layin'
all around. Ol' Kit came hobblin' out from'a open door,

carryin'a crooked ol' stick fer'a cane, an' jist
wearin'a big ol' grin on top of 'is chin.

Moonhead said, "Syd, I'll bet ya didn't know,
but that ole stick's Kit's pride 'an joy."

Then he went on t'explain that once it'd been'a bull's too, but
now it was jist dried rawhide with nothin' left'a th' critter's
lust, an' I'll jist have t'trust that ya know what I mean.

As we stood talkin', a big ol' bay was walkin'
in circles around'a stout wood post.

He was taller than most,with four white stockin's
above 'is hooves. Moon chuckled an'said

"He moves like he's never seen th' day he'll let somethin' like me
sit astride 'is ornery hide,
an' I'll bet that's jist what he intends t'prove."

Sittin' down on'a rock, he began t'roll a pair'a
Darlin's silk sox clear up t'each knee,

sayin' "Helps yer feet t'slide free in case
yer boots won't, don'cha see?"

Then he lifted'a scarred ol' chunk'a dry
leather from th' back'a th' truck,

an'waded once more across th' muck, t'set it
down on that powerful chunk'a mean,

green leather.

Just talkin' low an' slow all th' while, he tightened
th' cinch on that shiverin', quiverin' mound'a

meat. Replacin' th' halter with'a bridle, he sidled right on t'th'Bay.

Then he yelled "Let'er rip Satan, don't keep ol' Walter a'waitin'!"

An' then th' fun begun, fer that ornery Cayuse
had no use fer any'a mankind.

He plumb left th' world behind, headin'
high t'frolic around that big ol' sun,

way up high in the sky. He gave one hellova
grunt, then Moon did too,

as 'is boots went sailin' away.

'Round an' 'round they flew, an' neither one knew whether
he'd met 'is match fer quite'a spell, tho' Moonhead's face grew
grayer yet an' then th' end drew near. Fer'a look'a fear begun

t'show in th'eyes'a th' Bay, as he bowed 'is back ever' which way. An' we heard ol' Moon say, "Yer fulla scratch 'an awful stout, s'just buck'er out ya tough ol' sonovabitch!"

At last it'd ended an' was fin'ly over, s'th' Moon descended, t'stand in 'is stockin' feet,

right there in all that crap, 'cause there sure wasn't any clover. Darlin's sox, they were.

Th' Moon set quite some time back, I'm sad t'say, but I'm jist awful glad I got t'spend th'Spring'a "45" with'a damn fine friend, there at th' old Green Mountain Mine.

It was'a real nice time an'place, jist t'be alive.

Cloudy Weather

For some months now, it's been possible to develop a rather dark and bleak picture of life in this state of ours. But that's to be expected, since Alaska has always been noted for its long, dark winters. Lately though, there's been an over-abundance of gloomy forecasts, predictions and complaints, bombarding our senses with front-page headlines, and graphic scenes on the Late Night News reports coming from the boob tube.

Alaska has always reveled in doing things in a big way, so the long dark winter and long light summer are to be expected. But at times, we forget to open our eyes wide enough to find our way. For when a sad song is played long and loud enough, before you know what's happening, it seems like everyone's singing it. And whether you've noticed it or not, a lot of the suckers that are running around loose have been singing some awfully sour notes lately.

So with that in mind, I'd like to share something that happened to me recently. One morning just a short time back, as I was gazing out my window here on Skyline Drive, I saw what amounted to a double-dose of clouds. There was a solid blanket way up high, with a separate layer down below that was covering everything beneath the immediate location of our house. And since it gave me the impression of becoming cross-eyed while staring through fogged-up specs, I wiped mine off and took a really good look at what was going on.

The wind was hustling the upper blanket due north, just making humps and bumps all over the place. And since the lower layer was rolling right along too, in the opposite direction, I couldn't help wondering if I was hyperventilating or something.

But even though I never open the windows when the wind's blowing, and I hadn't put a single drop of Old Sockeye in my cup of coffee, I still felt like I was standing on the sidelines of some championship tennis match, watching all that back and forth action.

Every now and then a hunk of fluff would erupt from the bottom layer and shoot up to the one above, reminding me of the way the sheep I once owned always seemed to have a head on each end, with neither one containing the slightest sense of direction.

So as I continued watching, every so often a tentacle of cloud would reach down toward the other layer, but not once did any of them ever come in contact with the lower mass. Which I couldn't help comparing to the way some of us with high aspirations sometimes tend to go shooting off at things that are way over our heads.

This woolly circus lasted for a good twenty or thirty minutes, when a brilliant shaft of light suddenly angled down from the east, like the beam of some huge spotlight. And as it slowly burnt its way through the lower layer, a series of cottony wisps began drifting upward until finally, a fairly large grove of timber that was growing on one of the sandy bluffs across Knik Arm became the focal point of the show. So as I stood there, entranced for sure now, I once more realized what a privilege it is to live in Alaska.

T'ol' Moonhead's Darlin

It's really awful strange, ya know, th' way things go at times
b'cause when that slick-topped ol' galoot tilted back in 'is chair
I flat-out knew what he was a'fixin' t'do, but th' trouble was
I jist didn't have th' foggiest notion, on how t'beat 'im at it

S'when he pokes 'is fist in 'is pocket an' pulls out two dimes
I sucked in' a'big gulp'a air, an' jist kept on settin' there, where
an' I could almost see th' cogs goin' 'round in that ring'a fuzz
he called hair, 'tho most'a us kids said t'was jist dried up suet

At least when th' grin on 'is chin let us know 'is mood was good
which t'be truthful about it, was purty dang close t'bein' always,
unless a'course, ya rubbed 'im wrong when he had'a real snootful
a'fightin' whiskey, an' jist let me tell ya, that was plumb risky.

S'while I'm settin' an' listenin' t'them clickin' dang coins,
'is nasty tongue starts flickin' in an' out, jist like'a snake's.
An' I'm tellin' ya, even tho' t'was way back
in 1945 that it all took place,
it still makes m'ears burn, jist thinkin' about it.

Anyhow, when he kind'a sorta sighs, then rolls 'is eyes, I realize
    he's fin'ly satisfied as t'how he's got me
    sweatin' jist as much as I'm goin' to,
so he slips this half serious look on 'is face an' I swear,
    there wasn't even a'trace'a grin hid in 'is whiskers.

Then 'is mouth pops open, an' out drops th' bomb I was dreadin'.
    b'cause even tho' I truly would hate t'give ya th' impression
    he had'a mean streak, there was plenty'a
    times that what he come up with,
came awful dang close t'bein' downright obscene.

S'since what all he said more er less
    involved this gal I'd been seein',
by th' name'a Maxine, an' how, since he knew I was awful green
    'bout lots'a things, I really ought'a be
    careful how late, er how far I went,
when she an' me went out on a date.

An' Boy-howdy, if ya think I didn't blush,
    when that raunchy ol' sucker
    puckered up 'is lips, whilst winkin' an'
    blinkin' both of 'is eyes over at
that dadblame Darlin woman he was married to,
an' she jist sort'a gushed, real soft, sweet an' breathlessly

"Aw Walt, ya dang ol' tease, if ya don't stop mouthin' off like that,
    an' come gimme'a big ol' squeeze, I might d'cide
    t'park my rump on Ol' Huffy's knees,

jist t'see if he'll wind up sneezin' when he gits'a whiff'a what'a real
growed-up woman smells like."

Well sir, fer all you poker playin' folks
that happen t'wind up caught

in th' same fix I was in, that summer I blew
th' last few weeks'a my natural

naivete, I sure hope ya keep it in mind that
ever so often, even a'full house

might not stand up t'th' right pair!

An' that pair'a dang jokers sure as shootin' knew it, too! But
I'm tellin' ya true, I'd give an awful lot, jist t'live thru it again!

Potted Potential

For the second time in as many hours, the image of the slight, balding, and bespectacled man coming toward my wife and me brought a smile of recognition to my face. We'd earlier seen Pete and his rotund companion as thoroughly involved as we, studying the exhibits entered in the local Amateur Photo Contest that was on display in one of our city's larger shopping malls. Dee and I had gone there specifically to see if any of my first and only such offerings had been selected. After seeing what I'd been competing against, I was hardly surprised to find they hadn't, but was thoroughly delighting in our voyage of discovery and struggling to commit as many of the vivid scenes and settings to memory as possible.

Pete and I had recently been classmates in a couple of literary courses we'd enrolled in, and had become friends. As difficult as it was for me to comprehend, considering my lack of academic background, I'd completely enjoyed my initial poetry class and had been pleased to find Pete's smiling face in the next semester's prose class. He possessed a natural talent for word manipulation and although he poked them into some rather strange situations at times, I'd definitely relished uncovering the depth of thought he poured into his work. He was in the process of continuing a college education that had been interrupted for some reason, while I was racking up my first credits, since the universal University I'd enrolled in back in 1946 has always offered a diploma I'm in no hurry to collect.

For the benefit of those not familiar with the process involved in matters of this sort, allow me to clear up some of the muddy water that always seems to dog my footsteps. Each masterpiece our fertilized brains spewed out in both these courses first had to be shoved through a reproductive system that had more than likely given birth to far more deformities and maiming than any of the network soaps. Then these packages of consolidated material were distributed to each of our colleagues and allowed to ferment until the next class-night, when they were open for oral as well as written critique. And even though Jack the Ripper would have had a devil of a time stirring up any more blood than what flowed out of those sessions, our professor seemed to think we would eventually profit from them.

Even when you know full well that you need to go easy because your turn's coming, constructive criticism is an elusive and almost impossible ingredient to come up with whenever you're talking about something as fragile as a fledgling author's firstborn offerings. It's far easier to say "I like it" and to gloss over or ignore what's wrong with them, but that does neither of you any significant good. I've never been accused of being overly perceptive, but I tried as hard as I knew how to cushion any negative comments with a little humor whenever possible.

One thing I have been accused of though, is having a cynical outlook and I've had to accept that it isn't too desirable a trait. I even went so far as to find out what it meant, by spending a substantial amount of time browsing through my dictionary, which claimed the original Cynics were a group of Greek philosophers who eventually decided that the rest of society was far too interested in material things. Consequently, when Pete whipped out a piece that seemed to find more that was wrong with our city than was right, I felt the need to ask if there was any possibility he too might have a dusty old Greek lurking in his background.

Since I'd made a point of including myself in the category, I didn't feel I was being unduly critical or cutting. Yet when he later came up to me and said the reason he was no longer able to write was because of what I'd asked about his ancestry, I couldn't help wishing it was possible to undo my words. But the fact that his voice was decidedly slurred, while his breath seemed to possess the aromatic content one usually associates with proof or percentage, soon led me to conclude I was being used as a scapegoat or crutch.

So as I stood mutely watching his retreating back, wishing I had the courage to tell him to stop hiding in his bottle, yet too afraid to take the chance, I could only hope he'd someday wake up and put all that God given talent to work.

Ol' Gert's Night To Howl

Things was goin' along 'bout like most any other
night, ya see, out at our place on Hardrock Hill

Altho' things hardly ever sailed all that
smooth fer my little woman an' me

Since there really wasn't all that much as'd
grow, out on them steep ol' hillsides

'Cept fer rocks an' thistles, an' there was always a
whole buncha lamb's-quarters an' chickweed

Kinda funny 'bout them last two ya know, because even
tho' I'd thought at times, I oughta catch some'a their seed

Jist t'show my little girls they wouldn't really grow lambs an'
chicks, er quarters, er any other kinda spendin' money

But I never did, even tho' there's times that I still wish I
had, since there ain't too much most kids like better

Than funnin' around with their goofy ol' Dad. That's the way
it goes tho', so there ain't no use in cryin' over spilt milk

Which is why I didn't, the night ol' Gert pert near
sent me an' my bucket flyin' clean over the moon

Might have too, if 'er aim'd been better. T'was really jist the
barn door I flew thru tho', so I was real glad t'was open

Because when that right foot'a hers smacked me clean off the
stool, I sure was hopin' nothin'ud wind up bein' broken

What'd brought it all about ya see, was her
switchin' that dang fool tail'a hers

Not that it ever come as any big surprise, but it sure
come wrapped in a buncha crap, that's fer certain

Pure too, er as close as stuff like that ever gits! So
the first thing that popped inta my mind

Right after that nasty whip whopped me in the teeth, was
jist t'bite a chunk right out of it, at least if I could

But even tho' I really tried, I didn't quite succeed,
even if did bleed, at least a little, I think

There wasn't time t'do anymore'n blink, before the silly
fool started soundin' like she was plumb gonna croak

An' ya can talk about luck 'til yer brown in the face, fer
by the time I got unstuck from all the patties I'd lit in

She was stretched out most as tight as she could git, between
'er grub-box an' the big post I'd hobbled 'er left hind leg to

T'was the chain 'round 'er neck, a'course, that was causin'
'er t'choke, since the one on 'er leg kept 'er from gittin up

But if ya think she didn't look grateful when I fin'ly got
the chains unhooked from that post an' feed trough

Why I swear, it fair brought tears t'my eyes when she
batts them long lashes a'hers an' kinda sorta sighs

But then, when she cuts loose with'a big ol' belch, follered by
the most heart-renderin' MOOOOOOooooo I ever heard

The big-eyed bird that always kept both of 'em peeled up
on the roof, jist had t'grab hisself the very last word

Which, an' ya prob'ly ain't gonna be too
inclined t'believe this, sounded jist exactly like
MOOOOOOooooHOOOOooo-WHO-hooooo!

Yessiree, some purty weird things went on at times, out
there on Hardrock Hill, an' that's a flat-out fact!

Mom's stepmother, Josie Cooper, Mom in middle, and her father, Fred Allan Cooper on the right.

Now I Lay Me Down To Sleep

The year of 1935 was less than two weeks old, and as was usual for me, I'd teased Kayo until he'd suddenly burst into tears. And even though tears were something that came very easily for my four year old brother, Mom had turned from her breakfast chores at the cookstove just long enough to stamp her foot and shout "Buzzy, you stop that this instant."

I'd responded then by sulking all through breakfast, for even though I knew she hadn't been feeling well for several weeks, it seemed to me that for some time she had been much more susceptible to Kayo's needs than to mine. After all, in slightly over six weeks I'd be having my seventh birthday, so surely that was deserving of a little extra consideration. But all that my dawdling over my oatmeal had elicited from her was "Hurry up and finish eating, so I can get things put away before Daddy and I have to leave."

Then, just as soon as the dishes were washed, she and Dad had gone into their bedroom and changed into their "going somewhere special" clothes. I was still pouting when they came back into the kitchen of course, and I immediately ducked behind the door to sit with my back to the corner. There were unshed tears glistening in Mom's eyes as she came into the kitchen and reached down for my hand. And as she pulled me up to give me a hug, she said "I'm sorry I yelled at you like that Honey, but you know you shouldn't tease your little brother so much. Now be a good boy and take care of him for me until I get home from the hospital. I probably won't be gone for more than just a few days, but it would really be nice to know that I can count on you to look after him."

At that moment there was a knock on the back door, so she let go of me and straightened up just as Dad let in the neighbor lady who was going to look after us until Mom got back. A few minutes later, when I headed out the door on my way to school, our old Chrysler had already disappeared down the street.

All recollection of the next two days has long since departed, but several of the events on the day following them are still very sharply etched into my mind. My first-grade class had let out less than ten minutes earlier, and I was wading down the snow-covered street alone, just slightly over a block from home. A black Chevrolet coupe rounded the corner near our house just then, and came chugging slowly up the gentle grade toward me. And at times it seems that I can almost still hear the clank and rattle of the chains on its rear wheels. As it drew closer, I moved out into the deeper snow at the side of the street, to let it pass. But when it stopped right beside me, I was more than a little surprised to see Dad sitting in the passenger seat.

By then I'd recognized the car as belonging to the man who was then Ridgway's only barber, Jack Simmons. When Dad swung his door slowly open and I saw that both he and Mister Jack had tears running down their cheeks, my surprise changed swiftly to fear. You see, that was the very first time I'd ever seen grown men cry. But by the time Dad knelt down and wrapped his arms around my shoulders, then told me that Mom had died just a few hours earlier, I was undoubtedly crying too. I can't remember my own tears though.

At least two full days have since fallen through the cracks of time, for the next thing I remember was when we took my Aunt Margaret up to the mortuary, so she could see Mom. Margaret was Mom's only sister, and she'd come all the way from Texas on a bus. A tall young man who Dad called Tuffy, took us into a room that had a long, gold-colored box sitting on a low platform that had wheels on its legs, then he went out and closed the door. Dad was carrying Kayo and Aunt Margaret was holding my hand when we walked over to the box, but since I was too short to see what was inside, she picked me up.

It was Mom that was in the box of course, or at least what was in there looked a lot like Mom. Except for the fact that its skin was so pale, and its brown hair was combed differently from the way Mom usually wore hers. Then Dad said "It was the nicest coffin they had, Margaret, I hope you feel that it's alright."

I could feel Aunt Margaret quivering, so I knew she must be crying. But the quivering finally stopped when she sniffed really hard. Then she asked "Would you like to kiss your Mama, Buzzy?"

I'd have given anything right at that minute to be able to kiss my real Mama, but I knew that what she meant was would I like to kiss what lay there in that fancy "coffin" box, so I just shook my head. So she put me back down on the floor then.

My next clear memory is when we walked into the church the following day and I saw our preacher and the man called Tuffy, standing on either side of the doorway. And as I walked past him, Tuffy reached out his hand and squeezed my arm. I looked up and tried to smile at him, but when I saw his eyes brimming with tears, I knew I was going to start bawling if I didn't keep moving. So I pulled loose from his hand and continued walking.

The church was so full of people that I didn't think there was going to be enough room for the four of us, but then some lady came over to Dad and whispered something, just before she led us into the small alcove at the rear, where my Sunday School class usually sat. The whole church seemed to pulsate with noise, but it was the quiet kind that always comes when a roomful of grownups are squirming around in their seats and trying to get comfortable, in clothes that still look brand-new, but somehow seem to have shrunk two full sizes since they were last worn. And the air was so full of the scent of flowers, that in just a little while it felt like I was going to be sick to my stomach. Then I saw that gold-colored box again and felt a shiver shoot straight down my back.

In a few minutes our preacher stood up and began talking, and as was usual for me, the longer he talked the sleepier I got. When I felt Kayo begin to lean against me, though, I turned just enough to see that he was sound asleep. Since Aunt Margaret was wiping her eyes with a handkerchief and Dad was just sitting there, looking down at his hands, I slipped my arm around Kayo to keep him from falling off the seat. Then I looked over to where Tuffy was standing by the door, and saw that he seemed to be looking straight at me. And when he just barely nodded his head and winked, I tried to smile at him again.

The preacher finally got through talking, but when he sat down some fat lady got up and began to sing "Lay My Head Beneath A Rose." That had always been one of Mom's favorite songs, but when she sang it, it didn't hurt your ears. Then the fat lady sat down and everyone else stood up and began marching up to the gold-colored box. Most of the women were wiping their eyes with handkerchiefs the same way Aunt Margaret was, but all I could hear was the squeaking sounds the floor made.

Then Dad and Aunt Margaret stood up and I knew we were going to have to go look at what was in that awful box again. Dad picked Kayo up then, and Aunt Margaret took hold of my hand, gripping it so tightly that it made my fingers ache. But when we got up to the box, she let go of my hand and lifted me up, so that I had to look at what was inside again. This time though, she didn't ask me, she just said "Kiss your Mama now Buzzy, you'll never have another chance."

Then she lowered me down until I was almost touching that pale face and I knew I'd have to kiss it before she'd let me back up. Its lips were cold and stiff, not warm and soft like Mom's had always been. And once I'd gotten down past the perfume of all the flowers that were piled around the box, it smelled almost like the time Doc Bates had sewed my face up and had put me to sleep with ether. But this odor was much worse than the ether had been. It made me feel like I couldn't breathe at all, and I got so scared that I began crying and struggling to get loose. Aunt Margaret nearly dropped me into the box then, but she finally managed to get a better grip on one of my arms and backed quickly away from the box.

Her face was all red but she didn't say a word when she lowered me back to the floor. By that time Kayo had begun crying too, so we turned around and walked outside, where we got into a long, black car that soon started up the road, toward the cemetery.

The horror didn't end out there though, for within the matter of only a few weeks after the funeral, I had the first in a series of nearly identical nightmares. Our house had only two bedrooms in those days, and as soon as Aunt Margaret had gone back home to Texas, Dad moved me into the other bedroom so that it wouldn't be so crowded in the one where he and Kayo slept. It must have been only a day or so after I changed bedrooms that the nightmares began.

The closet in this bedroom was long and narrow, and since there wasn't a light in it, it was also quite dark. And clear down at the far end there were several of Mom's best dresses that Dad hadn't wanted to give away when he and Aunt Margaret were disposing of the other clothing. In the ceiling up above the dresses there was a covered hatchway that provided access into the attic, but the only way that even Dad could reach it was with a ladder. And the door into the closet itself always seemed to stick, so that you had to jerk and tug on the knob in order to get it open.

So in my dream I'd get out of bed and begin trying to open the door. But in a little while I'd get so tired from jerking on the knob that my arms would start aching. Then all of a sudden the door would swing open and there'd be a loud rush of wind that would almost blow me off my feet. I'd be so thoroughly frightened by then that all I wanted to do was turn around and run, but it seemed like the only direction my legs would ever take me was on into the closet. And after I'd worked my way past where my own clothing hung, I'd finally come to where Mom's dresses were.

And it was at this point that I'd begin smelling the odor I'd first been introduced to at the church. But even though it still made me feel like I was suffocating, something seemed to force me to pull each dress aside, one by one, until I'd finally reach the last one.

I'd be so completely terrified by now that I could hear my own heart hammering, but I was powerless to stop, and I'd slowly pull that dress out of the way, to find Mom standing there, still wearing the white gown she'd worn at her funeral. But even though her eyes were open now, they looked like bottomless, black pools of ink, and there was never any sign at all that she recognized me. Then she'd start walking toward me, reaching out with both hands. And it was at this moment that I'd always begin screaming "No, Mama, Oh please no Mama. I'm sorry I didn't want to kiss you, I'm sorry, I'm sorry, I'm."

Then just before her hands would reach me, I'd wake up. For three long years I had that same dream at least once a week, and there were times when it seemed like it came almost every night. And all of this despite the fact that I'd get to move back into Dad's bedroom whenever he found a housekeeper. My screams apparently never passed beyond my own lips though, for I was the only one who ever seemed to hear them. Finally, in June of 1938 Dad married one of our housekeepers, and for a little under five beautiful months Mom's ghost left me alone. Then in early November, Effie too died and the dreams began all over again.

At some point during the first three years, an alternate dream had been born. And I firmly believe that it came into existence solely because my mind had to find reprieve, or snap. For even though this dream began in exactly the same way, once I'd shoved that last dress aside, instead of Mom's ghost, I'd find a stairway leading up through the ceiling. At the top was a small door which opened to the right. And the room on the other side was completely filled with a brilliant light, even though there were no windows visible at all. Within the room there was an assortment of toys that had once been favorites of mine; a large racing-car, a dump truck, a tiny piano, and a miniature wind-up train that went round and round on a plate-sized platform.

There was also a small rocking chair, where I'd sit and rock whenever I grew tired of playing with the toys. And even though this dream always began with the same terror that the other one held for me, once I'd gotten beyond that door and closed it, I knew deep down inside of me that I was safe. At least until the next time. But even after I'd become completely familiar with each of the dreams, up until the moment I'd finally get beyond that last dress, I never, ever knew which dream I was going to have.

And since there were numerous periods of time when Dad was unable to find a housekeeper to look after us, at least after Kayo entered school, as the older of his two sons I was expected to provide as much help around the house as I could. During the winters this meant that I had no excuse for stopping off at a friend's house after school, the way Kayo invariably seemed to do. Simply because there were chores that had to be done, even though I positively dreaded what lay ahead of me, each evening I'd open our back door as quietly as I could, tiptoe all the way into the livingroom with one of the buckets from the back porch, and try to replenish the coal in our Heatrola stove without waking Mom's ghost in my adjoining bedroom.

After that was accomplished, I'd ease one of yesterday's Denver Post sections out of the magazine rack, tiptoe back to the kitchen and crumple the paper as soundlessly as possible, then place it into the cookstove, glancing every few seconds toward the doorway back into the main part of the house. The kindling and larger pieces of wood were likewise slipped into the firebox, where a match was soon applied. And while I was waiting for the wood to burn hotly enough so that I could dump in some of the slack-coal from yet another bucket, the ashpans had to be removed from both stoves, then taken outside to be dumped by the back gate.

So when the pans were safely replaced, there were generally three buckets of lump-coal to be carried into the house from the coal-shed, and two of slack-coal. Then the wood and kindling boxes had to be filled. Lastly, the eggs had to gathered from the henhouse and put down in the root-cellar just outside our backdoor. And if Kayo wasn't home by then, I'd creep back into the kitchen and either sit behind our blue-enameled Banquet cookstove, or slide in under its protective chrome-skirt, just as far as I could. But unless the warmth put me to sleep then, my eyes would invariably remain riveted on the doorway through which Mom's ghost would have to come, in order to reach me.

For some reason, one evening when I was feeling especially vulnerable I'd locked the backdoor, then crawled down under the stove to wait for Dad or Kayo to come home. And when Dad's angry hammering on the door finally roused me, I nearly ripped one of the rear pockets completely off my corduroys in my haste to get out from under the stove and unlock the door.

For some reason though, I could never bring myself to tell him about my problems, more than likely because I felt guilty or embarrassed about being so afraid of my own mother and my own home. But whatever the reason may have been, Mom's ghost gave me very little peace until Dad re-married yet again in 1944. This lady was a true godsend if ever there was one, not only because she brought an end to the dreams and fear, but also because I came to love her so very, very much.

It would be grossly hypocritical of me not to admit that I spent a great many years being extremely resentful of the part my aunt played in the birth of my mother's ghost. For even after I got old enough to know better, I still wouldn't accept that, as the product of an era when sending a loved one on their final journey with a kiss was all but mandatory, Aunt Margaret had very little choice in the matter either. She'd also loved Mom so much, and was so burdened with her own grief that she just didn't stop to realize how I might feel about what she asked me to do.

But if there is anyone reading this story who still feels it's necessary for a small child to attend a loved one's funeral, whether to satisfy propriety or to come to terms with their loss, won't you please give it a little additional thought?

Shady Deals From Out Of The Past

Now that the statute of limitations has no doubt expired, I suppose I might just as well confess to something that's been bothering me for quite awhile, albeit not an awful lot. For just because Dad was quite a bit older than the other kid's fathers back when I was growing up, at times I was more than a little envious of their having dads who'd occasionally take a swing at the old baseball with them, or even indulge in something as juvenile as a game of tag. But it sure didn't take me long to figure out that his need of a short nap at noon was a blessing in disguise, as well as one that the other kids didn't get to enjoy as often as I did.

So even though it had a tendency once in awhile to make me feel a trifle dishonest, as soon as he'd wake up and head back to the Post Office, I'd nearly break the sound-barrier in getting to the he'd just vacated, at least I did once my little brother, Kayo, got smart enough to figure out what was going on. Because lying beneath the cushions, or clear down in the tight little groove between the spring-compartment and the back of the couch, it was ever so frequently possible to find enough cold, hard cash (even though it was often still warm) to buy a candy-bar or two with.

But on the rare occasions when I'd find a quarter, or even a half-dollar, I couldn't help wonder whether Fate, or maybe even God, was testing me. Just to see if I'd split it with Kayo, or perhaps do something so rash as return it to its rightful owner. Almost invariably, though, I'd find some way to justify my larcenous nature, by remembering the days when Dad was guilty of offering me the choice of taking a nickel or a dime from he coins he held in his hand. And I'd always choose the nickel, just because it was bigger than the dime. Ah me, the things we poor foolish mortals are subject to.

But just because I once showed my oldest daughter, Sharon, who was then around five or six years old, how to test whether our electric-fence was turned on, she's still trying to get even with me. For even though I used a slender blade of grass to demonstrate the technique, how could I help it if she later chose a fat, juicy dandelion-leaf to show her little sister how smart she was? And how was I to know she'd also be kneeling, with both bare knees firmly in contact with the moist ground? Good grief, Gertrude, any dummy knows better than to pull an idiotic stunt like that!

So even if I did have her believing it was necessary to unscrew the handle and pour five water-buckets of air into our old tire-pump whenever it wouldn't work, and her bicycle tire needed pumping up, wouldn't you think she'd be able to let bygones be bygones by now? After all, the buckets weren't all that heavy, and once she'd managed to get the handle-gasket back into the cylinder, the fool thing almost always began pumping air the way it was supposed to.

Yet that ungrateful and thoroughly vindictive dang female spent most of one summer twenty-five or so years later, just trying to con me into going on a kayaking expedition with her and a bunch of her goofy friends. And since she even offered to loan me one of her kayaks, I was stupid enough to take her up on it. Which is the main reason my arms, shoulders, back, hips, and knees are so stiff I can barely even navigate anymore. Because after fourteen of us launched our armada of three canoes and eight kayaks one Friday evening, then paddled like mad to get far enough down the dinky little crick that everyone around Kenai calls the Swanson River, just to find a big enough spot to pitch our tents and spend the night, I was sure as the devil wondering what kind of monster I'd helped create!

But at least I managed to catch two dinky little rainbow-trout before crawling into my sleeping-bag for what remained of the night, sometime just a few seconds before midnight. Which just incidentally, is when it once more gets dark when you're as far up the crick as we were that night. So when I finally crawled though my little pup-tent's tube-like passage-way at somewhere around 6:00 that morning, hoping to find a clump of trees that would offer enough privacy to do what dang well had to be done, by the time I finally did, Sandy, my youngest idiot was just getting around to heating enough water so that each of us could have a cup of so-called Instant Coffee.

Consequently, when Roger, her sluggard of a husband, joined us shortly, all three of us had eaten breakfast and then headed down the fool crick almost an hour before the others. Which was just as well I guess, since it eventually allowed us to beat another party of four similar imbeciles to glom onto the onto the only other chunk of unreal-estate that was big enough to accommodate a herd of fools as big as ours. But by the time the rest of the bunch showed up at 4:00, we had our tents pitched, and were thus able to assist them ashore, since it was necessary to carry all but the canoes up to the top of the bluff we were on. And due to the unfortunate fact that I'd been the only one in advance party wearing knee-length rubber boots, it was up to me to scrounge up the night's firewood from the other side of an adjacent swamp. In case you weren't already aware of it, though, there's almost always a swamp adjacent to wherever you happen to be up here in the far North. But at least this one didn't go over the top of my boots.

On this particular evening, even though my fishing efforts proed totally unsuccessful, I enter my khaki-colored little cocoon at 10:00. And due to the fact that the sky looked more than somewhat threatening by then, I took the precaution of encasing the lower two-thirds of my sleeping-bag in one of the long plastic bags I had with me, since I'd forgotten to bring a full-length of plastic along, for draping over the tent. But even though it rained most of the night and most everyone wound up discovering a few more leaks in their tents before morning, the only thing of mine that got wet was my sox, which I'd lain on top of my boot to dry out. I had dry ones along though, so it really didn't amount to that much of an inconvenience.

On this morning we all started out together, paddling non-stop for three and a half hours, just to reach the spot where Sharon's sister-in-law, Dolly, wanted to stop for lunch. But as luck would have it, when a gal by the name of Barbara, and myself, each managed to find a spot to nose the prow of our tippy little craft far enough into the bank so we could get out without getting wet, the other six kayakers were forced to exit theirs were forced to use extreme caution and whatever else they could lay their hands on. Then they had to pull their kayaks up onto the steeply sloping bank to make room so the canoes could tie up to the very limited length of available creek-bank.

So when Roger and I started down stream in advance of the others immediately after lunch, we missed seeing Jim take a bath when he decided to launch by sliding straight down the bank and into the water. Luckily, though, he'd taken the precaution of handing his camera and vest-pocket radio to one of the others before attempting it. Because everything else that he had with him got soaked.

We eventually reached the haul-out point on the river somewhere around 4:00 that afternoon, but by the time Sharon took three of the kayaks and a like number of people into Kenai in her little red Ford station-wagon, then returned two hours later to haul Sandy, Roger, and me back to where we'd left our rigs on Friday evening, it was 8:15 before we parted company and I could start the two and a half hour drive back to Homer. Although I'd truly enjoyed the outing, paddling twenty-five miles in a damn fool kayak still comes awfully dang close to being work, despite what anyone else tells you. There's an extremely remote chance that I might be tempted to go on another one someday, just as long as Sharon either agrees to rent me an outboard motor, or a two-party kayak and is willing to do all the paddling herself. Which is almost as likely to happen, as pigs are to sprout wings.

Three Cheers For Candy

Once a long time ago, in this here cold ol' land'a ice an' snow
　　Ever'man here in Dawson town was huntin'
　　his own chunk'a Eldorado
An' most'a th' women, or what few was there, was already married
　　Then one day, a'boat come driftin' down
　　from Whitehorse town an'
　　th' single men could hardly believe all that it carried.

Fer standin in th' bow a'that little scow stood sweet Candy LaRue
An'right there close b'hind 'er, th' gals numbered twenty an' two
All'a them looked s'grand, dressed in gingham, n'ribbons, n'lace
But Candy, Oh sweet Candy, put th' shame on 'em all, just bowin'
　　an' a'wearin' such an angelic smile on 'er purty face.

Well now sir, within not more, an' maybe less'n two hours er so
Th' good ladies a'Dawson had up'n decided Sweet Candy had t'go
Why they just ranted an' raved, as t' how depraved was th' fact
That Sweet Candy must be fixin' t'stablish nothin' more'n a
　　Sportin' Goods store, considerin' all th' finery she packed.

> But th' menfolk a'Dawson town, from
> th' Mayor right straight down
>
> Wouldn't heed that howlin' mob, after
> seein' Candy's lowdown gown
>
> An' even tho' Emmaline McBean, whose
> dear Augustus owned th' bank
>
> Exercised `er rights'a rank, by makin'
> herself spokesman fer that whole
>
> indignant group, th' fella's all knew who t'thank.

Fer 'twas Ol' `Gustus hisself, who'd mailed Sweet Candy th' dust

T'pay fer th' fare from Seattle t'Skagway on'a ol' bucket a'rust

Called "Star of Deliverance." So as `propriate as that may sound

> There was quite'a bit'a ambivalence in
> Ol' Dawson Town, th' night

they got word that th' Star had gone down an' th' Cap'd drowned.

Now I know, there's a'plenty who'll howl that I'm wrong t'dispute

   How tainted are th' souls'a th' gals in'a ol' House'a Ill Repute

But maybe, altho' I really kind'a doubt it, if they knew how kind

Was th' dear soft heart, of th' infamous Sweet Candy LaRue, they

   could come t'accept there's worse things t'peddle than behind.

Cause y'see, `twasn't much more'n six months er so b'fore another

Boat come floatin' round th' bend, bringin'a child home t'Mother

   Now afore ya go hoppin' clean over th' wrong kind'a solution

Just let me make it clear, this little blue-eyed girl had ripped a hole

   right thru Candy's heart one day at'a Seattle institution.

Boy Howdy, if you think that didn't set Emmaline's gang t'carpin'
Why them stingy wives, n'their self-rightous tongues s'sharp'n
All whackin' away like butcher knives, just flat refused t'admit
'Twas better by far fer orphan Genevieve t'be raised by someone
like Candy, who loved her, than'a dang ol' do-good hypocrite.

S'they kept yakkin' away, just night n'day, fer twelve long years
An' you shoulda heard 'em rejoice, at th' sight'a Candy's tears
> Th' day Genevieve climbed aboard
> another boat, an' stood a'wavin'

At 'er Mom an' all 'er Aunts, an' it really made us proud'a her
when she called "G'bye Uncle Augustus!" Man did Em go t'ravin'.

But by th' time th' little darlin' had got herself a'fine diploma
At some big Institute, Em's gang'd got used t'Dawson's carcinoma
As they'd been callin' Candy's place, s'they hopped on th' wagon
An' just started braggin', like 'twas them as was responsible fer
> Dawson's Pride an' Glory. But Candy, God
> bless'er, just didn't seem t'give a'hoot!

Our daughter, Sharon Kay, on the rocking horse I made for her on her first Christmas. We had one hell of a time getting her to sit still long enough to take her picture. And by the time she finally got old enough to have climbed on it by herself, I'm fairly sure we'd already burned the fool thing in the stove. But do you have any idea how much we could have gotten for it if we'd only sent a picture of it to "BELIEVE IT OR NOT BY RIPLEY"?

Epilogue For A Collection Of Stories And Poems

Primarily because I couldn't afford to take a chance that too many of you who were considering whether you ought to buy this book or not, I decided to withhold the information I still need to dump on your shoulders at this time. Because after reading the last story in this rusty little bucket of mine, it's finally time to let you have it right smack between the eyes. For simply because I can't help thinking that those of you who qualify for already having paid your membership dues in the "OVER THE HILL GANG", have more than likely experienced exactly the same thing I did, just shortly after DeVon hauled off and sailed away into the Wild Blue Yonder.

But after having her pull the same stunt at least three or four times in a row, it seemed like it might be a real good idea to make an appointment with our regular "NUT NOODLER", Dr. Bill Bell, just to see whether he thought I'd sailed clear of the far side of what passes for normal with Ol' Homeroids like me. So even though I've already managed to forget what cockamamie reason I'd made the appoint for, when I asked him whether he'd ever heard of anything as downright spooky as having DeVon come back from the grave at least three or four times in the last two or three weeks, after sitting there and eye-balling me for a few seconds, during which I could almost feel the boys in Homer's Butterfly Brigade homing in on me, he said "I sure as the devil have Syd. You'd really be surprised at how many of my patients have told me exactly the same thing you just did. I don't pretend to know just why it happens, and it doesn't matter whether it's a spouse, parent, or young child that comes back, as long as they've loved and been loved by the person they return to, it's been going on for an awfully long time."

Despite the fact that I only saw Dee once, due to her wearing a long white gown that looked just like the one my mother was wearing in my nightmares about her ghost, when I involuntarily sucked in my breath, she just backed into the wall beside the picture of the aunt and uncle who'd raised her after her parents had been divorced, and disappeared. But whenever I get really down in the dumps about something, she'll either knock on our bedroom door or ring the doorbell on the main entry into the house. And even though there were any number of times this past winter when there was at least an inch or more snow on the porch floor, there were never any tracks or sign that anyone had been there. Barely over a week ago I got so discouraged about some things that had been going wrong with my damned "Crabapple" computer, that I begged her to come back just one more time, since she hadn't visited me for several weeks. And less than an hour and fifteen minutes later, she rang the doorbell again. So after running out to jerk the door open and answering her "ding-dong" with three of my own, I then came back and literally jumped into bed, so downright ecstatic that it took me at least an hour to go back to sleep.

There have also been two separate times when I woke up to find the scent of her cologne so strong that I'd get out of bed and go open the bottle again, just to make sure that's what had woke me up. And one night after spending most of the afternoon mowing the lawn, my shoulders were so sore it seemed to take me at least an hour to fall asleep. Before I was able to, though, she began massaging my neck muscles until they finally relaxed enough to allow me to go to sleep. So whether you choose to believe it or not, every last one of these things have happened during the past year and sixty-one days since my beloved Sweetheart left. As God is my witness, simply because she came back to let me know how much she loved me, she gave me back the belief in Him that I lost the night my first step-mother died, all the way back in November of 1938.